I0128786

For My Legionaries

Corneliu Zelea Codreanu

Introduction

by Kerry Bolton

Historical Overview and Background

by Lucian Tudor

For My Legionaries

Corneliu Zelea Codreanu

Introduction by Kerry Bolton

Historical Overview and Background
by Lucian Tudor

ISBN-13: 978-1-913176-59-4

Sanctuary Press Ltd
71-75 Shelton Street
Covent Garden
London
WC2H 9JQ

www.sanctuarypress.com
Email: info@sanctuarypress.com

Contents

Contents

Editor's Note

This new edition of *For My Legionaries* improves and expands upon all previous editions of this work in English in multiple ways, providing the reader with new material to better understand the book and its meaning.

It includes new footnotes to explain various historical names and events mentioned throughout the book. In terms of new texts, one will find in this new edition an Introduction by Kerry Bolton (p1), a second essay (p35) dealing specifically with the historical background for the book to inform the reader of certain aspects of Romanian history that most non-Romanians would not be knowledgeable in, and also several appendices which were not included in previous editions, which will help readers better appreciate the character of Codreanu and his movement.

Lastly, this edition includes "The Iron Guard: Its Origins, History and Legacy,"(p441) an essay which not only recaps and expands upon the basic history, biographical information, and philosophy discussed in the book and various texts attached to it, but also provides a comprehensive history of Codreanu's movement, going beyond Codreanu's life and up to present day, so that readers may fully realize the impact and importance of the Legionary Movement and its founder.

Lucian Tudor

Chicago, Illinois

Introduction

A Martyr's Life

> Rest assured, I beg you, that after ten years of suffering we have sufficient moral strength left to find an honourable exit from a life we cannot support without honour and dignity.[1]

The life and death, thoughts and deeds of Corneliu Codreanu have excited a fascination over new generations of youth over the course of the past several decades. Codreanu shared some notable characteristics with José Antonio Primo de Rivera in Spain: both were young and charismatic, both were motivated by their Christian Faiths, and both met a similar martyr's fate.

A particularly perceptive characterisation of Codreanu comes from Julius Evola in a short essay written about the Romanian in 1938, describing the man he personally met in Bucharest. The first thing that Evola comments upon was the fact of the Iron Guard having built the 'Green House', their headquarters, with their own hands', 'intellectual and craftsman' having joined together to build the residence of their 'Captain' 'as a type of symbol and a rite'.[2] As can be discerned from Evola's impression, the basis of the Movement was Faith and Work; that is to say, the movement had again made work a sacred duty. Evola described his first seeing Codreanu: 'A young, large and slim man, in sporting behavior, with an open face which immediately gives an impression of nobility, force and honesty, comes to meet us. It is precisely Corneliu Codreanu, Head of the Iron Guard.'[3]

Codreanu explained the differences of doctrine of Legionnairism, Italian Fascism and German Nationalism Socialism by analogy with the human body: While Italian Fascism revives the Roman form of politics, representing in the human organism the physiological form, German

1 C Z Codreanu to Prime Minister Vaida, 20 July 1933.

2 J Evola, 'Ascetic Legionnairism: Meeting the Head of the Iron Guards', *Fascista Mode*, Italy, 22 March 1938.

3 J Evola, *Ibid.*

National Socialism focuses on the 'race instinct' of the 'vital forces' of the organism, and the Romanian Legionary movement represents 'the element of the heart: on the spiritual and religious aspect'.[4]

Codreanu continued that the Legionary movement aimed to awaken the spirit that had been with Romanians even prior to Christianity, 'to create a man spiritually new'. 'Spirit and religion are for us the starting point', and once that had been rekindled the Roman form of political organization could proceed, the Romanians having inherited the Roman political form from ancient times. The Legionary concept was primarily metaphysical, based on principles that are 'eternal and immutable', with a rejection of 'utilitarianism and materialism'; principles for which 'one must be ready to fight, to die and in all things subordinate'.[5]

The Legionary lived as an ascetic warrior-monk, fasting three days a week, praying, practicing celibacy, and working freely for the people. If the Life of Christ was the figure by which the Legionary strived to emulate, so too his Martyrdom was readily accepted, and that was the culmination of the life of Codreanu.

Eight months after Evola's essay appeared in Italy the 'Captain' was murdered in a cowardly fashion by soldiers on orders of King Carol whom Stanley G. Payne has described as 'the most cynical, corrupt, and power-hungry monarch who ever disgraced a throne anywhere in twentieth century Europe.'[6]

Formative Years

There were not many years of Codreanu's life which were not engaged in struggle for his native land. Codreanu was born on 13 September 1899 in Hushi, a small town in the province of Moldavia. His father, Ion, descended from several generations of foresters, was a schoolteacher with avid nationalist sympathies. His mother, Elise, was of Bavarian descent.[7]

4 J Evola, *Ibid.*

5 J Evola, *Ibid.*

6 S G Payne, *A History of Fascism 1914-1945* (London: UCL Press, 1995), p. 278.

7 T O'Keefe, 'Codreanu & The Iron Guard', *National Vanguard*, Washington DC, No. 60, May 1978, p. 14.

Codreanu's education, that helped establish the course of his life, began at the famous Military Academy Mănăstirea Dealului (The Cloister on the Hill, 'where the head of Michael the Brave reposes'. He was to write of this:

> In fact, my military education will be with me all my life. Order, discipline, hierarchy, moulded into my blood at an early age, along with the sentiment of soldierly dignity, will constitute a guiding thread for my entire future activity. Here too, I was taught to speak little, a fact which later was to lead me to hate 'chatter boxing' and too much talk. Here I learned to love the trench and to despise the drawing room. [8]

Although only 17 when his father's regiment set off to the front in 1916 Codreanu briefly joined him. The war was over by the time Codreanu had completed his military training in 1919. That year he entered the University of Iasi. He had already been imbued with nationalism from the books he had read in his father's library and from reading the classic literature of Romania. This reading had early imbued him with what he regarded as the three principle ideas 'of life for the Romanian people':

1. The unification of the Romanian people.
2. The elevation of peasantry through land reform and political rights.
3. The solution of the Jewish problem.[9]

However it was at the University that Codreanu received a formal tutelage in the faith of Romanian nationalism from the Professor of Political Economy, A C Cuza.[10] Cuza had founded the Nationalist Democratic Party in 1910, of which Codreanu's father was a leading member. The party focused on the youth, campaigned against usury, and in favour of land reform and workers rights, while opposing liberalism and democracy. Hence, one might see that even prior to the Great War a spontaneous and nativist 'fascism' was arising in Romania without any outside inspiration.[11]

---

8 C Z Codreanu (1936) *For My Legionaries* (Madrid: Editura Libertatea, 1976), 'Stepping into Life'.

9 C Z Codreanu, *Ibid.*, 'At the University of Iasi',

10 C Z Codreanu, *Ibid.*, 'At the University of Iasi'.

11 F L Carsten, *The Rise of Fascism* (London: Batsford Academic & Educational Ltd., 1980), p. 182.

Codreanu entered Law School when former students, having returned from the war, were resuming their studies. These student war veterans formed nationalist groups centred especially around the faculties of Letters and Law. On the other hand there were many more students who were Jewish, coming from Basarbia, whom Codreanu describes as all being communist agents and propagandists.[12] Additionally most of the faculty were sympathetic to communism. Codreanu remarks on a situation remarkably reminiscent of the situation that has pertained in the academia of the 'West' since 1945:

> Such an attitude on the part of the professors who considered 'barbarous' any nationalistic idea or note, resulted in the total disorientation of the students, some openly supporting Bolshevism, others - the greater part - saying: 'Say what you will, nationalism is passé, mankind moves toward the left'.[13]

The nationalist students were in a minority, and were the object of increasingly aggressive attitudes.[14]

However, outside the University, Codreanu also found Iasi to be rife with Bolshevik agitation among the workers and chaos in the workplace. Demonstrations of 10,000 to 15,000 filled the streets every day; 'starved workers, manoeuvred by the Judaic criminal hand from Moscow, [who] paraded the streets while singing the *Internationale*, yelling: "Down with the King!", "Down with the Army!", and carrying placards on which one could read "Long live the communist revolution!", "Long live Soviet Russia!"'[15] Codreanu saw in this bolshevisation of the masses not the possibility of a Romanian people's revolution, but the prospect of a total Judaisation of Romania and the liquidation of its peasantry.

It was this urgent need for a movement that would not only thwart bolshevism but that would also reconstitute Romania as a strong nation predicated on the necessity of a social and ultimately a spiritual ethos, that prompted Codreanu to establish a movement that would capture the zeal of the working masses and the peasantry.

---

12 Codreanu later provides the names of the Jewish propagandists: Dr. Ghelerter, Gheler, Spiegler, Schreiber, Ilie Moscovici, Pauker, et al. C Z Codreanu, *For My Legionaries*, op. cit., 'The Leaders of the Romanian Workers'.

13 C Z Codreanu, *For My Legionaries*, 'At the University of Iasi'.

14 C Z Codreanu, *Ibid.*

15 C Z Codreanu, *Ibid.*, 'Revolution Being Prepared'.

The Guard Of The National Consciousness

In 1919 Codreanu attended a meeting of the newly formed Guard of National Consciousness. At the meeting room Codreanu found one dejected-looking individual, Constantin Pancu, the President of The Guard, hopefully waiting for people to arrive. However about twenty people did arrive, and what is of interest is that Codreanu notes the broad social base of those attending: labourers, a student, a lawyer and a priest.[16]

Pancu was a plumber and electrician who had little formal education, but was a deep thinker who had been preoccupied with the problems of workers, had served as president of the metallurgical union, and was an impressive public speaker. He was a popular figure and was noted for his physical strength. His weekly meetings over the course of a year attracting audiences of up to 10,000. The Guard spread throughout Romania, and daily clashes also occurred with the Reds. The culmination of this fight with the Reds came in February 1920 when, at the instigation of Codreanu, the movement marched on the Agency of State Monopolies (ASM), where Bolsheviks had raised the Red Flag and taken over the building as the start of a General Strike. Pancu, Codreanu and a hundred followers stormed the building, Codreanu reached the roof, and replaced the Red Flag with that of Romania and launched into a speech, after which the military took over the situation. Within several days the Pancu movement had organised 400 workers to get the ASM working again, and within two weeks most of the striking workers demanded a return to work.[17]

Within a month, however, the communists had taken over the railway works at Nicolina. The Guard mobilized and marched on the works and again Codreanu climbed atop a building to replace the Red Flag with the Tricolor, speaking to a crowd to thunderous acclaim. The Reds outside the gates challenged Poncu and Codreanu to come forward, which they did, accompanied by a third compatriot, walking toward a bolshevised mob out for their blood. As they approached, the mob parted allowing the three to walk through, whilst their compatriots followed, everyone in complete silence.

The heroic action had caused uproar throughout Romania, and that

16 C Z Codreanu, *Ibid.*, 'The Guard of National Conscious'.

17 C Z Codreanu, *Ibid.*, 'The Occupation of the Agency of State Monopolies by the Guard of National Consciousness'.

was the moment when a Romanian national awakening was born.[18] It was now time to formulate a doctrine and create a movement that would tap into this awakening and establish a new Romania.

National-Christian Socialism

The Guard of National Consciousness had been formed to defeat Bolshevism. This had been done with valor. However, Codreanu was at pains to point out to Pancu that:

> It is not enough to defeat Communism. We must also fight for the rights of the workers. They have a right to bread and a right to honour. We must fight against the oligarchic parties, creating national workers organizations which can gain their rights within the framework of the state and not against the state.[19]

These issues were being formulated in 1919. Romanian 'National-Christian Socialism', as the doctrine was already termed, was a creed that developed independently of, but parallel to, other such movements simultaneously arising in France, Germany, Italy, Hungary and elsewhere. The *zeitgeist* of the era called for a widespread response to the etiolating tendencies of materialism, whether in their capitalistic or Marxian forms, and many from both Left and Right were seeing the need for synthesis.[20]

It is also notable that one of the central principles of this new national-social synthesis in many countries was the incorporation of syndicalism as a means of achieving social unity upon which any real nationalism must be predicated. Hence Poncu and Codreanu began organizing workers into national unions while forming the Guard of National Conscious into a political party.

Although the Bolshevik revolts had been thwarted by the Guard of National Consciousness, Jewish influence in the press kept up a steady

18 C Z Codreanu, *Ibid.*, 'The Tricolor Flag Over the Nicolina Works',

19 C Z Codreanu, *Ibid.*, 'National Christian Socialism and the National Syndicates'.

20 Zeev Sternhell, *Neither Left Nor Right: Fascist Ideology in France* (New Jersey: Princeton University Press, 1983). Over the past several decades there have been several notable efforts to provide a scholarly definition for 'generic fascism'. See also: R Eatwell, *Fascism: A History* (London: Vintage, 1995). R Griffin, *Fascism* (Oxford: Oxford University Press, 1995).

agitation against the historic institutions of Romania: Church, Army and Monarchy. Codreanu said of the press:

> By reading those newspapers which crisped my soul, I came to know the real feelings of these aliens, which they revealed without reticence, at a time they thought we had been knocked to the ground. I learned enough anti-Semitism in one year to last me three lifetimes. For one cannot strike the sacred beliefs of a people or what their heart loves and respects, without hurting them to the depths and without blood dripping from their wound.[21]

Hence, while it is easy for academia and others to pontificate about the anti-Semitism of such movements at the time, the anti-national and anti-Christian sentiments that were being openly expressed among Jewish communities, and the messianic feelings that were aroused among them by the rise of Bolshevism were major factors in arousing those sentiments. Across the border in Hungary the short-lived, hysterical Bolshevik regime of Bela Kun, noted for the predominance of its Jewish commissars, including Timor Szamuelly, head of the 'Lenin Lads' who inflicted the 'Red Terror', was noted. *The New International Year Book of 1919* published by Dodd, Mead & Co. commented that 'the government of Bela Kun was composed almost exclusively of Jews who also held the administrative offices'. Kun's three months reign brought deaths to around 30,000 Hungarians. A more recent authoritative source confirms that:

> The new regime also employed a terror gang, in imitation of the Russian *Cheka* ('The Lenin Lads'), led by Tibor Szamuelly, a ruthless and brutal man. Torture chambers were set up under the old Parliament and for a short period the countryside was administered by gangs of itinerate revolutionaries. [22]

The Kun regime was largely destroyed with the occupation of Budapest by the Romanian army.[23]

With the opening of the University of Iasi in 1920 the decision not to include the traditional religious service was met with jubilation by most of the faculty and the many Leftist and Jewish students.

---

21 C Z Codreanu, op. cit., 'The Attitude of the Jewish Press'.

22 Norman Stone, 'Hungary 1918-19, Bela Kun', *History of the Twentieth Century* (London: Purnell, 1968), Vol. 3, p. 924.

23 Norman Stone, *Ibid.*

Codreanu and a small group resolved to take action. Codreanu relates: 'Communist students were jubilant, Jewry triumphant, while a few of us pondered sorrowfully: we wondered how long it would be before churches were torn down and priests in their vestments crucified on their altars?'[24] That after all was the situation that had pertained across the border in Hungary, and was ongoing in Russia.

The handful of students decided to prevent the opening of the University. They erected barricades and Codreanu put up a notice reading: 'I bring to the attention of the students as well as to that of the professors that this university is going to open only following the traditional religious service'. Standing alone at the University entrance, Codreanu was overwhelmed by a communist-led mob, taken into the lobby and beaten. Soon after, Codreanu's few comrades arrived. Miraculously, the University's sectary came along to post a notice stating that the University would be closed for several days, then opened with the traditional religious service. This was yet another victory, despite the physical odds, based wholly on courage founded on Faith.

When several days later the auditorium was filled for the service, it was Codreanu who received accolades, and Professor Cuza spoke with 'unsurpassed eloquence'. This was the defining moment for Codreanu. 'It was at that moment that the belief took hold in me - and it has never left me - that one who fights for God and his people, even if alone, will never be defeated'. A movement of zealous youth could defeat the odds.[25]

Thus a nucleus was formed at Iasi University and they, never more than forty, confronted the anti-Romanian forces at every occasion. Outreaching beyond the University, they also confronted the press, and invaded the premises of the Jewish-owned newspapers, *The World* and *Opinion* - which purveyed slurs against the Church, Army and King - smashing the printing presses.[26] However, a fistfight in the streets between Codreanu and the editors of the two newspapers resulted in Codreanu's expulsion from the University. The Law Faculty, under Professor Cuza, responded by declaring the Faculty independent from the University. Codreanu was elected president of the Association of Law Students, which introduced the study of Jewish issues into the studies of the association. The law students' association thereby become

---

24 C Z Codreanu, op. cit., 'The Opening of Iasi University in the Fall of 1920'.

25 C Z Codreanu, *Ibid.*

26 C Z Codreanu, *Ibid.*, 'The 1920-21 University Year'.

an institute for the study of the Jewish question in Romania.[27]

The law students' association attracted such interest that students were drawn to it from further afield, and it eclipsed the other associations. The association gained the adherence of the majority of Christian Basarabian students, and these were to form a significant cadre in the future nationalist movement. The primary intellectual influence was that of Professor Cuza, who was regarded as a leading world expert on the Jewish question.[28]

In April 1922 Professor Cuza began publishing *Apărarea Naţionala* ('The National Defence'). The following month the nationalist students at Iasi were able to replace the General Students' Association with their own Association of Christian Students. Codreanu then left for Berlin to resume his studies.[29]

Interestingly, Codreanu arrived in Germany with a view to promulgating his ideals – termed from 1919 'National-Christian Socialism' – in other states. He saw from the earliest period the world-wide dimension of his struggle. Registering at the University, his traditional Romanian dress prompted much curiosity. For his part, Codreanu noted the misery of the country while Jewish capitalists were able to close lucrative deals. He moved to Jena where he could live more cheaply.

He only heard about Hitler from a worker in October 1922, and at the same time Mussolini's march on Rome. Codreanu felt a bond with the embryonic movement for national awakening in Italy, and other movements that were emerging:

> There is, among all those in various parts of the world who serve their people, a kinship of sympathy, as there is such a kinship among those who labour for the destruction of peoples. Mussolini, the brave man who trampled the dragon underfoot, was one of us, that is why all dragon heads hurled themselves upon him, swearing death to him. For us, the others, he will be a bright North Star giving us hope; he will be living proof that the hydra can be defeated; proof of the possibilities of victory.[30]

27 C Z Codreanu, *Ibid.*, 'President of the Law Students' Association'.

28 C Z Codreanu, *Ibid.*

29 C Z Codreanu, *Ibid.*, 'In Germany'.

30 C Z Codreanu, *Ibid.*

It is significant to note that 'National-Christian Socialism' had already been formulated in 1919 as a Romanian creed when German National Socialism and Italian Fascism were unknown.[31] Professor Cuza had already started building the foundations via a periodical founded in 1906 and the Nationalist Democratic Party was established a few years later.[32] Cuza also adopted the swastika at this time; hence, the use of the swastika by the Romanian nationalist movement owes nothing to German National Socialism.[33]

Student Protests & League of National Christian Defence

Codreanu was still in Jena when huge student demonstrations erupted in Romania on 10 December 1922, converged on Bucharest and other cities, and closed the universities, protesting against the predominance of Jews.[34] Codreanu quickly returned to Romania, and went to Cernăuţi. The students wanted to proclaim a General Strike to keep the universities shut down until their demands were met. However, Codreanu began to formulate a strategy to build this student protest into a movement of Romanian awakening. A national assembly of delegates would be called to establish a movement.[35] It would be led by Professor Cuza. The student leadership was directionless and Codreanu had difficulty getting agreement in Bucharest for such a movement under Cuza. Codreanu proceeded with his plans, albeit with only a handful of supporters, and at the assembly in Iasi the League of National Christian Defence was formed on 4 March 1923, the name being suggested by Cuza.[36]

Delegates from 42 groups arrived, each carrying a flag comprising a black background (for the darkness surrounding them), with a white circle in the centre representing the hope of national awakening, within which was a swastika, the flag being edged by the Romanian tricolor red, yellow and blue. 10,000 supporters gathered at the Cathedral and the flags were blessed before the altar. These 42 flags were sent into counties throughout Romania to serve as the rallying symbols of resistance.

31 The Italian Fascio was formed in 1919.

32 F L Carsten, op. cit. p. 182. Carsten gives the date as 1909; Codreanu, 1910.

33 The National Socialist German Workers; Party adopted the swastika in 1920.

34 C Z Codreanu, op. cit., '10 December 1922'.

35 C Z Codreanu, *Ibid.*, 'The Return to Romania'.

36 C Z Codreanu, *Ibid.*, 'The Founding of the League of National Defence'.

Codreanu was appointed national organiser of the League, under the direction of Cuza. Codreanu's father, Ion, a long-time and well-known supporter of Cuza,[37] was among the speakers at the founding rally.[38]

While engaged with the organization of the League throughout Romania, Codreanu was also still involved with the student movement that had emerged from their General Strike. These activities converged, and Codreanu formed youth corps. Codreanu was developing a military-style organization, but the practicalities of such an organization were beyond the scholar, Cuza. A dispute arose between Cuza and Ion Codreanu, the senior supporting the aims of his son. However, Cuza relented, made amendments to the League's founding document, and it – *The Good Romanian's Guide* - became the manual of the movement until 1935.[39]

The changing of the Constitution in March 1923 to allow citizenship to Jews resulted in an uproar, and the League organised the opposition throughout Romania, with demonstrations being organised by Codreanu in Iasi.[40] While we might today pontificate with moral indignation about the lack of humanity of such widespread anti-Semitism, a more realistic assessment can only be made by a detached consideration of how the Jewish communities, especially in Eastern and Central Europe, had identified themselves – for whatever reason – with anti-national, anti-Christian and often Bolshevistic movements. Even the diplomatic and military intelligence sources in the West and the USA often remarked on such influences among the Jews.[41] As a result of the demonstrations and battles Codreanu was arrested for the first time and jailed for a week.[42]

The student strike continued into June 1923. Clashes ensued after the army tried to keep the universities open. In Iasi, the evening prior to the intent of the army to open the University, Codreanu

37 Ion Codreanu and Cuza had been elected to Parliament after the war as Deputies for the Nationalist Democratic Party.

38 C Z Codreanu, op. cit., , 'March 4 1923'.

39 C Z Codreanu, *Ibid.*, , 'The Romanian Action'.

40 C Z Codreanu, *Ibid.*, 'The Granting of Civil Rights to Jews'.

41 For example, Winston Churchill was to write of Bolshevism as 'this movement among the Jews'. W S Churchill, 'Zionism versus Bolshevism: A Struggle for the Soul of the Jewish People', London, *Illustrated Sunday Herald*, 8 February 1920, p. 5.

42 C Z Codreanu, op. cit., 'My First Arrest'.

and his supporters staged a pre-emptive occupation. After renewed clashes elsewhere, the universities remained closed.[43]

In August 1923 Codreanu accepted responsibility for organizing a national student congress in Iasi. One of the mainstays of the student movement was Ion Mota, son of a priest, who became Codreanu's deputy.[44] The Cathedral was chained to prevent the students from entry, and gendarme guarded the University. Refusing to turn back, the students, led by Codreanu, forcibly occupied the University, but were soon surrounded by the army. As the students proceeded with their Congress, townspeople clashed in the evening with the army when they attempted to bring the students food.

For the following two days the congress continued elsewhere in Iasi. Codreanu, Mota and their supporters had formally assumed leadership of the student movement. The movement would now take on a political direction in support of Cuza's League. On concluding the fourth day of the congress, Codreanu proceeded to Buconvina, a warrant out for his arrest, to attend the leadership congress of the League.[45]

The authorities also tried to ban the League congress, and the delegates had to break through the cordons. The congress resolved to send a peasant delegation to the Prime Minister to appeal for a halt to the exploitation and deprivations of the local peasantry by a Jewish merchant, Anbaub, who had gained ownership of Buconvina forestry. Codreanu arrived in Bucharest in advance to arrange their reception by students.

When the peasant delegation arrived they were met with blows from the sticks and rifle butts of gendarmes. The furious students placed the elderly peasants in the centre of their group and forced their way through three cordons. Three days later, after being told that the Prime Minister would see them, the police told them to disperse. The old peasants in travelling to Bucharest had spent more on the journey than they could afford. Codreanu was not inclined to take such drawbacks passively. Codreanu and the peasants forced their way into the government buildings and threatened a rampage. They were permitted to proceed to the Prime Minister and his Ministers. While

43 C Z Codreanu, *Ibid.*, 'June 1923'.

44 In 1936 Mota formed a Legionary unit to fight the Reds in Spain and was killed on the battlefield on 13 January 1937.

45 C Z Codreanu, op. cit., 'The Congress of the Student Movement's Leaders'.

Ionel Bratianu promised to settle the grievances of the peasantry against Jewish merchants, nothing was done. Indeed, several hours later, the leaders of the delegation were arrested.[46]

Codreanu went on to the League congress at Campul-Lung. Ion Mota had concluded that the student strike could not continue, and that the leaders must concede defeat, but that they must also set an example by taking up arms and executing those 'most guilty of betraying Romanian interests'. Eight students, including Mota and Codreanu, formed together to decide the most apt targets. The first to be executed should be Romanian traitors, and six Cabinet Ministers were chosen. The next to go would be the Bucharest rabbis, followed by the primary bankers who controlled the political parties, and then by the Jewish press directors. The group left Iasi for Bucharest.

They had not long met in Bucharest, when they were surrounded by police, and taken to Police Headquarters. The police already had the handguns they had hidden and the letters they had left. Several others were arrested, including Codreanu's father. Codreanu was innately incapable of lying even to save himself, and he defiantly admitted the plot. Ironically, due to the rapidity with which Codreanu and his colleagues had been detained, they had not even had time to formulate their plans; hence there was insufficient material with which to prosecute.[47]

In jail awaiting trial, the group planned a movement that would be the militant youth arm of the League for Christian National Defence. Discussing a name for this association on 8 November, 'the feast of Saints Archangels Michael and Gabriel', Codreanu suggested the organization be named in honour of Saint Michael.[48]

After several months jail most of the group, including Ion Codreanu, and the individual who was soon after discovered to have been the Judas, were released, with six remaining.[49]

From outside, the strike had been halted, but the students were nonetheless solidly in support of Codreanu and his colleagues. Of particular importance, the peasantry were on their side too, sent the

---

46 C Z Codreanu, *Ibid.*, 'The L.A.N.C. Congress at Campul-Lung'.

47 C Z Codreanu, *Ibid.*, 'The October 1923 Student Plot'.

48 C Z Codreanu, *Ibid.*, 'In the Văcăreşti Prison'.

49 C Z Codreanu, op. cit., 'In the Văcăreşti Prison'.

prisoners money and said Masses for them in the Churches.[50] By early 1924 the plight of Codreanu and the others had caught the sympathy of increasing numbers of Romanians.

In March the trial was held, and the jury took just half an hour to reach an acquittal.[51] In the interim Mota had been given a revolver and shot the judas within the prison.

Codreanu was not long back at Iasi when he was attacked without provocation by police, as he talked with his two sisters and a group of students. The police were under orders to provoke Codreanu. The Government aimed to crush the student and the nationalist movements in Iasi. While Codreanu had been in jail, the police had enacted a brutal regime upon the students. The choir conductor of the University had been beaten, had been detained in great misery, and had died in hospital. A group of female students had been dragged through the streets and beaten.[52]

The Nest

On 6 May 1924 Codreanu gathered together 60 high school and university students forming the first Brotherhood of the Cross, the youth branch of the new movement. The youths began building a meeting place in Ungheni, working from 4:00 am until evening. This as the first of the historical 'Work Camps' that were to be one of the foundations of what became a mass movement. Locals came to help, and food was donated. Other student teams cultivated several acres of donated land.

As the building was being constructed so too was an important ethos: curios townspeople gathered to see the *intelligentsia* covered in clay, sweating and working. This was 'National-Christian Socialism' in action.

These folk were witnessing the crumbling of an up-to-then dominating concept, i.e., that it is shameful for an intellectual to work with his hands, particularly at heavy labour, formerly allotted to slaves or despicable classes.[53]

50 C Z Codreanu, *Ibid.*, 'Outside'.

51 C Z Codreanu, *Ibid.*, 'Avenging the Betrayal and the Trial'.

52 C Z Codreanu, *Ibid.*, 'At Iasi'.

53 C Z Codreanu, *Ibid.*, 'The First Work Camp'.

The first to appreciate this new phenomena for Romania were the workers and the peasants, who felt that for the first time their labours had dignity and that in these youth were the making of a new order. However the provocations continued, and on 3 May 200 armed gendarme attacked the garden being worked by the youngsters. Codreanu was bound and beaten.[54] Thirty interrogators at the Police Prefecture attempted to intimate the young Brothers into incriminating Codreanu. The soles of the feet were beaten, and their heads pushed into pails of water.

Cuza accompanied by the public prosecutor, a medical examiner and the parents of the youngsters who were being tortured, arrived at the Prefecture. The youths were released, while Codreanu was detained for several days, before being freed by the examining magistrate. Codreanu defiantly told the magistrate that he would extract his own justice. Cuza naively thought that justice could be had through the Minister of the Interior.[55]

Codreanu felt defeated. He boarded a train for Bucovina, where he had been so well received by the hard-pressed peasants. He climbed 4500 feet up the Rarau Mountain. Here he built a shelter, and for a month and a half lived in solitude, eating a meagre diet brought to him by shepherds. Doubts wracked him.

Descending the mountain six weeks later, he returned to Iasi and perceived an increased arrogance among the Jewish community and a close relationship they had developed with the police.[56]

Trials

The trial of Mota, and Leonida Vlad, the student who had procured the revolver with which Mota had shot the judas under the noses of the police, began in September 1924. That there was such an outpouring of mass support for Mota, for his having shot a 'traitor', seems indicative of the deep, widespread dissatisfaction with Romania. Mota was acquitted.[57]

---

54 C Z Codreanu, *Ibid.*, 'Overwhelmed by Blows at the Garden'.

55 C Z Codreanu, *Ibid.*, 'Upstairs, in the Prefect's Office'.

56 C Z Codreanu, *Ibid.*, 'On the Rarau Mountain'.

57 C Z Codreanu, *Ibid.*, 'The Mota/Vlad Trial'.

As for the police atrocities against the youngsters, which Cuza thought could be resolved through the legal system, the complainants were themselves subjected to further beatings. In October 1924 Codreanu presented himself to the Court to represent a young, tortured complainant. The Prefect showed up in Court with twenty staff and attacked Codreanu. He drew his revolver and brought down three of the attackers including the chief culprit, Prefect Manciu, who was killed. The life of a brutal and stupid man had been justly ended, from whom the people of Iasi had endured much. Several thousand Jews gathered outside the Court House waiting to mob Codreanu. He drew his revolver and, accompanied by a lawyer, walked through the mob, as they parted. However, police jumped Codreanu and took him in chains to the Prefecture.

The news of Codreanu having been again attacked by a police mob provoked a student riot. The army came out, with bayonets fixed. Codreanu was placed under arrest and transported to a jail in Iasi. Again, the stalwarts of the student movement, along with Ion Codreanu, were arrested. The jail was cold and even the strength of Codreanu began to deteriorate.[58]

Codreanu's trial, scheduled for January 1925, was transferred to Focşani, which Codreanu states was a 'liberal stronghold'; the only town in the whole of Romania where 'the nationalist movement did not catch on'. Codreanu's supporters worried that he would be shot in transit on the pretext that he was attempting to escape.

Something of the miraculous then occurred in liberal Focşani: there was a groundswell of support for Codreanu. A mass agitation occurred throughout the country, and people from all over Romania converged on Focşani. The authorities and the Jewish power-brokers and opinion-makers began to think that prosecuting Codreanu would only add to his popularity.[59]

The Trial was then transferred to Turnul-Severin at the other end of Romania. There, however, the prison officials received him 'like an honoured guest', and his prison conditions were much improved. The noon of his arrival Codreanu could see out from the courtyard onto the street, where a gathering of over 200 children, 6 and 7 years old, had gathered, waving at Codreanu, having heard that he had been brought to their town. Every day the children waited on the pavement to greet him.

58 C Z Codreanu, *Ibid.*, 'The Fatal Day'.

59 C Z Codreanu, *Ibid.*, 'The Trial is Transferred to Focşani'.

The President of the Tribunal treated Codreanu with courtesy. Again, there was a groundswell of support. The little children in greater numbers continued to gather – solemnly - outside the prison until the authorities prevented them. However, officialdom in the town was by no means adverse to Codreanu, and the Mayor in particular showed support.[60]

The Tribunal had received a petition from 19,300 lawyers throughout Romania, wishing to defend Codreanu. Trainloads of sympathizers from throughout the country began to arrive. Over 10,000 people gathered outside. The prosecution witnesses denied everything, including the beatings and torture of the detained, and the veracity of the medical certificates issued by the examining doctor. The perjury of those who had sworn an oath upon the cross caused increasing outrage among the spectators. Suddenly one of the spectators jumped up and threw Commissar Vasiliu Spanchiu, who had been responsible for the torture of the youngsters, out of the building. Thereafter the attitude of the prosecuting witnesses became craven.

It took the jury just minutes to reach an acquittal of the seven defendants, who were taken back into the hall, carried on the shoulders of a jubilant multitude, where the jury now sat, each wearing the swastika and tricolor insignia of the movement. Even the presiding judge was caught up in the enthusiasm. The defendants were lifted up again and carried out to the waiting crowd of 10,000, who formed a column and carried the defendants on high through the town, the townsfolk showering them with flowers[61]

The following day Codreanu boarded the train for Iasi, the carriages festooned with flowers, while thousands gathered to farewell him and an entourage of 300.

A Marriage Becomes a Celebration of National Joy

At each train stop people came to cheer Codreanu; school children, peasants and priests, the elderly with tears of joy… At Craiova, a crowd of 10,000. At Bucharest, 50,000.

Codreanu remarks that with such a spontaneous rising of the country the State could have been seized then, but Cuza did not understand

60 C Z Codreanu, *Ibid.*, 'At Turnul-Severin'.

61 C Z Codreanu, *Ibid.*, 'The Trial'.

the possibilities. The movement was never again to see such an opportunity.

Several days later Codreanu reached his hometown of Husi, where he was married in a civil service.[62] The wedding entourage proceeded to Focşani where the religious ceremony would be performed. Codreanu describes the scene of '2,300 wagons, carriages and cars all embellished with flowers and the people dressed in national costumes'.[63] The wedding was preformed in front of 100,000 spectators. It had been a great celebration of national joy, with the traditional costumes and dances. A movie of the festivities was shown in theatres in Bucharest until quickly confiscated and destroyed by the authorities.[64]

In August 1925 Codreanu was to become god-father to 100 babies who had been born that month in and near the county of Putna, with the baptism to take place at Focşani. Even now the Government moved in and decreed a state of siege. The baptisms took place instead at Ciorasti in secret.[65] It indicates the state of desperation of those who sought to stop Codreanu, who emerged stronger with every persecution.

After nearly a year of interruptions, Codreanu returned to Iasi where the work of building a headquarters and organizing the youth was resumed. Now the movement had caught the imagination of the masses, and donations were even received from Romanians in the USA. The phenomenon of students undertaking hard labour was new, and caught the national enthusiasm. Office workers would join in after their work-day, taking up shovels and wheeling borrows cement. Brotherhoods of the Cross had formed throughout the country, and they would go to Iasi to help.[66] The building was serving as a focal point for a great national and spiritual movement that was transcending class and generational differences.

Yet despite such successes the League of National Christian Defence lacked the ability to take advantage of the situation. The success of the movement, which did not require any strict membership criteria, brought in opportunists and swindlers, others lacked discipline or strength of faith and will, while others were infiltrators. Codreanu

---

62 C Z Codreanu, *Ibid.*, 'Returning to Iasi'.

63 C Z Codreanu, *Ibid.*, 'My Wedding'.

64 C Z Codreanu, *Ibid.*

65 C Z Codreanu, *Ibid.*, 'The Baptismal Ceremonies at Ciorasti'.

66 C Z Codreanu, *Ibid.*, 'After one Year, Work Resumes'.

always believed that the national movement had to be of the hardest discipline. Because of its very popularity the League was becoming 'a real hell'. However, Cuza could not be persuaded to act.[67]

Cuza was a great theoretician and scholar. Codreanu's father, Ion, had been one of his leading supporters, and Cornelieu had learned about the nationalist creed at a young age from his writings. But the professor did not have the qualities of an organiser, or those that could inspire heroic sacrifices. 'When a leader hears that inner command he must have the courage to draw out his sword',[68] wrote Codreanu, and Cuza had already missed the opportunity for the seizure of the State. Nor had Cuza ever initiated any of the great events that had taken place, although he had been of great help when they had occurred.[69] Cuza nonetheless was denied his Chair of the Faculty of Political Economy at Iasi University for supposedly having been the instigator of the student strike, to which he responded with defiance: 'I am an instigator of the national energies'.[70] Following this blow, while walking alone on the streets, he was stuck by a Jew. In response, the students, including the ever-ready Ion Mota, went through the pubs in Iasi striking any Jew they found.[71]

On 23 September 1925 the corner stone to the movement's building at Iasi was laid. Codreanu now considered it time to resume his education, also being motivated by the need to recuperate his health that had been undermined by his jailing, and at a time when his relations with Cuza were declining. He also needed time to reflect in regard to the state of the League, as it was showing signs of added strength, having united with Romanian Action, and The National Fascia. These groups had brought many worthy men. Important support was also added by the affiliation of the widely read newspaper *Libertatea*, edited by Father Mota, father of Codreanu's close comrade Ion. The young Mota, having been expelled from the University, decided to join Codreanu abroad to continue his education, and they set off for Grenoble, France.[72]

---

67 C Z Codreanu, *Ibid.*, 'Dangers that Threaten a Political Movement'.

68 C Z Codreanu, *Ibid.*, 'The Critique of the Leader'.

69 C Z Codreanu, *Ibid.*, 'A Case of Conscience'.

70 C Z Codreanu, *Ibid.*

71 C Z Codreanu, *Ibid.*

72 C Z Codreanu, *Ibid.*, 'In France, At School'.

Democracy In Action

With the fall of the Liberal Government, elections were to be held in May 1926, and Codreanu returned home. The reception from Cuza to Codreanu's return was cool. At first assisting with the campaigns of others, he was soon asked by several of the movement luminaries to stand in Focşani, although Codreanu had a detestation of 'this heap of putrefaction' called democracy.[73]

With Focşani still under siege since the time of the baptisms, the Prefecture attempted to prevent Codreanu from entry, the first effort being stopped by police gunfire. Codreanu went to the Prefect, but despite the appeals of his comrade, General Macridescu, that they were legally entitled to enter, the Prefect would not relent. Codreanu stated that if he were shot at again in attempting to enter, he would come back and fire upon the Prefect. The following day Codreanu was arrested and questioned by the Council of War. He was told not to enter Focşani, despite being a parliamentary candidate. After being confined for three days, then going to Bucharest to complaint to the Interior Minister, Codreanu managed to get into Focşani just two days before the elections. Showing up at the first village, there was an atmosphere for fear, and he was told by the gendarmes that he would be permitted to speak for one minute. This was the situation pertaining to all the villages – one minute speeches.

On election day our delegates were beaten, covered with blood and otherwise prevented from getting to polling places; whole villages could not get near polling stations. The result: I lost, though in the town of Focşani I won over all the political parties.[74]

However, the League had garnered 120,000 voted and secured ten Deputies, including his father, and Cuza. Codreanu was happy with such results despite all the obstacles, and returned to France, but with the feeling that the State could never be taken by 'democratic' means.[75]

In May 1927 Codreanu received an urgent message from Mota and others stating that the League had split and for him to return urgently. Codreanu successfully took his examinations and went back to Focşani. He arrived in Bucharest and found the League in disarray,

73 C Z Codreanu, *Ibid.*, 'General Elections Back Home'.

74 C Z Codreanu, *Ibid.*

75 C Z Codreanu, *Ibid.*

with widespread demoralization. However, Cuza was jubilant, and patronizingly asked that Codreanu mind his own business.[76]

Codreanu concluded that the problems rested with lack of coordination between parliamentary and extra-parliamentary activities; and a lack of spiritual unity, caused ultimately by a lack of leadership. The movement was failing to adequately educate its supporters or to consult with them. Cuza had been a brilliant scholar, but had failed to issue any directives since the founding of the League in 1923. Cuza had also, oddly, given praise to the Liberal and People's parties in Parliament, as sincere servants of the nation; giving legitimacy to a regime that had persecuted and tortured his own followers.

Cuza unilaterally expelled Deputy Paul Uiescu from the League, demanding that he be thrown out of Parliament. Most of the Deputies, including Codreanu's father, issued a declaration condemning Cuza's action. All the signatories were expelled from the League. In response they formed a Statutory League of Christian National Defence.

This was the situation when Codreanu returned from France.[77] Codreanu hastily convened a meeting of his student supporters at Iasi, in the hope of forming a youth bloc that could ward off the demoralization of the older generation. Only a minority supported Codreanu's efforts. Nonetheless, Codreanu's supporters went to Bucharest to talk with both factions of the League. Cuza was intractable.[78]

Formation of The Legion of St Michael

Codreanu decided to proceed with his youth movement and taking the icon of Saint Michael he had first seen when jailed at Văcăreşti prison in 1924, the image of their Holy Patron was installed at the House they had built at Iasi. On 24 June 1927, the Văcăreşti prison veterans and a few others, met to found The Legion of Michael the Archangel; the realization of Codreanu's plans he had formulated during the hardship of his imprisonment three years earlier.

The meeting lasted a minute; long enough for those present – even the

76 C Z Codreanu, *Ibid.*, 'At Bucharest, the League of National Christian Defence is Broken in Two'.

77 C Z Codreanu, *Ibid.*, 'What Happened?'

78 C Z Codreanu, *Ibid.*, 'My Reaction'.

Văcăreşti prison veterans – to digest all they needed for reflection. The following day the group went to Cuza and asked to be released from their vows to the League. The Professor wished them well, shaking the hand of each. They had a similar meeting with Professor Sumuleanu, head of the 'Statutory' faction.

The Legion began with about 15 students, too poor to afford the postage for a letter. It was a challenge from God that one might live by spirit and not matter. 'We were striking a blow at a mentality which placed the golden calf in the centre and as the main purpose in life'.[79]

Despite the goodwill expressed by Cuza, both League factions bitterly condemned the youths, and the Iasi students also withheld support.[80] The first action of the Legion was to prepare a room suitable for the housing of the icon of Saint Michael. The walls were painted white and draped with Christian axioms. Unlike the democratic movements and political parties, the Legion would not seek members. They would declare their faith simply, so that those who had the dedication might come to them. Nor was it a time for political platforms, of which there were many in Romania. A new faith and a new man were needed. [81]

As for Cuza's party, in the 1927 elections its vote dropped to 70,000 from the previous 120,000.[82] With a bleak outlook for Romania, the League having lost an historic opportunity to take state power, the Legionaries accepted the possibility of martyrdom, which might redeem the Romanian masses and awaken them from the demoralization to which they had returned.[83]

For a new publication that would carry their Faith, the name chosen was *The Ancestral Land*; connotating more than politics, but a mystical union with their forebears who had sanctified the land with sweat and blood. *The Ancestral Land* came out on 1 August 1927 as a bi-monthly magazine printed by Father Mota. [84] During 1927-28 'Nests' of 3 to 13 members were formed, the Legionaries continued working on the buildings, and on the gardens, the selling of vegetables at the markets becoming a means of raising funds. However, Codreanu and his wife lived in poverty, while the

79 C Z Codreanu, *Ibid.*, 'The Legion of Michael The Archangel'.

80 C Z Codreanu, *Ibid.*, 'Against Treachery'.

81 C Z Codreanu, *Ibid.*, 'The Beginnings of Legionary Life'.

82 C Z Codreanu, *Ibid.*, 'Aspects of Romanian Public Life',

83 C Z Codreanu, *Ibid.*, 'Our Apprehensions Facing this World'.

84 C Z Codreanu, *Ibid.*, 'Stages of the Legion's Development'.

press insisted that the movement must be funded from outside Romania to be able to buy a truck. Codreanu opened a legal practice in Ungheni, and gained a modest income, but he continued to live a very spartan life with neither small luxuries nor entertainment.[85]

Codreanu made time to traverse the countryside, and speak to the peasants, to fully understand their plight. In the summer of 1929 he organised the first of the 'long marches' of the Brotherhood of the Cross and the Legionaries, the latter to undergo the toughest of conditions, carrying 'heavy loads through rain, wind, heat or mud; in formation and in step, with talking forbidden for hours; through a Spartan life, sleeping in forests, eating simple fare'.[86]

With the nucleus of a movement created over the course of two years, in December 1929 the Legion held its first public meeting in the market town of Beresti. As seems to be the case in every action Codreanu had sought to take since his student days, the gendarmes stated he was not permitted to speak. Codreanu replied with his customary defiance that the meeting would go ahead. The authorities agreed, providing that Codreanu did not cause any 'disturbance', somewhat to his bemusement, as if it were in Codreanu's interests to allow disturbance at the first public meeting. Few showed up, because the authorities had prevented attendance. Codreanu then proceeded on horseback, accompanied by a handful of Legionaries, with the intention of speaking to every town in the Horincea district. The locals came out to hear Codreanu at each village, where he spoke with customary brevity with a straightforward message of building a new society where one is based on character and faith. He was welcomed with jubilation at every village, as the country folk put aside all superficial differences to come as Romanians and as Christians. Codreanu picked up followers along the way. They adorned their hats with turkey feathers and entered the villages singing hymns. Word spread by word of month ahead of Codreanu, and thousands were now greeting him.[87]

Codreanu continued to travel throughout Romania the following year, and into Basarabia where the student movement had been strong, but where the Jewish communities had communist sympathies. With thirty horsemen riding into Basarabia, white cloth crosses sewn onto their jackets and with Codreanu holding a large cross, they entered

85 C Z Codreanu, *Ibid.*, 'Fighting Misery'.

86 C Z Codreanu, *Ibid.*, 'The Summer of 1929'.

87 C Z Codreanu, *Ibid.*, 'December 15 1929'.

Cahul township, riding along the streets singing 'Awake, awake, ye Romanian!' They stopped at the town square where 7000 peasants soon gathered. A few minutes into his speech, predictably, the police and local authorities arrived, telling Codreanu he could not speak in the square. Codreanu then appealed to the crowd to meet at a private courtyard, but the army attempted to stop the villagers. Codreanu and his followers were confronted by an army detachment, whose colonel pointed his revolver at Codreanu. The soldiers began to jab the Legionaries with their bayonets. Codreanu withdrew, leaving word that he would return in a few days.

Codreanu sent out a call for Legionaries to descend upon Cahul on 10 February. He went to Bucharest and obtained approval from the Interior Minister, although he was told that such permission was not necessary. Not only Legionaries, but thousands of peasants converged on Cahul.

A hundred riders, many wearing a green shirt adorned with a white cross, led the procession. A marching column of 100, flanked by about 80 wagons, followed. 20,000 peasants waiting at the square greeted this procession in respectful silence. Ion Codreanu was among the speakers assuring the Basarabian peasantry that they would not be left to the devices of the exploiters and the communists. Ion spoke for two hours with great affect and from then he was committed to the Legion.

Jewish elements were displeased at the perfect order and solemn dignity of the occasion, and after the crowd had returned home, a Jewish shop window was smashed. Two Jews were caught in the act. It was lesson that the movement must maintain perfect order, otherwise conflict would justify the state in crushing the Legion.[88]

Iron Guard

Codreanu was home a week when he was receiving pleas from the peasantry to return to Basarabia, as the news of the Legion had spread. This time Codreanu staged an expedition across the whole of southern Basarabia. It was now that Codreanu formed the Iron Guard with the aim of combating the communists. The movement aimed to win the workers over to the national cause, as they were winning youth and peasants. The approval of the Interior Minister was again received, with the assurance that order would be maintained by the Legion.[89]

88 C Z Codreanu, *Ibid.*, 'In Basarabia Again'.

89 C Z Codreanu, *Ibid.*

Meanwhile, in June 1930 Codreanu was visited at his home in Iasi by a delegation comprising two priests, a peasant and a youth. They had travelled by wagon for two weeks from Maramureş, to appeal to Codreanu for help against the despoilers of the land. The peasantry had appealed for State intervention, but they had revived no reply. The priests said that their people were dying form privation. Codreanu sent organizers to Maramureş.

The peasantry was coming over to the Legion en mass. The exploitive interests had to act, and did so by again resorting to incendiary action with which to blame the Legion. Fires had been set in Borsa, and Jews were claiming that a pogrom was imminent and that the State must repress the Legion. The two priests who had visited Codreanu, one Orthodox, the other a Greek-Catholic, were beaten and chased out of town by a Jewish mob, then arrested as 'agitators' along with the Legionary local organizers and peasant leaders.[90]

Codreanu's plan was for columns to march through Basarabia over the course of a month. After intense lobbying by the press, the Interior Minister withdrew his consent on the day the march was to begin. Codreanu issued an appeal for a mass demonstration in Bucharest. However, provocateurs were again at work, and a youth, Beza, who had recently sought membership of the Legion, had shot a Government Minister, inflicting minor wounds. Legion literature was found with Beza. When Codreanu publicly stated that Beza's motives were just in the cause of Macedonian Romanians, this was sufficient for him to be arrested.[91] Again in the Văcăreşti prison where the movement had been born in the minds and hearts of Codreanu and his comrades, he met Sterie Ciumeti, who became one of the great martyrs of the movement.[92] Codreanu was acquitted, but the prosecutor appealed and Codreanu remained in prison. Again he was acquitted, and released after six weeks.

Codreanu then went into Basarabia with a small group, including Ion Mota, to assist of the two priests who had been beaten and jailed for having led the peasant appeal to for the Legion's help. The plight of the families of the jailed priests and peasant leaders was one of destitution, hunger and sickness. The plight of the peasants throughout Basarabia was not much different, while Jews were widely perceived as an

90 C Z Codreanu, *Ibid.*, 'Troubles in Maramureş'.

91 C Z Codreanu, *Ibid.*, 'The March into Basarabia is Forbidden'.

92 Ciumeti was arrested on the night of 30 December 1930, falsely accused of shooting Prime Minister Duca, murdered by three policemen, and thrown into the icy waters of the Dambovita, fished out, and secretly buried.

extravagant middle class. Codreanu, Ion Mota and two others formed the defence team for the priests and the peasants. All were acquitted.[93]

In January 1931 the Interior Minister, Vaida, was replaced by Mihalache, who stated that he would act against the movement. The opportunity came when a Legionary youth, sickened by the calumny against the movement, unsuccessfully attempted to shoot Socor, a communist and director of the newspaper *Dimineata* ('The Morning'). Codreanu was summoned to Bucharest, found by the magistrate to have no connection to the shooting, returned to Focşani, where he was surrounded by police and jailed for eight days.

The Legion and the Iron Guard were dissolved by the Council of Ministers at the instigation of Mihalache. Homes of Legionaries were ransacked, records seized and offices shut. On 9 January Codreanu and other Legionary and Guard officers were in Văcăreşti prison. Forged documents were published in Socor's newspaper *Dimineata,* supposedly proving Codreanu had planned a revolt, and a faked letter he supposedly wrote to Hitler asking for support, was produced, which the authorities would not allow to be expertly examined. [94]

The case against the defendants collapsed. The jury could find not evidence of an intended revolt, despite the paramilitary organization of the movement.[95] Activities had always been open. However the prosecution appealed and the defendants remained in their cells. Again there was a unanimous acquittal and the defendants were released after 87 days in jail. The case went to the Supreme Court of Appeals, again with an acquittal.[96]

---

93 C Z Codreanu, op. cit., 'The March into Basarabia is Forbidden'.

94 C Z Codreanu, *Ibid.*, 'Dissolution of the Legion and the Iron Guard January 11, 1931'.

95 Paramilitary formations became the vogue for political parties during the 1930s, throughout Europe, from both Left and Right. In Germany the Social Democrats had the Blue Shirts and the Communist Party had the Red Front.

In Romania, Cuza's movement, which became the National Christian Party in 1935, had a Black shirted military called *Lancieri* (Lancers). The ruling National Peasant Party formed its own militia in 1936. See: S G Payne (London: UCL Press, 1995), pp. 284-285.

96 C Z Codreanu, *Ibid.*, 'The Trial'.

Elections

In 1931 Codreanu decided that regardless of his distaste for party politics and democracy the movement should contest elections, which was hoped to dispel some of the allegations of unconstitutionality that had smeared the movement. The National Peasant Government fell in June 1931, and a General Election was called. Although the Legionary Movement and Iron Guard were still banned, the movement continued under the name of The Corneliu Z. Codreanu Group, with the iron grid as its symbol. Despite the meagre of resources and the usual intimidation by the authorities, the Movement won 34,000 votes.[97] Two days after the General Election a seat fell vacate in Parliament for the county of Neamţ, and although all resources had been exhausted, Codreanu won by a large majority; 11,300 votes; Liberals, 7,000; National Peasants, 6000.[98]

Codreanu entered Parliament as the movement's lone representative, and despite the bitterness of his enemies, he never stooped to vitriol against them whatever the provocation. He did show however that many prominent politicians were in debt to the bankers; namely the Marmorosch Blank Bank.[99]

Four months later a Congressional seat fell vacate in Tutova. Again the authorities attempted illegalities against the Movement, and Ion Codreanu and other Legionaries were jailed. Gendarmes clubbed one Legionary team with rifle butts. Every Legionnaire was beaten unconscious and lay in the snow in pools of blow, then they were dragged to the gendarme post at Băcani. Other Legionaries went to their rescue and despite being fired upon, occupied the gendarme post. But despite the hardships, the Legion again won the election, obtaining 5,600 votes and beating the Liberals by 400.[100]

Another General Election was called for July 1932. The campaign was marked by increased violence against the Legionaries, and their supporters, including many priests. However, the Legion gained 70,000 votes and five seats.[101]

97 C Z Codreanu, *Ibid.*, 'The Legionary Movement in the First Elections, June 1931.

98 C Z Codreanu, *Ibid.*, 'The Campaign of Neamţ'.

99 C Z Codreanu, *Ibid.*, 'Democracy Against the Nation'.

100 C Z Codreanu, *Ibid.*, 'The Battle of Tutova April 17, 1932'.

101 C Z Codreanu, *Ibid.*, 'New General Elections July 1932'.

Parliamentarianism was not the major focus of the Legionary Movement. Codreanu regarded the primary purpose for the Legion as being to educate a leadership cadre and forge the 'new man'. The Movement had its real strength outside Parliament, where it was the major force among the university students, and younger youth who were being prepared within the Brotherhood of the Cross. The Legion was the primary force among the youth of Macedonia, and was gaining support among the peasantry.[102]

The press now focused on smearing the Legion as being in the pay of Mussolini, and as being 'foreign agents', and that it was even getting Jewish money, and also money from the Nazis. The press then had an about face, stated that the accusation of foreign funding was unfounded, but that the Movement was counterfeiting currency.[103] While the lies of the press and the parties reached new depths of outlandishness, so too did the violence increase.

'The Death Team'

If 'The Way of the Samurai is Death',[104] then this too was the ethos of the Legionaries, each of whom expected to meet his Calvary. Every Legionnaire felt that he was likely to pay the ultimate physical sacrifice for his Faith and land. In May 1933 a team, including a priest, Father lonescu, was formed that would travel throughout Romania spreading the Legionary message. They called themselves 'The Death Team'. They were attacked by armed police, and arrested on the outskirts of Gravita. The following day the local Prosecutor found them innocent; they had done nothing other than travel in a truck, singing hymns.

At Resita Codreanu met them to hold a public meeting, to give a public account of his Parliamentary work to his electors. The army occupied and surrounded the town. Codreanu did not to give the authorities another fraudulent pretext for acting against the Movement. The team moved on to the county of Arad. In the village of Chier the police and Jewish representatives told the village folk that the Legionaries were Red bands coming over from Hungary. The team was severely beaten

---

102 C Z Codreanu, *Ibid.*, 'The Condition of the Legionary Organization 1932-1933'.

103 C Z Codreanu, *Ibid.*, 'Printing Counterfeit Banknotes'.

104 Y Mishima, *Yukio Mishima on Hagakure*, (New York: Basic Books, 1977), p. 6.

by peasants and arrested. They were acquitted and gained much sympathy from the peasantry of Arad. Due to such actions, Codreanu decided to accompany the Team, and was received by the peasantry with customary enthusiasm.[105]

Leaving the Team, Codreanu proceeded to Teius, where his father, as a Member of Parliament, was to speak. He found his father in the home of a peasant, covered in blood from the blows he had received from the gendarme who had attacked the meeting hall. The Death Team and other Legionaries reinforced the town, but the gendarme prevented entrance to the hall. Codreanu wished to avoid a confrontation, but the peasantry confronted the gendarme and were shot at, one being killed during a battle that lasted for over two hours. The Death Team, some seriously wounded, along with 50 students, were detained without charge. Again the Legionaries were acquitted, when it was shown that the authorities had provoked violence.[106]

Labour Service

The next stage of the Legion was the formation of Work Camps to provide practical service to the people to alleviate their privations, as well as to act as a social microcosm of the Legionary ethos. During the Winter of 1932 a Legionary leader had written to Codreanu describing how the farmers of Visani were annually subjected to the flooding of the river Buzău. Entire villages were appealing to the Legion for help. All local Legionaries were directed by Codreanu to arrive at Visani on 10 July 1933, where the first Work Camp was formed. It was to be the start of a programme intended to create new villages and a new life outside the inaction of officialdom. A giant dam would be constructed.

200 young Legionaries arrived on the first day, but several companies of gendarmes, under orders from the Ministry of Internal Affairs, attacked them. A priest, Father Dumitrescu, there to say Mass before the start of work, was among those beaten. The 200 young men, in humility before their God, met the attack by laying in the mud and singing "God is with us', while the gendarmes, led by the local Prosecutor, trampled over them. Codreanu states of this: 'I understood then, that all avenues were closed to us, and that from then on we must prepare for death'. He appealed to Prime Minister Vaida, who

105 C Z Codreanu, op. cit., 'The Death Team'.

106 C Z Codreanu, *Ibid.*, 'At Teius'.

had two months earlier commended Codreanu for his intention of constructing the dam.

It was to be an example for other scores of thousands of youth. It was to be a school for the great popular masses who for years had gone along with their bridges and roads in disrepair, waiting for the state to come fix them, when in a single day their work in common could have repaired them.[107]

Dr Ronnett, a prominent Chicago physician, recalled decades later:

> Without asking for any remuneration, the Legionaries proceeded to help the peasants with their work in the field, repairing here and there a broken bridge, building a house for a needy family, digging ditches for water drainage, becoming caretakers of cemeteries and churches.[108]

What the 'Legionary Voluntary Workers' did receive in return is the redemption value of work and service, while showing the practical application of 'National-Christian Socialism'.

A month after the Visani incident Codreanu opened a Labour Camp in New Bucharest, a ward of the capital. Here a convalescent home was built for those Legionaries wounded in battles. This later became 'The Green House', headquarters of the Iron Guard. Throughout 1933-1934 the Legionary Voluntary Workers continued to be constantly harassed by the authorities. However by 1935 there were five labour camps in Romania; in 1935 over twenty and by 1936 all district organisations had opened camps. Other than the camps there were also thousands of construction sites. [109] Even this charitable work could not be left alone by the regime, and in 1937 a law prohibited voluntary labour in camps' as 'a subversive act'.[110]

Calvary

The leader of the Liberal Party, Duca, regarded the Vaida Government as too weak to crush the Legionary Movement, despite all the

107 C Z Codreanu, *Ibid.*, 'The Dam of Visani, July 10 133'.

108 A E Ronnett, *Romanian Nationalism: The Legionary Movement* (Chicago: Loyola University Press, 1974), p. 28.

109 A E Ronnett, *Ibid.*, p. 30.

110 A E Ronnett, , *Ibid.*, p. 31.

atrocities that had been perpetrated against them under the aegis of that regime.[111]

In December 1933 the Legion was again prohibited, and 11,000 Legionaries were jailed. In the forthcoming polls, Prime Minister Duca ordered that the Legionaries be kept from the polls. On 29 December 1933, three students killed Duca. Although the Legionary leadership had known nothing of the assassination 18,000 Legionaries were arrested, which was finally reduced to fifty including, of course, Codreanu. Before a Military Tribunal only the three students were found guilty. Thereafter, the Military judiciary was to be subjected to the authority of the Government. [112] Impartial juries and tribunals had found the Legionaries innocent time after time over the course of a decade, and on each occasion Codreanu emerged stronger.

Despite the unprecedented persecution from the regime, the Legion had grown to 200,000 by late 1937.[113] It should be recalled that the Legion, despite such a large membership, was an elite and hierarchical movement organised into 'Nests' or small cells. Each member took a blood oath, and expected death to be the likely result of membership. The hardships of the Legionaries make such a large membership all the more incredible.

Campaigning in the December 1937 elections – which Payne describes as 'customarily corrupt and partially manipulated', under the name of 'All for the Fatherland', the movement achieved an official count of 15.58%; although the real count was, according to later statements by Romanian police chief Eugen Cristescu, 25%, or 800,000 votes.[114]

King Carol dissolved Parliament in January 1938 and scheduled elections for March, but carried out a 'royal coup' in February. He chose a ministry under a figurehead, Patriarch Cristea, head of the Orthodox Church. The King wavered between having Codreanu murdered and trying to co-opt him into his regime, but the latter proved impossible. Codreanu ordered the Movement to lay low until the regimen started falling apart. However Interior Minister Calinescu was determined to finally crush the Legion.

---

111 C Z Codreanu, *Ibid.*, 'The Liberal Party Assumes Responsibility for Exterminating the Iron Guard'.

112 A E Ronnett, op. cit., pp. 36-37.

113 S G Payne, op. cit., p. 285.

114 S G Payne, *Ibid.*, pp. 286-287.

Several hundred leaders of the Movement were arrested on the night of Palm Sunday, 16 April 1938. Despite declining health through years of persecution in the regime's jails, Codreanu was thrown into the dungeon of the Jilava fort, in 'a sort of cave about six by four yards'.[115] His lungs were wrecked by years of persecution.[116]

Codreanu was charged with 'high treason' and 'the preparation of a social revolution in Romania with the aid of the foreign power'. The trial began on 23 May 1938 under the jurisdiction of the Council of War of the Second Army Corps. Under previous military tribunals that were impartial Codreanu had always been acquitted. Since December 1933, after the assassination of Prime Minister Duca, the military tribunals were no longer independent. Testimony of defence witnesses was not permitted, and the lawyers were intimidated. Although the defence had been able to disprove the charges the tribunal ruled Codreanu guilty and sentenced him to ten ears hard labour. Another trial the following month condemned other leaders of the Movement.[117]

Late in the night of 29 November 1938, under the pretext of being transferred to Bucharest, Codreanu and thirteen other Legionaries were taken from their cells at Ramnicul Sarat, loaded into a truck and tied with ropes. On a deserted road the truck stopped, the prisoners were garrotted; their bodies were taken to Jilava, their heads shot, their bodies thrown into a common grave and covered in sulphuric acid, and the grave covered with a thousand-pound concrete slab.[118]

The martyrdom of the Legionaries did not halt with the murder of their Captain, nor could the Movement be ended. From then until the 1960s Legionaries were the victims of the regime of General Antonescu, a nominal Legionary; the Germans, their supposed sponsors, and the post-war Communist regime[119] inaugurated by the veteran Communist Ana Pauker.[120]

---

115 C Papanace, citing Codreanu's posthumously published 'Notes from Jilava', 19 April 1938; Bob Eccles and Michael Walker, *Legion* (London: Rising Press, ca. 1980s), p. 15.

116 C Z Codreanu, 'Notes from Jilava', 19 June 1938, *Ibid.*, 16.

117 A E Ronnett, *Romanian Nationalism*, op. cit., p. 45.

118 A E Ronnett, *Ibid.*, p. 46.

119 A E Ronnett, *Ibid.*, pp. 46-56.

120 Ana Pauker, a veteran communist since Codreanu's youth, emerged after World War II as the ruler of Romania. This is how *Time* described her and her regime: Ana Pauker lives in three great houses, moving almost every night because of fears of assassins… The power of the aristocrats, the industrialists,

Codreanu, of all the 'fascist' leaders, was the most persecuted. Since his adolescence every day had been one of struggle for his Faith and Nation. Perhaps Codreanu embarked on a life as Christ-like as it is humanly possible to reach.

Kerry Bolton

Kapiti Coast, New Zealand

---

the royal playboys and the royal concubines passed into her hands. She runs Romania. Ana Pauker was born (1893) in Bucharest, where her father, Zvi Rabinsohn, was a shohet, i.e., the man who kills animals in accordance with Jewish rules. Ana went to the Jewish school at Anton Pan Street. A recent visitor described Bucharest as a 'city with the air of a pawnshop.' *Time*, 20 September 1948. Cited by Maj. R H Williams, *Know Your Enemy* (Santa Ana, 1950), pp. 29-30.

Historical Background to *For My Legionaries*

For My Legionaries is often described as Corneliu Zelea Codreanu's *magnum opus*, for it is Codreanu's autobiography and serves as the primary and most crucial source on his life and thought. However, as Codreanu himself pointed out at the very beginning of his book, his composition of the work was done in the midst of numerous other preoccupations and was written "hastily on the battlefield." It is for that reason that the book's contents were selected and organized in a rather irregular fashion, and it is also partly due to that fact that the book does not provide one with fully detailed explanations regarding historical occurrences that would allow a non-Romanian reader to properly grasp why Codreanu developed his particular beliefs, and why he undertook the life path he describes in this book. Concerning this problem, one must keep in mind that Codreanu originally intended that the book be read specifically by Romanians of his own time, and so the average, modern reader living outside of Romania will most likely not have an adequate knowledge of Romanian history and culture necessary to comprehend the causes and consequences of many of the events and philosophical concepts written about in this book.

Therefore, the purpose of our introduction here is to attempt to convey to the reader some of the essential knowledge of history, culture, and philosophy to better understand Codreanu's life experiences and ideas. Essentially, this introduction serves to provide the necessary background for understanding *For My Legionaries* in simple terms for the general reader; it has a clarificatory, not an academic, purpose. We must emphasize, in this regard, that our explanations here certainly do not encompass all of Romanian and Legionary history and ideas, only what is most essential to comprehending Codreanu's autobiography.[1]

1 A more comprehensive and academic explanation of Legionary history as well as the Movement's doctrine, along with referenced resources for further reading, can be found in our monograph "The Romanian Iron Guard: Its Origins, History and Legacy," included as an appendix to this present edition of *For My Legionaries*.

Some Prominent Events in Romanian History

1. The Quest for Unity and Independence

The history of Romania is dominated by struggles related to two goals: (1) independence from foreign control, and (2) the unification of all territories composed of majority Romanian people. This is because for much of its history, ever since the Middle Ages, Romania was divided into three sections: Transylvania, which was ruled by Hungary ever since the eleventh century, and the kingdoms of Moldavia (equivalent to modern-day northeastern Romania and the current country of Moldavia) and Wallachia (equivalent to the southern half of modern-day Romania). Some of the most famous Romanian kings, which one may see referenced throughout *For My Legionaries*, include:

- Stefan the Great (1433–1504), ruler of the kingdom of Moldavia, who successfully maintained Moldavia's independence from the Ottoman Empire, Hungary, and Poland.

- Vlad Tepes (1431–1476), who later became known as Vlad the Impaler and "Dracula," was ruler of Wallachia, and, despite the harsh punishments he imposed, was renowned for maintaining Wallachia's independence from the Ottoman Empire.

- Michael the Brave (1558–1601), also a ruler of Wallachia, struggled to regain Romania's independence from the Ottoman Empire after all of the three Romanian territories were conquered by the mid-1500's, and also eventually united all of the Romanian territories under his rule by the year 1600, thus becoming the first Romanian to politically unite Romania, if only until his death in 1601.

By the seventeenth century the Ottoman Empire solidified its rule over all the Romanian territories. Though, by the late 1600's, Transylvania was re-conquered by the Austrian Hapsburg Empire, thus, once again, falling under the rule of the Hungarians, albeit with Hungarians in turn being subordinate to Austrian Germans in this case.

However, during the eighteenth and nineteenth century, the ideology of ethnic nationalism, which held first and foremost that each ethnicity deserved its own independent state, spread across Europe. As it grew in popularity among the Romanian people sought independence from the foreign powers dominating them even more greatly than before.

Eventually, revolts against both Austrian-Hungarian and Ottoman rule broke out. Some of the most well-known were:

- The revolt of 1784 in Transylvania led by Horea, Closca and Crisan, which was an attempt for Romanians to gain equal rights and status with Hungarians and Germans, both of whom were more privileged than Romanians in the social structure of the Austrian Empire.

- The Wallachian uprising of 1821 against Ottoman rule, led by Tudor Vladimirescu, also known as Domnul Tudor.

- The Revolutions of 1848, which were an attempt by all three Romanian regions to unite and gain independence from both the Austrian and Ottoman Empires, and during which Avram Iancu led a revolt in Transylvania.

Unfortunately, all of these endeavors failed and Romanians continued to be ruled by foreigners. Yet, in 1859, Romania got closer to reaching its goals when Moldavia and Wallachia announced their unification and elected prince Alexandru Ioan Cuza as their common ruler. This became known as the "Union of 1859," and was also a prelude to Romania uniting once more to gain its independence.

It was in 1879 that Romania finally gained independence from the Ottoman Empire, along with several other Balkan states, due to Russia's victory over the Turks in the Russo-Turkish War of 1877-78, for Romania had fought alongside Russia in this conflict. However, Romania was not allowed to emerge whole at this time, as it was required to relinquish Bessarabia to Russia, while Transylvania remained part of the Austro-Hungarian Empire. Its complete unification occurred after World War I, thus forming then what is commonly referred to as "Greater Romania" throughout Codreanu's book.

2. Social Problems of the Early Twentieth Century

During most of its existence, Romania was primarily an agricultural, peasant nation. The country had just barely exited a quasi-feudal system in the years following the First World War. Nevertheless, prior to World War I, Romania was in large part an economically and socially stable nation. Yet, the aftermath of the war caused conditions to change and worsen due to certain new policies that were implemented.

Firstly, an agrarian reform was undertaken which involved arranging for the boyars (traditional nobles who functioned as large landowners) to relinquish much of their agricultural land and redistribute it to the peasants. This involved roughly ninety-two percent of Romania's arable land. This reform was thus expected to make the peasants more productive, and as a result also more able to pay what they owed for receiving the land.

While one might assume that such a reform would benefit the peasants, it ironically did just the opposite. The peasants, who now became small landowners, lacked the proper equipment and capabilities to make full use of the land. They were also unable to sell whatever agricultural products they produced to foreign markets or to obtain reasonable loans in order to cope financially. Thus, they were forced to agree to financially difficult deals and gradually fell into debt as a result. Additionally, the laws behind the reform also ruined the boyars along with the peasants, for the boyars were provided with only one-third of one percent of the worth of the land they just lost.

Certain political parties that claimed to represent the common people appeared in the 1920's promising to resolve these issues, the most notable being General Averescu's People's Party and the National Peasant Party. However, each consistently failed to fulfill expectations. It appeared as though no political party was capable of correcting this grave problem.

The situation was also coupled with the sort of unbridled capitalism that was being practiced in Europe at this time. During this time period, capitalism was completely unrestricted, in the sense that capitalists could modify the conditions, hours, and wages of their workers in whatever way they pleased, since workers had no state organizations or laws to use as leverage. It should also be noted that in the post-WWI era, wages and conditions for Romanians workers became dismal compared to previous eras. Furthermore, capitalists were also unrestrained in reaping the land of its resources; there were no restrictions to expanding economic interests even when it harmed the livelihood of the people, as Codreanu notes in some portions of his book when discussing the sources of livelihood of various groups of peasants being abused by certain companies. In fact, it could be said that perhaps the only people who benefitted from the agrarian reform and the situation it created were capitalists and speculators.

These are some of the significant aspects and facts of modern Romanian history that one must understand in order to grasp not only some of the events Codreanu describes in his book, but also why he and other Romanians living in this era developed the sort of beliefs they did regarding politics, culture, and economy.

Codreanu's Ideology and Beliefs

Throughout Codreanu's book one is able to consistently see expressions of anti-Semitism, Nationalism, Monarchism, anti-democratic thought, a unique type of economic theory, and a fervent religiosity. Most people are not knowledgeable enough in regards to why Codreanu and many other Romanians held such attitudes during this time period, and would therefore misguidedly dismiss them as the result of xenophobia, ignorance, or reactionary tendencies. Here we will examine the facts of these ideas, so as to illuminate to readers their origins and logic.

1. Nationalism

The sort of nationalist and anti-Semitic thought expressed throughout the book may perhaps be some of the most significant aspects of Codreanu's thought that many typical modern, Western readers would likely find difficult to properly understand and may even dismiss as nonsensical. This may be due to the fact that people living in Western nations today have developed the attitude that human beings are merely masses of individuals, and that elements such as ethnicity have no real, long-term importance. However, Romanian nationalists recognized that humans are not merely a collection of disconnected individuals, that they are in fact affected and united by the collective groups they belong to, such as ethnicity or nationality, and that these groups are sacred and need to be preserved with necessary measures. They understood that each ethnic group possesses, in its depths, its own unique spirit or soul, which expresses itself through its particular culture and traditions.

Understanding this concept may help give meaning to one of the quotes Codreanu reproduces from professor A.C. Cuza: "Nationality is the creative power of human culture, culture is the creative power of nationality" - a quote which was taken from Cuza's 1908 book titled *Naționalitatea în artă* ("Nationality in Art"). Here it is also important to highlight the fact, recognized by all Romanian national conservatives, that unique ethnic cultures only exist because there also exist different and separate ethnicities, not an undifferentiated "humanity," as egalitarian and universalist ideology teaches. "Culture would not be possible if the earth would be populated by a humanity which was ethnically undifferentiated," wrote Horia Sima[2] in *Doctrina legionară* ("The Legionary Doctrine"), "Culture is the product of national genius, a projection of the world of dreams, ideals, and aspirations of a people."

It is important to clarify here that these ethnic particularist ideas did not suggest that Romanians should not engage in dialogue and exchange with other ethnic groups in Europe, for it is obvious that Romanians were always accustomed to and benefitted from occasional contact with neighboring ethnic groups. Rather, it simply meant that dialogue and contact with other cultures should be controlled and limited to a reasonable extent, so that Romanians could preserve their unique ethno-cultural identity. To elaborate, it is natural and healthy for different ethnic groups to exchange cultural products and ideas between themselves, but an ethnic group must moderate such interactions so as to not allow foreign groups to dominate their culture, if they are to maintain the authenticity of their own ethnic culture.

Finally, we must mention here the complications of terminology, for it is necessary for readers to be aware of the meanings of certain terms related to the nationalist theory present in Codreanu's text. The terms "nation" and "national" are frequently used, but hold a sense different from what one finds in the West, where "nation" is synonymous to a "state," or a "civic nation." By contrast, Eastern Europeans often use the term "nation" as synonymous with "ethnos" or "ethnicity," and "national" as synonymous with "ethnic," or otherwise pertaining to the "nation" as an ethno-cultural structure. Of course, at the same time the word "nation" is still oftentimes associated with the state, which may contribute to confusions over its meaning among Westerners.

Additionally, we may mention that the term "race" holds two different meanings in Codreanu's writings: in some cases, such as in the excerpts from Cuza and Vasile Conta, it holds a biological meaning, while in other cases it is used as a more generic reference to

2 Horia Sima (1907–1993) became the second major leader of the Legionary Movement in 1940 (two years after Codreanu's death in 1938) and remained so until his death in 1993. He is also the author of many important books on Legionary history and doctrine (most of which remain un-translated).

an ethno-cultural group or a people, not a racial group in the sense of scientifically-defined biological categories. In relation to this fact, we may also mention that while Codreanu and many Legionaries believed that racial constitution in the biological sense had some importance to national identity, race was only a background, and ethnic groups and peoples were thought of as being primarily spiritual and cultural entities.

2. Anti-Semitism

The nationalist philosophy described above could help explain the Romanian anti-Semitism of this time, for the anti-Semitism of the Romanian people was not entirely baseless or without reason for existing, as many people today typically dismiss it. It must be understood that the Jews in Romania at this time were - with only the exception of a minority of the Jewish population - an entirely separate and unassimilated group, sharing almost no cultural or social connection to Romanians, very much unlike what can be seen in Western nations today. They felt very alien and hardly ever seemed sympathetic to the Romanian people they lived among. This was even more problematic when by the late nineteenth century and early twentieth century, a large portion of the Jews became economically and politically influential, increasing their numbers in the fields of law, journalism, politics, trade, banking, speculation, finance, business, company management, etc.

This situation had its origins in the granting of citizenship to the Jews in 1879, which was a requirement of the Treaty of Berlin that Romania had to submit to in order to be recognized as an independent state by the great powers of Europe at the time. In *For My Legionaries*, Codreanu refers to the prominent Romanian intellectuals, writers, and political leaders who protested this development, namely Vasile Conta, Vasile Alecsandri, Mihail Kogălniceanu, Mihai Eminescu, Bogdan Hasdeu, and A. D. Xenopol, as the "great men of Romania of 1879."

After being granted citizenship, the Jews steadily gained the influential positions described above through an ever-increasing presence in the universities, eventually reaching the point where they would outnumber ethnic Romanian students and, consequently, dominate future elite occupations. It must be understood that Romanians - as any people with a homeland and a healthy, natural cultural identity - would logically be led to feel that their people were in danger of being totally subordinated to a class of foreigners. It becomes clear with these facts in mind that Romanian anti-Semitism was not based strictly on xenophobia, for as Horia Sima wrote in *Istoria Mişcarii Legionare* ("The History of the Legionary Movement"):

> The anti-Semitism our people never had a religious or racial character. From the religious point of view, the Romanian people is the most tolerant in the world. There is not a single known case of religious persecution in Romania in all of its history. Romanian anti-Semitism had a social and economic origin. It was incited by the disproportionate number of Jews which were established in Romania in the nineteenth century, and who received preponderant economic positions, pretending to dominate the country. The tension between the Romanian people and Jews increased after World War I, due to the obvious and provocative participation of Jewish minorities in Communist agitation.

One may, however, occasionally see Codreanu make protests about the cultural influence of the Jews. A notable example can be found in a beginning section of the book titled "The Summer of 1922," where he discusses the issue of Jewish plays and music being performed in Romanian theaters for the first time, which he believed would corrupt Romanian culture. Many reading such portions of the book may find these attitudes to be very extreme, and while they are to some extent exaggerative, they do in fact have some basis in realistic concerns. One must consider that Codreanu and his fellows were not afraid of the impact of the exhibition of merely a few local plays, but rather of the possibility that this event was a prelude to further and more extensive changes. If an ethnic people is to maintain their cultural integrity, they must protect the sources of their culture and not allow them to be dominated and controlled by a foreign ethno-cultural group.

This may appear to some to be a chauvinistic attitude at first, and while Romanian nationalism and anti-Semitism occasionally expressed itself in chauvinistic ways, Codreanu's own views never originated in xenophobia or hatred of other cultures, but rather merely in a concern for the well-being of his own culture and people. The Legionary or Iron Guard Movement, which Codreanu would found in 1927, was in actuality meant to break with the old form of chauvinistic nationalism, to form a new nationalism based on Christian ethics and mutual respect between different cultures. To quote Sima once more: "In foreign policy, nationalism suffers an attenuation…" but when "subordinated to the Christian conception, nationalism does not degenerate into chauvinism or imperialism. True nationalism respects other peoples' right to live."

This law applied equally to the Jews, for it must be recognized that few Romanian nationalists at the time had any thoughts of exterminating Jews, despite all their hostile rhetoric, and had always advocated some type of deportation program. Thus, Codreanu's form of nationalism defies the sort of xenophobic nationalism that mainstream academics today try to obsessively categorize all nationalisms into.

We, nevertheless, do not mean to imply that Codreanu does not occasionally express outdated or unrealistic attitudes regarding the Jews throughout the book. For example, the notions of Jewish-Freemasonic conspiracy, or the idea that Communism and liberal-capitalism were conspiratorially united under Jewish leadership, or the belief that Jews were consciously attempting to physically poison Romanians with alcohol by taking over taverns, or the notion that Jews were spreading atheism in order to demoralize Romanians while at the same time maintaining their own religious beliefs, are all obviously unrealistic and based on a failure to recognize that Jews and other social-political forces are nearly always divided, heterogeneous, and thus would rarely be unified into the kind of large-scale conspiracy often discussed at this time.

However, our main argument here is that while Romanian anti-Semites did exaggerate in their analyses of how Jews functioned, they nevertheless made several undoubtedly valid points, especially in that Jews were a real cultural and political threat to Romanians because of the way they were taking over education, business, government, and other elite institutions. Furthermore, it must be kept in mind that while we may regard the conspiracy theories of the time as unrealistic, the reason they spread among Romanians and were taken so seriously is because they were supported by well-respected and even erudite professors such as Cuza, Paulescu, among many others whose names are mentioned throughout *For My Legionaries.*

3. Monarchism

Codreanu was an ardent, lifelong supporter of the Romanian monarchy, along with many other Romanians, to the point where he made Monarchism a key feature of his Legionary ideology. Our discussion of the specific developments in the modern history of Romania may help better explain why many of the Romanian people maintained such a loyalty to the monarchy. In most modern Western nations, the notion of supporting monarchy – that is, a monarchy which has more political power than what is seen in the modern British form, for example – may seem reactionary and absurd. This is because it not only appears outdated, but also because in many Western countries, historically speaking, the common people, the traditional nobility, and the monarchy were oftentimes in conflict. Yet, the situation was not quite the same in Romania, as Prince Michel Sturdza, who eventually became a member of Codreanu's movement, explained in his memoirs (*The Suicide of Europe*):

> It is generally pretended that the contacts between landowners and peasants in Rumania were more remote than in any other European country. This time, the misinformers chose not to alter the truth but to effect its complete reversal. Rumania's feudality was a paternal feudality, the character of which seems to have escaped many superficial Western observers....
>
> Help was always to be found at the court, as our homes were called, where the church of the village was also to be found. Every newly married couple received as a present a pair of oxen and a plough. Marriages and christenings, at which the boyards [boyars] often played the part of godfather and godmother, created a real spiritual relationship between the landlord and the villagers... The friendly and familiar relations between the peasants and the boyards are borne out by Rumanian folklore. The *haiduc*, the beloved Robin Hood of our legends and of our history, is never represented as hostile to the boyards, but only to the *ciocoi*, the *parvenu* (newcomer), generally of foreign origin. *Haiducs* and boyards often in popular ballads, and sometimes in reality, coordinated their activities.

In summary, Romania was a country in which the peasants and the nobility historically had a positive and almost familial relationship. The same could, of course, be said of the monarchy, for it was connected to the nobility. This knowledge may help readers understand why Codreanu's pro-monarchist views are something more than just a reactionary or irrational tendency, and are, in fact, grounded in historical reality and experience.

4. Economic Theory

The type of economic position that Codreanu advocated – which he had termed "National-Christian Socialism" – belonged to a general category that is typically labeled as "Third Position" economics. However, if one is to understand Codreanu's economics, one must first understand what Third Position economics and politics is in general. People are frequently deprived of an education in Third Position economics, because the two predominant political-economic ideologies today, liberal-capitalism and Marxism, both, rather ironically, attempt to brush aside the Third Position as being merely an offshoot of the other. In other words, the typical liberal-capitalist today dismisses the Third Position as being simply an offshoot of Marxist-Socialism, while the typical Marxist dismisses it as merely a concealed form of capitalism. Both perspectives are wrong and analyze Third Position movements and ideologies in an incorrect manner, as we shall reveal in this section.

There are a multitude of Third Position ideologies, the most well-known today being Fascism and National-Socialism. However, it is important to remember that there are several different types of Third Position ideologies which have significant differences from Fascism and National-Socialism, and thus cannot all be reduced and simplified as being merely a variety of "generic Fascisms." Yet, at the same time, all Third Position philosophies share certain traits and emerge out of a similar line of thought. The key idea behind Third Position economics is to create a society in which people of all classes, occupations, and social positions are spiritually united and live in a cooperative and harmonious manner. This concept accordingly rejects both the notion of class warfare present in Marxist thought as well as the sort of unrestricted competition and economic expansion favored by capitalists, which leads to workers becoming prey to blind economic forces.

Thus, Third Positionists generally advocate enacting laws and creating organizations which would regulate relations and alleviate tensions between employers and employees, between the upper classes and the lower classes. The reasoning behind the formulation of this kind of system is that neither Marxism – which advocates only the rights of the workers – nor Capitalism – which advocates only the rights of the financially and economically powerful – are sufficient for creating worthy societies to live in. In contrast to the other two positions, Third Positionists believe that the workers deserve a voice in the administration of their place of work, but they reject the Marxist idea of establishing a "dictatorship of the proletariat," because they realize that workers are not the sole bearers of justice, and that all classes and social positions have the potential for good as well as wrongdoing. In brief, it can be said that the central reason for the formulation of the Third Position is to avoid the injustices of both capitalism as well as Marxism.

To provide one example, the most significant and earliest developed type of Third Position economics was corporatism. This system referred to the medieval guild system - and similar corporative economic practices in the ancient world - and involved organizing the economy into units or estates (called cooperatives or corporations) based on type of labor, which included both employers and employees, and thus allowed for bargaining and cooperation between workers' and employers' organizations, with the state functioning as a mediator. This general system is known for being used in some manner by Fascist states, but it must be remembered that it was not a Fascist invention, for it was conceived and advocated by various theorists long before Fascism even existed, some of the most prominent being German Conservative intellectuals such as Friedrich List, Adam Müller, Othmar Spann, and Arthur Moeller van den Bruck. Corporatism could also be practiced in a variety of ways, and corporatist thinkers oftentimes neither advocated nor supported dictatorial states such as the Italian Fascist state.

Additionally, another fundamental goal of Third Position systems is to create a nationally organic form of socialism, which involves combing nationalism with socialism. The root of this notion is that Marxism correctly asserts that workers need rights and that capitalism should be rejected, for it is a system that, with its sole goal being endless profit, leads to social strife and the creation of a predatory society in which traditional communal and social bonds are broken. Yet, Marxism taken as a whole is also erroneous because it is inorganic to the nation in that it wrongly assumes that the past customs, traditions, and values of a nation can simply be totally brushed aside, thus making the same materialistic error as capitalism in seeing man as a soulless animal guided by merely economic motives.

The idea of organic socialism recognizes that people are more than just groups of classes driven solely by material interests, that people have higher motives related to spirituality, to patriotism, to loyalty to their ethnic group and cultural traditions. Thus, traditionalist nationalism, which upheld these higher purposes, would be combined with the socialistic idea of workers' rights to form a "national socialism." We should note that it is important to realize that this term does not strictly refer to Hitler's ideology or values, for the term was not actually invented by Hitler, and was used by numerous thinkers before him, some notable examples being Johann Plenge, Hans Zehrer, and Moeller van den Bruck.

Codreanu's proposed form of economics was in fact a kind of organic socialism in the sense described above, and also a form of corporatism. It must be noted here, however, that to read "National-Christian Socialism" as a Christian form of "national socialism" is a mistake; for what it truly referred to was a *national form* of *Christian socialism* – i.e., a socialism based on Christian ethics. In other words, it is not, as so many people make the mistake of thinking, a Christianized form of something similar to Hitler's economics, but an entirely different economic theory which combined Christian ethics, national loyalty, and workers' rights.

Codreanu essentially advocated workers organizing themselves into "syndicates" (another term for guilds or cooperatives), as he outlines in his chapter on "National-Christian Socialism." These organizations were meant to give workers the rights they deserved, so as to not be oppressed and mistreated by capitalist forces and oligarchs. To supplement the theory of National-Christian Socialism, in 1935 Codreanu also developed the concept of "Legionary Commerce," which was meant to be a new way of doing business which would be based on Christian honesty and honor, as opposed to doing business in a manner designed simply to maximize profit. In that same year, he also established the "Corps of Legionary Workers," the first Legionary unit formed specifically for the purpose of organizing workers to fight for better working conditions.

On another note, many Marxist or Left-leaning academics today attempt to analyze the Legionary Movement as having been supposedly based in Romania's small bourgeoisie, similarly to Western Fascist movements. This is an attempt to portray the Legionary Movement as purely reactionary and opposed to workers' rights, in order to make it appear as though Marxists have a monopoly on representing the interests of the lower classes. Aside from the fact that such a movement as the Legionary Movement cannot be analyzed in a strictly class-based manner, for it transcended class by recruiting and uniting people of all classes (from the old nobility, the industrial workers, and the peasants alike), it originated with and was largely based among rural people and peasants. Additionally, Codreanu always expressed a great concern for the lower classes, desiring to give them something beyond even what Marxism could offer, as he stated in his 1938 book *Circulars and Manifestos*:

> The Legionary Movement will give the workers more than a program, more than a whiter bread, or a more pleasant bed. It will give the workers the right to feel as masters throughout the country, along with all other Romanians. The worker will pass by with the stride of a master, not of a servant, along streets full of lights and luxury, where today he dares not lift up his eyes... because this master-worker will have laws, and an organization within the state....

Codreanu completely rejected Communist ideas, despite the Communist Movement's claim of representing workers, for the same reasons as other Third Positionists; although in his autobiography he frequently gives its supposedly Jewish nature as the primary reason. It must be pointed out, however, that he rejected Communism not just because he believed it was "Jewish," but also be he recognized its materialistic nature and absurd antagonism toward ethnic traditions and culture. He realized that the victory of Marxist-Communism would lead to "the abolition of the Monarchy, the destruction of the Church, the ruin of family life, the end of private property, and the death of freedom... everything that constitutes our *moral patrimony*," as he wrote in *The Nest Leader's Manual.*

5. Political Values

Another key feature of Codreanu's political position which must be explained is his anti-democratic attitudes. Comprehending the social and economic problems that arose after World War I should help one understand the source of these attitudes. As mentioned in our previous discussion about events important in understanding the historical background of the Legionary Movement, not a single democratic – that is, republican – political party was able to bring about satisfactory results in resolving the problems brought about by the agrarian reform. Democratic parties and leaders appeared to be meaningless, deceitful entities which were interested only in short-term goals and selfish desires that were in opposition to the common good of the nation as a whole.

Codreanu also found the liberal formula of putting the rights of the individual before the rights of the community and the nation as problematic. To clarify, he did indeed believe that individuals were entitled to certain rights, but he believed in the rights of the people as a collective entity held a greater value in a hierarchical sense; meaning, that the rights of the individual had to be subordinated to the rights of the nation. Although Romanians had not developed anti-individualist philosophy as extensively as sociologists in nations such as Germany, they typically had holist and anti-individualist instincts. The liberal concept of individualism was alien to Romanian tradition and culture, as Nae Ionescu, a famous professor and philosopher who influenced Codreanu, wrote in his book *Fenomenul legionar* ("The Legionary Phenomenon"):

> Property in the West was individualistic, in the West the formula was: *jus utendi, fruendi et abutendi* [Latin: "the right to use, enjoy, and dispose"]. We have no such thing in our country. Take, for example, rural property. A few years ago the newspapers wrote about the numbers of family members. This means that in our country, property is not an individual right, but of the family; it is linked to the work of the family. The relationship between right and property is also different in our country, for the peasant is not the owner of the land in the sense of the Roman formula, but rather the servant of the land. The concept of individualism does not exist in Romania... In our country, liberalism does not find the necessary material.

It should be clear that Romania's social, cultural, and political background in this epoch was very different from those of Western nations where liberalism and individualism had been powerful for a long time. For these reasons, it was natural for many Romanians to conclude that "democracy" was something to be rejected and replaced with a different form of state. Of course, at the time in Romania, the term "democracy" was seen as equivalent to the liberal, individualistic, and republican conception of democracy. There are different conceptions and theories of democracy (some of which even reconcile democracy with traditionalist political values), but that is well outside the scope of the present discussion. Our purpose here is only to clarify what Codreanu himself meant when he proclaimed a rejection of "democracy" in the liberal-republican sense.

Codreanu argued for the creation of a state without parties, mass voting, or elected leaders, and in its stead, one with a strong authority, with elitist practices, and with hierarchically selected leaders. However, while this state is posed as non-democratic and non-electoral, it was not meant to be a dictatorship or totalitarian state, but rather an open aristocracy and a monarchy in a traditional, universal sense.

Contrary to the mainstream scholars, who prefer to depict Codreanu as a Romanian version of Hitler or Mussolini, Codreanu was not interested in becoming a dictator, nor was he even interested in obtaining the position of chief political leader of the nation. Likewise, although in the section titled "The National Movements and Dictatorship," one may see Codreanu implying a similarity between the Fascist and National-Socialist states and his own envisioned Legionary state, it must be kept in mind that Codreanu had never actually seen first-hand either Fascist Italy or the Third Reich, and thus he was not fully aware of their policies and practices. Hence, the reader should not simply assume that Codreanu intended to create a state modeled on Fascist or National-Socialist principles.

Codreanu's vision – in contradistinction to the other movements – was to essentially merge a monarchy with his own movement, thus forming a state which would be more like a traditional monarchy, but one which would also avoid the problems typically associated with an all-powerful monarchy by combining it with the populist and socialist character of his movement. The values of respecting the will of the people, freedom, social justice, and the populism which one sees in the Legionary Movement, is also the reason why some Legionaries would later argue that despite rejecting democracy in the formal republican sense, the Legionary Movement was in fact democratic at heart. Horia Sima, for example, pointed out in his *Doctrina legionară* that despite Codreanu's vehement attacks against the farcical democracy that existed in Romania at that time, he had never rejected the fundamental principles of democracy:

> Corneliu Codreanu was right to revolt against this type of democracy, which was in reality nothing more than a disguised dictatorship of a caste of politicians. But if he denounced the system of government in Romania with all severity, at the same time he did not take a step in his entire political activity without invoking the right of the nation to secure its own fate, beyond the existing forms of the state. However paradoxical it may seem, Corneliu Codreanu professed a true cult of democracy, in which one finds this form of government more profound, more expressive for its own essence. At its core, in its intimacy, the democratic edifice has a central column, which is called the will of the people. Well, before this will, the Captain had never failed with anything.

Organization and Composition of the Book

The final issue which needs clarification regarding *For My Legionaries* is the organization of the book. Readers will notice that the book is not organized in the manner expected in a standard autobiography, but rather as a collection of disparate, although still chronological entries describing events at different dates, news articles, excerpted documents, brief philosophical reflections, manifestos, and speeches or addresses. As we noted in the beginning of this introduction, Codreanu had evidently written the book in haste and in conditions where he was too distracted to compose the work in standard fashion. He noted himself that "I do not pay attention to any regulation imposed on book authors. I have no time." This certainly explains why the book was composed as a compilation of heterogeneous documents and entries, but it does not necessarily explain why certain pieces where placed as they were.

It is apparent enough from Codreanu's own writing that articles from newspapers, manifestos, and speeches are all placed into the chronological context of the autobiographical entries which pass from date to date; they are organized by their relevance to a particular point in the story. It is not as obvious why the philosophical or ideological entries where organized as they were, on the other hand. Concerning the excerpts from professors, intellectuals, and political leaders in the section of the book titled "The Jewish Problem," we may presume that they were organized by chronological relevance (i.e., the documents in question were read at the point in the story in which they are presented) or organized so as to emulate the order in which Codreanu had personally learned the ideas presented in those texts.

As for the philosophical reelections and ideological explanations, it can be inferred – if not stated clearly by Codreanu himself – that the reason one will find each of them presented at a certain point in the book is because of their relevance to that portion, or because Codreanu thought that that particular point would be the most opportune moment for explanation. The portions concerning Legionary ethics, values, and practices, which are presented in the section titled "The Legion of Michael the Archangel," were clearly placed there because they are most properly presented at the beginning of the part of the book dealing with Legionary history *per se*. The reflections on political forms and practices, democracy, and monarchy in the section titled "Democracy Against the Nation," on the other hand, could have been placed in many other locations in the book. However, there is reason to believe that they were placed there because Codreanu thought it would be most appropriate to present them after he had already mentioned his experiences in electoral campaigns and in the parliament. Keeping all this in mind, the reader can interconnect the disparate entries and documents in this book into an organic, coherent whole.

Lucian Tudor

March 2015
Chicago, Illinois

For My Legionaries

Corneliu Zelea Codreanu

This volume contains the story of my youth, from 19 to 34 years of age, with its feelings, faith, thoughts, deeds, and its errors.

Corneliu Codreanu

December 6, 1935
Carmen Sylva

LEGIONARIES,

I write for our legionary family. For all legionaries: those in villages, in factories and in the university.

I do not pay attention to any regulation imposed on book authors. I have no time. I write hastily on the battlefield, in the midst of attacks. At this hour we are surrounded on all sides. The enemies strike us treacherously and treason bites us.

For two years we have been bound by the chains of an infamous censorship.

For two years our name and that of legionary are tolerated by the press only to be insulted. A rain of treacheries is heaped upon us while our enemies applaud and hope that we shall perish. But these knights of cowardice, as well as their masters, will be convinced, in fact, soon, that all the attacks in which they pooled their hopes of destroying the legionary movement, all their agitation and desperate efforts, will remain fruitless. Legionaries do not die. Erect, immovable, invincible and immortal, they look forever victorious over the impotent convulsions of hatred.

The opinion created in the non-legionary world by the lines that follow is of no consequence to me and their effect upon that world does not interest me,

What I want is that you, soldiers of other Romanian horizons, while reading these recollections, recognize in them your own past and remember your battles; that you re-live the suffering you endured and the blows you took for our people; that you fill your hearts with fire and stand firm in the difficult and righteous struggle in which you are engaged and out of which we all have the command to emerge either victorious or dead. I think of you as I write. Of you who will have to die, receiving the baptism of death with the serenity of our ancestral Thracians. And of you those who will have to step over the dead and their tombs, carrying in your hands the victorious banners of the Romanians.

Corneliu Codreanu

Ion Mota, Ion Zelea Codreanu, and Corneliu Zelea Codreanu.

Map of Romania showing principle cities.

Stepping Into Life

In The Dobrina Forest

Here we are, congregated one afternoon in the spring of 1919 in the Dobrina Forest which stands sentinel on the heights around Husi. Who? A group of about 20 high school students, sophomores, juniors and seniors.

I called these young comrades together to discuss a grave problem, though our life was but budding. What are we going to do if the Bolsheviks invade us? My opinion, with which the others were in accord, was this: if the Bolshevik army crosses the Dniester, then the Pruth, reaching our region, we shall not submit, but will take refuge in the woods armed; we will organize there a center of Romanian action and resistance, and by skillful action shake up the enemy; we will maintain a spirit of non-submission, and keep alive a spark of hope amidst the Romanian masses in villages and towns. We all took an oath in the middle of the ancient forest. This forest was a corner of that famous woods of Tigheciu on whose paths, throughout Moldavia's history, many an enemy found death.

We decided to acquire weapons and ammunition, to maintain total secrecy, to engage in reconnoitering and battle exercises there in the forest and to establish a front which would mask our intentions. We easily found this front and we soon brought it into being: a cultural-national association of the students at the high school of Husi which we named "Mihail Kogalniceanu." It was approved by the high school principal. Then we began get-togethers and lectures in town. We treated the customary subjects in public, while in the woods we simulated battle exercises. In those times one could find weapons everywhere, so that within about two weeks we collected all we needed.

There was then such a chaotic state of affairs in the country that we, though but children hardly over 18 years of age, understood all too well. Everybody was thinking about the Bolshevik revolution which was well underway only a few steps over the border. The peasantry was opposed to this destroying wave out of instinct, but completely disorganized, could not put up a serious resistance. But industrial workers were vertiginously sliding toward Communism, being systematically fed the cult of these ideas by the Jewish press, and generally by the entire Jewry of the cities. Every Jew, merchant, intellectual or banker-capitalist, in his radius of activity, was an agent of these anti-Romanian revolutionary ideas. The Romanian intelligentsia was undecided, the state apparatus disorganized. One could expect at any moment, either an internal eruption of some determined and organized elements, or an invasion from over the Dniester. This external action, coordinated with that of the Judeo-communist bands within—who could bear down on us, destroying bridges and blowing up stores of ammunition—would have then decided our fate as a people.

It was in such circumstances, our thoughts in turmoil, worrying about the life and liberty of our country just unified at the end of a difficult war, that in our youthful minds the idea that led us to the oath in the Dobrina Forest germinated.

I had had five years at the Military Academy in Manastirea Dealului (The Cloister on the Hill), where the head of Michael the Brave reposes, under the searching eye of Nicolae Filipescu[1]. There, under the orders of Maj., later Col. Marcel Olteanu, the school's commandant, that of Capt. Virgil Badulescu, of Lieut. Emil Palangeanu and under the guidance of the professors, I received a strict soldierly education and a healthy confidence in my own powers.

In fact, my military education will be with me all my life. Order, discipline, hierarchy, molded into my blood at an early age, along with the sentiment of soldierly dignity, will constitute a guiding thread for my entire future activity.

Here too, I was taught to speak little, a fact which later was to lead me to hate "chatterboxing" and too much talk. Here I learned to love the trench and to despise the drawing room.

The notions of military science I was receiving then will make me later judge everything through the prism of this science.

This cult of the sentiment of human and military dignity, in which the

1 Former cabinet minister (1900-1913) who founded the Military Academy bearing his name.. (Translator's note.)

officers brought me up, was to create for me difficulties and expose me to suffering, in a world oftentimes lacking both honor and a sense of dignity.

I spent the summer of 1916 at home in Husi.

My father had been recalled into the military for the last two years and left with the regiment for the Carpathians.

One night my mother woke me up and, crying and crossing herself, said: "Wake up, all the bells of all the churches are ringing." It was August 15, 1916, the Feast of St. Mary. I understood that mobilization had been decreed and that at that moment the Romanian army had crossed the mountains.

Seized by emotion, my whole body trembled. Three days later I left home to trail my father, pushed by my yearning that I too, be among the fighters on the front. Finally, following many adventures, I reached the regiment in which my father was commanding a company, the 25th Infantry Regiment under the command of Col. V. Piperescu, as it was advancing into Transylvania on the Oituz valley.

My misfortune was great, for, being only 17 years old, the regimental commander turned me down as a volunteer. Yet I took part both in the advance into and the retreat from Transylvania, and on September 20th when my father fell wounded above Sovata on the Ceres-Domu mountain, I was useful to him ahead of the enemy's advance. Though wounded he refused to be evacuated, leading his company throughout the retreat and later in the heavy fighting that followed at Oituz.

At two o'clock one night the regiment received orders to advance. The officers inspected their troops massed in a tomb-like quiet on the highway.

My father was asked to report to the colonel. Returning after a short while, he told me: "Would it not be better for you to go back home? We will soon be engaged in battle and it is not good that both of us die here, for Mother then is going to be left with six small children, with no support. The colonel called me and told me he does not want to take the responsibility of your remaining here on the front."

I could tell his heart was in doubt: he hesitated at leaving me alone in the middle of the night, out in the open, on unfamiliar roads, 25 miles

Corneliu and Ion Zelea Codreanu in 1914.

from the nearest railroad. Noting his insistence, however, I turned in my carbine and the two cartridge holders while the columns of the regiment moved on, disappearing into the quiet and darkness of night. I remained alone on the edge of a ditch, then started in the direction of the old frontier and home.

When, a year later, on September 1st, I entered The Military School of Infantry at Botosani, the thought was still in my mind—to be able to reach the front. Here I completed my education and military knowledge, from September 1st, 1917 to July 17, 1918, in the Military School's Active Company. The four distinguished officers, Col. Slavescu, Capt. Ciurea, Lieut. Florin Radulescu and Maj. Steflea, guided my steps in the ways of battle and sacrifice for my country.

Another year passed—1919 brought peace, and we, the children ready to die, were scattered, each to his home.

My father, a teacher in secondary schools, had been a lifetime nationalist fighter. My grandfather was a forester, likewise my great-grandfather. The people of my nation have been from the very beginning, in any difficult historical times, a people of woods and mountains. That is why my soldierly upbringing and the blood in my veins impressed on the action at Dobrina—a naive manifestation—a note of seriousness, which our tender age would not have presupposed.

In those moments, we felt in our hearts, with their advice and experience, the presence of all our ancestors, who had fought for Moldavia on the same paths the enemies never penetrated.

At the University of Iasi
September 1919

The summer passed. I took my baccalaureate[2] in the fall and our group parted ways, each directing his steps toward a university.

From Dobrina we retained only the memories of defending our country against the waves of enmity menacingly raised both from without and from within our borders.

2 Comprehensive examination required before graduation from high school. (Tr.)

I was leaving Husi at this crossroad for every youth, the enrollment into a university, the long-awaited enrollment at the university! As preparation I had the capital of knowledge acquired in high school. Sensational literature, or that of spiritual perversion which today occupies such an important place in the formative years of a high schooler—to his misfortune—I have not tasted. In addition to the customary literature of the Romanian classics, I had read all the articles in the *Semanatorul* ("The Sower") and *Neamul Romanesc* ("The Romanian People") of N. Iorga and A.C. Cuza. My father had these in some boxes in the attic. That is where I climbed in my free hours to busy myself with such literature. The essence of these articles contained the expression in a high form, of the three ideals of life for the Romanian people:

1. The unification of the Romanian people.
2. The elevation of peasantry through land reform and political rights,
3. The solution of the Jewish problem.

There were two maxims printed on the jackets of all nationalistic publications of that time:

> "Romania of the Romanians, only of the Romanians and of all Romanians." - N. Iorga.
>
> "Nationality is the creative power of human culture, culture is the creative power of nationality." – A.C. Cuza.

I approached Iasi with great reverence—the Iasi loved and understood by every Romanian, the city everybody at least wants to visit.

Many towns in Moldavia have some fragment of glory. We cannot pronounce the names: Hotin, Barlad, Vaslui, Tighina, Cetatrea-Alba, Soroca, without feeling our souls uplifted.

But above all these rise Suceava and Iasi.

Suceava, the fortress of Stefan the Great; and Iasi, the city of Cuza-Voda,—the city of the Union of 1859, which through the founding of the university, became the city of youth and that of its noblest aspirations.

In Iasi lived: Miron Costin, Bogdan Petriceicu Hasdeu, Mihail Eminescu, Ion Creanga, Vasile Alecsandri, Costache Negri, Iacob Negruzzi, Mihail Kogalniceanu, Simion Barnutiu, Vasile Conta, N.

Iorga, Ion Gavanescul. Here, like a lighthouse, shines in Political Economy, the great personality of Professor Cuza. The university became a school of nationalism; Iasi, the city of the great Romanian thrust forward, of our national greatness, ideals and aspirations. It is great from the sorrow of 1917 when here in his troubled hours the tormented soul of King Ferdinand found refuge; great through its destiny of being in 1918 the city of union of all Romanians; great by virtue of its great past and great by its present tragedy—for the city of the forty churches—dies daily forgotten under the merciless Jewish invasion. Iasi, like Rome, built on seven hills, is and remains the eternal city of Romanianism.

How many glorious memories!

Here were heard for the first time, resounding, those harmonious verses of Alecsandri:

> Romanians of every feather,
> Come let us join hands together,

Here, as nowhere else, the student feels hovering in the air over silent Iasi, with their mysterious appeals and with their sacred urgings, the spirits of our ancestors. The Iasi student, in the quiet of the night, hears, as if maddened by pain, the phantom of Mihail Eminescu running through the tortuous streets of the city, moaning like a ghost:

> He who takes strangers to heart
> May the dogs eat his heart
> May the waste eat his home
> May ill-fame devour his folks,

This is the town I was approaching with profound reverence in the fall of 1919 being attracted by its great aura, but moved also because it was here that I was born twenty years earlier. And just like any child I was moved to again see and kiss my native earth.

I registered in the School of Law.

Iasi University, closed during the war years, had reopened a year earlier. The old students, returned now as veterans, retained the line of the traditional nationalism of student life before the war. They were divided into two camps: one, under the leadership of Labusca from Letters, and another, under that of Nelu lonescu, from Law. These groups, small in number, were overwhelmed by the immense mass of Jewish students coming over to school from Basarabia, all communist agents and propagandists.

The university's professors, excepting a very limited group headed by A.C. Cuza, Ion Gavanescul and Corneliu Sumuleanu, were supporters of the same leftist ideas. Professor Paul Bujor, one of the majority's exponents stated quite clearly in the country's full Senate: "The light comes from the East," namely, from beyond the Dniester.

Such an attitude on the part of the professors who considered "barbarous" any nationalistic idea or note, resulted in the total disorientation of the students, some openly supporting Bolshevism, others—the greater part—saying: "Say what you will, nationalism is passé, mankind moves toward the left." The Labusca group slipped totally in this direction. The Nelu Ionescu group, to which I adhered, scattered in time, following some elections in the university which they lost.

The advancement of these anti-Romanian ideas, supported by a compact mass of professors and students, and encouraged by all enemies of unified Romania, found among the student body no Romanian resistance. A few of us who were still trying to man the barricades were surrounded by an atmosphere of scorn and enmity. On the streets or in the halls of the university, colleagues holding other opinions, those with "freedom of conscience" and who preach every other kind of freedom, spat behind us as we passed and became increasingly aggressive.

Thousands of students in meeting after meeting in which Bolshevism was propagated, attacked Army, Justice, Church, Crown. There was only one association that yet maintained a Romanian character: "Avram Iancu" belonging to the Bucovinans and Transylvanians, under the leadership of Vasile Iasinschi, a student.

The university, traditionally nationalistic since 1860, became a nest of anti-Romanianism.

Revolution Being Prepared

But it was not wholly in the university that this situation existed, Iasi's mass of workingmen, almost entirely immersed in Communism, was at the ready to erupt into revolution. Little work was done in factories. Hours on end they held meetings and councils; mostly about politics rather than work. We found ourselves systematically sabotaged, according to plan and by command: "break, destroy machinery, create the state of general material misery which leads to the eruption of revolution." And indeed, the more this command was obeyed, the more the misery spread, hunger threatened menacingly and rebellion grew in the souls of the multitudes.

Every three or four days on the streets of Iasi there were huge communist demonstrations. Those 10-15,000 starved workers, maneuvered by the Judaic criminal hand from Moscow, paraded the streets while singing the Internationale, yelling: "Down with the King!" "Down with the Army!" and carrying placards on which one could read "Long live the communist revolution!" "Long live Soviet Russia!"

If these had been victorious, would we have had at least a Romania led by a Romanian workers' regime? Would the Romanian workers have become masters of the country? No! The next day we would have become the slaves of the dirtiest tyranny: the Talmudic, Jewish tyranny.

Greater Romania, after less than a second of existence, would have collapsed. We, the Romanian people, would have been mercilessly exterminated, killed or deported throughout Siberia: peasants, workers, intellectuals, all pell-mell. The land from Maramures to the Black Sea, snatched from Romanian hands, would have been colonized by Jewish masses. Here it is that they would have built up their true Palestine.

I was perfectly aware that in those hours the life and death of the Romanian people was at stake. And so were the Jews who were pushing the Romanian workers into revolution. They had no sympathy with the anguish which gripped our hearts in those moments or with the anxiety betrayed in our eyes. They knew what they were doing. Only the Romanian intellectuals were unconscious. The intellectuals who had gone to school and were supposed to enlighten the people in difficult times — for that is why they were intellectuals — were absent from their duty. These unworthy beings in those decisive moments maintained with a criminal unconsciousness that "the light comes from the East." Who was to oppose the revolutionary columns which marched menacingly through the streets of all our towns? The students? No! The intelligentsia? No! The police? Siguranta[3]? These, when hearing the columns approach, panicked and vanished. Not even the military could bar their way. For one did not talk of 1,000 men, but of 15,000, of 20,000, organized and hungry.

The Guard of the National Conscience

One rainy evening in the fall of 1919 in the mess-hall of The School of Arts and Crafts, where I was a councilor, a friend of mine showed me a newspaper notice:

"The Guard of the National Conscience
holds a meeting this evening, Thursday, 9 o'clock,
No, 3 Alecsandri St."

I left immediately, running with great impatience to know and to enroll in this organization whose anti-communist flyers I had read several months earlier.

In the room on No. 3 Alecsandri St., set up with newly-made benches, I found only one man already there. He was about 40, brawny and downcast, sitting at a table, waiting for people to come. A big head, two strong arms, heavy fists, of middle stature. He was Constantin Pancu, the President of The Guard of the National Conscience.

I introduced myself, telling him I was a student and that I wished to be admitted as a fighter into the Guard. He accepted me. I sat in at that meeting. About twenty persons came: a typesetter, Voinescu; a student; about four mechanics from R.M.S.[4]; two from the railways; several tradesmen and workers; the lawyer Victor Climescu, and a priest. Several questions were discussed in connection with the momentum gained by the communist movement in various factories and part of the city and with the problem of organizing the Guard.

From that evening on my road bifurcated: one half in the fight at the university, the other half with Constantin Pancu, among the workers. I became attached to this man and I stood with him under his leadership constantly till the organization disbanded.

3 The Security Service of Romania before the communist takeover. (Tr.)

4 The Agency of State Monopolies, hereafter called the A.S.M. (Tr.)

Constantin Pancu

Constantin Pancu, whose name was on the lips of all Iasians in both camps, uttered hopefully by Romanians, in horror by the others, was not an intellectual.

He was a tradesman, plumber and electrician. He never went beyond four primary grades. He had a lucid, balanced mind which he himself enriched with adequate knowledge. For twenty years he had been occupied with workers' problems. He had been for several years the president of the metallurgical union. He was a first class speaker. At the podium, before a crowd, he was impressive. He had a soul and a conscience that were clearly Romanian. He loved his country, the military, the King. A good Christian. He had the muscles of a circus fighter and force truly Herculean. Iasians had known him for a long time.

Before the war a circus came to Iasi which held fighting shows. There were among the combatants men from all nations: Hungarians, Turks, Romanians, Russians, etc. One evening, when one of them won over all the other fighters, from among the spectators a citizen stood up asking to fight the winner. He was permitted to do so. He undressed and the fight started. In two minutes the Hungarian circus strongman was thrown to the ground, defeated. The Romanian who won amidst the crowd's enthusiastic admiration, was none other than Constantin Pancu.

That is why when his call to battle appeared for the first time on the streets of Iasi, the public which worships strength, accepted it with trust.

His effort lasted one year, increasing as the Bolshevik menace grew, then decreasing as it diminished.

Small meetings were held at first, then rallies that reached 5, 6, even 10,000 people. These took place weekly during the critical period in the Prince Mircea Hall, or sometimes in Union Square. Among those who spoke regularly was myself. This is where I learned how to speak before a crowd. Undeniably The Guard of the National Conscience raised the conscience of Romanians at a critical time, in an important place as that of Iasi and placed it like a barrier before the communist wave.

This activity however, was not limited only to Iasi. We went to other towns. In addition, the paper *Constiinta* ("The Conscience") which was regularly published, penetrated with its cry of alarm into nearly all the towns of Moldavia and Basarabia.

Almost daily out in the field between the two camps, inevitable bloody clashes *occurred*, our side sustaining the most wounded. This tense situation lasted until spring, but after two great victories for our side, the offensive power of our adversaries was much reduced.

The Occupation of the Agency of State Monopolies by the Guard of the National Conscience

It was either on the 10th or the 11th of February, 1920. For two weeks die there had been talk of a nationwide general strike. The decisive battle was approaching. It was rumored in town that around noon at the A.S.M., where about 1,000 workers were employed, the strike was declared, the red flag raised, the King's picture lowered and trampled underfoot, being then replaced by those of Karl Marx, Trotsky and Rakowsky.

Our people there were beaten, the mechanics, members of The Guard, wounded. At 1 o'clock, about 100 of us got together at our headquarters. What to do? Pancu chaired the discussion. There were two opinions. Some claimed we should send telegrams to the government, requesting military intervention. My opinion was that those present should head for the A.S.M. and tear down the red flag at any risk. My point of view was agreed upon. We took our flag and at 1 o'clock led by Pancu we started marching on Lapusneanu and Pacurari singing *Desteapta-te Romane* ("Awaken, Ye Romanian"). Close to the factory in the street we broke up several groups of communists.

We entered the factory's courtyard and went into the building, carrying the flag all the way to the roof, where I planted it. From there I gave a talk. The military appeared and occupied the factory.

We retreated singing, then returned to our headquarters, considering our rapid incursion a success. The news of our attitude flashed through the town like lightning, yet the strike continued. The military could only defend the flag, it could not make the plant run. What was to be done? An idea occurred to us to search the city for workers in order to open the plant. In three days, 400 new workers, gathered from all quarters of Iasi, entered the plant. This began to run; the strike had failed. Two weeks later, half the strikers demanded that they be returned to work. Our victory was great.

The first step toward the general strike was rejected. The plans of the Judeo-communist consortium began to be frustrated. Our action had a resounding echo within Romanian ranks raising their morale.

The Tricolor Flag Over the Nicolina Works

The most powerful communist center was formed by the Romanian railway works at Nicolina. Over 4,000 men worked there, nearly all bolshevized. Residential areas around these works, Podul Ros, Socola and Nicolina, were invaded by a considerable number of Jews. That is why the leader of the communist movement in Iasi, Dr. Ghelerter and his aide, Gheler, fixed their point of resistance here.

A month had not passed since their defeat at the A.S.M. and as a signal to begin the general strike and the decisive battle, the red flag was hoisted fluttering over the works. A strike was declared. Thousands of workers were pouring out. The authorities were powerless.

Through flyers we convoked all Romanians to a meeting in the Prince Mircea Hall. After the speeches, we left the building with our flags and the whole crowd headed for Nicolina. In Union Square we were stopped by the authorities who advised us against continuing, for there were over 5,000 armed communists there waiting for us and much bloodshed would take place.

So we turned from Union Square toward the railway station, where we hoisted flags over the engine roundhouse and over the station. Then we commandeered a train on the track and went to Nicolina. Someone threw the switch in the Nicolina station and train and all entered the Nicolina works. We got off. In the shops, no one. On one of the buildings, the red flag. I climbed up a fire escape holding a tricolor flag between my teeth. With some difficulty, for it was at a great height, I reached the roof. I got on the roof and crawled to the top. I snatched the red flag and amidst the truly tremendous hurrahs, lasting several minutes, I hoisted and secured the tricolor flag. Then, from there I spoke. Outside the walls, the communists increasing in numbers, steadily grew into a compact mass and demonstrated menacingly. An infernal racket. Inside, hurrahs; outside, boos and cursing. Then I slowly descended to the ground. Pancu ordered our departure. But at the gate the communists barred our exit, yelling: "Let Pancu and Codreanu come forward!" We stepped 30 yards in front of our crowd and headed for the gate. In the middle, Pancu, on his right a tradesman, Margarint, with myself on the left. All three of us advanced saying nothing, keeping our hands in our pockets on the revolvers. Those at the gate watched us, quiet and unmoving. Now we were but a few steps away. I expected the whiz of a bullet going past my ear. But we kept on, straight and determined. However, this was a very unusual, soulful moment. We were now but a couple of steps away. The communists stepped aside opening up for us! For about ten yards we walked in tomb-like silence through their midst. We looked neither to the left nor to the right. Nothing was heard, not even human breathing.

Our men followed us. But as they came through, the silence was broken. Cursing began, with threats on both sides. But no fighting. In a body, we headed along the railroad toward the station. Behind us, over the works, the blowing wind fluttered the cloth of the victorious tricolor.

The moral effect of this action was incomparable. The whole of Iasi was in an uproar. Everybody on the streets spoke only about The Guard of the National Conscience. A current of Romanian awakening was felt in the air. The trains, carried further to the four corners of the country the news of this resurrection.

We realized that Bolshevism would be defeated because facing it, as well as on its flanks, a barrier of conscience had been raised which would prevent its expansion.

All roads to its further encroachment were now closed. From now on it must retreat.

Not long after, action by Gen. Averescu's administration was added to our efforts, enough so that this movement's prospects were altogether nullified.

National-Christian Socialism
The National Syndicates

The Guard of the National Conscience was a fighting organization designed to knock out the enemy.

I was talking with Pancu many time those evenings in 1919, for we were together constantly and almost regularly ate at his table. And I was telling him:

> "It is not enough to defeat Communism. We must also fight for the rights of the workers. They have a right to bread and a right to honor. We must fight against the oligarchic parties, creating national workers' organizations which can gain their rights within the framework of the state and not against the state.
>
> "We permit no one to try raising on Romanian soil another flag, save that of our national history. No matter how right the workers' class may be, we do not tolerate that it rise up against the country or that it make common cause with foreign movements outside our borders. No one will admit that for your bread you lay waste and hand over into the hands of a foreign people of bankers and usurers, everything that for two millenia the sweat of a people of workers and brave ones has saved. Your rights, yes—but within the rights of your people. It is inadmissible that for your right, the historic right of the nation to which you belong be trampled underfoot.
>
> "But we will neither admit that in the shelter of tricolor formulas an oligarchic and tyrannical class may install itself on the backs of the workers of all categories and literally skin them, while continually waving banners through the air for Fatherland—which they do not love; God—in Whom they do not believe; Church—into which they never enter; and Army—which they send to war empty-handed.
>
> "These are realities which cannot be used as false emblems for political fraud in the hands of some immoral prestidigitators."

Then we began organizing the workers into national unions, and even a political party: "The National-Christian Socialism[5]." It was then that Pancu wrote:

5 At that time we had not heard of Adolf Hitler and German National Socialism.

The Creed of National-Christian Socialism

"I believe in the one and undivided Romanian State, from Dniester to the Tisa, the holder, of all Romanians and only of Romanians, lover of work, honor and in fear of God, concerned about the country and its people; giver of equal rights, both civil and political, to men and to women; protector of the family, paying its public servants and workers on the basis of the number of children and the work performed, quality and quantity; and in a State, supporter of social harmony through minimizing of class differences; and in addition to salaries, nationalizing factories (the property of all workers) and distributing the land among all the ploughmen.

"It would distribute benefits between owner (state or private) and workers. The former owner, in addition to his own salary should get a percentage inversely proportional to the size of his original investment; furthermore, the State would insure his original investment; furthermore, the State would insure the workers through a 'risks fund;' would provide storehouses for food and clothing for workers and civil servants who, organized in national unions will have their representatives in the administrative boards of the various industrial, agricultural and commercial institutions.

"I believe in a great and strong 'father of the workers' and King of the peasants, Ferdinand the First, who has sacrificed all for the happiness of Romania and who for our salvation became as one with the people; who at the head of his troops at Marasti and Marasesti vanquished the enemy; who ever since, looks lovingly and trustingly upon the soldiers owing him allegiance, soldiers who will find their military duty to be a real school of their nation which they can finish in a year.

"I believe in one tricolor surrounded by the rays of National-Christian Socialism, symbol of harmony among the brothers and sisters of Greater Romania.

"I believe in one Sacred Christian Church with priests living the Gospel and for the Gospel, and who would, like the apostles, sacrifice themselves for the enlightenment of the many.

"I recognize the election of the Ministers by the Chamber, the abolition of the Senate, the organization of rural police, a progressive income tax, schools of agriculture and crafts in the villages, 'circles' for housewives and adults, homes for invalids and old folks, national homes, the determination of paternity, effectively bringing the knowledge of the laws to everybody, the encouragement of private initiative in the interest of the Nation, and the development of the peasant's home industry.

"I await the resurrection of national conscience even in the most humble shepherd and the descent of the educated into the midst of the tired, to strengthen and help them in true brotherhood, the foundation of Romania of tomorrow. Amen!

"The Guard of the National Conscience."

The newspaper *Constiinta* ("The Conscience"),
Monday, February 9, 1920.

Then we began the organization of the national unions.

The following document shows how one of our unions was formed, I publish it in order to emphasize the conscientiousness of the Iasian workers at that time:

Minutes!

"The undersigned tradesmen, workers and clerks of the tobacco plant A.S.M., met this evening, Monday February 2, 1920, at the headquarters of the Guard of the National Conscience, No. 3 Alecsandri St., under the chairmanship of Mr. C. Pancu, active president of the Guard.

WHEREAS the criminal tendencies of certain individuals who serve interests that are foreign to this people, and,

WHEREAS the propaganda in which they engage, namely to strike at the well-being of this institution and at the very existence of those of us who have been working all our lives for a slice of bread, which is our only food and that of our children,

WE, honest and law-abiding Romanian workers, wishing to march united beneath the flag of our country on the road dictated by the supreme interests of our people, for the well-being of this institution in order to help stop once and for all the propaganda of our enemy within our ranks,

DECIDED to constitute ourselves into a professional national union, for which we elected the following committee and a delegate of the Guard of the National Conscience."

There follow 183 signatures.

'*Constiinta*" ("The Conscience"),
February 9, 1920, Nos. 17 and 18.

A Truthful Picture of the Situation in 1919

I try to report the moment of 1919-20, taking from newspapers and manifestoes what I consider to be significant.

The first manifesto issued by Constantin Pancu at Iasi in August 1919, posted on all walls everywhere in Iasi, in a moment of general disorientation, is the signal to battle for the Romanian workers of Iasi:

APPEAL TO THE ROMANIAN TRADESMEN, WORKERS, SOLDIERS AND PEASANTS

Brothers,

"Following years of frightful battles the world celebrates peace among men; the wise leaders in all civilized countries endeavor to do away with war by establishing a law to guarantee a peaceful existence in the future.

"But lo, from the East one hears voices of hatred which indicate the attempt of our enemies to rip us apart through discord and misunderstandings among us. From Russia, ruled by the darkness of erroneous teachings, we are urged to battle and fire and to kill our brothers of like blood.

"From Hungary, which weeps over her former grandeur, one hears the same urgings. The enemies in the East have united with those in the West to disturb our peace so they can invade us.

"The foreigners beyond our borders try to pass the cup of poison among us, through the aliens living in the bosom of our country. They dare state that they prod us forward in the name of peace, justice and liberty, and in the name of the workers. Their word is a lie, their urgings a killing poison for:

"They say they want peace, but they themselves destroy it, killing the most worthy;

"Demand freedom, but by death threats, oblige people to submit to them;

"Wish brotherhood, while they sow hatred, injustice, and licentiousness within nations.

"Moreover, they say they want the abolishment of capital earned by the sweat of one's brow.

"They tell us they do not want war, but they war.

"They demand the army be abolished, but they arm themselves. They urge us to discard the tricolor flag, while in its stead they hoist the red flag of hatred. Do not lend any credence to their manifestoes and urgings just as you did not believe that of the enemy when you were fighting at Oituz, Marasti and Marasesti.

"The duty of every good Romanian is to see to it that in the future, too, the seed of dissention the enemy endeavors to throw among us does not take root.

"Perfect the work you began by your labor and your honor. Your enemies are the indolence, hatred and dishonor that rule across the borders, that threaten us as well.

"Beware! Keep clean your soul, do not forget that our salvation is work, unity and honor.

"Brother soldiers,

"With faith in God, you have broken the enemy's power. With your weapons you have carved for eternity the country's borders.

"With your blood you have perfected and sealed your sacrifice.

"That is why you must not allow foreign and lawless bands to destroy that which you perfected. Continue to hold your love of country and faith in your King. You took an oath to defend with your blood to the last drop the fatherland's borders. Guard them attentively against the evil intentions of the enemy, for that is what our parents and ancestors did.

"Brother peasants,

"The God of our parents took mercy on our suffering and gave us as bountiful a year as was rarely seen. Be grateful to the good Lord, through your labor and your faith. Renew your working powers, gather assiduously the yield of the land. Rest assured that the land from the Tisa, the Danube, and the Black Sea, was entirely won by you.

"Keep it in sacredness, defend its riches through your labor and your love.

"Brother Romanians, it is in you that the hopes and strength of this country lie. You are also the happiness of tomorrow. Do not gather for yourselves curses, but blessings.

"The enemy is attacking at the Dniester and at the Tisa. He also tries to disrupt the inner peace of our country,

"Our deliverance is in labor, honor, love of country and faith in God.

"Be careful, call onto the righteous path also those who straying have crossed over to those without a people and without a faith. United around the throne and under the shadow of the tricolor banner stand watch for the peace of the country.

"Tell the foreigners and foreign-lovers who try to disturb us, that around us a national guard has formed that watches, that will fight those wishing to sow among us discord.

"Romanians everywhere, workers craftsmen, soldiers and peasants, be worthy of our ancestors and of the call of these times in which we live."

(ss) the Romanian circle of tradesmen, the Railway Traction Union; the Society of the War Invalids; the Ironworkers' Guild, etc.

Constiinta ("The Conscience"),
August 30, 1919, 1st year, No. 1

The Leaders of the Romanian Workers

The leaders of the Romanian communist workers were neither Romanians nor workers. At Iasi: Dr. Ghelerter, Jew: Gheler, Jew; Spiegler, Jew; Schreiber, Jew, etc. At Bucharest: Ilie Moscovici, Jew; Pauker, Jew, etc. Around them, groups of lost Romanian workers.

Had the revolution been successful, the president of the republic that would have usurped the great King Ferdinand, would have been Ilie Moscovici. In Greater Romania's Parliament in 1919 while the deputies and senators of all reunited Romanian provinces, thrilled by the great act of the Union, stood up and applauded the unifier great King, this Mr. Ilie Moscovici refused to stand up, ostentatiously sitting down.

The Attitude of the Jewish Press

It is necessary to underscore the attitude of the Jewish press in those perilous times for the Romanian people. Every time the Romanian nation was menaced in its existence, this press supported the theses that best suited our enemies. As in fact, following the events, it can easily be seen that the same theses were doggedly opposed any time they were favoring a movement of Romanian revival.

For them, our worries were days of joy, while our joys for them were days of mourning.

Freedom

Freedom, so much today denied to the national movement, was back then considered dogma, because it was to serve the cause of our destruction.

Here is, for instance, what *Adevarul* ("The Truth") of December 28, 1919 wrote under the signature of Emil D. Fagure (real name Honigmann):

> "By according to the Socialist Party the right to freely demonstrate, one cannot maintain that said party is granted a privilege. No matter what the party that wants to demonstrate is, this right will have to be respected "

Hatred

We can read in the same paper:

> "Hatred must forever be the guide against the party of murderers that ruled, headed by Ion Bratianu[6]"

The Judaic hatred of the Romanians is blessed; is supported; one invokes it. It is not a crime. It is not a medieval shame.

But when it comes time for the Romanians to defend their infringed rights, their action is labeled "hatred" and hatred becomes a sign of barbarism, a debasing sentiment on which nothing can be built.

Legal Order

Adevarul ("The Truth"), October 5, 1919

> "It is finished! By the 'high' decree-law, for the duration of the electoral period a new regime is instituted, much rougher than before, one of siege and censorship, the opposition and the whole country being taken outside of the law.

6 Romania's Prime Minister during the First World War. (Tr.)

"It is pure and simple, the regime of military dictatorship in which the crown alone is all-powerful; the crown and the Liberal Party, and as an executor of these two wills, you have the government of generals......thus the decree-law forbids us to attack the Crown. If telling the truth be taken as an attack, i.e., that the crown took onto itself the heavy burden of governing the country with the Liberal Party, then still, this attack we must make,

"The decree forbids us from attacking the present form of administration, if by this is understood that we have no right to protest with all vehemence against the present government which is the result of the unconstitutional will of two persons, we will protest....

"If there is no other way open against this state of affairs, if we knew that the incitation to revolt or against the so-called legal order would have any effect—this unfortunately is not the case—we would not hesitate a single moment to do it, for there is no other means of fighting against such a dictatorial and tyrannical regime.

"We consider ourselves facing an armed band which places itself outside the law and uses brutal force....

"Despite all this we will raise this banner and falling we will yet cry: 'Down with tyranny;' 'Long live freedom'."

This then is the Jewish press of 1919.

In other words: inciting to rebellion against the Crown, against the form of government and the legal order.

Incitation To Revolt

Adevarul ("The Truth"), October 11, 1919

"The madmen! Where are the madmen?"

"As we said, we have too many well-behaved men and no madmen. Or, madmen is what we need. Those of 1848 were madmen and they uprooted the boyars[7] regime of the time ....

"We too, need madmen. With well-behaved men who split a hair into 14 still not arriving at a decision, there is nothing to be done. We need at least one madman, if not more of them. What is this madman going to do, how do I know?....

"One madman then is asked for. Let then the madmen come.

"Even the socialists have become well-behaved. In reality they have a party behind them and men who should fear no one. I see they are

7 Members of privileged landholding class. (Tr)

not afraid, but they are nevertheless well-behaved. As I. Nadejde did of old, they stubbornly stay within the legal framework. Those in power, civilians and military, wish to take them out, a useless endeavor. Their tactic is the legal state. Even when they are shot at, as on December 13, 1918, when they are beaten to a pulp, when Frimu is lowered by his henchmen into his grave, the socialists protest—granted, with great dignity—but they do not step outside the law.

"In any case we need madmen.

"Let the madmen who would begin the illegal action, or that against the law, against today's state of affairs, come forward."

The Crown

To the Romanians the crown always constituted a dear patrimony. As the guarantor of our unity and resistance facing any dangers, the Jews never hesitated to attack it, to insult and compromise it by any means.

Here is, for example, how *Dimineata* ("The Morning") of November 16, 1919, treats King Ferdinand.

"Because of an error"

"An animal has need of limited preoccupations, but its brain suffices to fulfill them. Rarely, extremely rarely, is the animal wrong. Likewise his intelligence, no matter how small, prevents it from falling into gross error.

"It is not the same with the King.

"I want to speak of the king of creation.

"The king of creation is much more intelligent than a dog, a horse, an ass. This is certain. But whereas none of these animals would step off the edge of a precipice, would not throw themselves into the waters to drown or would not attempt an unsafe move, the king of creation daily commits unpardonable errors

"Wisdom demanded that the King not permit himself to fall prisoner into the hands of a single man or party.

"With all due respect I am duty-bound to tell His Majesty he erred. The situation which is so unclear is the work of His Majesty. For His Majesty, giving in to some guilty and interested obsessions, has run away from the natural solutions that the internal situation demanded.

"If even today the crown will not decide to enter into the natural ways which are divorced from future interests, nature will exact its rights with even greater determination.

"Let the king of creation be advised."

The Christian Church

Opinia ("The Opinion"), August 10, 1919

"The nationalists of Iasi begin to agitate. There are too few of them and they are too scoundrely, that is why their agitating which in times past was revolting, is today ridiculous, pure and simple.

"The nationalists formed a 'Guard of the National Conscience.' Manifestoes were issued; meetings were held... Chauvinistic students were also invited. The customary priests also came... At a time when everywhere, out of the most despotic laws, differences among nationalities are being abolished, in our country nationalists want to accentuate these differences.... this particularly at the moment when the peace conference wants to impose by treaty the control of minorities....

"When everywhere the church is being separated from the state, remaining the private concern of every individual, in our country the nationalists appeal to the clergy for organized religious propaganda of principle...

"Then the priest intervenes: he gently grasps the people by the hair of their heads and beats their foreheads against the stones of the church until they are dazed. It is in the church that the people learn humility and resignation. Such is the will of God.

"No one is fooled by lies any longer. It is in vain that the nationalists pin tricolor bands on their sleeves, that they incite the plebeian intellectuals against the Jews, that they have the priests anathemize us in church. No one today fears their anathema.

"We preach love among people. And kick at the door of the temples which shelter hatred and revenge..."

Signed: *M. Sevastos*

The Procession

Opinia ("The Opinion"), October 26, 1919

"To the appeal of the 'Guard of the National Conscience,' the honorable clergy placed at the disposal of the demonstrators, their beards, vestments, and church banners.

"But the luxury of having at one's disposal a God with a whole staff must be paid for. We prefer that from our taxes a professor be hired, not a priest. We wish therefore the separation of church from the state. For we do not wish that our forced contribution serve to encourage obscurantism, renunciation and the spirit of resignation, thanks to which police regimes are maintained.

"Back to the Middle Ages? To the Inquisition? We are exasperated by the terror in striped pants and tails, and military tunic; nor can we any longer tolerate the terror wearing the religious habit. It hurts us to see street demonstrations prompted by political intrigues and the military, and no longer wish to witness parades of mitres and of red neck-kerchiefs...

"Enough!

"The cupolas of the churches weigh heavily upon the shoulders of humanity; the prostrations pull it to the ground,

"This procession is going to be an insipid one. One will see on the streets museum vestments, brilliant-studded scepters, miters... Crosses will be seen, and stoles.

"Beards will pass. Orators with contorted gestures will bare their chests showing the crowd their bloodied side—sucking between teeth sponges soaked in vinegar..."

Signed: *M. Sevastos*

It is clear. From here to attacking officers and tearing off their stripes is but one step. Also one step to knocking down the churches with picks or to their transformation into stables or places of sadistic parties for the little Jewish reporters from *Opinia* ("The Opinion"), *Adevarul* ("The Truth"), *Dimineata* ("The Morning") and their people.

I saw in the columns of these newspapers, at a time of great Romanian hardship, all the hatred and foxy plotting of an enemy race, settled and tolerated here by the pity and only by the pity of the Romanians. I saw how they flaunted their lack of respect for the Romanian Army's glory and for the hundreds of thousands who died in its sanctified uniform; their lack of respect for the Christian faith of an entire people. No day passed without venom being poured into our hearts from each page. By reading those newspapers which crisped my soul, I came to know the real feelings of these aliens, which they revealed without reticence, at a time they thought we had been knocked to the ground.

I learned enough anti-Semitism in one year to last me three lifetimes. For one cannot strike the sacred beliefs of a people or what their heart loves and respects, without hurting them to the depths and without blood dripping from their wound. Seventeen years have passed since and the wound is still bleeding.

May I be permitted once again to fulfill a sacred duty, mentioning here this hero, an athlete of Christian workingmen, the craftsman Constantin Pancu, under whose command I stood and by whose side I would stay until the "Red Beast," as he called it, was defeated. It is to this man—to his courage and steadfastness—that is owed the deliverance of the city of Iasi from destruction.

Seven years later, this giant, weakened by suffering and poverty, was walking the streets of Iasi like a shadow, seeking aid toward the treatment of a heart ailment. He died ill and poor, forgotten and unaided, in the midst of a country that cared not, and in a city which he defended with his own body in its most trying hours.

The First Student Congress after the War Cluj, September 4,5,6, 1920

This congress was held in the National Theater in Cluj, in an atmosphere of great enthusiasm, as a result of the unification of the Romanian people by force of arms and their sacrifice. This was the first meeting of the young intellectuals of a people who had been up to then scattered to the four winds by destiny and misfortune.Two thousand years of injustices and suffering were coming to an end. What enthusiasm! How many sacred emotions! How many tears did we all shed!

But as great as our enthusiasm was for the present which overwhelmed our hearts through its majesty, just as great was our disorientation with respect to what line to follow in the future. It was from this uncertainty that the Judaic power sought to profit, by suggesting to and ultimately exerting pressure on the ministries, Masonry and politicians to place on the agenda of the congress the possible admittance of Jewish students into the students' associations. In other words the transformation of the Romanian associations into mixed Romanian-Jewish ones was attempted. The danger was serious: on one hand Bolshevism knocking at the door, on the other the probability of being overwhelmed numerically by Judeo-communist elements in our own groups. In at least two of them, Iasi and Cernauti, the situation was tragic.

In spite of this, the leaders of the congress, Labusca, the president of the Iasi student association and his entire committee; Nazarie, Bucharest's president with his whole committee and all associations; and Puscaru, Cluj's president, were won over to this idea. Young students are influenced very easily particularly when they lack a faith. They let themselves be lured not so much by the immediate material advantages they might be offered but more particularly by flattery and by the prospect of a great future they were promised.

But the youth must know that no matter what position he will hold, he is a sentinel in the service of the nation and that permitting himself to be bought, flattered, lured, means a dereliction of duty, and could even lead to desertion or betrayal.

A small unofficial group of us from Iasi, unshakable in our determination, united with that of the Bucovinans, fought fiercely for two days. And ultimately we won. The congress passed the motion I proposed, by nominal vote, as opposed to the motion supported by the entire student leadership. I believe the congress voted thus not so much out of conviction, as out of admiration for the determination and desperation with which our fight was conducted.

The students from Cernauti, no more than 60, behaved admirably. Our small group of Iasians, not more than 20, likewise. If we add the Ciochina group of 20, also from Iasi, the two-day battle was won by 100 versus 5,000.

That victory of ours then was decisive. Had our point of view lost, the student associations would have also lost their Romanian character, and in contact with the Jews would have turned toward Bolshevism.

The Romanian student body was at a great crossroad. And later, in 1922, we would not have had the eruption of a Romanian students' movement, but perhaps an eruption of the communist revolution.

The Opening of the Iasi University in the Fall of 1920

In the other university centers there was quiet. Only ours in Iasi was condemned to continuous struggle.

For the first time in the history of Iasi University, the University Senate announced the opening of the academic year without the customary religious service. In order for someone to understand our sorrow, one must know that this solemn ceremony has been, without interruption, for half a century, the University's most beautiful event. This occasion embraced the entire University Senate, all professors, all students newly-registered, and the intellectual elite of Iasi. The service was always celebrated in the auditorium by Moldavia's Metropolitan or his vicar, blessing the start of a new year in the education of the Romanian people. But now our university was casting aside by a gesture of the University Senate this jewel of its half-century tradition.

Graver yet, the university of our Christian Iasi, the highest institution of Romanian learning was thus proclaiming in those difficult times, the fight against God, the banishment of God in schools, institutions and country.

The professors of Iasi University, excepting 4 or 5 known to oppose this trend, welcomed with great satisfaction the heathen decision of the Senate as a step forward that would take "Romanian science" out of "barbarism" and "medieval preconceptions." Communist students were jubilant, Jewry triumphant, while a few of us pondered sorrowfully: we wondered how long it would be before churches were torn down and priests in their vestments crucified on their altars?

About eight of us nationalist students in Iasi at the time knocked in vain at the doors of many of the professsors trying to convince them to rescind the measure taken by the Senate, but our repeated attempts failed.

And then, on the evening before the start of the academic year, we decided to take a grave step: we would forcibly oppose the opening of the university.

University of Iasi 1920.

In order to stay grouped, we all slept at No. 4 Suhupan St., the headquarters of our action. At six in the morning Vladimir Frimu and myself left for the university—the others were to follow. We closed and barricaded the rear door of the university leaving Frimu there to guard it.

I put up a poster in red pencil on the large entrance door reading, "I bring to the attention of the students as well as to that of the professors that this university is going to open only following the traditional religious service."

The rest of our comrades came late, too late. Students started coming at 8 o'clock. Alone at the entrance, I resisted until about nine thirty, by which time over 300 students had gathered.

When mathematics Professor Muller wanted to force his way in, I told him: "You swore on the cross when you became a professor at this university. Why do you now raise yourself against the cross? You are a perjurer, because you had sworn on something you did not believe in and now you break that oath."

Then, the students, headed by Marin the communist leader, Hritcu and Ionescu from Botosani, dashed at me, opened the university's main entrance, took me into the lobby hitting me over the head with sticks and fists. No defense, no riposte was possible, for I was caught in the middle, pushed from all directions, getting blows from everywhere.

Finally I was left alone. As I stood in a corner reflecting upon the misfortune of my defeat, in came the six students. However, the victory of the enemy did not last very long, for shortly the university's secretary came down from the rectorate and posted the following notice: "It is brought to everybody's attention that the rectorate has decided that this university will remain closed until Wednesday, when it will open with the religious service." This was a great victory that we welcomed with unsurpassed joy.

Wednesday morning, two days later, in the auditorium filled to capacity by city people, was conducted the religious service. I was congratulated by everybody. Professor A.C. Cuza spoke with unsurpassed eloquence.

It was at that moment that the belief took hold in me—and it has never left me—that one who fights for God and his people, even if alone, will never be defeated.

In the public opinion at Iasi, these battles, especially those at the A.S.M. and the Railway Works, and lastly that at the university, have had a powerful echo. The enemy began to realize that Bolshevism cannot advance without serious obstacles, even when it is supported by nearly all the university's professors, the entire press, all Jewry, the largest proportion of workingmen, while on the other side there is only a minimal group of youth opposing these huge waves, armed only with their great faith in the future of their country. These youth presented the barrier of their wills comparable to some jagged rocks in the ground over which one can easily see, but cannot climb over without great hurt, in fact one would not even ever think of trying to.

The enemies feared not so much us, but our determination. The sane part of the population, the Christian and Romanian Iasi, encouraged us and sympathetically watched us.

The University Year 1920-1921

Begun in the conditions mentioned earlier, this year was an unending series of battles and clashes. We, the fighting students, organized ourselves around the student "Stefan Voda" association whose president I was. From here we attacked our adversaries, vanquishing them time and again.

Despising Romanian culture, they looked down upon the university and everything we had in this country with pretentions of being savants and advisors, like some men arriving from a great country upon this sinful and backward Romanian soil.

They may have been right in certain points, but soon they would clash in our little country with a great centuries-old common sense, that they in their large empire there beyond the Dniester, proved never to have had at all.

At the university, meetings became impossible. No decision could any longer be taken. The great majority of students was made up of communists and their sympathizers. But they could not take one step forward because our group, never over 40, was always present; we attacked and did not permit the airing of communist ideas and practices.

The general strike tried at the Iasi University when the communist student Spiegler was arrested, failed after one day, because our group occupied the mess hall forbidding strikers entrance to meals on the grounds that, "Whoever does not work, does not eat." All pleadings of the rector and the professors to convince us that these students ought to be permitted to enter for their meals, were made in vain. Shortly thereafter, our group was to win another victory—the change of the uniform.

Communist students were wearing Russian caps, not that they had no other caps, but as an ostentatious sign of affirming Bolshevism. On the occasion of a clash at the university, these caps were grabbed and burnt in Union Square. Then, daily, at the university, on the streets, through pubs, the hunting started. All caps were burnt. After one week they completely disappeared.

Our group went even further and engaged the Judeo-cornmunist press in battle. We did not have any printing presses to spread our word. Following several disrespectful articles about the King, the

Corneliu Codreanu with fellow Iasi students in 1921.

Army and the Church, our group, running out of patience, invaded the offices and printing premises of the newspapers *Lumea* ("The World") published by the Jew Hefter and *Opinia* ("The Opinion") and wrecked the presses that had spewed poison and insult.

We provoked disorders, no doubt, but those disorders would stop the great disorder, the irreparable disorder that the hirelings of communist revolution were preparing for our country. But all this activity made me the principal object of their revenge.

The Jewish press attacked us; I violently responded. Meeting the editors of *Opinia* ("The Opinion") one day on the street, following a verbal exchange, after I demanded they account for their insults, we had a fight. My adversaries were soundly beaten up.

But the next day all newspapers in Iasi made common front against me, *Opinia* ("The Opinion"), *Lumea* ("The World"), *Miscarea* ("The Movement").

Expelled From Iasi University Forever

Things did not stop here. The university Senate took action immediately; it met and, without giving me a hearing, expelled me forever from Iasi University. Finally, both the university and city of Iasi would get rid of the disturber of the public order, who for two years disrupted the peace of Judeo-communists and opposed all their endeavors to unleash the revolution for the dethronement of our king, the burning down of churches, the shooting of the officers and the massacre of hundreds of thousand of Romanians. The men of order and legality were, in the eyes of the university Senate, the communists; I, the disrupter of this order.

The Council of the School of Law

But their plans fell flat, because a truly unique event intervened in the ordinary course of our student life. The Council of the Law Faculty took issue with the expulsion pronounced by the Senate, and, led by Professor Cuza, its Dean, along with Professors Matei Cantacuzino and Dimitrie Alexandrescu, opposed this move.

The endeavors of the council to moderate the fury of the University Senate failed. The Senate did not rescind the expulsion order.

Then the Faculty of Law withdrew is representative from the Senate, no longer opposed its decision and declared itself independent.

I was informed by the Law Faculty that I could continue to attend classes, for the professorial council refused to recognize the decision of the University Senate. Thus I continued to remain on as a student at Iasi University.

As a result of this incident the council of the Faculty of Law did not send its representative to the University Senate for three years. This conflict continued for years longer, even after I left the university.

Later on when I obtained my degree, the rectorate refused to issue my diploma. And to this day they have not issued it. To register in the bar and to continue my studies abroad I made use of the certificate issued me by the Faculty of Law.

The University Year 1921-1922

The new academic year opened under normal conditions—that is, with a religious service. Again, the university and the city of Iasi were in a festive mood. This great event passed almost unnoticed in Bucharest.

There, when students arrive, their number is lost in the multitude of hundreds of thousands of people, in the noise, the lights, and the many conflicting interests. In Iasi, when students leave, a general melancholy descends as when the cranes and the birds leave in the fall. When students return, the youth comes, the life. It is a holiday. In Bucharest the student feels alone in the middle of an immense world that sees him not, does not appreciate him or admonish or have any interest in him, does not love him.

The student's education at Iasi bears no similarity to that at Bucharest, for he develops like a child under the love of his mother, in the shelter of the Romanians' love. Here the nation raises her students. I myself owe this Iasi an important share of gratitude for anything that I was able to do. I have always felt the concern that this spirit of Iasi held for me, I have felt the ray of its love, I have felt its admonition, encouragement, urging, its call to the fight.

These are following us—the students of Iasi—even now, and they will follow us to the end of our lives, as the ever present memory of my mother's urgings and love. Out of all the student generations who passed through Iasi, how many were not stimulated all their lives by Iasi's call to fight! How many were not accompanied all the way to their graves, how many are even today haunted by its reproaches!...

It was noticeable at the beginning of the year that Judeo-Communism backed down, disoriented, its morale practically nil, and put up no resistance. All the newly-enrolled students had heard of our battles and had for a long time been waiting to come to our side. Once here, they joined our ranks.

President of the Law Students' Association

I was elected that fall president of the Association of Law Students. The University Senate refused my validation on the pretext that I had been expelled from the university. I validated myself.

Our Law Student's Association, like the associations in all the other colleges, had as its purpose the scientific activity of completing and deepening studies in their respective fields.

For instance, under the presidency of Nelu Ionescu, two years ahead of me, the Association of Law Students held meetings almost every week. Some student read a book on law or a related field, condensed it and in a meeting presented a critique. Contradictory discussions then took place. I retained this general format but I also added something new. All these themes and reports could not be treated unless they delved scientifically into the Jewish problem.

Works, treating this problem in Romania and abroad were read, on the international Jewish power, on the history of this problem at home and abroad. We were studying not only their methods of fighting us, but the Judaic spirit and mentality as well, and then we proposed various means of fighting back and defending ourselves.

Then, after each exposition, there followed discussions, completions, and lastly, the formulation of the established truth so that everyone could leave enlightened. Furthermore, in the same meetings we sought to accomplish:

1. the identification, at every step, of this Judaic spirit and mentality, that have stealthily infiltrated the thinking and feeling pattern of a large portion of Romanians.

2. our detoxification, namely, the elimination of Judaism that was introduced in our thinking through books in schools, literature, professors, through lectures, theater and cinematography.

3. the understanding and the unmasking of the Jewish plans hidden under so many forms. For we have political parties, led by Romanians, through which Judaism speaks; Romanian newspapers that are written by Romanians, through which the Jew speaks for his interests; Romanian lecturers and authors, thinking, writing and speaking Jewish in the Romanian language.

Studying all these, we began to realize, that for the first time in his history, the Romanian had come into contact with a people which use as weapons to fight and to destroy—as national weapons—slyness and perfidy.

The Romanian has always known only the honest fight. Faced with the new Jewish method, he was at a loss. We realized that everything comes down to knowing the enemy, and that as soon as we Romanians know him, we will vanquish him.

Our meetings continued regularly for the whole year. They attracted larger and larger numbers of students from other colleges, so that the General Association of the Iasi students became almost non-existent. The entire student body gravitated around the activity of the law group.

The auditorium became too small for the crowds of students who wished to take part in these meetings.

The Basarabian students were participating in greater and greater numbers. One half-year of activity brought us a real miracle: three fourths of the Christian Basarabian students woke up, felt themselves called to a new life, became enlightened.

In a short time, they were to become the most faithful soldiers in our fight, reaching through faith, devotion, purity of heart and spirit of sacrifice, the leadership of the movement that had just begun to bud, This moment of brotherhood in the same faith and of pledging to fight for our Christian country against the cheating Judaic hordes, will never be forgotten. We who were fighting each other but yesterday, were now embracing.

The orientation guidelines in our meetings were the writings of our national geniuses Bogdan Petriceicu Hasdeu, Vasile Conta, Mihail Eminescu, Vasile Alecsandri, etc. but especially the writings and lectures of Professor Cuza, the writings of Professor Paulescu, the lessons in national education of Professor Gavanescul.

All the writings of Professor Cuza were read not only once, but three, four times, and they were studied. Particularly his course in political economy treating brilliantly the Jewish question from his prestigious position, asking Romanians to understand this their gravest present problem, was for us a guide for every moment in our effort to get to know it. Our greatest good fortune, and that of Romanians, was thus having Professor Cuza, one of the most knowledgeable men on the world-wide Jewish problem. It was thanks to him that we were able to orient ourselves to any Jewish manouevre.

His courses, of the highest academic standard, were followed by all students with hitherto unprecedented attention. The auditorium of the School of Law proved always too small. For a long time to come this University of Iasi will not have a professor with sermons on nationalism that will inspire a similar enthusiasm.

During this time for many of us life began to reveal a unique purpose, over all other interests: that of fighting for our people whose very existence was threatened.

Visiting the Cernauti University

At the other universities, quiet prevailed. Since the spring of the previous year, 1921, in Cernauti there had begun stirrings around the Romanianization of the theater. A fierce battle of several days ended with the students' victory. Now, in the spring of 1922, I organized under the auspices of the Association of Law Students a visit of the Iasians to Cernauti. We were well received by both professors and students. We 100 visitors did nothing else the three days we stayed there but impart to our colleagues in Cernauti the new faith which was taking shape in our souls.

It was not difficult, for Cernauti, just like Iasi only more so, suffered from the Jewish invasion, with its streets, its commerce, its dilapidated churches, its land and Romanians, all groaning under Jewish domination. Briefly, between us a new and tight spiritual kinship was created, based on a yearning and our common dream to see for once our people awakened to the consciousness of dignity, power and rights as master of their own fate and that of their country. This kinship then grew stronger through the visit repaid us by the Cernauti students one month later. It was now that I met for the first time Tudose Popescu, that handsome figure of a young fighter resembling a pandur[8], who was later one of the leaders of the student movement, but who today sleeps in a poor cemetery under a forgotten cross.

The Review *"Apararea Nationala"*

On April 1, 1922 the bimonthly *Apararea Nationala* ("The National Defense") was published under the editorship of Professors Cuza

8 Soldier of the national army of Tudor Vladimirescu (1780-1821). (Tr.)

and N.C. Paulescu. Anyone can imagine what the publication of this magazine meant for us in the midst of our thoughts and concerns.

In it we found everything that we needed for our own complete comprehension and useable arguments. The articles of Professors Cuza and Paulescu were religiously read by all the youth and had everywhere upon students both in Bucharest and in Cluj a resounding impact.

We considered the publication of each issue a triumph, because it was for us another munitions transport for combating the arguments in the Jewish press. I deem it appropriate to reproduce here two articles published at that time under the signatures of Professors Cuza and Paulescu.

The Divine Spirit of Truth Will Forever Defend Mankind

"In resume, the Talmud—the politico-religious legislation of the Hebrews—in lieu of combating like the Gospel the passions of ownership and domination, on the contrary pushes these vices to an unheard-of peak in order to accomplish Judah's dream of being at the same time both the owner of the entire earth and the master of all mankind.

"But, while the Christian apostles preached their ideal in the open, the Talmud hides; and its two appendages, the Kahal and Freemasonry, are even more invisible.

"The three of them use, in order to remain in the dark, a scabrous and accursed means, namely the lie.

"In other words, the lie is the basis of the system used by Jews, to whom one can say: 'You speak, therefore you lie'

"But the lie has a mortal enemy, namely the truth.

"Or, truth is the distinctive trait of Christianity. Christ said: I am the truth' and that is why His doctrine is in execration by Israel.

"The lie, on the contrary, characterizes what is called the spirit of evil or of the Devil. Thus Jesus, speaking to the Hebrews, said to them:

" 'You are of your father the devil and the lusts of your father it is your will to do. He was a murderer from the beginning, and standeth not in the truth because there is no truth in him. When he speaketh a lie he speaketh of his own for he is a liar and the father thereof.'

"Leaving this world, Christ sent his disciples an invincible weapon, namely His Ghost. The divine spirit of truth, which will defend mankind forever against the devilish spirit of the lie.

"I bow before this Spirit of Truth saying from the bottom of my soul: I believe in the Holy Ghost!"

(Prof. Dr. N.C. Paulescu, from *"Philosophic Physiology. The Talmud, the Kahal, Freemasonry"* vol. II., Bucharest 1913, pp. 300-301)

The science of anti-Semitism

" 'Another horrible pairing of words: the science of anti-Semitism. How can anti-Semitism be a science?' will ask themselves indignantly the scientists with their rocks, those with their seals, the mathematicians with their x's, the philologists with their suffixes, the scientists with their pretended "fixed" ideas of culture.

"Anti-Semitism? For these scientists it is only a savagery, a blind manifestation of brutal instincts, vestiges of prehistoric times, the shame of our civilization which both science and the enlightened conscience of man, free of preconceptions and passion, condemn.

"This is the atmosphere created particularly by the Jews—and which those Judaized nurture—around anti-Semitism, fooling the naive or exploiting the naivete of the stupid with pretentions that they too be 'on a par with modern civilization.' And who does not want to be?

"For example, there is this interesting case of a Judaized individual, himself half Jewish, speaking several years earlier with the air of a terrific scientist about our anti-Semitism, which was then, as it is today, unchanged. And here is what this author, nomen-odiosum, tells us in *Viata Romaneasca* ("The Romanian Life"), second year, No. 11 of November 1907, pp. 186, 204-207—a traitor then of national thought as he was later a traitor of our national action during the war:

" 'I want to talk about the Jewish question... totally denatured by the vulgar and ferocious Judeophagy of our anti-Semites, who thus... compromise us before the civilized world...

'With rusted weapons dug out from the arsenal of medieval persecutions, with hatred propaganda, with impassioned incitement to excesses, with the stirring of bestial instincts in popular masses... one can only compromise a just cause—but the cause of anti-Semitism is not a just one...

'But, to give this conflict... a false air of persecuting a race, of religious persecution, in a word, of anti-Semitism, can serve only the enemy's cause, only too glad to exploit the divagations of some maniacs... anti-Semitic scandalmongers, prematurely places on the order of the day the entire question...

'No people, let alone our own, can fence itself in ad infinitum free of repercussions, against modern ideas, nor against external political action... (These dots are those of the author. That is, they are not suspensive, but threatening, seemingly containing a fantastic political prevision. Ed. [i.e. Cuza, Tr.]).

"Therefore, to place our question in the realm of anti-Semitism, of racial hatred, means for us being led to a shameful and fatal defeat... Asiatic urgings... violent demagoguery, unhealthy agitation... an endeavor of speculating dark passions....' (The last dots, again, are those of the author's, portending the same threat for such horrible crimes like those of anti-Semitism. Ed [i.e. Cuza, Tr.])

"I quoted this typical concept, typical of all who sold themselves to the Jews. And one sees what it comes down to: cliches ('the civilized world,' 'modern ideas'), but particularly to slander (Vulgar and ferocious Judeophagy,' 'rusty weapons,' 'bestial instincts,' 'divagations of some maniacs,' 'anti-Semitic scandalmongers,' 'Asiatic urgings,' 'dark passions').

"We find such 'appreciations' not only coming from the vulgar Jew lovers but sometimes even from some otherwise distinguished representatives of culture in other fields. Thus, for instance, the eminent jurist, university professor, orator, man of politics, former minister of public instruction, Mr. A.C. Arion, levelled at me because of my anti-Semitism, in the full session of the Chamber of Deputies the apostrophe—we can say 'famous' coming from such a man—calling me the caveman.

'As for the Jews, their explanation of anti-Semitism is more characteristic yet. In addition to the usual cliche, 'with hatred and savagery'—naturally with no motive, for they do not care to discuss motives—according to them, anti-Semitism is a madness, an intellectual degeneration, an affliction of the spirit. This is how we are considered by one of the most distinguished modern 'intellectuals' of the Jews, Dr. K. Lippe, of illustrious origin as great-grandson of the famous commentator of the Talmud in the Middle Ages, Rasi, who said *tob sebegoim barog* (kill the best of the Goyim).

"Dr. K. Lippe, M.D. came our way from Galitia and settled down in Iasi where he served time for having killed a woman while performing an abortion on her, even authored a special work in German entitled: *Symptoms of the mental illness—anti-Semitism (1887).*

"And as proof that the arguments used by the parasitic Jews against anti-Semitism are very poor, just as are those of the Judaized, and always the same, here is what *Curierul Israelit* ("The Israelite Courier"), official organ of the Union of Naturalized Jews says in the editorial of its issue of this Friday, September 15, 1922, under the title—to us who write at the *Apararea Nationala* ("The National Defense"), slanderous—'A band of rascals:'

'There exists with these anti-Semites a state of intellectual degeneration that reached the perversity of the senses, some kind of mental sadism by which those touched are pushed to lies and calumnies.'

"As you can see, this is a very simple explanation as well as an extremely naive one: all that is said against the Jews is lies and calumnies due to a specific intellectual degeneration.

"The definition of anti-Semitism—according to Jews and those Judaized—is, then, summed up in these two words, savagery and madness, naturally, of the 'anti-Semites.' As for the Jews as a social phenomenon, they do not even enter into this 'explanation.' As if they did not exist.

"It was this savagery and madness that compelled all peoples of all time, Egyptians, Persians, Romans, Arabs, as well as the modern nations up to this day, to consider Jews as a national menace and take measures against them.

"It was this savagery and madness which darkened the understanding of the most prominent representatives of the culture of all nations, such as Cicero, Seneca, Tacitus, Mohamed, Martin Luther, Giordano Bruno, Frederick the Great, Voltaire, Josef II, Napoleon I, Goethe, Herder, Immanuel Kant, Fichte, Schopenhauer, Charles Fournier, Ludwig Feuerbach, Richard Wagner, Bismarck, Rudolf Virchow, Theodor Billroth, Eugen Duhring—and countless others in all fields—to come out against the Jews.

"Savagery and madness, finally, explains the anti-Semitism of the most distinguished representatives of our culture, such as Simion Barnutiu, B.P. Hajdau, Vasile Alecsandri, Vasile Conta, Mihail Eminescu.

"Savage and mad: all these. Civilized and well-behaved: those Judaized. And the Jews: nonexistent. And venality of those Judaized—is incapable of explaining anti-Semitism as a social phenomenon, we will call it the anti-Semitic theory.

"According to this theory of ours, in the make-up of anti-Semitism we must distinguish three stages: instinct, consciousness, science,

"Instinct always made the crowd, firstly preoccupied by its immediate material interests, oppose Jewish parasitism through popular movements, oftentimes general and bloody, as it was among many others all over, e.g., the terrible movement of the Cossacks in the Ukraine led by Bogdan Hmelnischy in which over 250,000 Jews perished in 1649.

"Consciousness of the Jewish menace is awakened gradually, first in the educated classes. Then it spreads and penetrates the masses. The former group unites with the people in supporting their demands. The latter thus become progressively aware themselves.

"Science begins with partial researches, until it reaches—only in our day—the determination of its objective, namely, studying Judaism as a social phenomenon, lifted out from the medium in which it seeks to hide, concluding that it is a human problem, in fact the biggest, whose solution must be found. We could say, by virtue of the conclusions reached by partial studies so far, that they form the anti-Semitism of science. This is the basis, which is not to be confused with the science of anti-Semitism. What distinguishes them, is their different objectives. And here is the definition as determined by its objective, of this science, which clearly demonstrates it to be a true science with its own domain:

"The science of anti-Semitism has as its object Judaism as a social problem, being thus, necessarily, the synthesis of all sciences that can contribute to its solution, which sciences these are, that through their partial studies contribute to the knowledge of Judaism, we already have seen. And this is the way in which the science of anti-Semitism uses their findings in order to arrive at a solution:

"History establishes that from the earliest times the Jews have been a people wandering among others, nomadic, countryless. The science of anti-Semitism establishes that this nomadism is contrary to the well-being of agricultural, sedentary peoples and cannot be tolerated.

"Anthropology establishes that Jews are a mixture of unrelated races, differing among themselves, as the Semitic, Aryan, Negro, Mongolian. The science of anti-Semitism explains the sterility of the Jewish nation in the domain of culture, as a result of this mongrelization and shows that this mongrel cannot contribute anything to the culture of other nations, which they only falsify, denaturing their characteristics.

"Theology establishes that the Jewish religion is an exclusivist religion, based on the special covenant made between their God, Yahweh, and the Jews considered as a chosen, sacred (am codes) people, apart from other peoples. The science of anti-Semitism rigorously deduces that such a concept excludes the possibility of any peaceful cooperation or any assimilation with the Jews.

"Politics establishes that everywhere, within the other nations, Jews have their unique social organization, constituting a state within the state. The science of anti-Semitism concludes that Jews are an anarchic element, dangerous to the existence of all states. Political Economy establishes that Jews have lived in all times, even in Palestine, as a superimposed people over other nations, exploiting their labor, themselves not being direct producers. The science of anti-Semitism says that any people has the right to defend its productive labor from exploitation by Jews, who cannot be tolerated living like parasites, jeopardizing peoples' existence.

"Philosophy establishes that Judaism's concept of life is an anachronism contrary to human advancement. The science of anti-Semitism imposes, as a duty toward civilization, that this cultural monstrosity be eliminated by the united efforts of all nations. The science of anti-Semitism bases its conclusions on what various, but differing, special sciences objectively established—all of which lead necessarily to the same conclusion:

"The elimination of Jews from the midst of other people putting an end to their unnatural, parasitic existence that is due to an anachronistic concept opposed to the civilization and peace of all nations who can no longer tolerate it.

"This anti-Semitic theory differs, as one can see, from the Jewish theory and that of the Judaized, which reduced anti-Semitism to the two individual expressions—that in fact, the minute they are manifested en masse become themselves a social problem: savagery and hatred—and explains this as well. The instinct of anti-Semitism can sometimes be accompanied by savagery and hatred. For instinct is blind—so they say—though it is essential in defending life. The consciousness of anti-Semitism is added, however, to the instinct, enforcing its urges, no matter how 'savage.' For, in order to be 'civilized'—one must first exist.

"The science of anti-Semitism finally comes to explain this phenomenon, enlightening further the consciousness of people, fully satisfying their instinct and its violent eruptions thus legitimized by revealing their cause—the parasitism of the Jews. Thus it gives us the formula of the scientific solution for the problem of Judaism, which in order to realize we have only to apply.

"Modern anti-Semitism then, pools all energies: the energy of instinct, conscience, science, of fully revealed truth, forming a formidable social force, certainly capable of solving the greatest problem of civilization of our times, which is the Jewish problem. And what do the Jews and the Judaized put up against this great power, seeking to prolong the condemned existence of their parasitism? We have seen: cliches, slander and whims.

" 'The vulgar Judeophagy of our anti-Semites..,' 'they compromise us in the eyes of the civilized world..,' 'Rusty weapons, dug out of the arsenal of medieval persecutions..,' 'The stirring up of bestial instincts in the popular masses...,' 'Asiatic urges..,' 'madness..,' 'mental sadism..'

"These are all the arguments they oppose to our anti-Semitism, for they have no others, thinking they can do away with it by their stupidities. While within all the nations revolted by the nomadic Judah's parasitism revenging energies boil..."

A.C. Cuza, *Apararea Nationala* ("The National Defense") No. 16, Nov. 15, 1922, 1st year.

The Founding of the Association of Christian Students

On May 20, 1922, in a limited meeting we abolished the General Students Association of Iasi which had been still in the hands of a remnant of adversaries supported by the rectorate and we founded "The Association of Christian Students" which even today is still alive. We were a small group when we started, then we founded a student circle evolving later into the Association of Law Students, and now finally, from our labors, a real general student association was being born under the name - of The Association of Christian Students for which the hearts of all the Iasi students were beating, but a different student body, unlike that of 1919.

By now, not without considerable melancholy in my soul, following three years of battle and dear friendships annealed in the fire of so many trials, I was approaching the day of my departure from the university, from student life, and from my comrades in battle. I only had one month before taking my degree exam and I could not resign myself to the idea of having to leave, that we, the 1919 high school graduates, so tightly bound in heart, would scatter, God only knows to which comers of the country.

That is why, after we designated my successors, Sava Margineanu in the Association of Students in Law, and Ilie Garneata in the Association of Christian Students, 26 comrades who felt ourselves closer together, took a vow aiming to fight no matter where we were, for the creed that bound us together while students at the university. We all signed this vow placed it in a bottle, then buried it in the ground.

After I passed my degree exams, another vow was taken from a second group of 46, newer in battle.

These were my guests in Husi where for four days we held meetings, clarifying in our minds the minutest details regarding our future activity. Here, my father spoke to my comrades on several occasions, urging them to fight.

Then we parted ways carrying in our soul the yearning for better and more just days for our people.

Obligation of Honor

The undersigned, students at the University of Iasi, realizing the difficult situation in which the Romanian people finds itself menaced in its very existence by an alien people that grabbed our land and tends to grab the leadership of the country; so that our descendants not wander through foreign lands chased from their land by poverty and misery, and so that our people not bleed under the tyranny of an alien people, we determinedly rise around a new and sacred ideal, that of defending our fatherland against Jewish invasion.

It is around this ideal that we formed the Association of Christian Students at the Iasi University. It is with this ideal in our hearts that we leave the school halls today.

To fight wherever we may be, for our justice, for the threatened life of our people, we consider being our foremost honor-bound duty.

That is why, congregated today, Saturday, May 27, 1922, we pledge ourselves to a common obligation, that, scattering throughout the country, we take with us everywhere the fire which animated us in the times of our youth to light in the saddened hearts of our people the torch of truth, that of their right to a free life in these lands.

We shall maintain the closest contact with the Association which we leave behind today and in which we remain supporting members, it being the central point that shall always unite us in our common struggle. We will meet again in 8 years, namely in 1930, May 1-14 at Iasi University. The Association's Committee will see to it that all members shall be notified two months before this day and will prepare for their arrival.

We invite all student generations following us through this Association, who shall show an understanding of consecrating their labor on the fatherland's altar, to join us that year and that day at Iasi University. May 27, 1922.

Corneliu Zelea-Codreanu — Husi
N. Nadejde, 21 University St. — Iasi
Grig. Ghica, 23 Carol St. — Iasi
I. Sarbu, Rudi, — Soroca County
Grigoriev Eusevie, Caragaiani, Cetatea-Alba County
Ilie Garneata, 40 Muzelor St. — Iasi

Alexandru P. Hagiu, Chetresti — Vaslui
loan Blanaru, 35 Tabacari St.—Husi
Constantin C. Zotta, 13 Maior Teleman St.—Husi
A. Ibraileanu, 3 Ghica Voda St.—Galati
M. Berthet, Purcari, Cetatea-Alba County
lacob I. Filipescu, Tg. Falciu, Falciu County
Leonid Bondac, 5 I. Heliade Radulescu St.—Soroca
Madarjac, 71 Apostol St. —Galati
I. Miclescu, 165 Portului St.-Galati
Ionel I. Teodoreanu, Muzelor—Galati
Lascu Nicolae, 22 Sinadino St.—Chisinau
Bobov Mihail, 85 Podolskaia St.—Chisinau
Mihail V. Sarbul, Mascauti, Orhei County
Nicolae B. lonescu, 59 Constantin Brancoveanu St.—R-Sarat
Pavel Epure—Cetatea-Alba, Cathedral
Gh. Boca, Balaceana, Suceava County
Vasile Nicolau, 61 Lascar Catargiu St.—Husi
Andronic Zaharia, Partestii de Sus, Bucovina
Vasile N. Popa, Paunesti, Putna County
Vasile Corniciuc, Putrauti, Sueceava County
Nicolae N. Aurite, Tereblecea, Siret County
Gr. Mihuta, Scheia, Suceava County
Ciobanu Stefan, 9 Sturza St —Suceava
Eugeniu Cardeiu, Bilca, Radauti County
Eug. N. Manoilescu, Epureni, Falciu County
Vladimir Frimu, Calmatui, Cahul County
Gh. Zarojeanu, 40 Muzelor St.—Iasi
Prelipceanu Tit. Vasile, Horodnicul de Jos, Radauti County
Prelipceanu Gr. Vasile, Horodnicul de Jos, Radauti County
Constantin Dane, Horodnicul de Sus, Radauti County
Pascaru Ioan a Stefan Tereblecea, Siret County
Mihail I. Babor, Balaceana, Suceava County
Sava Margineanu, Stroesti, Suceava County
Taranu Traian, Stroesti, Suceava County
Al. Pistuga, Tarnauca, Dorohoi County
Dragomir Lazarescu, Tarnauca, Dorohoi County
Constantin C. Campeanu, Scheia, Suceava County
Porosnicu, Gurmezoaia, Falciu County
N. Gh. Ursu, Malusteni, Covurlui County
C. Ghica, 23 Carol St.—Iasi

At The End of My University Studies

At home, the three years spent at the university passed before my eyes and I was asking myself: how could we overcome so many obstacles; how could we defeat the mentality, the will of thousands of men; how could we vanquish university senates; and how could we soften the daring of an entire enemy press? Did we have money to hire mercenaries, to publish papers, to go out into the countryside, to feed this real war? We had nothing.

When I threw myself into that first battle, I did not do it because of someone else's urging, or as a result of some confab, or some earlier decision which I was charged to execute, or even under the impulse of the great prolonged inner turmoil or deep thinking in which I had considered this problem.

Nothing of the sort. I could not describe how I entered this fight. Perhaps as a man who, walking down the street with his worries and thoughts, surprised by the fire which consumes a house, takes off his coat, jumping to the aid of those engulfed by flames.

I, with the mind of a youth of 19-20 years of age, understood from all that I saw that we were losing our country, that we were no longer going to have a country, that by the unconscious collaboration of the poor Romanian workingmen, impoverished and exploited, the ruling and devastating Jewish horde would engulf us.

I acted on orders from my heart, from an instinct of defense possessed by even the least crawling worm, not out of an instinct for mere personal preservation, but one for defending the people of whom I was a part.

That is why, all the time, I had the feeling that the whole people was behind us, with all the living, with all those who have died for their country, with its future generations; that our people fights and speaks through us, that the enemy numbers, no matter how large, faced with this historic entity, are but a handful of human wretches that we will scatter and vanquish.

That is why all our adversaries failed, beginning with the thoughtless university senates, who, believing they were fighting in us a handful of crazy youth, fought and struck in reality their own people.

There exists a law of nature which puts everyone in his place; rebels against nature, from Lucifer to the present day, all these rebels, oftentimes very intelligent, though always lacking wisdom, have fallen thunderstruck.

Within the framework of this natural law, of this wise order, anyone can fight, has the right to fight for betterment. Outside it, against it, over this order, no one can activate unpunished and unvanquished.

In the human organism blood globules must remain within its framework and in its service. A rebellion would exist not only if a globule should bestir itself against the organism, but when it would do even less, namely, when it would be in its own employ, when it would only satisfy itself, when it would have no other purpose and ideal outside itself, when it would become its own God.

The individual within the framework and in the service of his people.

The people within the framework and in the service of their God and of God's laws.

Whoever shall understand these things will be victorious even if he be alone. Whoever shall not understand will be defeated. I finish my third university year under the imperium of these thoughts.

From an organizational point of view we had settled on the idea of leader and discipline. Democracy was excluded, not out of speculation or by conviction reached by way of theory.

We had lived anti-democracy from the very start. I always led. In three years it was only once that I was elected president of the Association of Law Students. At all other times it was not the fighters electing me leader, but I choosing them to follow.

I never had committees and never put propositions to a vote. However, whenever I felt a need, I consulted with everyone, but on my own responsibility I took decisions on my own. That is why our small group was always an unshakable unit. Factions of divided opinions, majorities or minorities, clashing among themselves on questions of action or theory, did not exist.

With all the other groups the opposite was true. That is why they fell defeated.

One great faith, like a flame continousiy burning in our hearts, lighting our way; a great and unforgettable love for one another, a great discipline, one decision during the battle, and a balanced weighing of the plan of battle; these, our Fatherland's blessing and God's, assured us the victory those three years.

The Summer of 1922

The summer of 1922 did not pass peacefully. On the stages of Romanian national theaters or communal ones in Moldavian towns, Jewish plays began to be performed in Yiddish by the "Kanapof" troupe. Our youth considered this a threat, for it saw a beginning of the alienation of this institution, meant to be for the national and moral education of the Romanian people. Expropriated in commerce, industry, in the richness of the Romanian soil and subsoil, in the press, we will see ourselves one day expropriated also from the stages of our national theaters. The theater, together with the school and the church, can elevate a decayed nation to the consciousness of its rights and historical mission. It can prepare and motivate a nation to liberating struggle. From now even this redoubt shall be taken away from us. Our theaters that were built by the Romanian's sweat and money will serve Jewry for the preparation and strengthening of their forces in the fight against us. And, on the other hand, from these Romanian stages they will serve us Romanians as "spiritual nourishment" everything that will contribute to our national demoralization and moral decadence and destruction.

It was the duty of others, namely, the government, or any authority, or the professors, to take a stance against this new anti-Romanian attack. But none was taken. Only youth reacted as best it could, risking blows, being showered with countless insults, finding nowhere any support.

This struggle was pursued in every town: Husi, Barlad, Botosani, Pascani, etc. by the group of Iasian students who were everywhere helped by high school students. They entered halls full of Jews, throwing at Satan's artists anything they could grab, thus chasing them off the Romanian stage.

Perhaps—some may say—in an uncivilized manner. I too, say, perhaps. However, how civilized is it that an alien nation dispossess me, one after the other, of all the goods of my country? How civilized is it that the same nation poison my culture, then serve it on the stage to kill me?

To what extent were the means used by Jews in Russia civilized? How civilized is it to slaughter millions of people without trial? To what extent is it civilized to set fire to churches or to transform them into cabarets?

For myself, in my poverty and with my poor powers, I defend myself against an assault as best I can—by the printed word if I can; with the aid of authorities, if they are still Romanian; by word, if someone listens; by force, as a last resort, and if everybody keeps quiet. Unworthy and a traitor is he who does not defend his country either because of selling out or because of innate cowardice, or does not react in any fashion.

Anyway, this fight was a protest, the only protest in the center of a cowardly and terrifying silence. Next day our comrades returned full of blows and wounds, for it was no easy matter for a group of 15 youth to enter a theater with 3 or 4,000 Jews; and particularly they returned borne down with the opprobrium and invectives from our Romanians.

Many a time I ask myself: what kept us going, such a small group, faced with so many blows, so many rebukes heaped upon us from all directions? We found support nowhere. In this fight against everybody we found the only support in ourselves; in our belief that we were on the great path of our national destiny, side by side with all those who fought, suffered and died as martyrs for our land and its people.

In Germany

I returned to Iasi in the fall of 1922. There, I shared with my comrades an old thought of mine, that of going to Germany to continue my studies in political economy while at the same time trying to realize my intention of carrying our ideas and beliefs abroad. We realized very well, on the basis of our studies, that the Jewish problem had an international character and the reaction therefore should have an international scope; that a total solution of this problem could not be reached except through action by all Christian nations awakened to the consciousness of the Jewish menace.

But I had neither money nor clothing. My comrades got me some clothes and borrowed the sum of 8,000 lei from engineer Grigore Bejan, which they were to repay monthly, each contributing according to his ability. With this money I left for Berlin, accompanied to the station by all those from whom I parted, who now were staying behind at home to fight on. Once arrived in Berlin, two student friends, Balan and C. Zotta, were of great help. I registered at the university.

On registration day I donned my national costume and went to that beautiful ceremony wherein the rector, following an old tradition, shakes the hand of each new registrant. In the university's halls I was the subject of general curiosity because of my Romanian costume.

Two questions in particular might interest the reader of these lines regarding Germany of 1922—a look at the general situation, and the status of anti-Semitic movements.

The wounds left by the war just ended in defeat were still bleeding. Material misery blanketed both Berlin and the rest of the country alike. Lately the Ruhr valley, an important center of riches, had been occupied too. I was witnessing the vertiginous and catastrophic downfall of the mark. In the workingmen's quarters, lack of bread, lack of foodstuffs, lack of work. Hundreds of children were accosting passers-by, begging. The fall of the mark also threw the German aristocracy into the same misery. People who had money, in a few days were left penniless. Those who sold their land and real estate holdings, being attracted by the mirage of high prices, became impoverished in the course of a few weeks. Domestic and foreign Jewish capitalists closed colossal business deals. Those possessing strong currency became owners of huge buildings of 50 apartments for only a few hundred dollars. Speculators combed through the entire city, scoring formidable coups.

Sharing this great misery were also several foreigners, among them myself, for I had no money at all. The 8,000 lei I came with were spent. Then began hunger. But, in the midst of general suffering, your own suffering is easier to bear. Being a type who does not bend easily faced by difficulties, I did not submit to misery, but I tried to fight it. I studied all possibilities and I decided to engage in commerce. I needed a very little capital to procure a stock of food items in the country, bring them into Berlin, then sell them to restaurants. This fact made me move to Jena before the holidays, where life was cheaper. There, in the midst of the misery in which the German people struggled, I was impressed by the spirit of discipline, the capacity for labor, sense of duty, correctitude, power of resistance, and the faith in better days. It was a healthy people and I could see it would not permit itself to be knocked down and that it would with unsuspected powers resurrect itself from under the rock of all the difficulties burdening it.

The anti-Semitic movement. There were in Germany several anti-Semitic political and doctrinaire organizations, with papers, manifestoes, insignia, but all of them feeble. Students in Berlin, as those in Jena, were divided in hundreds of associations and numbered very few anti-Semites. The student mass knew the problem but vaguely. One could not talk of an anti-Semitic student action or even of a doctrinaire orientation similar to that of Iasi. I had many discussions with the students at Berlin in 1922, who are certainly Hitlerites today, and I am proud to have been their teacher in anti-Semitism, exporting to them the truths I learned in Iasi.

Of Adolf Hitler I heard for the first time around the middle of October 1922. I had gone to a worker in North Berlin with whom I established a good relationship, who was making "swastikas." His name was Strampf and he lived at 3 Salzwedeler Strasse. He told me: "It is said that an anti-Semitic movement has been started in Munich by a 36 year old painter, Hitler. It seems to me he is the man we Germans have been waiting for." The foresight of this worker was fulfilled. I always admired his intuitive powers by which he could select with the antennae of his soul, a stranger among scores of men, ten years before his time, the one who would succeed in 1933, uniting under a single great command the entire German people.

It was also in Berlin and at about the same time, that I heard the news of the huge Fascist eruption: the march on Rome and Mussolini's victory. I rejoiced as much as if it were my own country's victory. There is, among all those in various parts of the world who serve their people, a kinship of sympathy, as there is such a kinship among those who labor for the destruction of peoples.

Mussolini, the brave man who trampled the dragon underfoot, was one of us, that is why all dragon heads hurled themselves upon him, swearing death to him. For us, the others, he will be a bright North Star giving us hope; he will be living proof that the hydra can be defeated; proof of the possibilities of victory. "But Mussolini is not anti-Semitic. You rejoice in vain," whispered the Jewish press into our ears.

It is not a matter of what we rejoice in say I, it is a question of why you Jews are sad at his victory, if he is not anti-Semitic. What is the rationale of the worldwide attack on him by the Jewish press? Italy has as many Jews as Romania has Ciangai [a quite minor ethnic group] in the Siret valley. An Italian anti-Semitic movement would be as if Romanians started a movement against the Ciangai. But had Mussolini lived in Romania he could not but be anti-Semitic, for Fascism means first of all defending your nation against the dangers that threaten it. It means the destruction of these dangers and the opening of a free way to life and glory for your nation.

In Romania, Fascism could only mean the elimination of the dangers threatening the Romanian people, namely, the removal of the Jewish threat and the opening of a free way to the life and glory to which Romanians are entitled to aspire.

Judaism has become master of the world through Masonry, and in Russia through Communism. Mussolini destroyed at home these two Judaic heads which threatened death to Italy: Communism and Masonry. There, Judaism was eradicated through its two manifestations. In our country, it will have to be eradicated through what it has there: Jews, communists and Masons. These are the thoughts that we, Romanian youth in general, oppose to Judaic endeavors to deprive us of joy in Mussolini's victory.

THE STUDENT MOVEMENT

December 10, 1922

I was still in Jena, when one day I was surprised by the news that the entire Romanian student body from all universities arose to battle. This collective demonstration of the Romanian youth, unsuspected by anybody, was a volcanic eruption rising from the nation's depths. It first manifested itself in Cluj, the heart of that Transylvania which took a stand any time the nation experienced an impasse, then almost concomitantly it violently erupted in all other university centers.

In fact on December 3rd and 4th great street demonstrations took place in Bucharest, Iasi and Cernauti. The entire Romanian student body rose to its feet as in a time of great peril. For the thousandth time this earthy race, menaced so many times throughout history, threw its youth to face the threat in order to save its being. A great collective electrifying moment, with no preparation beforehand, without any pro and con discussions, without any committee decisions, without those in Cluj even knowing those in Iasi, Cernauti or Bucharest. A great moment of collective enlightment like the lightning in the middle of a dark night, in which the entire youth of the country recognized its own destiny in life as well as that of its people.

This destiny runs brightly through our entire national history and it extends into our whole Romanian future pointing the way to life and honor both we and our grandchildren will have to follow, if it is life and honor we wish for our people.

Generations can follow this destiny, can stay close to it or depart from it, having thus the capability of giving to their nation a maximum of life and honor or a maximum of dishonor and shame. Sometimes only isolated individuals, abandoned by their generation, can reach this destiny. In that moment, they are the people, they speak in its name. All the millions of dead and of the martyrs of the past are with them, as well as the nation's life of tomorrow.

Here, the majority with its opinions does not matter though it might be 99 percent. It is not the opinions of the majority that determine this destiny of life for our people. They, majorities, can only get nearer or farther away from it according to their state of consciousness and virtue or that of unconsciousness and decadence.

Our people have not survived through the millions of slaves who put their necks under the foreigner's yoke, but through Horea, Avram Iancu, Tudor, Iancu Jianu, through all the haiduci[1], who, faced by the alien yoke, did not submit, but put their muzzle-loaders on their backs heading up the mountain paths carrying with them honor and the spark of freedom. It was through them our people spoke, not through cowardly and well-behaved "majorities." They would conquer or die, no matter what. For when they die, the whole people lives from their death and is honored by their honor. They shine in history like golden beacons on the heights bathed at sundown in the sun's rays, while over the vast lowlands, no matter how extensive and numerous, settles the darkness of forgetfulness and death. It is not he who lives and wins by sacrificing the destiny of his people's lives who belongs to national history but only he who, whether he wins or loses, will hold himself to this destiny.

Our Romanian destiny is predetermined by God's wisdom; it could be seen on December 10, by the Romanian students. And it is in this that the value of the day resides: the entire Romanian youth saw the light.

On December 10, delegates from all student centers congregated in Bucharest, fixed in ten points what they thought formed the essence of their movement and declared a general strike for all universities, demanding the realization of these points.

December 10 is not great through the value of the formulation of points agreed upon, as much as the delegates could formulate of the truth's essence that then troubled the entire Romanian youth. It is great by virtue of the miracle of this youth's awakening to the light its soul had seen; by its decision for common action to declare the holy war that was to demand of this youth so much strength of heart, so much heroism, so much maturity, so much known and unknown sacrifices, so many graves! December 10, 1922 called the youth of this land to a great test.

Neither those in Bucharest, nor I who was far away, nor others who

---

1 Robin Hood type legendary men. (Tr.)

were perhaps high school students, but who today languish in so many prisons or sleep under the earth, could believe that this day would carry us through so much danger, would bring us so many blows and so many wounds in battles to defend our country.

In Bucharest, Cluj, Iasi and Cernauti formidable eruptions of student masses took place, which, led by their own power of intuition—not by leaders— turn toward the enemy. They eye first the Jewish press: *Adevarul* ("The Truth"), *Dimineata* ("The Morning"), *Mantuirea* ("The Redemption"), *Opinia* ("The Opinion"), *Lumea* ("The World"), hot-beds of moral infection, poison and confusion for the Romanians.

They turn to these in order to destroy them, but also to show the Romanian people the danger of the enemy's front line against which they must be on guard. Demonstrating against the press means: declaring it an enemy of national interest and thus calling it to the attention of Romanians that they not permit themselves to be fooled, blinded, or led by the press written by Jews or Judaized Romanians.

This press attacks the religious idea, thus weakening Romanian moral resistance and breaking their contact with God.

This press disseminates anti-national theories, weakening faith in their nation and breaking them from their country's land, of their love for it, land that was at all past times an urge to battle and sacrifice.

This press falsely presents our Romanian interests, disorienting and directing Romanians on paths opposed to national interests.

This press elevates mediocre elements and men capable of corruption so that the alien can satisfy his interests, and downgrades the moral people who will not stoop to do Judaism and its interests any favors.

This press poisons the soul of the nation, daily and systematically publicizing sensational crimes, immoral affairs, abortions, adventures.

This press murders truth and serves up lies with diabolical perseverance, using slander as a weapon of destruction of Romanian fighters.

That is why Romanians must be careful when they read a Jewish paper, being on guard against each word, not one of which is haphazardly printed, and seeking to decipher the Jewish plan behind it. It is these matters the student movement wanted to call to the attention of all Romanians when it turned on Jewish editorial offices, declaring them enemies of the Romanian people, I emphasized that the formidable eruptions of the student masses were led by their power of intuition and not by leaders. For it is easy for someone to direct several individuals towards somebody's house to stage a hostile demonstration, but when great multitudes turn on someone with hostility by order of their instinct, then that person is condemned, with no right of appeal, as an enemy of the nation.

The "Numerus Clausus"

The formula "numerus clausus" passes from mouth to mouth during student battles, but not as a saving formula, for masses do not issue formulas, they point out threats. "Numerus clausus" means that, the Jewish menace being in its great numbers, we can no longer support them either in schools, in commerce or industry, or in the independent professions. "Attention to their great number" is what "numerus clausus" means to say, for it surpasses our powers of national resistance and if we do not take any measures, we die as a people.

This is the whole value of this formula. Or, if you wish, as a saving measure, it has the value of an emergency formula, of necessary first aid, though totally inadequate to cure the illness. "Numerus clausus" per se, means: the limitation of Jews in schools, professions, etc. To what numbers, this limitation? To the proportion between the number of all Jews in relation to that of Romanians within Romania. Namely, if there are in Romania 15 million Romanians and 3 million Jews, the proportion is 20%. According to the "numerus clausus" formula, Jews are to be admitted into schools, medical professions, the bar, etc. in the proportion of 20%: "numerus clausus" means the limitation of the number of Jews up to the proportion between their number and the total number of Romanians.

"Numerus clausus" is only a formula of redistribution of the Jews within nations, and not a formula for resolving the problem.

This formula resolves almost nothing, for it treats of respecting proportions but does not cut down the high proportion of Jews. If the Jews are 3 million that is what they remain. Especially it does not treat the cause of this high proportion and does not show the means by which it can be diminished; in fine, it does not constitute of itself the means for resolving the Jewish problem.

THE JEWISH PROBLEM

The Number of Jews

The large number of Jews raises a series of problems: 1. The problem of the Romanian land; 2. The problem of the cities; 3. The problem of the Romanian school and of the leading class; 4. The problem of national culture.

All these are impeccably treated by Professor A.C Cuza in his writings: The Peoplehood, Nationality in Art, Articles, Parliamentary Discourses, Course in Political Economy. The ideas that I give below belong essentially to Professor Cuza's thought.

The number of Jews in Romania is not known exactly. That is because the statistics taken were done with the greatest lack of interest on the part of Romanian politicians so that they could cover up their work of national treason and because Jews everywhere run away from the truth of statistics. A proverb says: "Jews live by lies and die when coming in contact with truth." As a matter of fact, for a long time the Director of the State's Statistics in the Ministry of Finance had been Leon Colescu, real name Leon Coler.

And from their point of view they are right, because were Romanians faced with the exact number of the Jewish population, they would realize they are confronted by a real national menace and would rise up to defend their fatherland. In other words, in the face of statistical truth, the Judaic power flickers out, dies. It can live only by hiding truth, falsifying it by lies.

We believe that there are from 2 to 2.5 million Jews in Romania. If there be but one million—as they claim—the Romanian people would face mortal danger. Because it is not only the number per se that matters, the quantity, but also the quality of that number, particularly the positions occupied by Jews in the functional structure of the state and the life of the nation in all its aspects.

Our land has been a land of invasions. But it has never throughout its long history known an invader to reach such formidable numbers as those of the present day Jew. The invasions passed over us; the present day invaders never leave. They settle down here on our land in more unheard-of numbers than ever before and hold on like scabies to this land's body and people.

When did this Jewish invasion begin? Only several thousand Jews were found around 1800 in all of Moldavia. In 1821, there were 120 families in Bucharest.

Such late settlement on our land is due to the fact that Jews have always engaged in commerce, and commerce demands freedom and security in which to develop.

These two conditions were lacking in Romania: on one hand the freedom to exploit Romanian soil, thus any prospect of extended commerce, and on the other, stability, security. Romanian land was the most unsecure land in the world. The Romanian peasant had no security of home, cattle, his labor or his crops from year to year. Our country was ravaged by invasions and served as a theater of war for centuries, oftentimes with the aftermath of foreign domination and bloody tribute.

What was Jewry to do on this land? Fight the Huns, Tartars, Turks?

The Jewish invasion began only 100 years ago. As a result of the peace of Adrianople in 1829, freedom of commerce was granted and at the same time horizons of a more peaceful life began to appear.

It was then that their invasion began, increasing year by year over our Romanian heads, especially those of the Moldavians, draining us of wealth, destroying us morally and threatening us with extinction.

In 1848 the Moldavian merchants and industrialists began to complain to Mihail Sturza, the ruler, demanding measures be taken against Jewish merchants and the dishonest competition practiced by them.

Since then, the invasion has steadily increased. "Invasion" may not be the right term, for it presupposes the idea of violence, of moral and physical courage. "Jewish infiltration" is a more suitable term, for it better encompasses the idea of sly penetration, cowardly and perfidious penetration. For it is no small matter to steal the land and wealth of a people, without justifying through battle, through facing risks, through great sacrifice, the accomplished conquest.

Little by little they took over Romanian small commerce and industry; then, by using the same fraudulent tactics, they attacked big commerce and big industry, thus acquiring control over the towns in the northern half of the country.

The attack on the Romanian middle class was conducted with that precision met only in the case of some predatory insects, which, to paralyze the enemy, sting it in the spine.

They could not have chosen a more suitable spot.

Successfully attacking the middle class meant breaking the Romanian people in two.

It is the only class having a double contact: down, with the peasant class, being superimposed on it and exercising over it authority by virtue of its better economic status and by education; up, with the governing class which it supports on its shoulders.

A successful attack on the middle class, namely its destruction, brings in its wake as a fatal consequence, no additional effort being needed on the part of the attacker: a) The collapse of the ruling class (This ruling class will end up collapsing), b) The impossibility of its reconstitution, c) The confusion and animalization, the vanquishing and enslavement of the peasant class.

In the last analysis, the Judaic attack on the Romanian middle class purports death. The death of the Romanian people does not mean the death of the last Romanian, as some imagine. This death means life in slavery. The lowering to slave life of several million Romanian peasants, who would work for Jewry.

Here are the findings of Professor Nicolae Iorga regarding the number of Jews and their arrival in our parts. Professor Iorga in "The History of Jews in our Principalities," a paper delivered before the Romanian Academy on September 13, 1913, exposing this question, specifies, among other things:

> "In Neamt, several Jews settle on the lands of the Monastery between 1764-1766 (p. 18).
>
> "In Botosani, no ruler's document like that of 1757 mentions Jews among the other inhabitants of the town (p. 17).

"Sometimes a Jew pops up in Suceava as tavern-keeper on church land; others as small merchants in Ocna, Harlau, Siretiu, Galati, Barlad (there was a time when one could say that Christian Barladians were engaged in commerce more than in any other occupation) (p. 10); then in Roman where in 1741 only 'Moldavians' and 'Armenians' were known; in Targul Frumos where in 1755 'two taverns' and a Jewish one are mentioned as existing there (p. 17-18)."

In Bucovina about the time of its annexation in 1775:

"In the regions of Cernauti and Campulung, to which were annexed parts of Hotin and Suceava — in all these regions — before the Austrian imperial domination there were only 206 'Jewish' families.

"In 1775, through overflow from Galicia their number reached 780-800 families.

"The country's first governor, Gen. Enzenberg, learned that they engage primarily in tavern-keeping, with wine, whiskey, beer...

"They are, says the general, 'the most outright wicked people, inclined to laziness, living, without much trouble, from the sweat of Christian workingmen'."

A commission operating in 1781 shows that:

"In this country Jews are in the habit of buying from the peasant the chick in the egg beforehand, the honey in flower, the lamb in its mother's womb, for a pittance, and through this usury entirely sucking the inhabitants dry, bringing them to poverty, so that the peasants thus burdened by indebtness find no recourse for the future to save themselves but by fleeing from the country,

"We see the administration of this country (Moldavia), then the boyars, particularly Constantin Moruzi, desperately defending themselves against them.

"...As the Kahals offered Enzenberg in writing 5,000 pieces of gold annually to tolerate the old state of affairs, corrupting our Ruler was also tried, but he rejected the MONEY rather than expose his country to total destruction "[1] (p.20).

---

1 One question: How much do present day Kahals pay the leaders of Romania?

And later, around 1840-48, this is what Professor Iorga determines:

> "One could count these establishments of exploitation and depravation by the score, tavern by tavern, with bottles of potato whiskey and other poisons, all across Moldavia, exhausting a race for the feeding of the civilized vices of the domineering class (p. 34).

And Professor Iorga writes on:

> "Still, the intervention by foreigners, fostered by Jewish elements in the country, did not cease. In 1878 they imposed conditions before they would recognize Romania's independence (won with so much sacrifice of Romanian blood) and heaped indignities on independent Romania which cannot but commit suicide by politically yielding half of itself to the power of the Moldavian Jews... And as Kogalniceanu defended villages from Jewish alcohol and usury, so Mr. Maiorescu defends Romania's dignity from the insult of granting civil rights to foreigners in the country as a result of the pressures of their co-religionists abroad." (p.39).

I cite these examples as reported by a great, recognized, and uncontested scientific authority, to clarify the start of Jewish settlements on Romanian soil.

The Problem of The Romanian Land

The Law of The Territory

There cannot be any people in this world, be they only a tribe of savages that, faced by a foreign invasion, would not consider with rending pain the predicament of its land. All peoples of the world, from history's beginnings to this day have defended the soil of their fatherland. The history of all peoples, as ours, is replete with battles in defense of its land. Would it be an anomaly, a state of illness of ours, the Romanian youth, that we stand to be counted in the defense of our menaced land? Or an anomaly if we did not defend it when we see it endangered? It would be an anomaly for us not to defend it, namely, not doing what all nations have done. Placing us in contradiction to the entire world and our entire history would be an anomaly and a state of illness.

Why is it, I wonder, that all peoples have fought, fight and will always fight for the defense of their land?

Land is a nation's basis for existence. The nation has its roots like those of a tree deep in the country's soil whence it derives its nourishment and life. There is no people that can live without land, as there is no tree which can live hanging in air. A nation which has no land of its own cannot live unless it settles on the land of another nation—on its very body, sapping its sustenance.

There exist God-given laws which ordain the life of peoples. One of these laws is the territorial law, God gave each people a definite territory to live in, grow in and on which to develop and create its own culture.

The Jewish problem in Romania, as elsewhere, consists of the infringement by Jews of this natural law of the territory. They trespassed on our territory. They are the infractors and it is not we, the Romanian people, who are called to bear the consequences of their infraction. Elementary logic tells us: the infractor must bear the consequences of the committed infraction. Will he have to suffer? Let him suffer! All infractors suffer. No logic in the world will tell me that I should die for the infraction committed by others.

Thus, the Jewish problem is not born of "racial hatred." It is born of an infraction committed by Jews against the laws and natural order in which all peoples of the world live.

The solution to the Jewish problem? Here it is: the re-entry of infractors into the universal natural order and their respecting natural legality. But the laws of the land too, prohibit the Jewish invasion. Article 3 of the Constitution says: "The territory of Romania cannot be colonized by a population of foreign origin."

What does the fact of the two million Jews settling on Romanian territory mean, if not colonization?

But this territory is the inalienable and indefeasible property of the Romanian people. And as someone wrote, not after 50, not after 100, but even thousands of years later we will claim the right over this land, as we reconquered the Transylvanian land following 1000 years of Hungarian occupation.

We And Our Land

All peoples around us have come from somewhere else settling on the land on which they now live. History gives us precise dates regarding the arrival of Bulgarians, Turks, Magyars, etc. Only one people came from nowhere: ours. We were born in the mist of time on this land together with the oaks and fir trees. We are bound to it not only by the bread and existence it furnishes us as we toil on it, but also by all the bones of our ancestors who sleep in its ground. All our parents are here. All our memories, all our war-like glory, all our history here, in this land lies buried.

Here are the ruins of Sarmisegetuza with the immortal King Decebal's ashes, for whoever knows how to die like Decebal, never dies.

Here rest the ruling Musatins and the ruling Basarabs; here at Podul Inalt, Razboeni, Suceava, Baia, Hotin, Soroca, Tighina, Cetatea Alba, Chilia, sleep the Romanians fallen there in battles, nobles and peasants, as numerous as the leaves and blades of grass.

At Posada, Calugareni, on the Olt, Jiu and Cerna rivers, at Turda; in the mountains of the unhappy and forgotten Moti of Vidra, all the way to Huedin and Alba-Iulia (the torture place of Horea and his brothers-in-arms), there are everywhere testimonies of battles and tombs of heroes.

All over the Carpathians, from the Oltenian mountains at Dragoslavele and at Predeal, from Oituz to Vatra Dornei, on peaks and in valley bottoms, everywhere Romanian blood flowed like rivers.

In the middle of the night, in difficult times for our people, we hear the call of the Romanian soil urging us to battle.

I ask and I expect an answer: By what right do the Jews wish to take this land from us?

On what historical argument do they base their pretentions and particularly the audacity with which they defy us Romanians, here in our own land? We are bound to this land by millions of tombs and millions of unseen threads that only our soul feels, and woe to those who shall try to snatch us from it.

The Problem of the Cities

But within the breadth of this Romanian land Jews did not settle just anywhere, haphazardly. They placed themselves in towns, forming within them real islands of compact Jewish populations.

At first it was the cities and market towns of northern Moldavia that were invaded and conquered: Cernauti, Hotin, Suceava, Dorohoi, Botosani, Soroca, Burdujeni, Itcani, Briceni, Secureni etc.

Before them the Romanian merchant and tradesman gradually disappeared—today one street, tomorrow another, day after tomorrow a section. In less than 100 years Romanian centers of ancient renown lost their Romanian character, taking on the likeneness of real Jewish fortresses. The other Moldavian towns too, fell quickly: Roman, Piatra, Falticeni, Bacau, Vaslui, Barlad, Husi, Tecuci, Galati; and Iasi, the second capital of Moldavia—after the first one and our ancient Suceava—was purely and simply turned into a dirty Jewish nest, which surrounds the poor glorious ruins of Stefan the Great's fortress.

In Iasi now, one can walk through whole streets and sectors never meeting a Romanian, or seeing a Romanian home or a Romanian store. People pass by famous churches, today in ruins and decay: the Church of Talpalari[2] built by the Romanian cobblers guild, the Church of Curelari10 built by the Romanian harness-makers' guild. Everything is falling apart. In that large city of Iasi, there is no longer a Romanian cobbler or harness-maker. The Church of St. Nicholas the Poor of the old Moldavian nobility has totally collapsed; and over the tombs around it the Jewish eating places discard even today their slop, garbage and refuse.

The Church in Main Square, where one finds the greatest agglomeration of people—is closed, due to lack of churchgoers. And it is the Jewish population which constitutes that agglomeration of people now.

On Lapusneanu St., Cuza Voda's palace which almost groans as if in pain, has been transformed into a Jewish bank, and in its former garden a Palestinian-style Jewish theater can be seen. The foreign invader tramples underfoot everything we hold most sacred.

Our hearts groan in anguish. We children, our souls rent, ask

2 Plural for 'cobbler' and 'harness-maker' respectively. (Tr.)

ourselves: How could there be Romanians who behave with so much enmity toward their people? How could there be so many traitors? How come they were not lined up against the wall or burnt alive in the moment of their betrayal? How come everybody is impassive? How come we do nothing? These are problems of conscience that weigh upon us, which bother our souls, upset our lives. We know that in no way will we find our peace but in battles, in suffering or in graves. Our silence covers us with cowardice and every minute of delay seems to kill us.

We do not even mention the cities and market towns of Basarabia which are open sores on the country's exhausted and squeezed body.

Nor do we even mention Maramures where Romanians, in a state of slavery, daily die. There are no words that can describe the great tragedy of Maramures.

But the illness spread like a cancer; it reached Ramnicul-Sarat, Buzau, Ploesti and it penetrated the capital.

In 15 years fell Vacaresti, an old Romanian quarter; Dudesti fell entirely; likewise, the Romanian merchants on Calea Grivitei. The famous merchants in the Obor quarter die and are replaced by Jews; Calea Victoriei[3] has fallen. Today it has become in reality only a Romanian road of "defeat;" for three-fourths of the properties on Calea Victoriei are now Jewish owned. In the last ten years the Jews spread westward up the Danube plain into Oltenia and entered Michael the Brave's capital city of Craiova; they went into Ramnicul-Valcea, Severin, under the protection of the Romanian politicians who, well paid, pretend there is no Jewish problem. This betrayal by these politicians of their people is so frightening that, if they are still alive, the people should gouge their eyes out; if they are dead, their bones should be disinterred and burnt in public squares. Their children and grandchildren should be prosecuted, their wealth confiscated and they should be stigmatized with the epithet of "traitors' children."

The loss of our Romanian towns has for us devastating consequences, for towns are the economic centers of a nation. The entire richness of the country is accumulated in them. So that whoever controls the towns controls the means of subsistence, the wealth of a nation.

---

3 The Victory Way, a fashionable shopping boulevard (Tr.)

Congress of the Romanian Zionist movement. Iasi, Romania. 1921.

Could it be an indifferent matter to us Romanians as to who are the masters of our national wealth? Ourselves or the Jews? To no people in the world could this be an indifferent matter. Because a population reproduces and develops within the means of subsistence at its disposal. The fewer these means are, the less will be the growth of the population in question and the fewer the chances for its development, and vice versa. These truths regarding the law of population were studied by all economists and formulated by Professor Cuza with unequalled clarity.

The passing of Romanian riches into the hands of the Jews does not only mean the Romanians' economic dependence or the political one—for, whoever has no economic freedom, has no political freedom—but it means more: a national menace that grinds down our very ability to grow in population. To the extent that our means of subsistence vanish, to that extent we Romanians will die off on our land, leaving our places in the hands of the Jewish population whose number increases day by day both because of the invasion from abroad and because of seizing our means of subsistence, our riches.

Then, secondly, the towns are the cultural centers of a nation[4]. Here in towns one finds the schools, libraries, theaters, lecture halls, all of them serving the townspeople. A Jewish family can easily support five or six children in school, whereas the Romanian peasant, in some remote village far from town, can hardly manage to send one child to school to the end. And in this case he is completely exhausted of strength and wealth so that he endangers the well-being of the other four or five children at home. So, whoever controls the towns controls the possibilities for partaking in the culture.

But that is not all. It is through towns and schools that a nation fulfills its cultural mission in the world. How is it possible for the Romanians to fulfill their cultural mission through Jewish voices, pens, hearts and minds?

Finally, towns are the political centers of a nation. Nations follow the lead of the towns. Whoever controls the towns, directly or indirectly has the political leadership of the country.

What is left of the country, outside of the towns? A crowd of several million peasants, lacking humane means of existence, drained and impoverished, cultureless, poisoned by drink, led by the enriched Jews now become the masters of Romanian towns, or by the Romanians (prefects, mayors, police officers, gendarmes, cabinet ministers) who are administrators in name only because they are nothing but supine executors of Jewish plans. These officials are supported, flattered, showered with gifts, co-opted in administrative councils, paid by the month by the Judaic economic power (Judas was paid but once); their lust for money is roused, they are urged on to luxury and vice, and when disobeying Jewish directives and stances, are purely and simply thrown out even though they be cabinet ministers. Their pay and subsidies are cut, their thieveries brought to light and shady business deals exposed, implicating them, in order to compromise them. This is what remains of the Romanian fatherland since we lost our towns: a dishonest leader class, a people of peasants without freedom, and all Romanian children countryless and futureless.

4 See A.C. Cuza, *Apararea Nationala* ("The National Defense") No. 3, May 1. 1922.

The Problem of the Romanian Schools

Whoever controls the towns controls the schools, and whoever controls the schools today controls the country tomorrow. Here are some 1920 statistics:

The situation at the University of Cernauti School of Philosophy:

Summer Semester :	Romanians:	174
	Jews	574

School of Law: Summer Semester, according to denomination:

Orthodox:	237
Catholics:	98
Lutherans:	26
Other Religions:	31
Hebraic:	506

From *Situatia demografica a Romaniei* (The Demographic Situation of Romania) by Em. Vasiliu-Cluj p. 84

In Basarabia - Rural Elementary Schools:

Boys:	Romanians	72,889
non-Romanian	Christians	1,974
	Jews	1,281
Girls:	Romanians	27,555
non-Romanian	Christians	1,302
	Jews	2,147

Urban Elementary Schools:

Boys:	Romanians	6,385
non-Romanian	Christians	2,435
	Jews	1,351
Girls:	Romanians	5,501
non-Romanian	Christians	2,435
	Jews	1,492

Secondary and professional schools:

Orthodox	1,535
Hebraic	6,302

Coeducational secondary schools:

Orthodox	690
Hebraic	1,341

(Op.cit. pp. 84-5)

In the Old Kingdom[5]	Romanians	Jews
Lycee of Bacau .	363	198
Lycee of Botosani	229	127
Girls Lycee of Botosani .	155	173
Lycee of Dorohoi	177	167
Lycee of Falticeni	152	100
National Lycee, Iasi	292	201
Alexander the Good Gymnasium, Iasi	93	215
Stefan the Great Gymnasium, Iasi	94	120
Lycee of Roman	256	157
Lycee of Piatra-Neamt	343	179

Private Schools:	Romanians	Jews
Bucharest	441	781
Iasi	37	108
Gaiati	190	199

(Op.cit. pp. 85-7)

The situation at the University of Iasi	Romanians	Jews
School of Medicine	546	831
School of Pharmacy	97	299
School of Letters	351	100
School of Sciences	722	321
School of Law	1,743	370

(Op.cit, pp.87-8)

The Romanian system of education thus being destroyed by the large number of Jews raises two problems:

1. *The problem of the Romanian leading class*, because schools form the leaders of tomorrow, not only the political ones, but all leaders in every domain of activity.
2. *The problem of national culture*, because schools are the laboratory in which the culture of a people is molded.

In order to underscore the tragedy of this Romanian school system overwhelmed by Jews, I consider it particularly important to cite below the distressing findings of one of the most illustrious pedagogues of our nation, Professor Ion Gavanescul of the University of Iasi:

---

5 Moldavia and Wallachia before the unification of Romania in 1918. (Tr.)

> "We no longer wish to see the spectacle offered by the National Lycee of Iasi, where the crushing majority of students is composed of the Jewish element. The few Romanian students feel like strangers; during recess they retreat, uneasy, into corners. They constitute the tolerated minority.
>
> "The majority lives apart, talk among themselves about their preoccupations, their games, societies, Macaby, Hacoah, Macoah, etc., of their get-togethers and lectures, their sports, work plans and good times. And when they are doubtful of the discretion of the Romanians, the Jewish students (a majority in school, though a minority in the country), whisper among themselves or switch directly to Yiddish....
>
> "Pity the Romanian professors faced with such student souls! One involuntarily is reminded of the hen that hatched duck eggs. Look at her, how she stands cackling, scared, at the edge of the pond, how she desperately calls her ducklings, her chicks of another species which jumped into the water, gliding off to the other shore where she cannot follow. "What school of nationalism can you teach to such an audience? Can you talk, if you feel in yourself the flame of patriotism, of Romanian aspirations and ideals? Can you even open your mouth? Your jaws lock, your words freeze on your lips.
>
> "The great Kogalniceanu, in the face of such benches full of foreign students... could he have pronounced his famous discourse introducing the history of Romanians which he delivered on this very spot, where today the Romanian 'National' Lycee has turned into a Jewish 'National' one?
>
> "He would have lost the inspiration that derives its force from the sympathy of the shining eyes full of understanding and faith."
>
> 1. Gavanescul, *Imperativul momentului istoric* ("The Imperative of the Historic Moment") p.67.

And further:

> "And to limit ourselves to but one aspect of the national life, where did anyone ever see in England, France, Italy a school at any level, in which the preponderant number of students belongs to another people than the people constituting the indigenous population of the country and which founded the National State in question?
>
> "Can anyone imagine, for instance, that at some school of Law in some English university there might be 547 Jews versus 234 Britons, the same proportion of Jews to Romanians at the Cernauti School of Law in 1920?

"Or that, at a school of philosophy in Italy, there could be 574 Jews versus 174 Italians, the same proportion as that of Jews to Romanians in Cernauti?

"Are these ratios normal? Are they not inadmissible, inconceivable monstrosities of ethnic biology? Are they not an indication of criminal unconsciousness on the part of the Romanian people's responsible leading class?"

(I. Gavanescul, op.cit.)

The Problem of the Romanian Leading Class

But who are the pupils and students of today? The present day students are the professors, doctors, engineers, lawyers, prefects, congressmen, cabinet ministers of tomorrow, in one word, the future leaders of the people in all domains of activity. If present day students are 50, 60, 70% Jews, tomorrow we will logically have 50, 60, 70% Jewish leaders for this Romanian people.

Can one still raise the question whether a nation has the right to limit the number of alien students in its universities?

Here is how this question is answered in the Harvard University Bulletin by Morris Gray, a graduate of Harvard (1906) after he studied the Jewish problem there—as cited by Professor Cuza in "*Numerus Clausus*" p. 11.

Morris Gray began by formulating the problem in principle, asking:

"First of all, what is the function of a university? What are its duties?

"If its duty is a duty to the individual, the admission into the university must be based frankly and manifestly, on the democratic principle: any candidate must be admitted on the condition he pass his entrance examination and pay the first term of tuition. And this with no serious investigation of the candidate's personality or his latent possibilities of progress, his capability, or usefulness to himself or to others.

"But, if the university's duty is a duty toward the nation, its attitude regarding student admissions must naturally be based on a different principle.

> "In my opinion, the duty of a university is to form men in the various domains of human thought in such fashion that part of them at least can become leaders in their respective fields, thus serving the nation."

Here then is a well-established principle, adds Professor Cuza:

> "The duty of universities is toward their nation, for which they must prepare leaders in all fields and these must be necessarily ethnically native,
>
> "For it is intolerable that a nation educate for itself alien leaders in its universities."

From the preceding figures one can deduce the grave problem of the Romanian leading class of tomorrow.

There remains a well-established truth: Romania ought to be led by Romanians.

Is there anyone who claims that Romania ought to be led by Jews?

If not, then one has to admit that Romanian student youth is right and that all campaigns, all wrongs, all infamies, all provocations, all plots, all injustices that are heaped and are going to be heaped upon this Romanian youth, find their justification in the war waged by Jewry for the extermination of Romanians and of their best fighters.

The Problem of National Culture

A people, considering this the gravest of all problems, is like a tree concerned with the problem of its fruit.

When it sees itself overwhelmed by caterpillars, it can no longer fulfill its mission in this world, cannot bear fruit; then it would have to face the saddest problem, greater even than the problem of life itself, for, seeing its aim in life destroyed, it would be more painful for it that were it to be dead. The greatest pains are those of useless efforts, because they are the pains resulting from the frightful consciousness of the uselessness of life.

Is it not frightening, that we, the Romanian people, no longer can produce fruit? That we do not have a Romanian culture of our own, of our people, of our blood, to shine in the world side by side with that of other peoples? That we be condemned today to present ourselves before the world with products of Jewish essence?

That today, at this moment, when the world expects that the Romanian people appear to show the fruit of our national blood and genius, we present ourselves with an infection of Judaic cultural caricature? We look at this problem with hearts constricted with anguish and there will be no Romanian, who, seeing his entire history endangered, will not reach for his weapons to defend himself.

I reproduce here from Professor I. Gavanescul's "The Imperative of the Historic Moment," these immortal lines:

> "The principal concern of the Romanian people, just as important to its being as its physical preservation, is its affirmation in the realm of humanity's ideal of life—the creation of a culture specifically of Romanian character.

"It is impossible that a Romanian culture evolve from a school or an economic or political organization of alien character.

> "An institution, as a function of national life, has a Romanian character only when the human factor giving it birth is Romanian."

Faced with this sad situation, faced by the large number of invaders overwhelming us, Professor Gavanescul, posing the question of a national school and culture, asks himself full of anxiety:

> "Where can Romanian souls seek refuge? Where can they escape the obsessing painful impression of being exiles in their own country?
>
> "Excepting the church, where they enter to collect their thoughts in quiet, under the protection of the saving cross, their only refuge is the school.
>
> "The school is the ideal nest in which the national genius gathers its progeny to nurture it, to raise it, to teach it how to fly, to show it the way to heights that only that national genius knows and only it is meant to reach.
>
> "The school is the place of refuge where the nation's heartstrings and the spiritual organs of the people are tuned in order to intone a new symphony as yet unheard in the world, the first symphony of its natural talents predestined by God exclusively to its being.
>
> "The school is the sanctuary where the great mystery of a people's

life unfolds, where the ethnic soul distills in drops of light its immortal essence so that it be molded into the ideal form preordained to it exclusively by the world's creative thought.

"The melodic instruments of other ethnic souls cannot harmoniously participate in the symphony of our culture. By virtue of their make-up they know only how to sound the note of their people.

"What kind of Romanian symphony could they produce?

"The essence of national genius of other ethnic souls cannot crystalize in a different form from that determined for them by the creator of peoples. How can one produce a Romanian image from the Jewish, Magyar, or German national essence?"

(I. Gavanescul, "The Imperative of the Historic Moment," pp. 64-8).

Not only will the Jews be incapable of creating Romanian culture, but they will falsify the one we have in order to serve it to us poisoned.

The Romanian school being thus macerated, we are placed in the position of renouncing our mission as a people, of renouncing the creation of a Romanian culture and of perishing from Jewish poison.

The Return To Romania

In contrast to our colleagues from the other universities, we Iasian students knew all these things from the lectures of Professor Cuza, the writings of Professors Paulescu and Gavanescul, from our studies and research done at the Association of Law Students, and from what we saw with our own eyes and felt with our own souls.

A problem of great conscience posed itself for us. Every day brought us additional proof. We recognized the perfidiousness of the Jewish press, we saw its bad faith in all circumstances, we saw its incitations behind everything anti-Romanian; we saw the work of flattery and elevation of political figures, functionaries, authorities, writers, Christian priests, who stooped to do the bidding of Jewish interests; we saw the ridicule heaped upon those who adopted a correct, dignified Romanian attitude, or those who dared denounce the Jewish peril; we saw the indecency with which we were treated in our land, as if they had been masters here for thousands of years; we saw with evergrowing indignation the daring meddling of these uninvited guests into the most intimate problems of Romanian life: religion, culture, art, politics, they seeking to trace lines along which the destiny of the Romanian people should move.

Young as I was, almost a child, I was long troubled by these thoughts while searching for a solution.

The elements which impressed me most, that then determined me to fight and that comforted and strengthened me in times of suffering, were:

1. The consciousness of mortal danger in which our people and its future found itself.
2. My love for the land and the sorrow for every sacred and glorious place, today ridiculed and profaned by Jews.
3. The pity for the ashes of those who had fallen for their country.
4. The feeling of revolt against the offenses to, as well as the ridicule and trampling underfoot by this alien enemy of our dignity as human beings and as Romanians.

That is why, when on December 10, 1922, I heard the great news: the volcanic explosion of the student movement, I decided to return home so that I too might fight side by side with my comrades.

A short time later, the train was taking me home. From Cracow, I sent a telegram to the students in Cernauti, who were expecting me at the station. I stayed there two days. The university was closed. The students guarding it seemed like soldiers serving their country, their soul enlightened by God. No trace of personal interest clouded their beautiful and sacred action. The cause for which they banded together and fought as one went much beyond themselves and their constant privations and needs.

In Cernauti, the leading fighters were: Tudose Popescu, the son of the old priest from Marcesti, County of Dambovita, a third year student in Theology; then, Danileanu, Pavelescu, Carsteanu etc.

I inquired about the plan of battle. It was decided to declare a general strike until we won, namely, until the government satisfactorily solved the points raised in the motion of December 10, beginning with "numeras clausus."

To me this plan seemed wrong. In my head another one began to form:

1. The student movement ought to reach out to all the Romanian people. Limited now to universities, it should be extended into a Romanian national movement, because for one thing the Jewish problem is not limited to the universities but involves the whole Romanian nation, and for another, the universities by themselves cannot solve it.
2. This national movement must be incorporated into an organization under a single command.
3. The aim of this organization must be fighting to bring the national movement to power, which will resolve both "numerus clausus" and all other problems, for no other rule by political parties outside of this movement will resolve the national problem.
4. With these points in mind, the students should organize a great national assembly of Romanians from all social strata, which would men signal the beginning of the new organization.
5. In order to implement this assembly, each university should provide as many flags as there are counties in each province, the cloth for each being then given by a student delegation there to a known nationalist whom the delegation would consider the best qualified person for the job of gathering round him a group of town and country leaders. Then, upon receiving the telegram announcing a week ahead of time the date and place of the ally, he would start for that place with the flag and all his men.
6. Lest the government try to prevent the rally, all preparations should be made quietly, keeping the date unknown until the last minute.

I outlined this plan to about 50 fighters in one of the dormitories.

They considered it good. Then we all pitched in money, bought the necessary cloth and right away girl students started making flags for the counties of Bucovina.

At Iasi

In Iasi I met all my former comrades. I exposed my plan to them as well. Here too, the flags were made the first day, by girl students, for all counties in Moldavia and Basarabia. I could not find Professor Cuza. He had left for Bucharest together with Professor Sumuleanu and my father to attend a meeting in the capital.

At Bucharest

The next day I left for Bucharest. Here, I went to see Professors Cuza and Sumuleanu and my father, who for over a quarter of a century had been fighting together against the Jewish menace, being overwhelmed by ridicule, blows and even wounds, and who today experienced the great satisfaction of seeing the entire educated youth of the country numbering over 30,000 raising battle banners for the faith they had served for a lifetime.

But in Bucharest my thoughts were not received with the same enthusiasm. First, because I encountered some opposition from Professor Cuza. Presenting my plan, proposing the creation of a national movement, headed by him as chief, in the rally to be held, he did not consider my plan good because, said he: "We do not need to organize, our movement is based on a formidable mass current."

I insisted, comparing a mass movement to an oil well, that, unconnected to a pipeline, even when it gushes, it comes to naught, because the oil spills all over. I left, however, with no success but next day, Professor Sumuleanu and my father convinced him.

But I was soon confronted by a difficulty I had not expected. It was around the beginning of February. The great body of students was overflowing with enthusiasm. Though all its mess halls were closed down and the gates of all dormitories locked against us, being thus left out to starve in the middle of the winter, yet the students were enthusiastic, admirably protected by the capital's Romanians, who the very next day opened wide the doors of their homes, sheltering and feeding over 8,000 student fighters. There was, in this gesture, an approval, an urge to the struggle, a solidarization, a comfort for those being wounded.

But I had no contact with this mass. I knew no one there. Through the student Fanica Anastasescu, who was the manager of the review *Apararea Nationala* ("The National Defense"), I began to meet a few. I had the impression that the leaders of the student movement in Bucharest were not sufficiently oriented, for though elite elements endowed with distinguished intellectual qualities, a fact verified by the functions they later occupied in society, they found themselves unexpectedly heading a movement to which up to then they had given no thought. In fact, as there were many, each had a different opinion. Among the valuable elements of the leadership, figured in the forefront: Cretu, Danulescu, Simionescu, Rapeanu, Roventa, and others. The mass was warlike, but part of the leadership thought it wise to calm down such high spirits.

On the other hand, both their insufficient familiarity with the Jewish question, and the inadequate contact with politicians made at least some of them try to some extent to re-position the movement onto a material plane, something that in my opinion was inadmissible. For this would have been as if someone were to say:

1. We fight to take our country back from the Jews.
2. We fight for white bread on our tables.
3. We fight for two-course meals.
4. We fight for a more comfortable bed.
5. We fight for equipment in our laboratories, for dissection instruments, etc.
6. We fight for more dormitories; so that in the end the authorities would tell us loudly:

   "Student demands have been satisfied; the government has recognized the pitiful state of students' lot, their great misery, etc. Out of the six points demanded five were allowed: dissection instruments, laboratory equipment, two white loaves of bread daily, two-course meals, three student dormitories with comfortable beds, etc."

As to the first point: saving the country from Jewish hands, nothing would be said, on the pretext that the government conceded five points out of six.

From the beginning of the student movement the entire Jewish press sought to shift it onto this material plane: that the objective of the movement be 'a loaf of bread.'

Thus the real objective— the Jew—would escape unnoticed. In fact, if one troubles to re-read the papers, one observes that Romanian politicians also posed the problem in similar terms: students must be given dormitories, better food; etc.

As I have said, part of the student leadership in Bucharest were inclined toward this propensity. Had the students taken this course they would have strayed from their true mission.

My opinion was always contrary to this point of view—against any intrusion of a material order into the formulation of student demands.

For, I was saying, as I also say today, it was not the immediate needs or material wants that impelled students toward this great movement, but on the contrary it was the abandonment of concern for such things, of selfish interests, of their own or family sufferings: it was the forgetting of all these things on the part of the Romanian students, the identification of their whole being with the worries, needs and aspirations of their people. It was this abnegation and only this, that lighted the holy light in their eyes.

The student movement was not one of material demands. It raised itself above the needs of a generation, entwining itself with the superior aspirations of the nation.

On the other hand, here in Bucharest the idea predominated that the student movement ought to stay within the university's confines, to remain an academic movement, not become a movement of a political nature. But this opinion was a totally incorrect one, for it coincided with the design of the Jews and political parties who had the greatest interest in restricting this fiery movement to the university so that there, by one means or another, it could be extinguished.

Our opinion was not that we had formed a movement in order to agitate, but to gain a victory. Our student forces alone being insufficient for that, we needed to unite with all Romanians.

In addition, the Bucharest leaders opposed having Professor Cuza proclaimed president of an eventual organization, claiming he was not good for such active leadership. I insisted that we must support him, such as he is.

Finally, those in Bucharest held great reservations toward me. This pained me, for I was coming to them with what a man has most clean and most sacred in his heart, with the live desire to cooperate in the best possible manner, for our country. Perhaps, not knowing me, they were justified in having reservations.

For these reasons I encountered opposition in Bucharest. That is why I began to work outside the committee, and we only made 3 or 4 flags.

At Cluj

I left for Cluj together with Alexandru Ghica, one of Mrs. Constanta Ghica's three sons, of Iasi, who were the ruler's great-grandsons who throughout the student campaign acted admirably.

The president of the Cluj student center was Alexa, a moderate, good element. He received me with the same arguments regarding both student orientation and proclaiming Professor Cuza as president of the new movement. The student mass was staunch and full of enthusiasm. It was then that I met Mota, an agile, talented youth. He held the same opinions as Alexa. I tried to convince him but unsuccessfully. I had a difficult time. I knew no one. Yet, I found a few students on my side: Corneliu Georgescu, student in Pharmacy; Isac Mocanu from Letters; Crasmaru, in Medicine; Justin Iliesu, etc. We made only one flag, then in Capt Siancu's house, who from the first moment with great enthusiasm agreed to our plan of action, we took an oath on this flag.

The Founding of the League of National Defense

Once returned to Iasi I had before me two roads of parallel activity:

1. Laying the groundwork for the rally for which flags were made in all universities.
2. Continuing the student movement and keeping the general strike going.

Regarding the first point, the biggest difficulty was not the lack of men or lack of organization, or the government's measures. This time, the greatest obstacle was coming from Professor Cuza himself, who, though not disapproving it, showed lack of enthusiasm.

Professor Cuza was not sufficiently convinced of the necessity for organizing, and did not believe at all in the possibility of success for the projected rally.

Regarding the second point, I faced serious difficulties with the leaders in the Bucharest and Cluj centers, difficulties which prevented agreement on a single point of view toward a battle plan around which perfect unity of this new world could be realized, raising up with all its united strength in defiance of the enemy and all our past errors. Neither the leadership nor the body of these student centers:

Knew the Jewish problem, particularly did not know the Jew; were not aware of the Judaic power, its way of thinking and of action. They began waging war without knowing the adversary.

They believed the then Liberal government, or eventually the one to succeed it, to which we would promise our support, would satisfy our demands.

On this basis, they preferred to engage in diplomacy, believing that ultimately they would convince the politicians of the justice of our cause. I believe there is nothing more distressing than discussing a problem with men who are not even familiar with its most elementary aspects. Regarding this situation, I took the following steps:

1. That several good delegates of the Iasi center regularly take part in the meetings of the central committee in Bucharest (The meetings of this committee were regularly held two and three times a week. They began at 9 in the evening lasting to 3, 4, 5 and even 7 o'clock in the morning, in contradictory discussions. For many of those participating, the only recollections of the student movement were of these meetings with their rethorical encounters within the committee).

2. That at Bucharest and Cluj a group of the best fighters from the student body be formed in order to work independent of the directives by their respective centers.

At Cluj and Bucharest, these groups were formed very quickly. In Bucharest they were present right in the committee, where the leadership bumped into stiff opposition at each meeting. In Bucharest, Ibraileanu, the delegate from Iasi, was of real help. Likewise, the firm attitude of Simionescu, the leader of the medical students, had kept the student body in the true spirit.

Regarding the arrangements for the assembly, according to news received from Iasi, the outlook was as follows:

In only two weeks, over 40 flags had been issued in 40 counties, to trustworthy people. It was only natural that, after two months of student movement, of general strike in all universities, the soul of Romanians would bubble and that they would be ready everywhere to arise, awaiting but the word. The flags and the news of the rally came on time.

Professor Cuza wanted to fix the date for the rally sometime in May so that more people would come. I opined that the rally should be held as soon as possible for the following reasons:

1. All the people, on their feet, rallying around the student movement, were expecting to hear a command from somewhere, in order to form a unit, to know that a plan was established which they could follow.

2. I was afraid that Jewry and Masonry, getting wind of the situation, might initiate a pseudo-nationalist organization in order to tap the people and thus divert the movement onto a dead-end track. In any case, this would have created such confusion in the minds of the Romanians, that it was not at all to be contemplated.

3. I felt it was necessary to support the front line of the student movement, for waging war is not easy, with blows coming from all directions: government, local authorities, parents, professors; with poverty, hunger, cold. A mobilization of the Romanian masses coming to their defense, sending them a word of encouragement, would invigorate the entire front of this movement.

4. Finally, because thousands of students were inactive, not knowing what to do; they demonstrated once, twice; they held a meeting or two. But it had been two months. These youth had to have something to do. Once the new organization was born, the entire multitude that could not think of what to do next, would be offered a wide field of activity.

They could start working the very next day, heading for villages to organize them and to win them over to the new faith.

March 4, 1923

Professor Cuza decided the rally should be held on Sunday, March 4, 1923; the place, Iasi.

He had invited me to dinner. There, the question was raised as to what name should be given the new organization. Capt. Lefter said: The National Defense Party, as in France. I thought it appropriate. Professor Cuza added: "Not party, but league—'The League of Christian National Defense.' " And so it was called.

Then I sent out telegrams to Cernauti, Bucharest and Cluj, containing the same message: "Wedding in Iasi on March 4."

Following this I busied myself with arranging the smallest details of preparation for the rally. The schedule was determined by Professor Cuza in agreement with Professor Sumuleanu and my father: at the Cathedral—prayer; at the University—homage to Simion Barnutiu and Gh. Marzescu; in the Bejan Hall—public meeting.

Posters were printed announcing the great national assembly. The news of a big Romanian assembly in Iasi, having as its purpose the founding of a fighting organization, spread like lightning among the students of the four universities and then among Romanians at large.

On the evening of March the 3rd full trainloads began arriving, headed by leaders bringing with them the cloth for flags.

By morning, 42 groups had arrived with 42 flags. The cloth of these flags was black—a sign of mourning; in the center a round white spot, signifying our hopes surrounded by the darkness they will have to conquer; in the center of the white, a swastika, the symbol of anti-Semitic struggle throughout the world; and all around the flag, a band of the Romanian tricolor—red, yellow and blue. Professor Cuza had approved while in Bucharest the form of these flags. Now we affixed them to poles, wrapped them in newspapers and all of us left for the Cathedral, where the religious service was conducted before a crowd of over 10,000 people.

All 42 flags, at the moment when they were to be blessed, were unfurled before the altar. Once blessed, they were to be taken throughout the whole country, each to have a real fortress of Romanian souls rallying around it. These flags, sent into each county, would be coagulants to gather together all those of like thought and like feeling. With their solemn blessing, their impressive symbolism and their placement in each county, a great organizational and popular orientation problem was being resolved.

From the Cathedral, the thousands of people, banners unfurled, formed a procession through Union Square, Lapusneanu and Carol Sts., headed for the University. There, in a gesture of homage and veneration, wreaths were placed for Mihail Kogalniceanu, Simion Barnutiu and Gheorghe Marzescu, the last, defender of the article 7 of the Constitution of 1879 and, ironically father of the Liberal minister George Marzescu, defender of the Jews.

There in the University's amphitheater was signed the founding document of "The League of Christian National Defense." That afternoon the meeting took place in Bejan Hall, presided over by Gen. Ion Tarnoschi. Many people who could not be accommodated in the hall stood in the street. Professor Cuza was proclaimed president of the League of Christian National Defense with great enthusiasm.

The speakers were: Professor Cuza, Professor Sumuleanu, Gen. Tarnoschi, my father, each county delegate and those of the university centers: Tudose Popescu, Prelipceanu, Alex. Ventonic, Donca Manea, Novitchi, Sofron Robota. Among these, myself. At the end, following the reading of the motion, Professor Cuza, in conclusion, entrusted me with a mission, saying:

> "I charge with the organization of L.A.N.C.[6] for the entire country under my direct leadership, the young lawyer C.Z. Codreanu."

Then he named the county leaders. The rally ended in perfect order and great enthusiasm.

Other Anti-Semitic and Nationalist Organizations

Small anti-Semitic organizations of an economic and political character existed even before 1900 as well as after. These were weak efforts of people with foresight and love of country, to oppose the ever-growing Jewish invasion. But the most serious anti-Semitic organization was "The Nationalist-Democratic Party" founded on April 23, 1910 under the leadership of Professors N. Iorga and A.C. Cuza. This party had a whole administrative program. Its article No. 45 gave the solution to the Jewish problem:

> "The solution to the Jewish problem must be accomplished through the elimination of Jews, the development of the productive powers of Romanians, and the protection of their enterprises."

Following the enumeration of these points, one reads this solemn statement:

> "We will keep, spread and defend this program with all our steadfastness and power, considering this our first honor duty."
> *A.C. Cuza* *N. Iorga*

6 The Romanian acronym for "League of Christian National Defense". (Tr,)

This organization gathered together all veteran fighters since 1900. Among the prominent ones, one counted: Professor Sumuleanu, Professor Ion Zelea-Codreanu, Butureanu in Dorohoi, Toni in Galati, C.N. Ifrim and then later Stefan Petrovici, C.C. Coroiu, and others.

In 1914 all these were leading the movement that demanded Romania enter the war for Transylvania's liberation; and in 1916 most of them were on the front lines, brilliantly doing their duty.

Ever since 1910-11, the counties of Dorohoi, under the leadership of lawyer Butureanu; Iasi, under that of Professor Cuza; and Suceava, under that of my father, became fortresses of Romanian re-birth.

By 1912 the current in these counties was so powerful that in the elections the administration could not avoid a sound defeat without the use of terror. On that occasion my father was seriously wounded.

Immediately after the war when the peasants returned home from the front resolutely desiring a new life, the first elections brought into the Parliament Professor Cuza for Iasi and my father for Suceava. There they engaged in a fierce parliamentary fight applauded by the whole country. The fight was waged against the peace that the Germans, whose armies invaded our country, wished to impose upon us.

The echo of these truly remarkable clashes gathered the hopes of the country around the Nationalist-Democratic Party, so that in the elections that followed, real formidable victories were registered. In Suceava the victory was unparalleled. Out of seven deputy seats, the administration took one, the other groups none, and my father's list, six. In Dorohoi and Iasi, almost the same. The trains took toward Bucharest 34 nationalist deputies.

But, unfortunately for the Romanian people, this whole troop coming up from all corners of the country ended up in a great defeat. This struck like lightning over the heads of Romanians. The Judeo-Masonic forces succeeded in dividing the two party chiefs, Professor Nicolae Iorga from A.C. Cuza. Nicolae Iorga did not oppose the treaty imposing on us the "minorities' clause" declaring himself ready to sign it. Professor Cuza, on the opposite barricade, shows that this infamous "minorities' clause" represents a defiance of all the blood shed by Romanians, an impermissible meddling into our national affairs, and a beginning of misfortune for us. In effect, the imposition was placed upon us, to grant Jews political rights en masse. For some time, N. Iorga had not been an anti-Semite. It was clear that the break was an irreparable one.

And this unfortunate Romanian nation, again became heartbroken over its hopes for salvation. The majority of the party's membership and parliamentarians sided with Professor Nicolae Iorga, believing that Professor Cuza's position placed them farther away from any chances to gain power. With Professor Caza stood only Professor Sumuleanu and my father.

The Romanian National Fascia and The Romanian Action

In 1923, during the student movement and under the impetus of the wave of nationalism, "The Romanian National Fascia" came into being under the leadership of Vifor, Lungulescu, Bagulescu, and in Ciuj, "The Romanian Action" led by Professors Catuneanu, Ciortea, Iuliu Hategan, lawyer Em. Vasiliu-Cluj and a group of students headed by Mota.

The former published the weekly "Fascism," well written and spirited. But they did not know the Jewish problem. The latter published the bi-monthly "Romanian Action" and later "Romanian Brotherhood," also very well written, but they limited themselves only to publishing. They could not initiate any action or create a sound organization.

During this time, the student Mota translated from French "The Protocols" which were commented upon by Professor Catuneanu and Em. Vasiliu-Cluj, then published in booklet form. Also at about that time Em. Vasiliu-Cluj published his work "The Demographic Situation of Romania" in which he showed statistically the terrible state of Romanian towns.

These two organizations had neither power of action nor organization nor a doctrinal competence like that of "The League of Christian National Defense" lasting only till 1925 when they merged with the latter.

After the founding of "The League of Christian National Defense" my activity was to continue along two lines: that of the student movement as a separate unit organized by centers, having as an immediate objective its own battles in which it had been engaged for three months; and that of L.A.N.C. in which I was given the function of organizer under Professor Cuza.

On the student side I was to fight for:

1. Maintaining the posture of the general strike which involved the honor of the students, quite a difficult job considering the attacks, blows, pressures, lures that flowed over the heads of students everywhere. In addition, there were defeatist students, partisans of believers in defeat, who had to be checked.

2. Systematically using available student elements to recruit among all Romanian masses, thus organizing them into a single army: L.A.N.C.

On the L.A.N.C. side we had leaders and flags in some 40 counties. We needed:

1. The completion of flags for the remaining counties.

2. As tight a contact as possible with the respective leaders.

3. The immediate set-up of precise guidelines in organizational matters, so far non-existent but requested by county chiefs who did not know how to proceed.

In resume: defensive on student lines; offensive on L.A.N.C. lines.

The large mass of students acted, guided by their healthy instinct of our race and by the spirit of the dead. It followed its glorious path overcoming many difficulties.

With the League the problems were somewhat more serious. County chiefs were asking for clarifications and guidelines for organizing. People who were moved by this current had to be strengthened in their faith, indoctrinated, fully informed regarding the organizing and the objectives they had to reach in their fight. They had to be taught discipline and trust in their superiors.

We were not then giving birth to a movement, but already had a full-fledged movement which had to be organized, disciplined, indoctrinated and led into battle.

When I went to Professor Cuza with the letters and requests received, he was disarmed by them, for they introduced him to a strange new world. Shining like a sun, and unchallengeable on the heights of the theoretical world, when he was brought down to earth on the battlefield he became powerless:

"We have no need of regulations. Let them organize by themselves."

Or:

"We are not in barracks to need discipline"—he oftentimes told us.

Then I began to write up a statute myself, down to the last detail. But realizing this was a tough job for my age, I took it to my father and working at it several days I effected the needed modifications in form and substance.

The organizing system was simple, but different from that of the political parties up to then. The difference was that, in addition to the political organization proper, based on county village committees and members, I formed separately a youth corps organized by tens and hundreds. Our political organizations up to then had nothing like these. Later, they too adopted them in the form of Liberal Party Youth, National-Peasant Party Youth, etc.

When I presented the statute to Professor Cuza the matter took on the character of real war. He would not hear of such a thing. Then an embarrassing discussion ensued, for several hours, between Professor Cuza and my father, which literally froze me. Suspecting that it would possibly lead to an unfortunate conflict, I regretted being the cause of this discussion. My father, a violent and rough man, took the statute and left for the printer to have it published without Professor Cuza's approval.

But the latter, exercising more tact and calmer, as much as he was adamant in certain matters, was just as malleable in cases like these, and knew how to quiet things. He called my father back, telling him:

"All right, let us print it, but give me a chance to look it over."

He corrected it, rearranged it, added to it a doctrinaire section, appeals, manifestoes, then sent it to the printer. This then became "The Good Romanian's Guide" and later that of L.A.N.C., the fundamental book of the League until 1935.

I was satisfied that something good and absolutely necessary for the organization was really accomplished, but in my heart I was telling myself: "Things are going to be tough if we need so much discussion for such elementary questions. In an organization neither the lack of comprehension in a chief nor too much discussion are good."

Modification of Art. 7 of the Constitution March 1923

The Granting of Civil Rights to the Jews

It was rumored for a long time that the Liberal Parliament which was also the Constituent Assembly, thus having the mission of re-writing the Constitution, intended to modify Art. 7 in the sense of granting "citizenship and political rights to all Jews present in Romania."

Up to now, this article of the old Constitution prohibited the granting of citizenship to foreigners and thus constituted a real defense shield against the invasion and meddling of the Jews in the administration of our own Romanian destiny. Giving this privilege of meddling in Romania's public affairs to as high as two million Jews, and to the just-settled Jew on our land, the right of equality with the Romanian who lived on this land for millenia, was both an injustice crying to high heaven and a great national menace that could not but worry and profoundly shake every Romanian who loved his country.

Confronted by this situation, Professor Cuza had written a series of immortal articles showing the menace threatening the future of this nation and the League distributed petitions throughout the country to be signed by Romanians, by which it was demanded that Art. 7 of the Constitution be maintained as such. The petitions were filled with hundreds of thousands of signatures and forwarded to the Constituent Assembly.

I thought it indicated that we students, while this grave question was being deliberated, should go from all centers to Bucharest, where together with the local students and the population we would demonstrate in order to stop the act enslaving our future. I left for Cernauti, Cluj and Bucharest.

Students accepted my proposition and began organizing for the departure. In order to indicate the departure date it was agreed I should send a casual telegram.

But the plan failed. We had expected that the deliberations around this question would last at least three days during which time we could reach Bucharest. But on March 26 the deliberations lasted less than half an hour. The Liberal government, as well as the Assembly—

seemingly conscious of the act of great shame they were about to commit, sought to cover it, passing it as unnoticeably as they could.

The next day following this great act of national betrayal the so-called Romanian press, as well as the Jewish one, treated the infamous act with silence. '*Dimineata*" ("The Morning"), "*Lupta*" ("The Fight"), *Adevarul* ("The Truth"), daily printed in bold face the conflict between landlord's and renters in Bucharest and in a corner several words by which they announced simply and perfidiously: "Art. 7 of the old Constitution has been replaced by Art. 133."

The Liberal Party and the infamous Assembly of 1923 thus laid in the grave and sealed the tombstone over the future of this people.

No curse of our children, of our mothers, of our old folks, of all Romanians suffering on this earth, now and forever, will be adequate to punish these traitors of their nation.

Thus in silence and in an atmosphere of general cowardice was consummated this great act of national betrayal. Only Professor Cuza's voice, the personality now towering over the entire Romanian nation, could be heard:

> "Romanians,
>
> "The March 28, 1923 Constitution must be abolished immediately. Protest against its promulgation. Demand free elections. Organize, in order to insure your victory. A new Constitution must guarantee the Romanian Nation's rights of priority, as the dominant people in the State."

When I heard the news in Iasi, I burst out crying. And I told myself:

> "It cannot be! At least people ought to learn we protested. For, if the people on whose neck is placed such a yoke does not protest, it is a people of imbeciles."

Then I edited a manifesto addressed to Iasians, calling all Romanians to a protest meeting in the university. The news of the Jews being granted civil rights spread like lightning. The town was seething.

On governmental orders local authorities brought out the army, the gendarmes, the police; provocations arose followed by the interdiction of movement. Then the plan was changed. The rally, instead of being held at the university, took place at 14 points throughout the city. There is where the demonstrations and the clashes began that lasted all night.

Local authorities, the army and police forces were completely baffled by the abrupt change of our plans of battle, of our meeting place and by running from one end of the city to another, as they were informed by their agents regarding demonstrations which erupted every half hour at opposite points. The group under my command met at the toughest point: Podul Rosu (Socola) and Tg. Cucului where the Jewish impertinence maintained that never will an anti-Semitic demonstrator set foot and get out alive.

No Romanian lives there. Thousands of Jews woke up and ran to and fro like a nest of worms. When we were greeted with fire, we responded with fire. We did our duty, toppling everything that stood in our path and showing the Jews that Iasi, Moldavia's ancient capital was still Romanian and that there, it is our arm which rules, which can permit or forbid, which holds peace or war, which punishes or forgives.

The next day the cavalry from Barlad arrived in the city to help the two local regiments, the police, gendarmerie and the Jews, and the Bucharest papers came out in special editions with headlines such as: "Iasi had lived a night and a day of revolution."

This is how much we could do, merely children; this much we knew how to do, and at the moment the yoke was put on our shoulders. We did not accept it serenely, with a slave's resignation, with cowardice. That much we did, and took the sacred oath for all of our life to break this yoke, no matter how many battles and sacrifices would be expected of us.

I went to the police prefecture the following day to take some food to those arrested. There, Iulian Sarbu was just then being interrogated as he was suspected of being the author of the manifesto. Seeing that, I went before the investigator and I said:

"Sarbu is not the author of the manifesto, I am."

My First Arrest

At the police station I was told:

"Mr. Codreanu, you must go to the Court House accompanied by the agent."

"Why with the agent?", I replied back. "I go alone." This was the first time that my word was doubted. I felt offended.

"No, I do not go with the agent. He can, if he wishes, walk 60 feet behind me. I go alone. My word is worth more than 20 police agents." I left, with the agent walking 20 feet behind me.

I reached the Court House. The agent came along and took me before the Investigating Judge Catichi who told me:

"You are under arrest and I must send you to the penitentiary."

When I heard that, I saw black before my eyes. At that time, "arrested" was something degrading. No one among Iasians was ever arrested and no one heard of a nationalist student being arrested. Let alone me, with a patriot's past?

I approached his desk and told him:

"Your Honor, I do not accept being arrested and nobody is going to pick me up and take me to the penitentiary."

The poor man, in order to avoid further discussion, ordered the agent to take me to the penitentiary and advised me against opposing it. Then he left. The agent tried to take me. I told him:

"Go home, man, and leave me alone. You cannot take me from here." Then other agents came in. I stayed there from 11 A.M. till 8 in the evening. All efforts to take me out were fruitless.

I was thinking:

"I am guilty of no wrongdoing. I did my duty to my people. If there is a guilty party who ought to be arrested, that party is of those who wronged their people: the Parliament that accorded civil rights to the Jews."

Finally, all Court House employees went home one by one, down to the ushers. Only the agents by my side and myself were left.

Around 8 o'clock three officers arrived.

"Mr. Codreanu, we have orders to evacuate this Court House."

"All right gentlemen, I will go out."

We descended the stairs and got out of the building. To my surprise I saw there a company of gendarmes in semi-circle, prosecutors, judges, police. At that, I walked ahead and sat down in the middle of the courtyard. The authorities came to me and said:

"You must go to the penitentiary."

"I will not go."

They lifted me up, put me into a vehicle and I was transported to the penitentiary, slowly, followed by the gendarme company on foot. At the last moment, as we were going through the gate of the prison, our boys attempted to free me, but the agents' revolvers stopped them.

Was it a protest against the laws? No. It was one against the yoke of injustice. My obstinate refusal to let myself be arrested seemed to be for me a foreboding of much suffering to come my way, once taking the path which led me inside the cold walls of prisons.

I was kept there one week, until the eve of Easter. My first days in prison! Morally speaking I took them very hard, for I could not understand that someone could be arrested when he fights for his people and by order of those fighting against the people.

Upon being released I went home. Many Romanians came to meet me at the railroad stations showing sympathy for me and encouraging me to carry on the fight, which is the people's fight, which in the end will be won. The entire nation, in all its best elements, from peasant to intellectual, received with great pain the sad news of the Art. 7 modification; but it could do nothing, for it woke up sold out and betrayed by the leaders. I wonder what curse on our heads and what sins condemned us Romanians to have part of such scoundrelly leaders?

Here we have face to face two historical moments in two different Romanias, with two sets of people and with the same problem: The Constituent Assembly of 1879 in Small Romania, very small, that had the courage to withstand Europe's pressure, and the Constituent Assembly of 1923, in Greater Romania, emerged from the sacrifice of our blood, which out of venal servility, under the pressures of the same Europe, does not hesitate to humiliate and endanger the life of an entire nation.

The Great Men of Romania of 1879

The Veil of Forgetfulness

In the pages that follow, the readers of this book will encounter with some surprise a series of extracts from the works of several pinnacles of thought, patriotism and character of our people, who in 1879 fiercely fought for the right to life of the Romanian people, confronting with manliness the threatening lightnings of all Europe.

Though the inclusion of these extract overtax and complicate the normal unfolding of the present volume, disobeying rules customarily followed in such matters, I include them not so much wishing to use them as historical arguments, but to bring to light anew these pearls of reasoning and of expression of these great forebears, whom the conspiracy of the Judeo-Masonic Occult persecuted, locking them up under heavy seals and plaques of forgetfulness, just because they wrote, thought and fought like true giants of Romanianism.

Our student generation, jumping over fifty years of the abdication practiced by politicians vis-a-vis the Jewish peril, identifies itself with the same convictions, sentiments and character possessed by those of 1879, and in the moment of this sacred union bows its head in gratitude and reverence in the shadow of their greatness.

Vasile Conta

Consider the attitude our great Conta held in the Chamber in 1879. Fifty years earlier the Romanian philosopher demonstrated with unshakable scientific arguments, framed in a system of impeccable logic, the soundness of racial truths that must lie at the foundation of the national state; a theory adopted fifty years later by the same Berlin which had imposed on us the granting of civil rights to the Jews in 1879.

From this, one can see the frailty of the arguments of those who attack the national movement as being inspired by the new German ideology, when in reality, after so many years, it is Berlin that has taken up the line of Vasile Conta, Mihail Eminescu and the others.

"We, if we will not fight against the Jewish element, will perish as a nation.

"It is a recognized fact, even by those attacking us today, that the first condition for a State to exist and prosper, is that the citizens of that State be of the same race, same blood, and this is easy to understand. First, individuals of like race usually marry only among themselves, for only thus can they retain the unity of race; then marriage creates the family, feelings which are the strongest and the most lasting ties between individuals; and when we consider that these family ties spread out until they take in all the citizens of the State we see that the latter are attracted to one another by a general feeling of love, by what is called racial sympathy. Moreover, bearing in mind that the same blood flows through the veins of all the members of a people, one understands that all these members will have through heredity, about the same feelings, about the same tendencies, and even about the same ideas; so that in perilous times, on unique occasions, their hearts will beat as one, their minds will adopt one opinion, the action of all will seek the same purpose; in other words the nation made up of a single race will have only one center of gravity; and the State made up of such a nation, that and only that one will be in the best condition of strength, durability and progress.

In consequence, just as in the maintenance of a species, the first requisite for the existence of a State is that its people be of like race. Well, this is the truth on which the principle of nationalities is based, on which so much is being said in the civilized world. This principle of nationalities, naturally, refers only to race and not at all to what is called 'the subjects of the State regardless of race' for then the principle would have no application whatever. Well, this principle is today so deeply rooted in the conscience of all people, be they statesmen or simple citizens, that nowadays all States in the civilized world come into being or are reconstituted only on this basis. Then let the Jewish publicists or the Jew-lovers no longer say that the basis of the State is only a common material interest of its citizens, because, on the contrary, we see that it is exactly this, our century, that gave birth to the principle of nationalities; that prevails today more and more...

"True, this does not prevent foreigners from acquiring the citizenship of a State, provided they assimilate into the dominant nation; namely, to mix totally so that ultimately the State remain of the same single blood.

"These are the only scientific principles of naturalization. For naturalization to be useful, rational and conforming to scientific criteria, it must be granted only to those foreigners who assimilate or are inclined to do so by marriage to the indigenous. Otherwise, one can easily comprehend that granting citizenship to individuals who lack, or cannot have, this inclination of assimilation into the blood of the dominant race, would result in a country subject to perpetual struggles between opposite tendencies.

"I am not saying it is impossible for various races that would exist in some country to have sometimes a common interest, that the hereditary tendencies of one race be just as favored as those of another by the same circumstances. As long as this state of affairs lasted, both indigenous and naturalized would certainly live peacefully. But circumstances change and with them the interest of the various races could also change; and if not today, then tomorrow; if not tomorrow then day after tomorrow the tendencies of the naturalized will be in conflict with those of the natives, and then the interest of some will be at odds with that of the others, and then the interests of some could not be satisfied without sacrificing those of the others; and then we would have a fight for existence between two races, with fierce battles that could only be ended either by the total abolishment of the State, or when one of the races is totally crushed so that again only one dominant race remain in the State....

Well, our national history and everyday experience have proved to us that from among all foreigners who come to us, the Turks and particularly the Jews are the ones who never intermarry with us, while other foreigners: Russians, Greeks, Italians, Germans intermarry and fuse with us, if not on the first then during the second or third generation, but finally there comes a time when there is no distinction between these foreigners and ourselves, either as regards blood or love of country. But it is not the same with the Jews....

"... No matter how this question would be posed, or how it would be interpreted, we, if we will not fight against the Jewish element, will perish as a nation."

(From the discourse against the revision of the Art. 7 of the Constitution, delivered in the Chamber of Deputies, Extraordinary Session, held on September 4, 1879 and published in the Official Monitor No. 201 dated Wednesday, September 17, 1879, pp. 5755-6)

Vasile Alecsandri

While in the Chamber, Vasile Conta delivered the above-mentioned discourse, in the Senate, Vasile Alecsandri, the poet of the Union, expressed the feeling of Romanians as follows:

> "Today Romania comes to us holding in her hands her History Book so that we write in its pages either the humiliation and the loss of our people or its dignity and deliverance...
>
> "Faced with this situation, unparalleled in the historical annals of the world, we must know how to lift our hearts and minds to the height of our duty, without passion, without violence, but in quiet spirit, with enlightened patriotism and noble courage that is expected of men called to decide the fate of their country...
>
> "What is this new impasse? What is this new invasion? Who are the invaders? Where do they come from? What do they want? And who is the new Moses leading them to the new promised land, situated this time on the banks of the Danube?
>
> "What are the invaders? They are an active, intelligent people, never tiring in the fulfillment of their mission; adepts of the blindest religious fanaticism; the most exclusivist of all the inhabitants of the earth, the most unassimilable with other peoples of the world...
>
> "What do they want from us?
>
> "To become owners of the land of this people, turning the old masters of this country into slaves, as are today the peasants of Galicia and part of Bucovina.
>
> "This country is beautiful and rich; it has big cities, railroads, advanced institutions and a people rather unforeseeing as are all people of Latin origin... What is easier than substituting themselves for the inhabitants of this country and thus turning all of it into an Israelite property?
>
> "If this is the plan of the present day invaders, as everything leads us to believe, it once again proves the enterprising spirit of the Israelite people, and far from deserving blame, it is likely to attract the plaudits and admiration of practical men.
>
> "We Romanians would deserve the blame, if by our indifference or by the application of some fatal and absurd humanitarian theories, we would ourselves be helping in the fulfillment of this plan. The blame would fall upon our heads, if fooled by these theories, understanding them inside-out, or dominated by an imaginary

fright under the influence of imaginary threats, we would forget that the Romanian fatherland is a sacred storehouse entrusted to us by our parents to be transmitted whole and unstained to our children...

"What then would the whole country say, if we created for it such a situation? What would the Romanians say who had joyously fought for the independence of the ancestral land?

"Our country would turn her eyes away from us in pain.

"The Romanian would say: Ask no longer for my blood from now on, if the blood that was shed serves nothing but the fragmentation of my country and the demeaning of national dignity.

"For these considerations, when Romania comes before us today holding her History Book in her hand so that we may inscribe on its pages our veto, for myself I tear out the page meant for the inscription to humiliate our country, and on the other page write with my heart: its dignity, its deliverance!"

(From the discourse against the revision of Art. 7 of the Constitution, delivered in Romania's Senate, Extraordinary Session, meeting on October 10, 1879 and published in the Official Monitor No. 230, Thursday 11/23, October 1879, pp. 6552-8.)

Mihail Kogalniceanu

Here is the dignified attitude regarding the Jewish problem and the pressures exercised from abroad taken by Mihail Kogalniceanu, Minister of internal Affairs in 1869, titular head of that same ministry which today has become the place from which emanate the orders for torturing those of us who still fight to defend our people:

"All those possessing a live interest in their country have been preoccupied with stopping Jews from exploiting the people.

"In Romania the Jewish question is not a religious one, but a national and at the same time an economic one.

"In Romania, Jews not only constitute a different religious community; they constitute in the full sense of the word a nationality, foreign to Romanians by virtue of origin, language, dress, customs, and even sentiment.

"It is not a matter then, of religious persecution, for if this were the case, the Israelites would face interdiction or restriction in the exercise of their cult, which is not the case. Their synagogues would not be allowed to rise freely near Christian churches; their religious instruction, the publicity of their cult, likewise would not be tolerated.

"All those who visited the Principalities, in particular Moldavia, were frightened by the sad aspect, not to say worse than sad, revealed by the Polish Israelites populating our towns. When they looked more closely into the commerce, industry, and this crowd's means of livelihood, these travellers became even more frightened, because they saw that the Jews are consumers only, not producers. And that their largest, and I can say their only and principal industry is the retailing of alcohol...

"I evicted no Jew from his domicile on the simple basis that according to all the laws of the land the Israelites from Romania have no right of domicile in villages, as is also the case in Serbia.

"I restricted the future rental of taverns and nightclubs by Jews, especially by those called Galicians and Podolians. This measure was justified on the Organic Statute and on the law voted by the General Assembly, then sanctioned by Prince Mihai Sturza, which no succeeding law has to this day abolished, but on the contrary, a law all Ministers of Internal Affairs before and after the convention, maintained and enforced. Proof of this are the orders of my predecessors, namely: of June 17 and 28, 1861 during Minister Costa Foru; of February 5, 1866 signed by Gen. Florescu; on March 11 and April 11, 1866 issued to the Ramnicul-Sarat Prefecture by Prince Dimitrie Ghica, etc., etc.

"Under these conditions, not one minister, not even ten succeeding one another in office could do other than myself and my predecessors did.

"Ministers of Romania, a country with a constitutional regime, we cannot govern but according to the will of the people.

"We are duty bound to take into account the needs, wishes, and to a certain degree even the prejudices of this nation...

"This justifies the great irritation on the part of the Romanian populace, originating out of profound suffering and of a legitimate concern, for it is the voice of a nation feeling threatened in her very nationhood; and her economic interests. Foreigners can stifle this voice, but it is impermissible to a Romanian minister, of any party, not to listen to it.

"That is why, not only today, but always, in all times and under all administrations, all rulers, all statesmen of Romania, all those who possess a live interest in their country, have been preoccupied by the necessity of stopping the exploitation of the Romanian people by an alien people, the Jews."

(From the communication of the Minister of Internal Affairs Mihail Kogalniceanu, addressed to the Minister of Foreign Affairs, June 1869 regarding the Jewish question. Published in *The Collection of old and new legislation for Romania, promulgated up through 1870*, by loan M. Bujoreanu, Bucharest 1873, The new printing press of Romanian workers, Part F. Title '*Dispositions and Circulars*,' Chapter X, pp.813-6.)

Mihail Eminescu

"If today, when they do not yet have full civil rights or political ones, they have taken over all commerce and all small industry in Moldavia; if today they have flaunted themselves frightfully over Romanian plains; if today they are nesting in the hearth of the industrious Oltenians; what will it be like tomorrow when they will be granted equal rights, when they will be able to call themselves Romanians, when they will have inscribed into laws the formal right that this fatherland is theirs just as much as it is ours!"

(Complete works, *The Israelite Question*, p. 489, Iasi, the Ionescu-Georgescu Bookstore, 1914. Quoted by Alex. Naum).

And on page 481:

"By what labors or sacrifices have they won for themselves the right to aspire to equality with the Romanian people? Was it they who fought the Turks, Tartars, Poles and Hungarians? Was it they who were punished when the old treaties were broken? Was it through their efforts that the fame of this country spread, that this language was disinterred from the veilings of the past? Was it through one of them that the Romanian people won its right to sunlight?"

Ion Heliade Radulescu

"Do you not see that the Kikery in England and France do not only demand citizenship rights in Romania for their co-religionists, but privileges, a supremacy; do they want to establish an aristocracy of money, of the Golden Calf? They demand that which we cannot give were we to die to the last man.

"Does the Kikery in England and France believe, I wonder, do you gentlemen believe with them, that Romanians will watch calmly while among them will settle the most sordid and filthy, the most vulgar of aristocracies, the domination of clowns, Jews, ruffians of Mammon?

"Under what title and on what right could such an abominable domination be established before the atrium, before the gates of the twentieth century, where all humanity, except the sons of perdition, will come like a bride before the divine Groom?

"Dares the Kikery of England and France come out with the Right of Man based on equality, and yet have the audacity to pretend privileges and supremacy for themselves?

"And because they cannot invoke this right, they dare—as it struck their fancy to coin the paradox 'Romanian of Israelite Rite'—to push their specifically Jewish further audacity so far as to threaten us in the name of Europe's monarchs?

"With what then shall the Jews conquer us? By their numbers, their force?

"For the good that we wish and we have wished them, in the name of the regeneration of peoples and of the Jews themselves in the land of Palestine, we pity them and advise them as a Christian would—desirous for the salvation of all humanity, through Christ's wounds, Who from the Cross forgave his tormentors themselves—not to try anything of this sort, or dare to even contemplate it, let alone lay claim to something in our present era of agitation caused by Satan's angels who tempted them; they had better not dare something of the kind, for God only knows how far Romanians may go in their legitimate and most sacred of all tempestuous furies defending their rights as a nation having an instinct of preservation!"

(From *The Equilibrium Between Antitheses Or Spirit And Matter* by I. Heliade Radulescu, Bucharest, published from 1859 to 1869; Part III, entitled "*The Israelites and the Jews,*" Chapter X, pp. 80-3).

Bogdan Petriceicu Hasdeu

"Thus, two ways of Jewish behavior toward us are specified in the Talmud:

" 'If you are stronger than Christians, exterminate them.'
" 'If you are weaker than Christians, flatter them...'

"But someone weaker than I, in order to become some day stronger than I, has first to pass through a middle stage in which he is equal to me.

"Do you now understand, I wonder, what it means to grant so-called political rights to the Jews?"

(From "*Studies in Judaism. The Talmud as a Profession of Faith of the Israelite People*,"
by B.P. Hasdeu,
Director of the Historical Archives of Romania,
President of the Moral and Political Sciences' section of the Romanian Athenee, Bucharest.
Printing House Theodor Vaidescu,
Bossel House No. 34, 1866; pp. 30-1.)

Costache Negri

"Jewry, one seventh of our total population, is the saddest leprosy to which our weakness, our lack of foresight, and our venality condemned us."

(From the letter to Lupascu sent from Ocna, dated January 12, 1869, published in the volume *Verses, Prose, Letters* by C. Negri with a study on his life and writings by E. Garleanu, "Minerva" Publishers, 3 Academiei Blvd., Bucharest 1909, p. 116).

A.D. Xenopol

We permit ourselves to introduce in the same selection of extracts the opinion of the great historian A.D. Xenopol, professor at the University of Iasi; this in view of the uncontestable authority of the scientist who had lived and seen with his own eyes the painful reality of his findings:

"If a Romanian decides to open a store, no Jew will cross his threshold. Thus he would be by-passed by a large clientele, while Romanians are not averse to buying from Jews. It is clear that even without price-rigging the resistance of the Romanian merchant and tradesman can be broken.

"A Jew will never take a Romanian into his establishment if the latter stands to learn something thereby; for Romanians are received into Jewish homes only as servants or porters. This system of exclusiveness persists strongly. In the innumerable Jewish workshops and stores which cover Moldavia from one end to the other, there is not a single Christian or Romanian apprentice, worker, foreman, accountant, cashier, salesman.

"Jews then, practice against Romanians the most stringent economic exclusivism which they cannot renounce, for it is prescribed by their own religion."

(From *La question Israelite en Roumanie* by A.D. Xenopol, a study published in La renaissance latine, rue Boissy-d'Anglas 25, Paris, 1902, p. 17).

The Student General Strike Continues

After Easter the fight recommenced. On the L.A.N.C. front, Professor Cuza continued action via the papers while the rest of us busied ourselves organizing. The series of meetings in towns and villages began.

On the student front, the modification of Art. 7 of the Constitution brought with it changes. Student leaders in Bucharest and Cluj who believed that a student movement would ultimately persuade the government to recognize the just demands of the students, became bitterly disappointed upon seeing that not only does the government not recognize any of their demands but that it grants the Jews political rights; so they more and more thought of capitulating.

In Cluj, the president convoked a meeting in which he suggested the best thing to do was to go back to classes. The student mass rejected his proposal, declaring that they were fighting to preserve their honor, and that the fight should be fought to the very last limit of resistance. The supporters of this thesis were: Ion Mota, Corneliu Georgescu, Isac Mocanu, and all our groups.

Alexa resigned, and to replace him as president of the student center Petru Maior, Ion Mota was elected along with a new committee. The government's assault, to make students resume their classes, failed this time also, but the leaders were sacrificed: Ion Mota and six others were forever expelled from all universities for their uncompromising attitude.

In Bucharest, a group headed by Simionescu and Danulescu began to replace the leadership that had been becoming increasingly undecided and weak. Here too, the government failed in its attempt to open classes after Easter.

June 1923

Two more months of heroic resistance, misery, and pressures have passed, with students exhausted. In Bucharest the University was re-opened for exams, if only for Jewish and renegade students. On opening day, the army was posted in the university. Student dishes occurred out front but were too weak, to longer deter its opening.

The government's plan was to open the universities one by one, leaving Iasi for the last, and presenting Iasi with the fait accompli of three operating universities. A week later in Cluj, several days after that in Cernauti, the universities opened with the army present under the same conditions as in Bucharest. In another week the difficult hour of Iasi was to come. It was isolated by the government, alone, with its student forces considerably diminished.

On the opening eve, knowing tomorrow morning the army would enter the University, we planned to occupy it ourselves during the night. Before dark, I sent a trusted student who entered the lobby and pulled back the bolts of two large windows in such a manner that this would go undetected, so that being pushed from the outside they would open. Not yet sharing this plan with anyone, I convoked a 9 o'clock meeting of 100 students in the Bejan Hall. At 10 o'clock we occupied the University. We raised on its facade the swastika banner.

A little later the Rector of the University arrived, Professor Simionescu. He was let in. He talked to us urging us to leave the University. We replied explaining to him our reasons. Several hours later he left. We organized ourselves for guard duty and stayed there the whole night.

Next morning, the students arrived at the University in large numbers. Invigorated, they unanimously resolved to continue the fight. The Jewish papers were furiously attacking us.

Two days later, Cluj, in a fight, tried to retake their University from the hands of the gendarmes. After two more days Bucharest and Cernauti followed suit. These fights led to student risings again and to the closing anew of all universities. The academic year ended. The Romanian youth had passed a unique exam in resistance, character and solidarity.

Honor to the student body which for its steadfastness, taking so many blows, has given an example of collective will yet unsurpassed in the history of the world's universities. No country has ever witnessed students, united in a single soul and assuming unto themselves all responsibility and all risks, being able to maintain a general strike for one year in order to prove their faith, seeking through their demonstration to awaken the conscience of an entire nation, faced by the gravest problem of her existence.

This is a beautiful page, a heroic page written by the suffering of this youth, in the book of the Romanian nation.

The Plans of Judaism Against the Romanian Nation Against The Romanian People

Whoever imagines that the Jews are some poor unfortunates, arrived here haphazardly, brought by winds, pushed by fate, etc., is mistaken. All Jews over the entire world form a great collectivity bound together by blood and by the Talmudic religion. They are constituted into a very strict state, having laws, plans, and leaders making these plans. At the foundation, there is the Kahal. So, we do not face some isolated Jews but a constituted power, the Jewish community.

In every city or market town where a number of Jews settle, the Kahal, (the Jewish community there) is immediately formed. This Kahal has its own leaders, separate judicial set-up, taxes, etc. and holds the entire Jewish population of that locality tightly united around itself.

It is here, in this tiny Kahal of market town or city, that all plans are made: How to win over local politicians and authorities; how to infiltrate certain circles of interest to them, such as magistrates, officers, high officials; what plans to use to take over such and such a branch of commerce from the hands of a Romanian; how to destroy a local anti-Semite; how to destroy an incorruptible representative of local authority who might oppose Jewish interests; what plans to apply when, squeezed beyond endurance, the populace would revolt and erupt into anti-Semitic movements.

We shall not delve deeper into these plans here. In general, the following methods are used:

I. For winning over local politicians: 1. Gifts; 2. Personal favors; 3. Financing the political machine for propaganda, leaflet printing, traveling expenses, etc. If there are several bankers in town or rich Jews, each is assigned to a specific political party.

II. For winning over local authorities: 1. Corruption, bribery. A policeman from the smallest town in Moldavia, in addition to the pay he receives from the State, gets monthly another salary or two. Once he accepts a bribe, he becomes the Jews' slave and if he does not follow orders, then they use on him the second weapon: 2. Blackmail, if he does not comply, his bribe-taking is revealed. 3. The third weapon is destruction. If they realize you cannot be swayed or subjected they will try to destroy you searching well your weaknesses. If you drink, they will seek an opportunity to compromise you through alcohol; if you are a skirt-chaser, they will send you a woman who will compromise you or destroy your family; if you are violent by nature, they will send your way another violent man who will kill you or whom you will kill and then go to prison; 4. If you lack all of these defects, then they will employ the lie, whispered or printed calumny, and denounce you to your superiors.

In the market towns and cities invaded by Jews, local authorities are either in a state of bribery, a state of blackmail, or in a state of destruction.

III. In order to infiltrate into various circles or around some highly placed people, they use: 1. servility; 2. boards of directors; 3. base personal favors; 4. flattery.

Thus, all politicians are given Jewish secretaries, because they are handy at doing the shopping, shining the shoes, rocking the babies, holding the briefcase, etc., while at the same time cajoling and insinuating themselves.

A Romanian is not going to be as good for he is less refined, is not perfidious, comes from the plow, and particularly because he wants to be a faithful soldier, guarding his honor, refusing to be a valet.

IV. Plans to ruin a Romanian merchant.

1. Flanking the Romanian either with one or two Jewish merchants.
2. Selling merchandise below cost, the loss being made up by special funds given by the Kahal. This is how Romanian merchants were ruined one by one.

To these can be added:

(a) The commercial superiority of the Jew, resulting from a commercial practice much older than that of the Romanian.

(b) The Jew's superiority competing under the Kahal's protection. The Romanian enjoys no protection from the Romanian state but only miseries imposed by the local authorities corrupted by the Jews. The Romanian does not fight the next door Jew but the Kahal, and that is why one readily understands that the individual will be crushed if he fights the coalition. The Romanian has no one, a parent state to raise him, advise and help him. He is left by himself, to his fate, while faced by the powerful Jewish coalition.

It is easy to repeat the formula of all politicians of Mihalache's category: "Let the Romanian become a merchant." Let these Romanian politicians show us a single Romanian merchant who was assisted by the state, a single school that was meant to really educate merchants not bank officials or clerks. Let them show us only one institution built by them which helped with a small capital or guided the young graduate of a commercial school on the road to commerce.

It was not the Romanian who deserted the road to commerce, but these politicians who deserted their duty as leaders and councilors of the nation.

The Romanian, abandoned by his leaders, was left alone to face the organized Jewish coalition, the fraudulent manoeuvers and the dishonest competition, and he was defeated. But the hour will come when these leaders will have to account for their wrongdoing.

Against The Romanian Land

I repeat once again, we are not before some poor individuals who wandered here haphazardly, by themselves, in quest of shelter.

We face a Judaic State, an army that comes into our land to conquer us. Jewish population movements are effected against Romania according to a well established plan, the great Judaic council probably seeks to establish a new Palestine on a section of land extending from the Baltic Sea down through parts of Poland and Czechoslovakia, then covering half of Romania to the Black Sea, whence they could easily establish contact by water with the other Palestine. Where is the naive person who can believe that the population movements of Jewish masses occur unplanned?

They come according to plan, but lack the courage to battle, to face risks, to shed their blood in order to justify, at least by these traits, some right to this land.

How do we know these plans? We know them for certain by drawing conclusions from the enemy's movements. Any troop commander attentively following the enemy's action realizes the plans he is seeking. It is an elementary matter. Was there a leader in all the wars of this world who knew the adversary's plans because he sat in on their making? No! He knew them perfectly from what the enemy did.

In order to break all power of resistance of the Romanian people, the Jews will apply a truly unique and diabolical plan:

1. They will try to break the spiritual ties of the Romanian to heaven and to earth.

To break our ties with heaven they will engage in widespread dissemination of atheistic theories in order to separate the Romanian people or at least some of the leaders from God; separating them from God and their dead they can destroy them, not by sword but by severing the roots of their spiritual life.

To break our ties binding us to the land, the material source of a nation's existence, they will attack nationalism, labeling it "outmoded," and everything related to the idea of fatherland and soil, in order to cut the love thread tying the Romanian people to their furrow.

2. In order to succeed in this, they will endeavor to get control of the press.
3. They will take advantage of every opportunity to sow discord in the Romanian camp, spreading misunderstandings, quarrels, and if possible to split it into factions fighting each other.
4. Will seek to gain control of most of the means of livelihood of the Romanians.
5. They will systematically urge Romanians on to licentiousness, destroying their families and their moral fiber.
6. They will poison and daze them with all kinds of drinks and other poisons.

Anyone wishing to conquer and destroy a people could do it by using this system:

> Breaking its ties with *heaven* and *land*, introducing fratricidal quarrels and fights, promoting immorality and licentiousness, by material ruin, physical poisoning, drunkenness. All these destroy a nation more than being blasted by thousands of cannons or bombed by thousands of airplanes.

Let the Romanians look back a bit to see whether against them this system has not been used with precision and tenacity—truly a murderous system.

Let the Romanians open their eyes to read the press for the last 40 years since it has been under Jewish control. Let them re-read *Adevarul* ("The Truth"), *Dimineata* ("The Morning"), *Lupta* ("The Fight"), *Opinia* ("The Opinion"), *Lumea* ("The World"), etc. and see if from each page this plan does not constantly emerge.

Let the Romanians open their eyes to see the disunity in present day Romanian public life; let them open their eyes and see well.

The Jews use these plans like poison gas in a war, to be used against the enemy, not their own people. They propagate atheism for Romanians but they themselves are not atheistic, as they fanatically hold to respecting their most minute religious precepts. They want to detach Romanians from their love for the land, but they grab land. They rise up against the national idea, but they remain chauvinistically loyal to their own nation.

Against The Student Movement

Whoever believes that the forces of Jewish power have no plans for the student movement is mistaken.

Being so far fooled in their expectations, Jews remained disoriented for a moment. They tried to oppose the students by manoeuvering the workers in the communist movement, namely other Romanians, but they were not successful, because on one hand these workers were drained of strength and on the other they too, began to realize that we fight and suffer for their rights and for the Romanian nation. Many of them were, in their hearts, on our side. The Jews, realizing their failure to put the workers across our path, then set *the government* and all the politicians against the students.

By what means?

Political parties need money and loans from abroad; and when in power, votes; favorable press when in opposition.

Jews threatened to cut off financing needed for election propaganda of various political parties; threatened with the cooperation of Jewish international finance to turn down loans to the government; threatened to control a large mass of votes through which, now that they had civil rights, they might decide victory or defeat through the democratic system; they threatened to manipulate the press, which they control almost entirely and without whose support a political party or government can be defeated.

Money, press and *votes* determine life and death in a democracy. The Jews control all of them and through these the Romanian political parties turned into simple tools in the hands of the Judaic power.

So that we who had begun fighting the Jews find ourselves all at once fighting the government, political parties, local authorities, the army, while the Jews sit quietly on the side.

Jewish Arguments And Attitudes

"What will foreign countries say of the Romanian anti-Semitic movement which takes us back to barbarism? What will men of science, civilization, say?"

Our politicians will repeat to us at every step this Jewish "argument," printed daily in all the papers. When finally, after eight years, Germany, notwithstanding all her civilization and culture, rises up against Jewry and defeats the hydra through Adolf Hitler, that argument is dropped. Then, they bring forth another: "You are in Germany's service, paid by the Germans to engage in anti-Semitism, Where do you get the funds?"

And again Romanian politicians—soulless, characterless, honorless—mimic the tune of the Jewish press: "Whence the money? You are in Germany's pay."

In 1919, 1920, 1921, the entire Jewish press was assaulting the Romanian state, unleashing disorder everywhere, urging violence against the regime, the form of government, the church, Romanian order, the national idea, patriotism.

Now, as if by a miracle, the same press, controlled by the same men, changed into a defender of the state's order, of laws; declares itself against violence. While we become: "the country's enemies," "extremists of the right," "in the pay and service of Romanianism's enemies," etc. And in the end we will hear also this: that we are financed by the Jews.

I wonder, when will that day come, when every Romanian will understand the lies and perfidious argumentations of the Jews and reject them as something of Satanic origin? I wonder, when will that moment come in which they will comprehend the perversity of this race?

Here is how three Romanian university professors, A.C. Cuza, Paulescu, and Sumuleanu were treated in the Israelite Courier, official organ of the Union of Naturalized Jews of April 23, 1922 in the editorial titled "The Ghosts":

> "A clique of clowns and public offenders got together to set up a band of wrongdoers. And to the country's shame among them one finds three professors of our universities.
>
> "And these specimens, these belated ghosts want to revive anti-Semitism... and some retrograde clowns will succeed in this, now, when official anti-Semitism is vanishing and the universal vote will also inevitably bring along the democratization of our public and social life. No! It is in vain they work! These ghosts are not going

> to halt mankind in its onward march, nor will it be necessary to pierce their hearts with a sharp pole;[7] the ridiculousness of their treachery will definitively finish them....
>
> "We have reported earlier the savage action originated by the so-called "National Christian Union" (composed of some five and one half silly characters) in order to fix them once and for all in their infamous posture, and call it to the attention of Jews that there still are wrongdoers around, against whom they should defend themselves."

So then: clique of clowns, public offenders, band of wrongdoers, specimens, belated ghosts, treachery, savage action, infamous posture—this is what Professors Cuza, Paulescu, and Sumuleanu, teachers of Romanianism, are; and what their action to save the nation is!

We have taken outrage after outrage, ridicule after ridicule, slap after slap, until we have come to see ourselves in this frightening situation: Jews are considered as *defenders of Romanianism*, sheltered from any unpleasantness, leading a life of peace and plenty, while we are considered enemies of our nation with our liberty and life endangered and hunted down like rabid dogs by all the Romanian authorities.

I witnessed with my own eyes these times and lived through them, and I was saddened to the depths of my soul. It is dreadful to fight for years on end for your fatherland, your heart as pure as tears, while enduring misery and hunger, then find yourself suddenly declared an enemy of your country, persecuted by your own kind, told that you fight because you are in the pay of foreigners, and see the entire Jewry master over your land, assuming the role of defender of Romanianism and caretaker of the Romanian State, menaced by you, the youth of the country.

Night after night we were troubled by these thoughts, occasionally feeling disgusted and immensely ashamed and we were seized by sadness. Would it not be better for us, we reflected, to go out into the world, or would it not be more suitable to seek vengeance whereby all of us would perish: both we and the Romanian traitors as well as the heads of the Judaic hydra.

---

7 Popular superstition, according to which, in order to prevent a ghost from disturbing the peace of the living, the dead is disinterred and his heart is pierced with a rod. (Tr,)

The Congress of the Student Movement's Leaders

Iasi, August 22-25, 1923

In a limited committee in Bucharest, it was decided a first congress of the leaders and delegates of the student movement be held following one year of struggle.

This congress was to take place in Cluj on August 22-25, 1923. Mota, the president of the Petru Maior student center, wrote us that local authorities informed him they were ordered to interdict this congress. We, the Iasians, replied to Cluj as well as to the other centers, that we would take on the responsibility for this congress to be held in Iasi, even if the government wished to forbid it. Our offer was accepted and we fulfilled our duty of making the arrangements for the quartering of the 40 known delegates.

On the morning of 22 August we went to the railway station to meet the delegation from Cluj headed by Ion Mota, then the one from Cernauti headed by Tudose Popescu and Carsteanu, and the one from Bucharest led by Napoleon Cretu, Simionescu and Rapeanu.

At 10 o'clock we headed in corpore for the Cathedral to pray and have a Requiem celebrated in memory of student war dead, one of whom was the former president of the student center, Capt. Stefan Petrovici.

But to our great chagrin we found the gates of the Cathedral chained shut and guarded by gendarmes. Meantime, old Professor Gavanescul also arrived. Then, uncovering our heads we kneeled in the middle of the street in front of the church which not even the infidel Turks had closed to those wanting to pray. As the priest Stiubei happened to come by, seeing us kneeling, he approached us and read a few prayers.

Then, bareheaded, in silence and very saddened, we covered the distance to the University, walking down the middle of the street, with stares from the Jews being shot at us like arrows from their doorways and shop windows.

The local authorities, flanked by numerous police forces, expecting us on the University s steps, informed us that the Ministry of Internal Affairs forbade the congress. The prosecutor stopped and warned us to disperse. Irritated, I replied:

"Mr. Prosecutor, I know we live in a country ruled by laws. The Constitution guarantees us the right to meet, and you, Sir, know better than I that a Minister cannot abrogate these rights guaranteed us by the Constitution. Consequently, in the name of the law that not we, but you, disobey, we call upon you to step aside."

Hardened by the sacrilege committed an hour earlier when the church's gates were chained and we were prevented from praying; being now faced by a second unjust and humiliating provocation, that of being prevented from entering our own home, the University; realizing these measures constituted a brazen lawlessness, we upturned everything in our path and, after some fighting, forcibly occupied the University.

The 13th Regiment, arriving a moment later, surrounded the University. We barricaded ourselves in, guarding all entrances, while outside each window we could see three soldiers posted, bayonets at the ready.

The congress opened in the auditorium of the School of Law at 12 noon, under a heavy atmosphere in this inauspicious situation. The delegates, pale with indignation, muted by the sorrow of what happened at the Cathedral and here, felt throughout the deserted halls an air of profound sadness. Everybody was worried about a possible army assault on the University and of the inevitable consequences.

We delivered no discourses. The congress fathomed the seriousness of the situation and was apprehensive of grave repercussions.

I was chosen as president for the first day. We began by denouncing the day's events. Several asked for the floor to protest. Then we began discussions regarding the movement.

What attitude do we take as the new school year opens? Do we capitulate? Difficult! A whole year of struggle with no result. On the contrary, shamed, humiliated, beaten. Do we keep on? Again, difficult! Students are exhausted; they cannot carry on a second year of battle.

Yet, Mota, Tudose Popescu, Simionescu and myself, plead for continuing our fight; plead for sacrifice, as nothing would come from capitulation but shame and humiliation. And it was impossible that out of sacrifice something better would not bear fruit for our nation.

By 8 o'clock it was dark. Outside in the town we heard commotion and noise. Constantin Pancu, the veteran fighter of 1919, surrounded by the students, remained outside. A large number of townspeople, gathered at Tufli Cafe and carrying torches, tried to advance up the hill toward the University to bring us several sacks of bread.

We all jumped to the windows to look out. The demonstrators broke the cordon at Tufli Cafe and ran up the hill. A second cordon at Coroiu St. was also broken in a tough fight. We beard outbursts of "Hurrah's." Likewise, a third cordon was overcome. We got ready to make an assault from the inside, to get out, but our people on the outside could not break through the fourth cordon. One could hear Pancu's voice, his sack of bread at his feet: "They are our children."

We were crying tears of joy. It is for this people we fight, and it would not let us down.

At 9 o'clock negotiations began between us and the authorities through Napoleon Cretu. All the students were promised immediate freedom, provided I be turned in to them. The students refused. At about 11 they sent word to us we could leave in groups of three, naturally intending to apprehend me as we left. We accepted.

Every minute a group of three left. At the door they were closely scrutinized by four commissars and agents. I quickly took off my national costume, gave it to a comrade, and donned his clothes. I left with Simionescu and a third student. As the door swung open I dropped some coins out of my pocket. As they hit the pavement, all commissars looked downward and asked: "What did you lose, gentlemen?"

We; our heads also bent, looking for the coins, answered: "Some change." Simionescu lingered behind talking with them, searching for money by striking matches, while I escaped.

We fixed the continuation of our congress for the second day outside of town at the Cetatuia Monastery in the greatest secrecy. I sneaked up there disguised as a locomotive stoker and I was lucky enough to be unrecognized even by the delegates. Ion Mota presided. With our sentries placed in strategic positions, we could detect anyone's approach a mile away. We worked in quiet and stayed there until late that day. Propositions were made, decisions taken.

It was also at this meeting that December 10 was proclaimed a national holiday for the Romanian students.

On the third day deliberations continued in a small forest on the Galata Hill. By a majority it was decided to continue the strike. An action committee of five was elected to direct the actions of the entire student movement in all universities. The committee members were: Ion Mota in Cluj, Tudose Popescu in Cernauti, Ilie Gameata in Iasi, Simionescu in Bucharest, and myself.

By forming this committee, the old student leadership in Bucharest, insufficiently informed and indecisive, fell for good. It continued in name but no longer led.

For the first time it was officially decided to give the movement a new orientation: on one hand, to fight the political parties, considered by us to be estranged from our nation, and on the other, to strengthen the faith in a new Romanian movement which must be officially helped by the students to attain victory, "The League of Christian National Defense."

The congress concluded its work on the fourth day in the house of Mrs. Ghica on Carol St.

In the evening everyone left for his university and I left for Campul-Lung to organize the L.A.N.C. congress in Bucovina in which Professor Cuza and all leaders of the movement were to participate. I had a hard time getting there, for an arrest warrant had been issued for me.

As I was traveling I rejoiced over all the decisions made by the congress which were in the spirit of our views, but especially because we gained for our side a man: Ion Mota, the president of the Petru Maior center in Cluj.

The L.A.N.C.'s Congress at Campul-Lung

The congress at Campul-Lung took place on Monday, September 17, 1923.

We held it only after a tough battle, because the government had forbidden it, and to enforce its edict sent in troops from Cernauti under the command of a colonel. Strong troop cordons were set up at each entrance to the town.

We concentrated all our forces at the west entrance into town, from Sadova, Pojorata. There we broke cordons, thanks to the archers from Vatra-Dornei and Candreni, giving us a whole hour to get the entire convoy of several hundred wagons through.

The congress convened in the town's churchyard. The speakers were: Professor Cuza, my father, Dr. Catalin, L.A.N.C.'s president for Bucovina, Tudose Popescu; then brothers Octav and Valerian Danieleanu who enthusiastically had organized this imposing congress with the help of Dr. Catalin.

Those proud mountain peasants with their long locks, dressed in white shirts and thick-woven coats, upon hearing the sound of the long mountain horn, gathered in their town, many in number and stormy as never before.

They thought the hour had struck, awaited for centuries, for the Romanian to trample underfoot the hydra that has been sucking him dry and that he emerge to assume his rights as master of his country, his mountains, his rivers and his towns.

They carried the burden of the war. Their sacrifice of blood on all fronts created Greater Romania. But to their great chagrin and disappointment Greater Romania did not meet their expectations. Because Greater Romania *refused* to break the chains of Jewish enslavement that had been torturing them for so long.

Greater Romania abandoned them to further Jewish exploitation and brought down upon their heads the whiplashes of politicians who would send them into prisons when they tried to reclaim their stolen historical rights.

All forests in Bucovina, all those mountains laden with firs belonging to the *Orthodox Church*, which was now infused with politics, and estranged, were given to the Jew Anhauh for exploitation of the firewood at the unheard-of price of 10 lei[8] per cubic yard, while the Romanian peasant had to pay 350 lei.

The mountains' forests fall under the merciless Jewish axe. Poverty and sorrow spreads over the Romanian villages, mountains become barren rock, while Anhauh and his kin carry constantly and tirelessly their gold-laden coffers over the border.

The partner-in-crime of the Jew in exploiting the misery of thousands of peasants, was the Romanian politician who gorged himself on his portion of this fabulous profit.

The rally delegated 30 leading peasants to go to Bucharest under the leadership of Dr. Catalin and Valer Danieleanu, see the Prime-Minister, and ask him to take steps against the devastation of their mountains by revoking the Anhauh-Church contract and, to thus show their love for and gratitude to the young people who had aroused them to battle, beg him to put "numerus clausus" in the schools.

Tudose Popescu and I were also chosen by the rally to accompany the 30 peasants to Bucharest.

I left for Bucharest ahead of them in order to see to it that these peasants who came to the capital of their country for the first time were well received by the students. These peasants were approaching Bucharest with such purity of heart, with so much pain and so many expectations, to plead our cause as well as theirs. The expense of their trip was disproportionately great compared to their poor means.

Upon their arrival in Bucharest the students received them royally—these kings of all times of the Romanian people—and they got off the train in their sacred capital with eyes full of tears.

But behind the railway station there waited Prosecutor Rascanu, police commissars and cordons of gendarmes that prevented their going through. The gendarmes and police commissars were then ordered to strike us. Rifle butts and sticks rained blows upon the white heads of the peasants and on their serene faces. The furious students then, placing the old peasants in the middle of their group, charged,

8 The Romanian monetary unit. (Tr.)

and broke the first cordon, hastening toward the Polytechnical School where they broke the second one, then a third, and escaped into Matache Macelaru Square. The peasants wept. One of them, seized by uncontrollable indignation, tore his shirt.

Next day we all went to Gogu Cantacuzino St. to the Ministerial presidency to be received by the Prime-Minister. We were put off till the next day; finally, we were told we would be received on the third day. We came.

We entered a hall and waited about an hour, quietly, talking in whispers and walking tip-toe. The office chief showed up:

"Gentlemen, go home, the Prime-Minister cannot receive you. He is entering the Council of Ministers."

"But we came from afar," we tried to say. The door was closed in our faces. I was thinking: each man spent 1,000 lei on his fare alone. Shall we go back home not accomplishing anything? They can stay in Bucharest no longer.

I grabbed the door with both hands and began to shake it with all my might, shouting at the top of my voice:

"Let us in or else I'll break down the door and enter forcibly." I kicked at the door with my foot. The peasants raised a clamor and put their shoulders to the door.

The door opened and about ten frightened individuals appeared, their hair on end, their faces yellow. I think they were newspapermen:

"What is it you want, gentlemen?" they asked.

"Tell the Prime-Minister if he does not let us in we'll break everything here and force our way in."

Several minutes later the doors were opened wide before us and we entered. We climbed a flight of stairs. There in a hall, standing, tall and straight as a pole, stood Ion Bratianu; behind him, Ministers Angelescu, Florescu, Constantinescu, Vintila Bratianu, and others.

"What do you want, good men?" he asked.

The two of us, young students, were still full of indignation and we would have liked to appear fiercer, thus imparting the true note of the group's state of spirit, but the peasants having trod with their country shoes on marble stairs and plush carpets, softened up.

> "Your Highness, Sir Prime-Minister, we kiss your hands and keep ourselves respectfully at your feet. What do we want? We want Justice, for the Jews have invaded us. They take out our timber by the hundreds of train flatcars while it rains in our homes through leaks in the roof, for we even lack shingles with which to cover them.
>
> "We cannot keep our children in schools any longer. The Jews also filled our schools, and our children will become their hired hands."

Then other peasants spoke. Ion Bratianu listened, made no mention of our ruckus in the antechamber and finally, after the peasants added:

> "We also ask for the university students, our children, that numerus clausus be implemented as they have requested," he responded:
>
> "Go home and have patience because I will have the forest question looked into; as regards numerus clausus, it cannot be done. Show me but one single State in Europe that introduced this measure and I too, will introduce it."

But Europe would wake up only ten years later and introduce numerus clausus thus recognizing our just cause. However, lonel Bratianu would not live long enough to keep his promise, and his successors would be only low-level servants of Judaism who would raise their fists to strike us and kill us on order of their alien masters.

We all left, holding no hope. Nothing is going to be done.

As an immediate consequence of the audience, several hours later Dr. Catalin, who headed the delegation, and Valer Danieleanu were arrested.

A group of students that evening staged a hostile demonstration before the house of the Minister of the Interior. The student Vladimir Frimu was arrested and incarcerated in the Vacaresti prison.

The rest of us then left for Campul-Lung.

The October 1923 Student Plot

An Attempt at Revenge to Serve As an Example to Future Generations

Mota also came to Campul-Lung to join me in going to Petru Rares's[9] hermitage on the Rarau Mountain—the mountain I particularly love. As we climbed it, Mota shared with me his inner turmoil:

> "Students can no longer carry on next fall, and rather than all of us accepting shameful capitulation following a year of struggle, it would be better to urge them to resume classes and we, who have led them, end the movement nobly by sacrificing ourselves and taking down with us all those we find most guilty of having betrayed the Romanian interests.
>
> "Let us procure handguns and fire on them, giving a terrifying example to be long remembered throughout Romanian history. What will become of us after that, whether we shall die or whether we shall spend the rest of our days in prison, would no longer matter."

I agreed that the final act of our fight be, at the price of our downfall, an act of punishment for the pygmies who, deserting the posts of great responsibility they were holding, humiliated and exposed the Romanian nation to untold dangers.

We felt in that moment bubbling in our veins the blood which demanded vengeance for all the injustices and the long chain of humiliations to which our people had been subjected.

Shortly after this, there gathered at Mr. Butnaru's home on 12 Savescu St. Ion Mota, Corneliu Georgescu and Vernichescu from Cluj; Ilie Garneata, Radu Mironovici, Leonida Bandac and myself from Iasi; and Tudose Popescu from Cernauti.

The first problem we had to face was to decide who were the principal guilty parties; who were most responsible for the state of misery which seized the whole country: Romanians or Jews? We unanimously agreed that the first and greatest culprits were the treacherous Romanians who for Judas's silver pieces betrayed their people. The Jews are our

9 Ruler of Moldavia, 1527-1538; 1541-1546. (Tr.)

enemies and as such they hate, poison, and exterminate us. Romanian leaders who cross into their camp are worse than enemies: they are traitors. The first and fiercest punishment ought to fall first on the traitor, second on the enemy. If I had but one bullet and I were faced by both an enemy and a traitor, I would let the traitor have it.

We agreed on the names of several individuals who had betrayed their country, namely, six cabinet Ministers, George Marzescu heading the list. At last, the hour was striking for those scoundrels who never imagined they would have to account for their deeds in a country in which they considered themselves the absolute masters over a people incapable of any reaction—the hour in which they would have to answer with their lives.

This time the Nation was sending its avengers through the invisible ties of the soul. Then we took up the second category: the Jews. Which ones should we choose from the two million?

We pondered, discussed and finally concluded that the real chiefs of the Judaic attack on Romania are the rabbis, all rabbis in all market towns and cities. They lead the entire Jewish mass to attack and wherever a Romanian falls, he does not fall by chance. He falls because he was marked by a rabbi. Behind every politician who sold out, there is the brains of a rabbi who laid the groundwork and ordered the Kahal or the Jewish banker to close the deal and pay him off. Behind every Jewish newspaper to inspire slander, lies, instigation, there is a rabbi.

But there are only a few of us so we chose only "the big cats" in Bucharest. Had we had the numerical strength we would have taken absolutely all of them.

Then we picked the bankers: Aristide and Mauritiu Blank who corrupted all parties and all Romanian politicians by putting them on boards of directors and showering them with money; Bercovici, who financed the Liberal Party (Blank took charge in particular of the National-Peasant Party, but he felt capable of buying the Liberals too).

Then we looked over the Jews of the press. The most insolent ones, the poisoners of souls: Rosenthal, Filderman, Honigmann (Fagure), directors of the papers *Dimineata* ("The Morning"), *Adevarul* ("The Truth"), *Lupta* ("The Fight"), all these, the enemies of Romanianism.

We left for Bucharest in groups, saying to Iasi good-bye forever.

I left a letter for the students in which I explained the justification for our gesture, bade them farewell, and urged them to go back to classes, but fully to keep the faith till final victory. We all wrote to our parents and comrades-in-arms.

In Bucharest we met again at Danulescu's house. We had known him for some time now, and he had made a good impression on us. He was not included in this team, but he gladly put us up.

We left his place that evening at 8 o'clock to go to Dragos at 41 13th-of-September St. where we were to clarify details and determine when our action should begin.

We were hardly gathered together when a pale Dragos came into the room, saying:

"Brothers, the police have surrounded the house."

This was on the evening of October 8, 1923, at about 9 o'clock—a moment of confusion in which we had no time to even talk. We just directed our searching looks to one another.

Then I stepped out into the foyer whence I could see the figure of Gen. Nicoleanu and his commissars who were forcing the door. The next second the door gave way and the house was filled by commissars. Gen. Nicoleanu shouted:

"Hands up!"

But we had no time, as we were each grabbed by two commissars and placed in line: myself in the right flank, then Mota, Corneliu Georgescu, Tudose Popescu, Radu Mironovici, Vernichescu, Dragos.

"Turn over your revolvers!"

"We do not have any" we answered. Only Mota had a Browning 6.35 and Vernichescu.

Then they took us out of the house one at a time, each with his arms gripped by two commissars and put us individually into waiting cars.

Behind us in the house Dragos's old mother was crying.

The cars started. Where were they taking us, we wondered? We did not utter one word. We asked no questions of those who held us prisoner, who, themselves, also kept silent. After riding through a few streets we reached Police Headquarters. They had us get out and go into a room where they searched our pockets. They took away everything we had on us, including collar and tie. This frisking, this stripping of our collars, this treatment as if we were pickpockets was most humiliating. But we were only at the beginning of this road of humiliation. With faces to the wall, not allowed to turn our heads, and kept in this position for some time, we were thinking: "Free men several hours earlier, proud and determined to break the chains of our people, look what we have become—some poor, powerless unfortunates stiffly facing a wall by orders of some miserable police agents, frisked like robbers, stripped of our personal effects."

It was with this humiliation that our great suffering began, which little by little would rend our hearts.

I think there is no greater suffering for a fighter who lives in dignity and honor, than being disarmed, then humiliated. Death is always sweeter than this.

Next we were taken to a room and seated five yards apart on benches, with the agents at our side, being forbidden to look at one another. We sat there like that for hours until we were called for interrogation. Sharers in these long, burdensome hours were, besides myself, Mota, Tudose Popescu, Radu Mironovici, Corneliu Georgescu, Vernichescu, and Dragos.

After a while, one by one, we were called to be questioned, in a large room with the prosecutor, the investigating judge, Gen. Nicoleanu and some government representatives there. My turn came towards morning. There they placed before me some of my letters and two baskets containing all our revolvers that were hidden in a supposedly quite safe place. I could not figure out how they got there. I could understand we were caught but who told where the handguns were hidden?

My questioning began. I had no idea what the others had declared and we had no previous understanding among ourselves as to what to declare, for we had not dreamed we would find ourselves in such a predicament. That is why I weighed the situation and took the decision I considered best.

A minute at the crossroads.

When the first question was put to me, though three minutes had elapsed since coming into the room, I had not yet sized up the situation enough to take a decision. I felt overwhelmed by weariness and was profoundly shaken. And when I was asked to reply, I said:

"Gentlemen! Please grant me a minute of reflection before I reply."

The question was—to deny or not to deny? That minute I strained all the powers of my mind and soul and decided to deny nothing. To tell the truth. And not timidly or remorsefully, but courageously:

"Yes, these handguns are ours. We wanted to shoot with them the ministers, rabbis, and the big Jewish bankers."

They asked me for their names. When I started giving them their names beginning with Alexandru Constantinescu and ending with the Jews Blank, Filderman, Bercovici, Honigmann, all those present stared goggle-eyed more and more, terrified. From this I suspected that the comrades, questioned before me had denied everything.

"But why kill them?"

"The former because they betrayed their country. The latter as enemies and corrupters."

"And do you not regret it now?"

"No, we regret nothing... Though we have fallen it does not matter: behind us there are tens of thousands who think likewise!"

Saying this, I felt freed from the boulder of humility under which I would have further sunk, had I denied everything. Now I was standing on my faith that brought me here, proudly facing both my fate and those who seemed to hold the right of life or death over me.

Had I denied everything, I would have had to stay on the defensive against the accusation lodged against me, begging indulgence, gaining the good will of my inquisitors. At the trial to follow, and on the basis of written proof in their possession, we would have had to experience a painful and shameful test denying our own writing and our own beliefs, denying the truth, which went counter to our conscience and the honor of our movement. Representatives of a great student movement, should we lack the courage of taking responsibility for our deeds and faith?

In this case, the country and our comrades on the outside would not have learned our intentions, whereas the only fruit of our suffering—no matter how long it might be—was exactly that the country be enlightened so it could at least know its enemies better.

Then they demanded that I put these declarations down on paper in my own handwriting. I did so.

In the end I added: "The date had not been decided upon. They caught us while discussing this. I proposed to move in one or two weeks." At which the interrogators stopped me insisting more and more that I not put down these particulars.

It was only later that I realized their reasons for this insistence—because my last phrase blew the juridical value of the entire accusation, being our defense point, for a conspiracy demands four elements:

1. An association of individuals with one aim in mind.
2. The designation of victims.
3. The acquisition of weapons.
4. A date established for the action.

But since we had not yet decided upon a date for putting the plan into action, we were still in the discussion phase. The fixing of the date was of capital importance, for in two weeks we could have gotten ill, the victims could have died, the government could have fallen or given in, etc. Our entire juridical defense rested on this point.

Following my testimony, agents led me into a cellar where I was placed in a cell alone. The door was padlocked on the outside. I guessed my comrades were occupying the adjoining cells. I beat on the wall with my fist asking who else was there. I received an answer: "Mota." I then lay down on the boards to get some sleep for I was dead tired, but not having a heavy coat I trembled from the cold. Then lice began biting me. They swarmed over me by the thousands. I turned the boards on the other side, the lice came on top. I repeated this operation several times until I thought it must be daylight.

I heard a noise at the door. It was opened, and those of the others, and we were all taken out; then placed in cars, each accompanied by two gendarmes and two commissars. The cars then left one after the other. And the same question crossed our minds: "Where to?"

In the Vacaresti Prison

We passed through several unfamiliar streets on which the curious passers-by stared at us. We left the capital behind and the cars stopped in front of some large gates above which was written "The Vacaresti Prison."

We got out of the cars, flanked by soldiers with bayonets, spaced ten yards apart. A creaking of locks and chains was heard and the big gates were opened. One by one we crossed ourselves and stepping inside, were led upstairs to the prison offices where our arrest warrants were handed to us. We realized we were arrested for conspiracy against State Security, with forced labor as the specified punishment.

We were then taken to another yard in the middle of which rose a tall church. All around there were walls and along them cells. I was put into a cell way back, one yard wide, two deep, then it was locked on the outside. There was only one plank-bed inside, and near the door, a small iron-grilled window. I wondered where my comrades were. Then I laid my head on the boards and fell asleep. I woke up after two hours, shaking. It was cold and no sun's ray penetrated into the cell. Dazedly I looked around me and could hardly believe where I was. I looked well and saw the misery of the cell. I told myself: "Difficult situation." A wave of pain ripped my heart. But I consoled myself: "It is for our People."

Then I began gymnastic movements with my arms, to warm myself up.

At about 11 o'clock I heard footsteps. A guard opened the door. I looked at him. Perhaps I had met him at some time, I hoped. But he was a stranger, and a surly man. He looked at me with mean eyes. He gave me a loaf of bread and a dish of borsch. I asked him:

"Mister Guard, might you happen to have a cigarette?"

"No! I do not!"

He locked me up again and left. I broke the black bread and swallowed a few spoonfuls of borsch. Then I placed them down on the cement floor and began to collect my thoughts. I could not comprehend how they discovered us. Could it be that one of us was careless enough to speak about our project to someone? Did someone betray us? How come they found our revolvers?

Again I heard footsteps. I looked through the window. A priest and several men were nearing my cell. They said:

"Well gentlemen, is it possible that you, educated youth, could do such a thing?"

"If it is possible for this Romanian people to perish invaded by Jewry and by being overwhelmed by the sell-out, licentiousness and ridicule of its leaders, then what we did is possible too."

"But you have so many legal means!"

"We have gone by way of all the legal paths till this time. If just one had been opened to us, it may be we would not have landed in these cells."

"And now, is it good? You will have to suffer for your deeds!"

"Perhaps from our suffering something better will emerge for this people."

They left. At about 4 o'clock, a guard came bringing me a worn-out blanket and a large sack full of straw in lieu of a mattress, I evened-up the sack as well I could. Then I ate a little more bread and lay down.

I was meditating on the discussion I had had with the priest and I was thinking: "A people never gained anything out of the partying and easy living of its sons. It was always the suffering that resulted in good gains for it."

I succeeded in finding a purpose for our suffering and at the same time some moral support for these sad hours.

Then I got up, knelt and prayed:

"Lord! We take upon ourselves all the sins of this nation. Receive this our suffering now. See that a better day for this people be forthcoming through this suffering."

Then I was thinking about my mother and those at home who may have heard of my fate and might be thinking of me. I prayed for them and I lay down to sleep.

Although I was dressed and covered with the blanket, I was cold, and I slept poorly on that straw mattress. I was awakened at 8 o'clock when a guard opened the door and asked me if I wanted to go out for several minutes. I got out and did some gymnastics to warm up.

The row of cells of which mine was one was somewhat higher than the rest, so I could see the entire courtyard. All at once I saw someone wearing national dress walking among the inmates. It was my father. But I could not believe it. What was he doing here? Was he also arrested? I made a few signs and he saw me. The guard stopped me:

"Mister! You are not allowed to signal."

"He is my father," I answered.

"That may be, but you are not allowed to signal."

I looked at him and said:

"Comrade, leave us alone in God's care with the suffering He gave us; don't you add more to it." And I went back into my cell.

After lunch they took me out again. They flanked me between bayonets and led me out of the prison, where, on the road, all of us were placed in a single file at 10 yards apart, each between two bayonets. My father was leading the column between two soldiers, bayonets at the ready. There were some new arrestees: Traian Breazu from Cluj, Leonida Bandac from Iasi, and Danulescu. We were not permitted to turn our heads or to signal one another. For just a second I got a glimpse of the sunken' faces of my poor comrades-in-suffering.

What gnawed at my heart was the injustice to which my father was being subjected. He was guilty of nothing. A lifetime fighter for this nation, a professor in secondary schools, a major, former battalion commander on the front line all during the war, several times a member of Parliament, and not an obscure one at that, he was now paraded on the streets of Bucharest between bayonets.

We left thus in a column trudging toward the Tribunal. Romanians looked at us with indifference. But when we reached the Jewish quarter, all the Jews came out to doors and windows. Some threw at us outrageous looks and laughed; others commented loudly, others spat. We bent our heads and walked thus, the whole way, our hearts full of pain.

At the Tribunal our arrest warrants were confirmed. We were defended by the attorney Paul Iliescu, who was the first lawyer to offer to plead our case.

We were then sent back in the same formation, on the same route. We could see on newsstands the headlines of *Dimineata* ("The Morning")

Vacaresti Prison a former monestry where Codreanu was held. It was in this prison where Codreanu was inspired by a painting of the Archangel Michael.

and other Jewish papers, "Student Conspiracy. The Arrest of the Plotters."

And again I got to my cell. For two weeks I stayed there in the cold, with no further knowledge of the others or any news from outside.

After two weeks seeming like two centuries, we were taken out of our cells and placed in heated rooms, in threes. We were permitted to cook and eat together. When we saw each other again it was like a true holiday.

I was to share a room with Dragos and Danulescu. Meantime, Garneata, the president of the Association of Christian Students turned himself in so that our number grew to 13. My father, free of any guilt; Mota, Garneata, Tudose Popescu, Corneliu Georgescu, Radu Mironovici, Leonida Bandac, Vernichescu, Traian Breazu and myself, charged with conspiracy; Dragos and Danulescu, detained for having sheltered us. In addition to these, there was Vladimir Frimu, who had been arrested when we demonstrated in front of the Minister of Interior's home. We obtained a primus stove on which we cooked the groceries sent from the outside by relatives and friends. The regular prison food was something frightful, and the misery in which the inmates lived, indescribable.

My father got permission from the prison administration for us to go each morning at 7 o'clock into the church in the courtyard to pray. We all knelt before the altar saying the "Our Father" and Tudose Popescu sang *Prea Sfanta Nascatoare de Dumnezeu* ("Most Blessed Virgin Mary").

There, we found solace for our sad prison life, and hope for tomorrow. Each of us set up a work schedule for himself. Mota busied himself with matters related to the forthcoming trial; Danulescu studied for his exams in medicine. I was working on plans for the organizing of the youth in the national struggle: organizing the student centers, the youth in villages and the students in secondary schools. I worked this out down to the smallest detail, till Christmas time, so that if we got out of prison we could put it into practice; if not, we decided to find someone on the outside to implement it. This was to be done within the framework of the League which was to be the political arm, while our section would be for educating the youth and for fighting.

On November 8, the feast of Saints Archangels Michael and Gabriel, we were discussing the possible name for this youth organization. I said: "Let it be 'Michael the Archangel'."

My father said: "There is in the church, on the left hand door of the altar, an icon of St Michael."

"Let us go see it!" Mota, Garneata, Corneliu Georgescu, Radu Mironovici, Tudose and I went to look at it and we were truly amazed. The icon appeared to us of unsurpassed beauty. I was never attracted by the beauty of any icon. But now, I felt bound to this one with all my soul and I had the feeling the Archangel was alive. Since then, I have come to love that icon.

Any time we found the church open, we entered and prayed before that icon. Our hearts were filled with peace and joy.

The torture of our trips to the Tribunal was resumed. On foot, between bayonets, through mud, with our worn-out shoes and our feet wet.

Some Jewish crooks who defrauded the State of several hundred million lei were driven to the Tribunal in cars, while we walked. Many times our trips were made unnecessarily, only to harass us. I was called to the Tribunal 25 times, to be interrogated by the investigating judge only twice. We changed no part of our early depositions.

One thought preoccupied us constantly: "Who betrayed us?" Night after night we sought to solve this enigma. We reached the stage where we were suspicious of one another.

One morning I went to church to pray before the icon to reveal to us the traitor. That evening as we sat down to dinner I spoke to my comrades:

> "I am compelled to bring you sad news. The betrayer has been identified. He is in our midst sitting at the table with us."

Everyone was looking at everybody else. Mota and I followed everyone's face hoping for an indication. I put my hand into my breast pocket saying:

> "Now I will show you the proof."

At that moment Vernichescu stood up, hesitated for an instant, gave Bandac the key to the food box and said: "I am leaving."

We were puzzled by his departure, but resumed our discussion regarding the proof I refused to produce, for I had none.

When we left the table, we found Vernichescu alone. He addressed us:

> "Codreanu suspects me." I told him I suspected no one; thus we were reconciled.

Weeks and weeks passed and our prison life was dragging on. We marked in pencil on the wall every passing day. Life in prison was difficult, exhausting for the man who was born free, who lived in dignity. It was horrible to feel in chains, within high unfriendly walls, far from your loved ones of whom you hear nothing. And not even here can you move around much, for three fourths of the time we were kept locked in our cells. Every evening the sinister noise of bolts being drawn at your door plunged one into a mood of sadness. The enemies of this nation were free outside, enjoying respect and the good life, while we, in addition to moral indignities, oftentimes went to bed hungry and shivering from the cold the whole night on plank-beds and straw.

But finally, joyous days came our way. After two months of imprisonment we received the news that the order for my father's and Danulescu's release had been received.

For us; indeed, great joy. We helped them pack and shortly they were taken away. We watched as they left until they passed through the first gate. I asked my father to tell mother and the others not to worry at all.

Anyone's liberation is an occasion of great joy for those left behind. Everybody is glad. Perhaps, by one's liberation, each grows stronger in the hope of obtaining his own freedom.

After a short while, Dragos, Bandac, Breazu and Vernichescu left, having been taken out of the case as were my father and Danulescu. Only six of us were left and charged with "conspiracy against State security."

Several days later Dragos sent the news that it was Vernichescu who betrayed us; he also made copies of the latter's testimony which was on file. We received this news with hearts full of bitterness. Our nation had always had her share of traitors.

Outside

In all the universities, students returned to classes. It seemed there was a moment of disorientation. For two months they had been living under the terror of the Jewish press which incessantly exaggerated the gravity of our attempt at revenge and its "disastrous" consequences for the country. It shouted that we had lost the confidence of the "civilized world;" that we were a Balkan state. They constantly asked: "What will Berlin say?" "Vienna?", "Paris?" And so, transformed into the defenders of the "permanent interest of the State," Jews daily urged the country's leaders to take radical measures against the national movement which must be suppressed "with the utmost violence."

A year earlier, when Max Goldstein planted the bomb in the Senate building and the police were rounding up communist Jews, the same press was yelling:

> "A state cannot maintain itself against popular will by the use of violence. Where is the Constitution? Where are the laws? Where are the constitutionally guaranteed freedoms? What are foreign countries going to say when a state takes such restrictive steps? A state cannot survive through arrests, prisons, bayonets, terror. For this violence the state uses will be returned by the multitude or isolated individuals. Force will be answered by force. Terror, with terror. And they will not be guilty, but the State that provoked them."

And now, with a shamelessness which only the blindfolded fail to see, the same press wrote:

> "It is not enough that these terrorists be arrested. They must be condemned in such a manner as to make them an example. Even this is not enough: all those who propagate such anti-Semitic 'ideas' which cause so much damage to our country, ought to be arrested. This anti-Semitic weed ought to be pulled out, root and all. And this question must be dealt with mercilessly and without clemency."

To this torrent of hostility, the national press opposed a fierce resistance. In addition to *Universal* ("The Universe") which always expressed a correct attitude regarding the manifestations of national conscience, the nationalist movement had the support of the following newspapers:

Cuvantul Studentesc ("The Student Voice") put out by the Bucharest students, which only recently came under the editorship of our indefatigable comrades who were free: Simionescu, Rapeanu, Fanica Anastasescu, Danulescu, and others whose names escape me.

Dacia Noua ("New Dacia"), organ of the students in Cluj, directed by Suiaga, Mocanu, Iustin Iliesu, the poet and author of "*The Students' Hymn.*"

Cuvantul Iasului ("The Word of Iasi"), organ of the Iasi students.

Desteapta-te Romane ("Awake, Ye Romanian"), organ of the Cernauti students, recently moved to Campul-Lung, directed by Dr. Catalin and Danieleanu.

Apararea Nationala ("The National Defense"), official organ of the L.A.N.C., Bucharest, with the unsurpassed articles of Professor Paulescu, from which we reproduce the following lines:

> "...The same constraint through cold, hunger and terror, successfully used by Bolshevik Jews, was used on the students.
>
> "Who could ever imagine that the time would come when our children, the flower of the Romanian nation, would be compelled to celebrate the holiday of the unification of all Romanians locked up in the cellars of some prison or chased into the cold without shelter, without food?

> "Probably you did not realize that you were waging war against the entire Romanian nation."

Unirea ("The Union"), organ of the L.A.N.C., Iasi, directed by Professor Cuza, containing articles of immortal logic.

Nationalistul ("The Nationalist"), popular organ of the League in Iasi.

Libertatea ("Freedom"), popular newspaper in Orastie, belonging to Father Mota who revealed our gesture in its true light, being thus the first to unhesitatingly cut the curtain of silence that surrounded us those very first moments.

The student body understood our sacrifice. That is why the student movement rallied more and more around these walls of the Vacaresti prison in which each student center had its imprisoned representatives.

Peasants, too, began showing concern in our lot. They sent us money, had masses said for us in churches, particularly in Bucovina's mountains and Transylvania where *Libertatea* ("Freedom") penetrated. Here is a small example:

The Mite of the Moti for the Students in Vacaresti

(*Cuvantul Studentesc* No. 7, Year II, March 4, 1924)

> "Among the gifts of money received by the students locked up in Vacaresti prison from the peasants from all regions, there is one more brilliant and more precious than all the others. It is that sent by the Moti of the Apuseni Mountains. Scraping the bottom of their leather belt pockets or a corner of their kerchiefs, they gathered their 2, 3 or 5 lei to send down their valleys, on paths trod by Iancu, their defender of old, and sent them along with their hearts, over the long, long way to Vacaresti across the mountains, where they had heard their sons were imprisoned for wanting to save them from want and injustice, from poverty and chagrin. These contributions were sent from the poorest corner of our country, of which the song says with so much bitterness and sorrow,
>
> 'Gold lies in our mountains' core
> While we beg from door to door.'
>
> "The most precious gift was sent to the students in Vacaresti: a

> handful of change and a fragment of a beggar's soul 'hungry and naked, without lodging,' a soul that hides beneath a rag, its greatest treasure, moral health, that inexhaustible source of strength from which in times of great tribulation springs the salvation of the people!
>
> "The Moti think of the students! Their soul begins to understand, to stir, to forge a new ideal. This is the best and most eloquent sign! Listen to some of their names, from the town of Risca, near Baia de Cris:
>
> "Nicolae Oprea, 2 lei; Nicolae Florea, 3 lei; N. Haragus, Aron Grecu, Tigan Adam, A. Hentiu, N. Bulg, Ion Asileu, Al. Vlad, N. Borza, N. Leucian, Antonie Florea, A. Leucian, each 5 lei; N. Ciscut, A. Riscuta, Ion Ancu, Saliu Faur, each 10 lei; N. Florea, priest and N. Rusu, each 15 lei; N. Baia, notary public and Dutu Riscuta, each 20 lei. Total 210 lei."

The peasants will soon understand and will come to our side with their strong and long-enduring soul, in the expectation of the hour of justice.

Thoughts of a New Life

Christmas holiday is here. There in the Vacaresti prison we thought constantly of our families back home and especially during the long sleepless nights were relentlessly worried. When will our side win, we wondered? When will we get out of here? If we are sentenced to 10-15 years will we be able to weather the imprisonment or will our suffering and worries sap our health day by day till we perish?

We floated in the unknown. This state of uncertainty consumed us. We should have liked to have the trial date set once and for all in order to know sooner the fate awaiting us.

The suffering and common fate we had in store bound us together more and more, and discussions over the innumerable questions raised led us to the same conclusion, little by little shaping a uniform pattern of thinking. The smallest questions regarding the national movement preoccupied us for hours and days. There is where we learned to think deeply and pursue a problem in all its ramifications, down to the finest detail. We resumed the study of the Jewish problem, its causes, its chances for solution. We established organization and action plans. After a while, discussions were finished and we passed on to laws, to indisputable truths and axioms.

We watched Romanians on the outside of our group gropingly delving into our national problem and giving birth either to a newspaper or a parody of an organization. We could see they were reaching false conclusions in matters of doctrine, were uncertain in matters of organization, and totally lacked original ideas in matters of action.

We realized then even better as a result of more profound reflection, that:

1. *The Jewish problem* is no utopia, but a grave life and death problem for the Romanian nation, the country's leaders grouped by political parties becoming more and more like toys in the hands of the Judaic manipulators.

2. This *present political system* through its concept of life, its immorality, and its democratic set-up from which it springs, constitutes a real curse fallen upon the Romanian people.

3. The Romanian people will not be able to solve the Jewish problem unless it first solves the problem of its political parties. The first aim to be reached by the Romanian people on its way to topple the Judaic power that oppresses and strangles it, will have to be the toppling of this political system. A country has only the Jews and the leaders it deserves. Just as mosquitoes can settle and thrive only in swamps, likewise the former can only thrive in the swamps of our Romanian sins. In other words, in order to win over them we will have first to extirpate our own defects. The problem is even deeper than Professor Cuza had shown it to us to be. The mission of this fight had been entrusted to the Romanian youth which, if it wants to take up the challenge of this historical mission, if it wants to go on living, to continue having a country, must prepare and gather all its forces to carry on the fight and win. We decided that when we should get out of prison, by God's help, we not part ways, but stay united to dedicate our lives to this one aim.

But before busying ourselves with our people's defects, we began by looking at our own sins. We held long meetings in which each of us told the defects he observed in the rest. And we endeavored to correct them. This was a delicate matter, for so is man made: he does not take lightly the critique of his own defects. Each believes or wants to show he is perfect. But we say: first we should know and correct our sins and then we shall see whether we have the right or not to engage in improving upon others.

This is how the holidays passed and then the winter. Spring arrived. We knew as yet nothing regarding our future fate. Only that a great popular current in our favor was born on the outside supporting our cause in spite of all desperate endeavors of the Jewish press to stem it. This current was steadily growing among students, townspeople and peasants, uniformly strong in Transylvania, Basarabia, Bucovina and the Old Kingdom. Now, we were receiving letters of support and encouragement from all parts.

Spring finally brought us a great joy. Trial was set for March 29 before the Assizes' Court of Ilfov. We began to get ready. But what kind of preparation could we make? We admitted everything. We said all we had to say. Lawyers who signed up to defend us came to visit us. They called to our attention the gravity of our position in view of our testimony, suggesting we change it as well as our whole attitude; that it would be more prudent to deny. We categorically refused and asked them to defend us within the framework of our testimony, that we did not intend to alter it the least bit, no matter what might be the outcome of the trial.

If by any chance we should be acquitted, how could we do without the icon before which we prayed each morning?

We searched among all the inmates till we found a painter. We asked him to make us a copy, and in three weeks time he made an exact replica, six feet high, and a small one for me to carry on my person, and a third of medium size for my mother. Mota also had one made for his parents.

Then we figured that on the basis of our testimony we would most certainly receive at least five years. And we knelt before the icon:

> "Lord Almighty! We consider these five years lost to ourselves. If we are acquitted we pledge to consecrate them to the cause of our nation."

We decided that all of us would move to Iasi in case we were acquitted, there to establish our center of activities. From there, following the plans we had readied, we would begin organizing the country's entire youth, beginning with high school boys and girls and even younger students; those in the normal schools, trade schools, seminaries, commercial schools, and finally, youth in the villages. After that, the university centers would be revamped. All these young people, we hoped, would grow in the spirit of the faith that animated us, so that as young adults they would enter the political arena, where the fate of our struggle was to be determined, and, being further augmented by new graduates year after year, would become like waves of assault endlessly coming on.

The Isolation of Politicians

The political system has infected our national life. Organization of the youth is needed, as is also emphasis on the necessity for their further self-education, to protect and separate them from the infection of the political system. To permit the infection of the Romanian youth to continue means annihilation for us, and a definitive victory for Israel.

Moreover, our organizing of this youth will take care of the very problem of our political system, which by lack of young recruits will starve to death. The slogan of the entire younger generation must be: No youth must ever enter the gate of a political party; he who does so is a traitor to his generation and his nation. For in effect, by his presence, name, money, work, he strengthens the power of the politicians. Such a one is a traitor, just as he is a traitor who leaves the side of his brothers and goes over into the camp of their enemy. Though he may not shoot back with a weapon, if he only carries water for those who do shoot, he is an accomplice to the killing of those falling among his betrayed comrades, consequently a traitor to his cause.

The theory urging us to all join political parties in order to improve them—if we pretend they are bad—is false and perfidious. As it has been from the beginning of the world, day and night uninterruptedly, it is only sweet water that has flowed into the Black Sea from thousands of rivers, this never resulting in sweetening the sea's salty water but rather the opposite: likewise with us, entering the cesspool of political parties, not only will we not better them, they will corrupt us.

These were the thoughts and resolutions uppermost in our minds to implement when we would have been acquitted. Our organizational set-up was ready. Our plan of action established down to the minutest detail. Everybody's part was set. The newspaper that was to be put out was to be named *Generatia Noua* ("The New Generation") and our organization as a whole was to be named *Archangelul Mihail* ("The Archangel Michael"). All our flags would have to carry the image of St. Michael the Archangel from the church in Vacaresti prison. This organization, as we saw it, of the entire youth generation, was to be the youth section of the political organization L.A.N.C., having as its aim the education of this youth. For us, this program, conceived within the Vacaresti prison walls, was a beginning of a new life. It represented something complete in inspiration, organization and plan of action, different from anything else we had thought of earlier. It was the beginning of a new world, a foundation on which we could build for years to come.

Upon leaving the prison we were to go to all university centers and share with the students our decisions, showing them that street demonstrations and clashes no longer have a raison d'etre in view of our new plan. We would still cling to our past expressions, not denying them as ours, would not be ashamed of them. But their time is gone. We must all engage now into a great organizing task that will bring us victory.

Avenging the Betrayal, and the Trial

We saw Mota pensive. He was constantly telling us that once out we would not be able to make any headway unless we punished the betrayer. It had always been betrayal that sapped the nation's strength, but we Romanians had never turned our weapons on the traitors; that is why treason took root and traitors multiplied in all walks of life; that is why Romanian public life was nothing now but a permanent betrayal of the people. If we did not solve this problem of treason, our work would be compromised.

We were very excited the night before our trial began. At last our fate was to be decided.

In the morning we were taken to the office for our families to see us. Corneliu Georgescu's parents were there from Poiana Sibiului. Shortly, Vernichescu came in. Mota took him by the arm as if he wanted to tell him something and both went into a nearby room.

Several minutes later we heard seven gun shots and shouts. We stepped out into the hall. Mota had shot Vernichescu to punish him for his betrayal.

I jumped to Mota's side to defend him, for he was surrounded by police officers and functionaries threatening him. When the commotion subsided we were immediately taken away and put in separate cells.

Through little windows we could see Vernichescu carried out of the infirmary on a stretcher on the way to a hospital. In our cells we all began whistling "Christian Students of Greater Romania," our fighting hymn, to accompany him thus till he disappeared through the prison gates.

Two hours later the Investigating Judge Papadopol arrived. He had us brought upstairs one by one to appear before him. We all made common cause with Mota.

The next day, following a night spent sleeping on cement floors, we were taken to the Tribunal. Our situation was now very grave, yet we, in the basement of the Court House, sang our fighting songs the whole time.

The trial was to begin at one o'clock. Since 10 o'clock thousands of students and citizens had been gathering around the Tribunal. At around noon all the capital's regiments had been called up to control the crowds.

At one o'clock we were led into the Court of Assizes. Presiding was Mr. Davidoglu and prosecutor was Mr. Racoviceanu. On the defense bench sat Professor Paulescu, Paul Iliescu, Nelu Ionescu, Teodorescu, Donca Manea, Tache Policrat, Naum, etc. After the jurors were drawn, the definitive writ was read amid great silence. We listened. We realized that our fate was being decided. Then it came our turn to speak. The interrogation began. We admitted everything with the exception of having reached a final decision. We did not determine the date, but we showed the motives pushing us into this action. We showed the menace of the Jewish problem and accused the politicians of corrupting and betraying the nation.

In spite of many interruptions by the presiding officer, we continued our testimony to the end.

There followed a severe and oftentimes unjust and insinuating indictment delivered by the prosecutor. We felt the balance tipping in his favor. But the prosecution's success was short-lived. Professor Paulescu read his declaration in the church-like silence imposed by his great prestige and saintly figure. It was a short declaration, but for the prosecutor who seemed to embarrassedly sink into his easy chair, a devastating one.

A recess was taken; it was now 8 o'clock in the evening. Outside, the crowd waited in increasing numbers.

Nelu lonescu, Tache Policrat and others, and at the end, Paul Iliescu, spoke brilliantly. It was 5 o'clock in the morning by this time. The prosecutor, through a new indictment, tried to regain his position and win over the Court. Our lawyers answered him. At 6 o'clock we had our last word. Then we were taken out. The jurors began their deliberation. We waited over half an hour that seemed to us half a year. A little afterwards we heard "Hurrah's." An officer brought us the news: "You are acquitted!"

We were then taken back into the courtroom where the acquittal verdict was read to us. Outside, people were still waiting. Upon learning we were acquitted they broke into "Hurrah's" and singing.

We were loaded in a car which took us through unfamiliar streets back to Vacaresti for the completion of customary discharge formalities.

We gathered up our belongings and icons, ready to leave that grave with its long nights of turmoil and its sufferings. But poor Mota had to stay on, who knew for how long, to suffer henceforth all alone. We took leave of him. We embraced him, tears in our eyes and parted from him in profound pain. We left to be free; he entered his cell anew, in solitary. Oh, how many more weeks he would have to lie there alone on that cement!

As soon as we were out, the first thing we did was to go to Danulescu and Dragos to ask forgiveness of their families for the trouble we caused them and to thank them for their concern for us during our imprisonment. Then we left for our homes where our mothers and the whole family expected us, rejoicing with eyes full of tears.

At Iasi

At Iasi I was impatiently expected by the younger comrades. I no longer found any of my classmates there; since last fall they had all scattered to their home towns. I took my icon to St. Spiridon Church where I placed it within the altar. One after another I met all my friends and we rejoiced to see each other again. But our joy did not last long, for, as I was promenading on Lapusneanu St. with my two sisters and about ten students, the police jumped on us out of the blue sky, striking us over the head with their rubber clubs and hitting us with their rifle butts.

Provoked in this manner and struck for no reason in the Iasi in which we had seen so many battles? In the Iasi in which we beat Judeo-Communism at the University in 1919, 1920, and 1922? In the Iasi in which we put in their place and kept at bay for years the overwhelming Jewry and its press? Struck in my own house?

Then I turned to deliver a riposte. Indignation seemed to give me the strength of a lion and I would have been able to take on the whole police force. But my student friends grabbed hold of me, some my arms, some my legs. Held thus, I received several additional blows with rifle butts. Passers-by began booing the police and shouting. I left for home dejected, furious at those who held me. But they were telling me:

"They have orders to provoke you. If you retaliate, to shoot and get rid of you."

In the afternoon, together with Garneata and Radu Mironovici, I went to a student dormitory where in a large room were gathered the student leaders. They told us how for the six months during which we did not see each other they had fought, and how much they had taken; how they went back to classes and how they handled the situation so as not to be humiliated; how on November 1st, on opening day, a religious service was held in the auditorium before all the students and professors and what student Lazarescu said on that occasion:

"We will go back to classes, but not right away. First we will address a memorandum to our professors and the University Senate, expecting a satisfactory reply."

Then he related to us how this memorandum was presented and how university professors headed by Bacaloglu, the Pro-rector, granted the greatest part of the memorandum's points. On November 6, the students resumed classes. The professors knew how to avoid an unjust humiliation of the students who fought a whole year for their beliefs.

They went on telling us how Marzescu, the Interior Minister, brought his own man in as Police Prefect, giving him free rein to crush the student movement and national movement in Iasi; how this man, with the help of his entire police force, engaged in this work. Because the students went back to classes and quiet was re-established, and at a loss as to how to win his laurels and get paid, he began to provoke them.

They further related to us how on December 10, the girl students headed for the Cathedral were met by intoxicated police who beat them with their rubber truncheons, grabbed them by the hair—right in view of the professors—and dragged them through mud on the street; how, one by one, the students were beaten; how on December 10 the student Gheorghe Manoliu, the choir conductor, was beaten on his ankles with sticks, then arrested; how he, kept by the police in a state of great misery, contracted jaundice and died in the hospital.

The students in Iasi went through tough times in those six months.

We, in our turn, told them of our tribulations, reminding them that it was our duty to get Mota out of prison.

In the end we gave them an account of our plans for the future. How we must organize our entire generation, raise it and educate it in an heroic spirit; how we would have to isolate the political system so that no youth would ever enter its ranks, and how it could be defeated and the L.A.N.C. with Professor Cuza could get in; how only through a nationalist government, the expression of our Romanian conscience, force and health, could the Jewish problem be solved, by taking legal measures to protect the Romanian element and putting brakes on the Jewish invasion. How our generation has the great and sacred mission to revive this conscience, this force and this vitality. That we, the "Vacarestians," have decided that all of us are to come to Iasi and establish here the center of this action which we would place under the protection of St. Michael the Archangel.

Our comrades listened and received our plans for the future with much joy. After the meeting we paid visits to Professors Cuza, Gavanescul, Sumuleanu, etc. sharing our thoughts with them as well.

A YEAR OF GREAT TRIALS

MAY 1924 - MAY 1925

The Christian Cultural Home

Our meetings, in view of the plan we were trying to follow, were held with difficulty because we did not have a meeting place of our own. All of us being poor, we could not afford the rent for at least two rooms in order to commence organizing the youth. We met in a wooden barracks left since the war in Mrs. Ghica's yard. One day we decided to build ourselves a home of several rooms. But how should we go about it?

On May 6, 1924 I gathered some 60 youngsters, university and high school students (the members of the first Brotherhood of the Cross[1] founded in Iasi). And this is how I talked to them:

> "Dear comrades, how long are we going to sweat it out by holding our meetings in this barracks? Up to now, Romanian students had the right to meet in their own university buildings. But we were chased out. Until yesterday we had the right to meet in our dormitories. We were chased out of here too. Today we meet in run-down barracks in which we get rained on. In all cities, students receive help in their noble pursuits. Here, there is no one to help us, because the population around us is composed of enemy Jewish crowds and of politicians devoid of feeling. Our Romanians are pushed out to the periphery of towns where they live in black misery. We are alone. The power to carve for ourselves another destiny, now as tomorrow, we will find only in ourselves. We must get used to this idea, that between God and us, there is no one to help us.

---

1 The "Brotherhoods of the Cross" are the "nests" in which "brothers of the cross," young men in high schools are grouped. See also the chapter "The First Beginnings of Organization" in the section "The Legion of Michael the Archangel" p. 305; see also footnote on p. 310. (Tr.)

> "That is why there is no other solution but to build with our own hands the home we need. Granted none of us has built houses or made bricks. I can understand that we need in the first place the courage to break down the mentality in which we have grown up, the mentality that makes the young intellectual who, the second day after becoming a student, is ashamed to carry a package on the street. We need the courage and the will to start from scratch, the will to uproot obstacles and overcome difficulties."

Olimpiu Lascar, a small building contractor with a big heart, who owned a house in Ungheni on the Pruth river, encouraged me in my idea, telling us:

> "Gentlemen, I suggest you come make the bricks in Ungheni, where I have a plot I will let you have. I also place my house at your disposal."

We accepted his proposition. But we had no money to pay our fare to Ungheni. We needed about 300 lei for about 20 persons. This money too was given us by Olimpiu Lascar.

The First Work Camp May 8, 1924

On May 8 we left for Ungheni, some by train, some on foot. There were 26 of us.

We had nothing: neither shovels nor any kind of tool, nor money, nor food. Lascar, who was expecting us, took us in.

> "Welcome gentlemen! The market town Ungheni is full of Jews, like a hive. Perhaps, seeing you, they will act less impertinently. We Christians, only a handful, are terrorized by them."

Finally we formed some delegations to go to the homes of Christians, trying to borrow shovels, spades, and other needed tools. Next day we went to the plot of land on the shore of the Pruth river. The local priest said a prayer for us. We worked for over a week to get down to the good soil, for it was our bad luck that for about 50 years townspeople had dumped their trash there, forming in some spots a layer six feet thick. Helped by several professional brick-makers, among whom I lovingly remember old Chirosca, we began working the clay and making bricks.

Legionary volunteers at the Ungheni work camp. May 1924.

We were divided into teams of five, each making 500 bricks daily, thus attaining a total of 3000 per day. Later, when our numbers grew, we made even more, working from 4 o'clock in the morning till the evening. The big problem was food. At first it was the Ungheni people who helped us; later groceries were sent to us also from Iasi. Our old professors, Cuza and Sumuleanu, looked somewhat distrustfully upon our endeavor. They found it childish, thinking we would not be successful. A while later though, they began to appreciate our efforts and even helped us.

When Corneliu Georgescu left the University in Cluj where he had completed a year of pharmacy, and came to Iasi, in common agreement with the others, we turned over to the brickyard the 17,000 lei donated to us while we were imprisoned at Vacaresti, and which he had kept for us.

Yet, as the feeding problem was serious, Mrs. Ghica lent us a two acre garden plot, which was planted by other student teams, to grow the vegetables needed at Ungheni. Our work was now in two places, one group of the students working at Ungheni, another at Iasi in the garden, interchanging every three or four days.

Our first work camp had the effect of generating a revolution in the thinking of the day. Everybody from all around—peasants, workingmen, and no less intellectuals—came to watch us, full of curiosity. These people had been used to seeing the students promenading, elegantly dressed, on Lapusneanu St. or singing songs of joy around tables in beer halls in their free hours. Now they saw them working clay with their feet, muddy up to the waist; carrying river water in pails from the Pruth river; bending over the shovel in the heat of the sun. These folk were witnessing the crumbling of an up-to-then dominating concept, i.e., that it is shameful for an intellectual to work with his hands, particularly at heavy labor, formerly allotted to slaves or despicable classes.

The first ones understanding the camp's value, from this point of view, were precisely the members of the humble classes. Peasants and workers, socially separated from the other categories, shy, because their labor was not appreciated, showed their delight on their faces, seeing in this at the very first glance a sign of appreciation of their exhausting labor and one of esteem for them.

They felt honored and perhaps envisaged in the future better days for themselves and their children. That is why, out of the little they possessed, they brought us daily, gladly, food.

Student life passed quietly. There were no longer street demonstrations and incidents. We worked full of joy, hopes, thinking we would soon have: our own home.

A New Blow

One day my father went to Iasi and I met him there. At about 10 o'clock in the evening I was headed back to my place. At Union Square I heard some commotion at a restaurant and I stopped to see what was going on. Two students, the Tutoveanu brothers from Barlad were having an altercation with Professor Constantinescu-Iasi. The Prefect of police arrived on the scene, handcuffed the students and took them away toward police headquarters, beating them. I, saying nothing, just watched this scene sorrowfully. Then I noticed that Commissar Clos accompanied by 3 or 4 police officers was coming toward me. Two paces from me he shouted:

"What are you doing on the street at this hour, you good-for-nothing?"

Bewildered, I just looked at him. Because he had known me for so many years, I could not imagine that he could ever address me like that. I thought he took me for somebody else. But I felt myself grabbed by the neck and shoved back. Then again:

"You stare at me, yet? Vagabond... crook!"

I said nothing, but I stood my ground looking at them. Then under blow after blow, pushed by the four policemen, I was "walked" more than 30 yards to the corner at Smirnov's. Here, I tipped my hat, saluted them and said:

"I thank you, gentlemen."

Deeply hurt, crushed by grief and shame, I went home to spend that night in torment. It was for the second time in my life that I was struck, both times within the month. I controlled myself. But you, oppressors in the entire world, do not count on the power of one's self control. He who controls himself, one day will explode terrifyingly.

The following day I told my father what befell me.

"Leave him in peace" he said. "Do not do anything. Two slaps on the face of such a person, just dirties your palms. The time of his justice will come, rest assured. They are probably ordered to provoke you. But you must control yourself and try not to go out alone any more."

I accepted his advice. But it seems that a man who was beaten and did not retaliate is no longer a man. He feels ashamed, dishonored. I carried this dishonor like a big boulder on my heart. But worse was yet to come several days later.

Overwhelmed by Blows at the Garden

The garden was all spaded. We came from Ungheni to put in tomatoes. At 5 o'clock on the morning of May 31, 50 students were ready to start work. While still in formation, as we finished the roll call I noticed several soldiers at the back of the garden. Then, over 200 of them burst into the yard loading their weapons. They surrounded us. I told the boys: "Everybody stay put. Do not react."

At the same moment, I saw like a black cloud a group of about 40 men around the gate, running in step, revolvers at the ready, shouting and swearing. It was Manciu the Prefect and his police. They were beside us in no time. Two commissars and the chief of police placed three revolver barrels against my forehead. They looked at me with bloodshot eyes, cursing. Manciu shouted: "Tie his hands behind his back!"

He struck me. Two others lunged at me, pulled out my belt and tightly tied my hands behind with it. Then a blow from behind hit me on my right jaw. Another, Vasiliu Voinea, came near and whispered in my ear:

> "Before evening we'll kill you! You will not live to chase out the Jews!"

He cursed and kicked me; then blows rained upon my face and some spat into my face. Our entire front, blocked now between rifles and revolvers, stood immobilized watching, helpless to come to my aid.

Mrs. Ghica came downstairs, demanding: "What is the meaning of this, Mister Prefect?" And he replied: "I'll arrest you too!"

Somewhat on the side I spotted Prosecutor Buzea, witnessing the scene.

Revolvers in hand, those in custody were then searched. Whoever moved was struck and thrown to the ground. After that, flanked by eight gendarmes with fixed bayonets, they placed me 10 yards out front; the others were likewise flanked by 200 gendarmes. And they marched us off. I was ahead, hands tied behind my back, my face spat upon, followed by the others. We were escorted thus all along Carol St., before the University, on Lapusneanu St., Union Square, on Cuza-Voda, to the Police Prefecture.

The Prefect and his policemen walked on the sidewalks rubbing their hands. The Jews, jubilating in front of their stores respectfully greeted them. I, saddened, could hardly see in front of my eyes. I felt that from now on everything is finished. Several high school students passing by me stopped and tipped their caps to me. They were immediately apprehended, manhandled and put with the rest of us.

After being paraded like this better than a mile through the middle of town before the Jewish population, in this state of utter humiliation, we were taken into the Police Prefecture. They threw me tied as I was, into a filthy hovel; the others were kept in the yard.

Upstairs, In The Prefects Office

One by one the young prisoners were taken upstairs into the Prefect's office for interrogation. The Prefect sat at his desk and the other interrogators, over 30 of them, were on chairs around him.

"What did Codreanu tell you?" he demanded.

"He did not tell us anything, Mister Prefect" answered the student or young high school boy.

"You are going to declare now everything he told you!"

The shoes of the individual being interrogated were taken off and his ankles chained together. A weapon was introduced between these and he was lifted upside down, the weapon being held on their shoulders by two soldiers.

Manciu, his coat off, began beating the soles of the victim's feet with an ox sinew. Poor children, hung heads down, thus beaten on their feet, unable to support the pain, began to scream.

Realizing they faced these henchmen-commissars who were sneering with gusto at the frightening tableau—in which the Romanian nation's children were being tortured by some enemy-paid scoundrels—far from any heart that could weep for them and intervene on their behalf, they cried out:

"Help!"

Then the Commissar Vasiliu had their heads lowered into pails of water so that their cries of pain and despair could not be heard outside.

When finally, the pain became unbearable and they felt their bodies could no longer take it, they shouted they would admit everything. The Prefect went to his desk in the expectation of their confession and the victims, their legs freed, looked around dazed. Then they burst out crying, falling to their knees before the Prefect:

"Forgive us, Sir, but we do not know what to declare."

"No? You do not? Get him up again!" he ordered his commissars and gendarmes.

And each poor child, his heart frozen, watched as the preparations for his agony recommenced. Again lifted upside down on the weapon, again beaten on the feet. Again they felt one by one the Prefect's blows falling on their feet. Their feet became bloody, ebony-black, swollen so that they could not put their shoes back on. Among those thus tortured were: the son of the present prosecutor of Ilfov County, Dimitriu; the son of Maj. Ambrozie, his eardrum broken and who in later life became a commissar at the same police prefecture.

Beaten in this manner, they were then carried into a separate, secret room. At around 9 o'clock I was called. My hands still tied and numbed, two gendarmes escorted me into the Prefect's office. There, he sat behind a desk and around him sat the more than 30 men, commissars, commissar-aides, and agents.

I looked into their eyes. Maybe among them I might find one compassionate heart. But I found nothing but general satisfaction; they were all smiling: Botez, the Chief of Security, Dimitriu, the Director of the Prefecture, Commissar Vasiliu, Clos and the rest. The Prefect took a sheet of paper. Wrote down my name. Then:

"What exactly is your name?"

"I am Corneliu Codreanu, candidate for a juridic doctorate and attorney in the same bar as you."

"Put him down!"

Three individuals, servile scoundrels, lunged at me and knocked me down in front of his desk.

"Take off his shoes!"

They took them off, one man for each shoe.

"Put chains on him!"

They chained my feet. I told them:

"Mister Prefect, you are now the stronger, master over life and death; but tomorrow when I shall leave here, I will take revenge upon both you and him who cursed me."

At this moment I heard some noise and voices in the hall. Professor Cuza was arriving with Professor Sumuleanu and parents of the children: Col. Nadejde, Maj. Dumitriu, Butnariu, Maj. Ambrozie and others, accompanied by the prosecutor and medical examiner, Professor Bogdan.

The Prefect and the others jumped off their chairs and went out into the hall. I heard the Prefect saying:

"What do you want here? I ask you to get out!"

Then Professor Cuza's voice:

"Who do you think you are throwing out? We came to see you so that you would throw us out? We have come accompanied by the prosecutor as complainants against you."

"Gendarmes, throw them out!" ordered the Prefect.

Professor Sumuleanu posted himself at the door of the room in which were locked the victims and said:

"Mister Prosecutor, we will not leave here until this room is opened for us."

Several commissars:

"There is no one in this room. It is empty,"

Professor Sumuieanu:

"Let this room be opened now!"

Upon the prosecutor's intervention the room was opened and six youngsters were helped out by their parents and brought into the Prefect's office. The medical examiner, Professor Bogdan, examined all of them, issuing medical certificates. Several hours later all those in the yard were freed. I was kept in for two more days after which I was sent to the examining magistrate.

He let me go. I told him:

"Your Honor, if I am not given justice, I am going to get it myself."

I went home. Professor Cura with Liviu Sadoveanu came there to see me.

"We heard that you said you wanted to take the law into your own hands. Do not do anything of the sort. We will report this to the Ministry of the Interior demanding an investigation. It is impossible that we shall not receive satisfaction."

On The Rarau Mountain

I was morally crushed. All my plans collapsed. I left to fate both the brickyard and the garden and I boarded the first train to Campul-Lung in Bucovina, where, on the green paths, I slowly climbed up the mountain, carrying on my soul burdens and the humiliation of yesterday as well as the puzzling torments regarding the future.

It seemed I had no friend in the world except the mountain—the Rarau, with its hermitage. When I was about 4500 feet up, I stopped. I looked over mountains and hills for hundreds of miles, but no view before my eyes could replace the picture of infamy and humiliation to which I had been exposed together with my comrades; I could still hear their sobbing, and it hurt.

It was getting dark. Not one living soul around. Only trees with vultures shrieking around the barren cliffs. I only had with me my heavy coat and a loaf of bread. I ate some bread and drank some water springing from among the rocks. I gathered pieces of wood to make myself a shelter, a hut. Here in this habitation I lived for a month and a half. The little food I needed was brought to me by shepherds from old man Piticaru's sheepfold. I was brooding and ashamed to go down among people. I wondered, what sins may I have committed that God sent this misfortune upon my head right now when I was ready to launch such a grand and beautiful plan?

I wrote Mota: "I do not know what ails me; it seems I am not myself! Good fortune abandoned me. Misfortune has been following me for some time, step by step; in anything I start, I fail. And when fortune no longer serves you in battle, all those around you begin to desert you. You bring them together at the cost of 30 victories and one defeat is enough for them to leave you."

My soul was ravaged by doubts. I was at a crossroad. We were fighting for the good of the country and were treated like enemies of the people. We were mercilessly hit by the government, police, gendarmes, army.

Should we also use force? They are the State; by tens of thousands, by hundreds of thousands. We, a handful of youngsters, exhausted in body by hardships, hunger, cold, prison. What force do we represent to expect at least a small chance of victory? Were we to try we would be crushed. And in the end, the country, dazed by the Jewish press, would say we were some madmen.

Not to use force and violence as they do? They provoke, torture your men, scatter them and kill you. Shall we permit ourselves to be killed? But at our age we have not yet written anything down and it would not even be known why they killed us. Better for all of us to leave the country. To leave and to curse; to wander throughout the whole world. Better for us to beg in country after country than be so humiliated to the utmost here in our own land, or descend from this mountain weapon in hand and do justice, that I may do away with the beast blocking the road and stifling the life of our nation. But what about our plans afterwards? I will die in my endeavor or die in prison; for I cannot bear a prison regime. I love liberty. If I do not have it, I die. But what about Mota? For such a move means both my martyrdom and Mota's, whose chances for acquittal will vanish completely. Our entire group will be crushed. All our well-meant thoughts, all our plans for organizing will have been in vain—for all would have ended here.

For six weeks, there on top of the mountain, I was tormented by these thoughts, failing to find a solution. Under the weight of my worries and anguish, my chest began hurting and I felt my powers waning. I had been an impetuous man who never gave in to anyone. I was sure of myself and confident in my powers. Wherever I went, I won. This time, present difficulties bent me!

I descended from the mountain. I left everything to fate; I could not find any solutions. But from then on I carried on myself a revolver which I intended to use at the first, slightest provocation: nobody was to budge me from that resolve.

I went to the brickyard. There, Grigore Ghica, left in charge of the work, exemplarily had met his responsibility. The number of bricks in storage increased considerably. Two new ovens, each of 40,000 brick capacity, were built. This was around July 15th. The boys received me affectionately. Nothing unusual happened in the yard.

In Iasi though, I found changes. Police commissars who earlier hardly had shoes on their feet, were now newly outfitted from top to bottom by the Jews who felt like absolute masters. The Police Prefecture had an automobile at their disposal given by the Jews. They exhibited an impertinence we had not encountered since 1919 during the communist movements when they imagined themselves to be on the eve of revolution and when every little Jew, in Iasi or over the Pruth, assumed the airs of a people's commissar.

Codreanu at the Rarau Mountain cabin built in 1934 by legionaries in memory of their leaders "40 days and 40 nights" spent on the mountain following the brutal assaults on the students by Police Chief Mancio. The cabin was subsequently destroyed by communists in 1945.

Efforts To Break Up Our Bloc

The Judeo-Liberal power had heard of our group, of our vow taken at Vacaresti, realizing that around this bloc the students would rally as one. Nothing frightens Jews more than a perfect unity in others: the unity of feeling in a movement, in a people. That is why they will always be for "democracy" which has but one advantage, and that one for the nation's enemy. For democracy will break up the unity and the spirit of a people, which, faced with the perfect unity and solidarity of Judaism in Romania and the rest of the entire world, once divided into democratic parties, thus fragmented, will be defeated.

This was also true of the student movement; as we had no perfect unity, Jews found factions or leaders whom they could convince, in Masonic-fashion, namely, suggesting to them all sorts of ideas which had no other purpose but that of breaking up our unity. Or, as our group this time presented an unshakable oneness with possibilities of rallying around itself the entire student movement, we were confronted with an interminable series of lies and intrigues carefully woven, aiming to split Mota away from me, and the others from one another.

Jews found among students weak elements who could be used as unwitting tools. Pretending that they were sharing great secrets with them, Jews launched intrigues which caught on even among students' parents, some of whom becoming the fiercest advocates for breaking the ties of their sons with this group.

How were we able to resist? Only through the foresight of our plans made at Vacaresti. We realized from the very first moment that this classic attack used by Masonry and Judaism would be aimed at us. We were ready. So that, the moment it started, we resisted even our closest relatives. As soon as we detected an intriguer at work, we got together and informed the whole group.

I now give here advice to all organizations, calling their attention to this system, commonly used everywhere. In order to parry the attack:

Never believe a tendentious information, no matter where it comes from. Immediately report the intrigue attempt to the group in question, to the involved persons and the leaders. In this way the attack could be repulsed.

My Betrothal

On August 10, 1924, at the Ungheni brickyard, surrounded by my comrades and my parents, was celebrated my betrothal to Miss Elena Ilinoiu, the daughter of Mr. Constantin Ilinoiu, a train conductor. He was a man of great goodness and great tenderness of soul. After that I moved into their home where I was received with open arms, even though they had a family of five children. This family was to me a constant support in the fight I was waging. Their care for me and their love sustained me.

On September 13, I went home to Husi where I celebrated in my parents' home my birthday and nameday.

I had just turned 25.

The Mota-Vlad Trial

The trial of Mota and of the student Leonida Vlad who procured the revolver, was set for September 26, 1924. Vlad turned himself in several days after the shooting, and was kept in prison with Mota all the time.

I left for Bucharest where deliberations opened before the Court of Assizes. Mota energetically defended his thesis that treason must be punished. Public opinion, fed up with traitors, followed the unfolding of the trial with lively interest and enthusiasm. It saw in Mota's gesture a beginning of action against traitors and proof of moral health. His deed has burst like a light on the dark side of Romanian life where century after century fighters for the good of the people had been felled through treason.

All the students at all universities held huge demonstrations for his acquittal. Around the Tribunal in Bucharest, again, thousands of people were massed who wanted a new life for their country and demanded Mota's freedom.

At daybreak, popular justice brought a verdict of acquittal which was enthusiastically received throughout the whole country. Mota, after seeing his parents, left Cluj for Iasi where he settled down, in accordance with our vow.

Around What Happened in the Garden

The humiliation and dishonor to which we were subjected during the lawlessness of May 31st had crushed us morally; it became an open wound that deepened more and more, consuming our life and seemingly drawing us closer to the grave.

The humiliation you feel when both you and yours are dishonored, gives you a feeling of profound pain, making you shun people, ashamed to be seen. It would seem you feel this world despises you, laughing in your face because you are incapable of defending your honor; that you endanger society proper, letting it be believed through your cowardice that an oppressor can, unpunished, dishonor it and hurt it according to his whims.

These pains grew proportionately as our endeavors to obtain legal redress were rejected with a cynicism that led us to desperation. Victims who sued for legal satisfaction risked being beaten again by the police, this time within the very walls of the praetorium of justice and even before the judges. In the end, however, it was the complainants who were condemned.

What happened on May 31st did not remain without its repercussions.

I reproduce from newspapers the echo this event had in Romanian society along with attempts at getting satisfaction for the outrage.

Universul ("The Universe") on June 8, 1924 prints under the title:

THE POLICE OF IASI
STUDENTS WERE BEATEN BY THE
POLICE PREFECT HIMSELF

"We imagine Mr. Manciu, the prefect of the Iasi police, as being like one of the most notorious policemen of the last century, exemplified by violence and brutality.

"Mr. Prefect Manciu, though a policemen of only a year's experience in a university town like Iasi, inaugurated his system of anachronistic police violence last year at the congress of university professors. He was able to stop a congress of university teachers because that is what his police impulses dictated to him.

"The protests that followed, against the indignities heaped upon this most distinguished group of intellectuals, remained fruitless, for Mr. Prefect of the Iasi police had politically-backed support for doing what he did.

"And since then Mr. Manciu has assiduously continued his police methods which he particularly exhibited these past days, when he beat, he beat thirstily, he zealously struck, he maliciously bled the students, then ordered his subalterns to imitate him with the same brutal zeal.

"No matter what the students of Iasi had done, had they even been assassins, they should not have been beaten.

"First, an investigation should have been made, the public prosecutor's office should have been informed, they should have been arrested, possibly put in chains, but not beaten to a pulp.

"Mr. Prefect Manciu is certainly obliged in the course of his duties also to apply certain regulations regarding 'the protection of animals.' We even believe he enforces them.

"In other words he sees to it that horses are not beaten, that pigs are not tortured.

"And yet Mr. Manciu who as a student must have studied penal law and must have read something of the penal literature that perhaps was recommended to him by our distinguished penalist Mr. lulian Teodoreanu himself, a man who has been preaching the abolition of brutal sanctions in prisons, personally beat the students, tortured them, covered them with blood.

"But, what if the beaten students are not guilty of any of the absurdities of which they are accused?

"Then what? Should he in turn be thrashed?

"Certainly a judicial investigation is needed.

"But a sanction is also needed to make it impossible for Mr. Manciu to strengthen his muscles on the heads of students."

B. Cecropide

The paper continues on June 9, 1924;

THE STUDENTS OF IASI WERE MALTREATED

They were Provoked by the Police, Tortured for no Reason. A Brutal Police Prefect. Manciu Must be Fired.

"We wrote in an earlier issue on the banditry committed by Mr. Manciu, the Police Prefect of Iasi, against the students.

"Today we hall reproduce several passages from the memorandum the students forwarded to the Ministry of the Interior.

THE STUDENT BUILDERS

"In the memorandum they say:

'We Christian students of Iasi University took a decision a month ago to build through our own labor a cultural home....'

THE PROVOCATIONS OF THE POLICE PREFECT

'Hardly gathered we found ourselves surrounded by a gendarme company and the entire police apparatus headed by Prefect Manciu.

'While all of us stood very quiet, their weapons extended, they lunged at us, started swearing and struck us in the most barbarous possible manner. We were searched, as they thought they would find weapons on us, but nothing was found on any of us. During the search they tried to put into the pockets of our colleague Corneliu Zelea Codreanu, a revolver and some papers, which he protested. Because of this he was beaten by the Policeman Manciu, Inspector Clos, Commissar Vasiliu and, together with the rest of the agents, he was tied as if he were the worst of thieves. The same thing happened to a large number of those of us who were there. We were arrested, surrounded by military cordons, taken to the Police Prefecture.'

EVEN THE CHILDREN ON THE STREET WERE BEATEN

'We met on our way several students of various high schools who were going toward the sports park to practice the oina (Romanian baseball—Tr.), as they were directed by their principals to do. All of them were arrested and taken along with us to police headquarters, naturally after they were beaten by Policeman Manciu himself and the other policemen, for everybody to watch. They too, were kept at police headquarters the whole day. Some of us were beaten till we fainted, then were freed; others gave declarations under duress while some were freed with no declarations being taken'."

And in conclusion *Universul* added:

"The above-mentioned deeds cannot go unpunished. The Prefect of police Manciu, proved to be an agent provocateur and guilty of torturing students and high school boys in Iasi, must receive the punishment for such lawlessness."

Among others, Universul of June 10, 1924 prints:

IASI UNDER THE TERROR OF THE POLICE PREFECT

"... Transported to the police dungeons, these students were subjected to the most terrifying tortures.

"Some of them were hung head down, beaten on the soles of their feet with the ox sinew. The student Corneliu Codreanu was bound, then slapped and tortured by the police prefect himself. His health was shaken.

"The other arrested students show serious body lesions.

"Three hundred students have reported the above-mentioned facts to the general prosecutor demanding that the medical examiner look into the condition of their tortured colleagues."

The Word of Professor A.C. Cuza

In the special issue of the newspaper *Unirea* ("The Union") of June 1, 1924, Professor A.C. Cuza published a judicious article from which I extract:

"But in the face of these constant brutalities and innumerable abuses, groundless—especially committed so that they would worry the Romanian students through terror—two questions strongly pose themselves:

"Wbat does the government that keeps such a policeman at the head of such a city as Iasi want?

"Wbat does the policeman himself want?

"Do they want thoughtless reactions to be produced, as a result of this continuous frustration which seems to be provoked daily?

"This provocation is the more undignified and the more irritating because at the same time policeman Manciu frequents the meetings of the Jewish association 'Macabi' and ostentatiously leads these sport-minded Macabces in excursions, behind their white and blue flag.

"And one sees him daily lounging in his car—not the one he traveled in the other day to Ciurea—but in the new car that it seems was bought for him by the Iasi Israelite community through a public subscription, the same Kahal which encourages him in the press and at every opportunity in his attitude against the Christian students.

"Protesting with utmost indignation against this action of continuous provocation, we demand that the superior authorities intervene in order to put an end to an undignified and dangerous state of affairs, that neither Iasi nor Christian students can tolerate any longer."

A.C. Cuza

Protest Meetings Against Manciu June 3rd and 5th

The following telegrams were sent:

TO HIS MAJESTY THE KING

"Wishing to meet in order to protest the lawlessness of Policeman Manciu against our students and children who were daily beaten and insulted, we were prevented by police and gendarmes even though the prosecutor authorized our meeting.

"We respectfully submit to Your Majesty our complaint and ask to be protected." (There follow 1200 names).

TO THE MINISTRY OF THE INTERIOR

"Our children were picked off the streets, savagely maltreated by police Prefect Manciu. We demand immediate investigation followed by severe sanctions.

"Hurt in our parental feelings, losing all patience, we expect justice without delay."

ss. Maj. I. Dumitriu, Maj. Ambrozie, D. Butnaru, Elena Olanescu, Capt. Oarza, Gheorghiu, etc.

ACTIUNEA ROMANEASCA ("ROMANIAN ACTION")
First Year, No. 2, November 15, 1924

Actiunea Romaneasca in its Nov. 15, 1924 issue published over the signature of the renowned writer Dr. Ion Istrate:

"An impressive meeting of public protest was held on June 8, 1924 in the Bejan Hall, under the honor presidency of Gen. Tarnoschi, Manciu's conduct was branded by: University Professor A.C. Cuza, student Grigorescu representing Christian students, craftsman Artur Rus, metallurgist C. Pancu, University Professor C. Sumuleanu from the School of Medicine who gave an impressive description of what he saw at the police station: broken eardrums, swollen ears, bloody eyes, broken arms and legs bruised by the ox sinews of Manciu's savages. He declared that, had he had a son so tortured by the barbarian heading the police force, 'he would not have hesitated for an instant to blow the rascal's brains out.'

"Then spoke Maj. I. Dumitriu who concluded by saying: 'I trust the country's justice will give us satisfaction. If not, I swear here before you—and I shall know how to respect my oath—that I will take justice into my own hands.'

"Attorney Bacaloglu also spoke, then craftsman Cristea, attorney Nelu Ionescu and Professor Ion Zelea Codreanu. At the end a protest motion was voted upon in which the Ministry of Justice was asked for satisfaction on the one hand, and the government was asked to fire Manciu on the other,"

A Useless Warning

In *Tara Noastra* ("Our Country") No. 24 on June 15, 1924 the well known writer Al.O. Teodoreanu published an article from which we reproduce the last passages:

"Justice, called upon to speak up, declares all the 'arrested students' innocent and decides that they must be freed immediately.

"The student Zelea Codreanu is kept under arrest despite this, put on trial by Policeman Manciu who is a lawyer besides, for conspiracy.

"The most elementary law manuals and common sense tell us that in marriage, duel or conspiracy, one person alone cannot figure.

"In order to place such a label on a person as above, one who issues it must be in a particular state of inebriation which would make him see at least double.

"In other words, one cannot talk with him.

"But, in the name of the entire slandered Romanian population, from which we gladly exclude, with no loss to anyone, its timid representatives in Parliament and the press, we ask of the government whether it considers it best to leave the (inevitable) punishment of Manciu up to his victims, or more opportune to prevent it.

"Fortified by the decisive word of justice we do not hesitate to label 'the conspiracy' of Iasi as a treacherous frame-up..."

Al.O. Teodoreanu

An Administrative Investigation is Ordered

As a result of the numerous protests stemming from this event, the Administrative Inspector Vararu was sent out to investigate the case. Here is the memorandum forwarded to him by Maj. Ambrozie:

MEMORANDUM

"Mr. Inspector,

"Definitely wishing to establish the whole truth as to our telegraphic report on the torture of our sons, the Minister of the Interior has sent you to investigate; as we believe you wish to give full exposure to this case, we have put together this memorandum containing a narration of the facts.

"The event happened as follows: It was known in Iasi both by school principals and by the students' parents, that students were making bricks in Ungheni to build a home of their own in Iasi, and that they worked a garden placed at their disposal by Mrs. Ghica on Carol St. Some of the students and high school boys met once a week under the leadership of the student Corneliu Z. Codreanu, when work assignments were made, namely: 40 students were sent to Ungheni to make bricks, and 20-25 high school boys were sent to water the vegetable garden.

"The police prefect was aware of this; but he figured he might as well concoct something sensational, like a 'conspiracy,' particularly when newspapers in Iasi are practically owned by him and consequently would fall in with his game. Said and done. On May 31, 1924, between 4:30 and 5 o'clock in the morning, when he knew some 65 students had come to work in Mrs. Ghica's yard, his entire police force and many armed troops made a sudden charge against them because of the gravity of the contrived 'conspiracy.' The human mind refuses to comprehend what happened when students and high school boys were surrounded like ordinary criminals and were barbarously struck on the spot by agents, the military, and even by Policeman Manciu himself.

"A half hour later, all of them, headed by Corneliu Zelea Codreanu and under heavy escort, were headed down the main street toward police headquarters; on their way they met another group of high school students who by order of their professors were going to Copou to play 'oina'. These, because they permitted themselves the luxury of greeting those in chains, were immediately arrested, beaten and taken to police quarters, as accomplices of the former.

"Arrived there, the prefect, not bothering to inform the public prosecutor's office of the gravity of the situation, began a 'sui generis' interrogation all by himself; namely, he beat, manhandled and tortured these students and high school boys to force from them declarations that they were a part of the conspiracy, to make them tell what they knew. But what were they to tell, when they knew nothing of the sort? Almost all of them were beaten, but the most seriously hurt were:

"1. My son, Cezar Ambrozie, senior at the Pedagogic Seminary, who was personally whipped by the prefect over the head with an ox sinew, and in the end, because he did not produce the expected answer, was given a blow of the fist on the left ear, which broke his eardrum.

"2. High school student Dumitriu Sprinti, Maj. Dumitriu's son; his feet were chained together and he was turned upside down being hung on a rifle held by Sgt. Cojocaru and Cpl. Teodoroiu. He was beaten on his feet with the ox sinew by the prefect personally till he passed out.

"3. High school boy Gh. Gurguta had his hands and feet tied. Then he was placed on the floor face down and beaten with the ox sinew, and in order to stifle his screams, a pan of water was placed under his face and an agent posted there pushed his face down into the water when he screamed louder.

"During all this torture, two gendarme officers were also present: Capt. Velciu and Lieut. Tomida, whose soldierly dignity, we hope, will not prevent them from revealing the truth, since it was not dignified of them to witness such treatment; to use troops in the torturing as well as using a military weapon as a tool of torture, when it is well known what its use ought to be.

"According to what students and high school boys related, while

Policeman Manciu was engaged in such operations, Prosecutors Culianu and Buzea passed through his office. I believe they will tell the truth.

"The beatings and tortures stopped altogether only later, when First-Prosecutor Catichi came to police headquarters, as demanded by a committee composed of: Professors Cuza and Sumuleanu, attorney Bacaloglu, Col. Nadejde and Medical Examiner Bogdan who examined the children and legally established, there in the police prefecture, the wounds enumerated in the medical certificates attached to this report.

"As you can see, Mr. Inspector, we have followed legal procedures up to today, namely:

"1. We had asked the first-prosecutor and the medical examiner to come to the prefecture for them to verify the wounds of the students.

"2. We brought suit against the torturers before the Court of District II.

"3. We informed the public prosecutor's office, where the medical examiner's report was also sent, the case being referred to Investigating Magistrate Iesanu.

"4. As officers and men of honor we could have demanded from Mr. Manciu satisfaction by means of weapons, but he had disqualified himself when he refused meeting Capt. Ciulei in a duel.

"Honestly, this is the truth.

"We beg you to be good enough to consider that.among the offended parents, two of us are high ranking officers who, for having proceeded legally, are exposed for no one has yet given us satisfaction to this day. Our belief is that the Minister of the Interior will give us complete satisfaction, bringing Prefect Manciu before the bar of justice for his misdeeds, and will intervene to the Ministry of War for Manciu, though a reserve inferior officer[2], knowingly tortured the children of his superior comrades."

Maj. (ss) Ambrozie

2 Reserve Sublieutenant Manciu was in the 10th Regiment of the Mountain Infantry, but during mobilization he shirked his duties in the repair shops of the 3rd Army Corps.

The Result of the Investigation Was as Follows:

1. Prefect Manciu was decorated with Steaua Romaniei (Romania's Star) with the rank of commander.

2. All police commissars who tortured us were promoted.

3. Encouraged by these measures, the police unleashed further persecution against us, this time extending it over the whole of Moldavia. Any commissar, to increase his sources of revenue from the Jews or to get promoted, grabbed a student by the throat, beat him to a pulp in the street or at police headquarters, having to answer to nobody for his deeds.

The Fatal Day

This being the situation, on October 25, 1924 I presented myself at the Court House of District II of Iasi as a lawyer, together with my colleague Dumbrava, to represent the student Comarzan who was tortured by Manciu.

The prefect showed up with the whole staff and there, in full court session, before the lawyers and the presiding judge Spiridoneanu, threw himself at us.

Under these circumstances, risking everything, about to be crushed by the twenty armed policemen, I pulled out my handgun and fired.

I aimed at whoever came closest. The first to fall was Manciu. The second, Inspector Clos; the third, a man much less guilty, Commissar Husanu. The rest vanished.

In no time at all, in front of the Court House, several thousand Jews had gathered, their hands high in the air, their fingers like talons crooked in hatred, waiting for my departure in order to rip me apart.

Holding the gun in my right hand—in which I still had five rounds—I grabbed Victor Climescu, a lawyer in Iasi, by the arm, asking him to accompany me to the Tribunal.

We stepped out and walked thus through the howling mob of Jews which had the common sense, upon seeing the handgun, to step aside. I was caught by the gendarmes on the way, separated from Mr. Climescu and taken into the Police Prefecture. Here the commissars jumped on me to disarm me of the gun—the only friend I had in the midst of this misfortune. I gathered all my strength resisting them for about five minutes. In the end I was overpowered. They then chained my wrists behind my back and placed me between four soldiers with bayonets at the ready.

After a while they took me out of that office and far back in the courtyard, placing me in front of a tall fence. The gendarmes retreated leaving me there alone. I suspected they wanted to shoot me. I stood there several hours till late in the evening, waiting to be shot. However, this waiting did not phase me.

The news of this tragic vengeance spread with truly lightning speed. When it reached student dormitories it caused a real outburst. From all mess halls and dormitories students started running down the streets toward Union Square. There they demonstrated at length, singing, then they tried to head for the Police Prefecture. But the army, by now on the scene, succeeded in stopping them. Though chained, I was glad to hear their singing for that meant they had been freed of their tyrant.

Late in the day I was taken upstairs into the same office of torture, where Iesanu, the investigation judge, now sat behind the desk, the same man to whom I complained four months earlier, demanding justice. He interrogated me summarily after which he issued the warrant for my arrest. I was then thrown into a paddy-wagon and transported to Galata prison up on the hill above Iasi near the monastery built by Petre Schiopul, ruler of Moldavia.

There, I was put into a room with ten other prisoners, where my chains were taken off. My cellmates gave me a cup of tea. Then I lay down to sleep. Next day I was placed in solitary in a room with cement floor, one bed of boards, no blanket or pillow; the door then was padlocked. The room had two windows whose panes were whitewashed on the outside. I could see nothing. One wall was so damp that water ran down it. The first day in that room, a guard—old Matei—brought me a loaf of black bread. He opened the door a crack, thrust his hand in with the loaf, for he was not permitted to enter. I was not at all hungry. At night I stretched out on the boards and covered myself with the coat. I had nothing to put under my head. I shivered.

They took me out in the morning for two minutes, then I was locked up again. A student, Miluta Popovici who was also under arrest, was able to get near my window during the day, wipe the pane clean about the size of a finger tip so I could see outside. Then he walked away and when about 60 feet away carefully signaled to me with his fingers. I understood he was using the Morse code. Thus I learned that all Vacarestians were re-arrested: Mota, Garneata, Tudose Popescu, Radu Mironovici save Corneliu Georgescu whom they could not apprehend. They too were brought to the same prison and put together in one room. I learned that my father was also brought there. The second night was much worse. I was very cold and I could not doze off at all. Almost the whole night I paced the cell.

In the morning, again, I was taken out for two minutes, then locked back in; old Matei gave me another loaf of bread. At noon I was handcuffed, put into a paddy-wagon and taken to the Tribunal for the confirmation of my arrest warrant. Following this formality, I was brought back to Galata into the same dark room. Outside, the weather was getting worse. With no heat, I was beginning to shiver. I tried to get some sleep on the boards but I was able to doze off only for about half an hour at a time, for my bones ached. Because of the cold coming up from the cement floor my kidneys began to ache. Realizing I was losing my strength, I appealed to my will and to gymnastics. Throughout the night, every hour on the hour, I got up to exercise for ten minutes obstinately endeavoring to keep my strength.

The following day I felt ill. My strength was visibly waning despite my determination and willpower. The night that followed, the cold was even greater and my will no longer functioned; I felt broken. I saw black before my eyes and I collapsed. As long as my will lasted I had not worried. But now I realized I was in bad shape. I was shaking all over and could not stop. How difficult were those seemingly endless nights!

The prosecutor came in the next day to see me. I tried to hide the shape I was in.

"How are things here?"

"Very good, Sir."

"Have you nothing to report?"

"No, nothing."

It was thirteen days that I spent like this; then they made a little fire for me. They gave me bed linen, blankets and some matting that was hung on the walls. I was permitted to be outdoors one hour each day. One day I got a glimpse of Mota and Tudose deep in the back of the yard and I signaled to them. It was then that I learned that my father had been freed; likewise Liviu Sadoveanu, Jon Sava and another student who had been arrested.

Two Articles Regarding the Manciu Case

The next day following the events at Targul-Cucului, *Cuvantul lasului* ("The Word of Iasi") of Oct. 27, 1924 published an article signed by Nelu Ionescu, lawyer, former president of the Association of Law Students, from which I quote:

> "Comments made by the Jewish Liberal press concerning the death of C. Manciu, are slanted and in bad faith; they start with a gross falsification of facts — facts which were only the inevitable consequence of a regime of abuses and injustice—in order to turn into a hero, at any price, the man who was but an instrument, and to heap the blame on some imagined fascistic anti-Semitic conspiracy.
>
> "The students were forcibly prevented from entering the Cathedral to pray; were prevented from eating in common in a restaurant; were brutalized and prevented from walking the streets; were prevented from holding meetings in their own university and at their association's offices; were prevented from working their own garden for their own use; were beaten on the street, in police cellars and in public squares by the entire police force, from the lowliest cop all the way up to the one who was but yesterday the police prefect of this city.
>
> "Students, showing a self-mastery worthy of admiration and a trust in justice that honors them, initiated a series of suits against Prefect Manciu and his subalterns, for severe cruelty, abuse of power and individual liberty.
>
> "This gesture of the students was not understood. And regretfully we must say that Justice did not meet the expectations that an entire generation, animated by the purest sentiment of legality and order, placed in it.

"The coed Silvia Teodorescu, kicked in the back by Manciu in broad daylight on Dec. 11, 1923 on Carol St. in front of Col. Velsa's house—a fact stated and attested to in having numerous eyewitnesses—not only did not succeed in having Manciu convicted before the Court of Urban District 1, but she as plaintiff ended up convicted of slander, for at the trial it was learned that during the kicking she addressed to Manciu the words: 'this is savagery.'

"On the evening of Dec. 14, 1923, the law student, Lefter, from Galati, as he was entering Hotel Bejan where he resided, was with no reason surrounded by a band of policemen and gendarmes who, together with Manciu and by his orders, beat him with bludgeons, canes, rifle butts, kicks and fists, till he fell to the ground unconscious, following which he was dragged into a side street, dumped and left there without any assistance.

"Though Lefter sued, Manciu was exonerated, not having to bring any witnesses to his defense.

"But what is one to say of the barbarity and savagery of last summer, perpetrated on the students working in the garden of the Ghica residence?!

"Twenty five students, beaten on the soles of their feet like thieves for a full day, a fact that was verified by the first prosecutor and by the pathologist, for an imaginary conspiracy so insignificant that it did not even warrant an investigation,

"And not only this but when, upon the students' demands for an administrative investigation, one was conducted last summer by Mr. Vararu, he was profoundly shocked by the abuses he himself confirmed. However, Vararu's report to the appropriate Ministry resulted in Manciu being decorated with Steaua Romaniei (Romania's Star).

"This then is the man who died; one speaks only well of the dead, but this does not prevent us from telling the truth.

"Manciu suspended meetings; Manciu stopped those wanting to enter the Cathedral; Manciu beat students on the streets, at the police and in public squares; insulted those who complained and threatened, their defenders. Manciu, protected by cordons of police officers and gendarmes, beat—with the bestiality of one possessed—

the students, tied and foot, who could throw back at them through the rain of spittle and blows of his demented subalterns, only looks of contempt and temporary resignation.

"Behold the man of duty and behold the kind of order this man was dispensing!

"Public opinion is on Corneliu Codreanu's side. It likes his manly gesture and, appreciating the superior motive of this gesture warning a regime and serving an idea, absolves him of the customary incrimination for such a deed, justifying him completely and in fact, public opinion approves of him.

"Personally I salute Corneliu Codreanu's heroic gesture, who once again remains intransigent in matters of honor and determined when dignity is involved."

Several days later, the newspaper *Unirea* ("The Union") in Oct. 1924, published Professor Cuza's article,

Prefect Manciu's Death

The Fatal System and its Consequences

"For a full year now the police of Iasi have experienced a real tragedy, whose last act is known by all. Due to the fatal evolution of events the following victims fell:

"Prefect Manciu, Inspector Clos, Sub-commissar Husanu, and no less, the doctoral candidate Corneliu Zelea Codreanu.

"Prefect Manciu died; Sub-commissar Husanu fights death; Inspector Clos sustained a deep wound; Corneliu Zelea Codreanu lingers in jail.

"What is this tragedy that fells so many victims? In what manner can we speak of the fatal evolution of these events? Who are the guilty parties?

"Manciu was Mr. Marzescu's police prefect in Iasi.

"It was in this capacity alone that he was brought here and was maintained till the end—all the excesses of which he was guilty notwithstanding. Which makes it abundantly clear that his actions were approved. The abundant proof that he was approved, that he worked according to a pre-established plan at the direct inspiration of Mr. G.G. Marzescu who supported him, are the distinctions accorded him—his 'merits' in office and the promotion of his personnel.

"The fatal system inspired by Manciu was the terrorization of Christian students: to give the Jews satisfaction and to prove that 'order' can be maintained 'by energetic means'.

"The unfortunate Manciu, who had no special talents, put the fatal system into operation with an unusual brutality even when it came to university professors: commencing his career on the occasion of the general meeting of the Association of University Professors of Romania, held in Iasi on Sept. 23-25, 1923 under the presidency of our eminent colleague Professor I. Gavanescul.

"Prefect Manciu insulted the universities, brutalized and arrested innocent students, thus compelling their professors to protest and seek satisfaction.

"The four-university commission made up of Professors Dr. Hurmuzescu, Bucharest; Dr. Sumuleanu, Iasi; M. Stefanescu, Cluj; and Hacman, Cernauti, edited right there in the meeting the following telegram signed by Professor Gavanescul, which was then sent to:

1. The President of the Council of Ministers;
2, The Minister of Internal Affairs;
3, The Minister of Public Instruction:

"The General Association of University Professors of Romania, in its opening meeting, condemns the harassing interference of the Iasi police, and in total agreement with its president, demands from superior authorities customary investigation and complete satisfaction.

"President of the Association (ss) *I. Gavanescul*

"The same commission edited and sent the mayor of Iasi the following text:

"Mr. Mayor,

"The General Association of University Professors, in their opening meeting, in consequence of the harassing measures taken against our convention by Mr. Prefect of the Iasi police, regrets to inform you that under the circumstances they cannot take part in the banquet given by the City Hall, hereby thanking you for your good intentions.

"President of the Association (ss) *I. Gavanescul*

"Having received an imperative mandate to terrorize students, Manciu operated in conformity with its aims and according to the established plan—treading on the path of fatalism. We will briefly enumerate the events as they occurred:

"1. The introduction of police and army into the university on Dec. 10, 1923.

"On the occasion of the student demonstrations which followed, the student G. Manoliu was beaten by the police so severely that he was taken ill with jaundice and died several days later.

"2. Brutalities at the railway station. On the occasion of the arrival of Professor Ion Zelea Codreanu in Iasi, after he was released from prison, Prefect Manciu, totally unjustifiedly, threw himself, the police and the army upon the citizens and students who came to the depot to receive him, brutalizing them and chasing them away as if they were malefactors.

"3. Prince Carol's visit. On the occasion of this visit Manciu had staged other scandalous abuses which compelled the students to complain to His Royal Highness.

"4. The scandal at the Sidoli Theater. Upon arrival in Iasi of the Romanian retired opera artists, they were met by the students who staged for them a demonstration of sympathy. This absolutely peaceful demonstration was reason enough for Prefect Manciu to cause another scandal. He manhandled the students and scattered them with odious brutality.

"5. The Carol St. conspiracy. Thanks to the courtesy of Mrs. Constanta Ghica, the students planted vegetables in her garden offered for that purpose, in order to support themselves. On May 31, this year, as students were gathered to commence work, Prefect Manciu with his whole staff and the gendarmes with bayonets fixed, appeared and arrested all students present. Corneliu Zelea Codreanu had his hands tied behind his back with his own belt, and was led thus throughout the town together with the other 25 students and high school boys toward police headquarters where they were cruelly beaten.

"Corneliu Zelea Codreanu, a reserve officer, doctoral law candidate, was slapped over the face - and coarsely insulted with the most degrading vulgarities.

"The high school student Ambrozie, son of the veteran Maj. Ambrozie, was slapped so hard that his eardrum broke, a fact verified by the medical certificate signed by pathologist Dr. Gh. Bogdan.

"The other students and high school boys had their feet soles lashed by a bullwhip after being suspended, heads down. Their heads were lowered into pails of water to stop their, shouts.

The parents of the children so tortured are: Major Ambrozie, Dimitriu, Butnaru, etc. who forwarded to the Ministry of Internal Affairs a petition against Prefect Manciu, and then sued him. But Manciu continued to exhibit a revolting attitude even before the judge.

"Not only was Prefect Manciu retained in his post but he was rewarded for his attitude and encouraged to pursue his fatal system further.

"The Jewish press eulogized him daily, proclaiming him a savior of law and order and a superior being.

"The government, having at Iasi as its representative G.G. Marzescu, instead of accepting the findings of Inspector Vararu, pinned on Manciu's chest Steaua Romaniei (Romania's Star) and promoted the personnel he had used to commit his lawlessness. For instance, Commissar Clos, one of the guiltiest, was promoted to police inspector.

"The Department of Justice, headed by the same G.G. Marzescu, Manciu's supporter, in lieu of energetically and promptly stepping in against the perpetrated abuses, condemned the victims.

"The Jews of Iasi, well-pleased, presented Manciu with the gift of an automobile, which he accepted, scandalizing all Romanians and inducing greater resentment particularly among the students who could see Manciu's defiant insolence as he proudly drove the Jews' car through town.

"Upheld in his position, supported and encouraged in this manner, Prefect Manciu, by his impulsive temperament, lacking any self-control, imagined that he reached a pinnacle of glory by the application of his system,

"It ts this sequence of events that brought Prefect Manciu to the last act of this tragedy.

"Comeliu Zelea Codreanu acted in legitimate defense.

"The responsibility of Prefect Manciu's death rests first of all with him who placed Manciu at the head of the police department and supported him, namely the Minister of Justice, G.G. Marzescu.

"The responsibility rests with the Jewish press and all those who urged him on and encouraged him, congratulating him for applying his fatal system."

Hunger Strike

About ten days before Christmas, Mota, Garneata, Tudose and Radu Mironovici who had been arrested sixty days earlier, innocent of any wrongdoing, went on a hunger and thirst strike. They said: either our freedom, or death.

Endeavors on the part of various authorities to talk to them failed, for they barricaded themselves in their cell permitting no one to enter.

These youth have long since become an image of the entire Romanian studentry; a symbol. When news of their strike was heard, students and everybody else understood the gravity of their act in view of their well known strength of resolution. Should these youth die within the walls of Galata? In Iasi and Cluj, spirits became so agitated that a mass vengeance would have ensued on those the multitudes would have considered to be responsible. Not only students, but also old folks well established in society were loudly demanding: "If these children all die there, we will start shooting." The government began to fathom that it was facing a general determination and tension; that this nation began to show her will and dignity.

My father issued in Iasi a manifesto from which I reproduce the following passage:

AN APPEAL

"Romanian Brothers,

"The students: Ion I. Mota, Ilie Garneata, Tudose Popescu and Radu Mironovici, detained for two months in the Galata prison, declared Tuesday at 1 P.M. a hunger and thirst strike.

"They have taken this difficult step because they are completely innocent, because besides being innocent they were imprisoned at Vacaresti and because they came to realize that certain politicians wish to gradually ruin their health and life through imprisonment.

"These young heroes, the choicest flower of the country's future, were endowed by God among other qualities, with wills of steel. Consequently, their determination to die of hunger and thirst—in order to protest the injustice whose victims they are and the enslavement of our Nation by Jews through the aid of certain politicians—is not a joke, but a grave decision."

EITHER LIBERTY, OR DEATH!

"Romanian Brothers,

"Will we wait to see, 2 or 3 days from now, the four coffins holding the bodies of these heroes, being borne down the street?

"Old and young alike, think: one does not speak of the corpses of the four students, but of the death of our children, of all of us.

"The duty of all of us it is, to take quick measures of peaceful and legal protest, but energetic and determined, against this government, and thus prevent this iniquity, to stop the assassination of our sons."

At Christmas, following eleven days of hunger and thirst strike, they were freed. But they were so emaciated that they were taken out of the prison on stretchers directly to the hospital. Some had left a period of imprisonment only several months prior to this last detention, Mota only one month earlier having finished an uninterrupted one year, so that their strength was sapped.

The consequences of this strike are even today felt by some of them, ten years later, while poor Tudose took them with him into the grave.

Alone at Galata

In the same damp and dark cell, sitting on the hard edge of my bed, arms crossed over my chest, head bent under the weight of my thoughts, time passes slowly, minute after minute.

How terrifying solitude is!

With regrets I remember the verses:

"Gaudeamus igitur
"Juvenes dum sumus."

"Let us therefore rejoice, while we are young"! Verses that have warmed, cheered, crowned with the crown of joy the youth of all student generations. To be joyful, to have a good time is a right of youth, before that age comes when man's life is weighed down by hardships and worries, ever increasing, ever greater.

I was not granted this right. I had no time for enjoyment. Student life, during which everybody enjoys himself and sings, for me had ended. I did not even realize when it had passed. Over my youth had come worries, difficulties and blows too soon, and all these tore it to pieces. Whatever is left of it is further obliterated by these gloomy cold walls. Now they deprive me even of the sun. So many weeks have passed since I linger in this darkness and I can enjoy the sun only for an hour a day.

My knees are constantly frozen. I feel the coldness of the cement floor creeping up through my bones. The hours pass slowly; very slowly. I take a few bites at noon and in the evening. I cannot eat more. But it is particularly at night that the real torment commences; it is about 2 or 3 in the morning when I fall asleep. Outside is stormy weather. Here, on top of the hill, the wind is stronger. The snow is pushed by the wind through the cracks in the door until it covers a fourth of the cell area. By morning I always find a layer quite thick. The heavy quiet of the night is interrupted only by the hooting owls that live in the church towers and from time to time by the voices of the guards who shout as loud as they can:

"Number one! OK! Number two! OK!"

I was pondering, wondering, worrying, yet unable to clear the puzzle: A month? Two months? A year? How much? A lifetime? The rest of my life?

Yes, my arrest warrant threatened for me forced labor for life. Will trial be held? Certainly; but it is going to be a difficult trial. For there are three forces that are coalesced against me:

The government, which is going to try to make an example of my punishment, particularly in view of the fact that this is the first time in Romania when anyone has faced, gun in hand, the oppressor who trampled underfoot his dignity, offended his honor and ripped off his flesh in the name of the principle of the power of state authority.

The Jewish power within Romania which would do anything to keep me in its clutches.

The Jewish power from abroad, with its money, its loans, its pressures.

All of these three forces are interested in preventing my ever leaving here. Against them are poised the students and the Romanian nationalist movement. Which will win? I realize that my trial is more a test of forces. No matter how right I was, if enemy forces were only a little bit stronger than our camp, they would not hesitate for one moment to destroy me. It has been so many years since they waited to catch me, for I placed myself across all their plans. They will exercise all efforts so I will not be able to escape them.

At home, my mother, having heard so much terrifying news year in and year out, her home raided at night by prosecutors and searched by brutal commissars, was receiving blow after blow.

Reflecting upon my life coming to such a sad fate, she sent me the Akathist of Virgin Mary, urging me to read it at midnight for 42 consecutive nights. I had done so, and it seemed that as I neared my goal, our side was gaining strength while the enemy retreated and the dangers subsided.

The Trial is Transferred to Focsani

I was informed in January that the trial had been *ab officio* moved to Focsani.

Focsani, at that time, was the biggest Liberal stronghold in the country. Three cabinet members hailed from that town: Gen. Vaitoianu, N.N. Saveanu and Chirculescu. It was the only town in the whole country where the nationalist movement did not catch on. Our endeavors to accomplish something there had failed. There, we had no one, except Mrs. Tita Pavelescu, a veteran patriot with her paper *Santinela* ("The Sentinel") which preached but to the wind. The students in Iasi, upon learning about this transfer, became very worried.

Numerous groups, upon each train's departure, waited in the railway stations around Iasi to accompany me to Focsani, for it was rumored that my escort would try to shoot me on the occasion of this transfer under the pretext that I tried to escape.

Some two weeks later, Botez, the Chief of Security, came with several agents, put me into a car which was escorted by a second car. We drove out of Iasi through the Pacurari barrier to the Cucuteni depot.

There, I found a group of students and on the train that pulled in there was another group. But I could not talk to any of them. While the police got me into the prisoners' railcar, they demonstrated in my support. We traveled almost the whole night. I approached Focsani certain of my condemnation. Local police and the prison warden were expecting me at the station. I was immediately whisked away and incarcerated.

At first the regimen was stricter than at Iasi. Gavrilescu, the county prefect, who seemed to be a mean man, without any justification—for no prefect has the right to interfere in the prison's regimen—wanted to impose upon me a severe regimen. He even came into my cell where we had an altogether not too pleasant discussion.

The miracle, that neither I nor particularly those who brought me to Focsani expected, was that three days after my arrival, the entire populace, irrespective of political party and in spite of all endeavors on the part of the authorities to turn it against me, spontaneously came over to my side.

Liberal politicians were abandoned not only by their own supporters but by their families as well. For example, the Chirculescu high school girls sent me food and sewed for me, together with other girls, a regional national shirt. I even heard they refused to sit at the table for meals with their father.

It was then that I met Gen. Dr. Macridescu, the most venerable figure in Focsani; Hristache Solomon, a moderately rich property owner, but a man of great moral authority to whom even his enemies tipped the hat; Mr. Georgica Niculescu; Col. Blezu, who through his little daughter, Fluturas sent me food; Vasilache, Stefan and Nicusor Graur; the Olteanu, Ciudin, Montanu, Son, Maj. Cristopol, Caras, Gurita Stefaniu, Nicolau, Tudoroncescu families, and others. All these, and many others, from whom I received their more than paternal care. Yet my health was not in good shape. My kidneys, chest and knees ached.

Trial date was set for March 14, 1925.

With that in mind, thousands of flyers began to be printed in all university centers as well as in other towns. In Cluj, Capt. Beleuta printed, and distributed throughout the whole country, tens of thousands of such flyers. His home, open day and night to nationalist fighters, was changed into a veritable headquarters. In Orastie, at Father Mota's printing shop, scores of thousands of popular poetry brochures and hundreds of thousands of flyers were printed. Also here my comrades had some of my letters written by me in the Vacaresti prison printed as a brochure titled: Letters of an imprisoned student.

The government came out with contrary subject matter to be spread near and far. But they had no effect whatsoever, for the wave of national feeling grew imposingly and irresistibly. Two days before the trial was to begin, hundreds of people and students from throughout the country began arriving at Focsani. From Iasi alone over three hundred came, taking up a whole train.

I was transported by the authorities in a carriage to the National Theater where the trial was to take place. But this was ordered postponed, though the jury was drawn. They took me back to the prison. But outside, the unjustified postponement of the trial produced a general indignation that quickly changed into an enormous street demonstration that lasted throughout the afternoon and late into the night

The efforts of the army to quell the spirited crowd got nowhere. The demonstration was directed against the Jews and the government. Jews then realized that all their pressures in the case would backfire. This demonstration was overwhelmingly important for the outcome of my trial. It put Jewry out of the fight, because they realized that my being sentenced could have disastrous repercussions against them. Although Jewry did not beat a total retreat, it lessened its pressure on the authorities.

Meanwhile I received the suggestions to petition to be freed and assurances that I would be freed, but I refused to do it.

Easter arrived. I celebrated the Resurrection alone in my cell. When the bells of all the churches in town began pealing, I knelt and prayed for my fiancee and myself, for my mother and mine at home, for the souls of the dead and those fighting outside—that God may bless them, fortify them and grant them victory over all enemies.

At Turnul-Severin

At about two o'clock one night I woke up as someone tried to open the padlock. Prison officials came to fetch me, for unexpectedly my trial was transferred by the government's intervention to Turnul-Severin at the other end of Romania.

I hastily gathered my few belongings; then, surrounded by guards, I was placed in a lorry which took us to the edge of town near a rail line. Shortly thereafter a train stopped and I was put into the Black Maria rail car.

So I was leaving this town of Focsani which at the opportune moment bravely faced the tremendous pressures of officialdom, and whose citizens broke their party ties, or sometimes family ties, to appear in a superb and impregnable unanimity of sentiment.

As I traveled I was wondering what kind of people I should find in Turnul-Severin? I had never been there. I knew no one in that town.

Wherever the train stopped, I heard people talking, laughing, descending or boarding the train, but I was unable to see anything, for the car I was in had no windows. It was only one inch of wall that separated me from the rest of the world, from freedom. Perhaps among those who crossed the tracks out there in those railway-stations there were many who either knew me or were my friends. But they were unaware I was inside that car.

Everybody is headed somewhere. Only I was unaware of where I was headed. All walk lighty and gaily while I carry on my soul, heavier than a millstone, the burden of this immense unknown that awaits me. Shall I be sentenced for life? For less? Shall I ever leave the ugly and black walls of prison or shall it be my fate to die there? I realize full well that my trial is not a matter of justice, it is a question of force; whichever of these two forces is the stronger will win. Will our nationalistic current be stronger or the Judeo-governmental pressure? But, it cannot be like this! Whoever is right shall be stronger and consequently will inevitably win.

And as the train kept rolling I felt my pain more poignantly. My heart was seemingly attached to every stone in Moldavia and as I was leaving everything further and further behind me I felt as if bits of it were gradually being chipped off.

All day I traveled like this, locked alone in a jail car. We reached Balota I believe, toward evening. A gendarme officer accompanied by agents came in and asked me to step out. They led me behind the station where we got in a car and drove off. They seemed to be very good men, trying to strike up a conversation with me, to crack a joke. But I, borne down by other thoughts and needs, was not inclined to converse. I answered them with good will, but briefly.

We entered Turnul-Severin. Driving along several streets I experienced real joy in my heart, and delight, for my eyes again saw people walking the streets.

At the prison gate we stopped. Once again, the padlocked gates opened, to again close behind me.

The warden and personnel received me like an honored guest. The good room they assigned to me had a wooden floor, not a cement one as earlier ones. Here too, detainees approached me as they had in the other prisons, with affection; and I helped them later in their unending material and moral misery.

Next day I stepped out into the courtyard. From there I could see out in the street. Around noon I noticed massed before the prison gates over 200 small children between 6 and 7 years of age, who upon seeing me pass by began waving their tiny hands at me, some using handkerchiefs, some caps. They were school children who heard I had come to Turnul-Severin and was there in prison. Those children were to be there daily from then on to show me their sympathy. They waited for me to pass, to wave their tiny hands.

At the Tribunal, President Varlam, a man of great goodness, treated me very courteously. Less so Prosecutor Constantinescu of whom it was rumored he took it upon himself that together with Prefect Marius Vorvoreanu he would obtain my conviction, but I did not believe it. They were at first rather severe, behind which I detected some meanness. But little by little they were softened up by the wave of public opinion, by the enthusiasm emanating from small children to old folks. At that time everybody was feeling Romanian and saw in our fight a sacred struggle for the future of this country. They were aware of my misfortunes and saw in my gesture a gesture of revolt for human dignity, a gesture that any free man would have made.

These people, descendants of Iancu Jianu and Capt. Tudor Vladimirescu, whose pistols had been brandished in the defense of the nation's honor against the humiliation of centuries, understood readily what happened at Iasi. No argument could budge them. It was in vain that the prosecutor and the prefect shouted. I was surrounded by the affection and care of all the families in town, even of those who played an official role, like that of Mayor Corneliu Radulescu for whom I developed a great admiration; but especially was I surrounded, as nowhere else, by the children's love and understanding for my tribulations. They were the first ones to demonstrate on my behalf in Turnul-Severin. I remember with tenderness how small tots from the suburbs, who hardly knew how to walk, seeing the bigger ones regularly gathering in front of the prison in large numbers, waving their hands, daily began to come also. I watched them assemble from all parts, at a given time, as to a program they had to put on. All of them were quiet and well behaved. They did not play or sing. They just watched, waiting to see me pass by an opening so they could wave at me; then they left for home. They understood that there is something sad in this prison and their common sense told them there was nothing to laugh about here. One day the gendarmes started chasing them away. The following day I no longer saw them. Sentinels were posted to stop them from coming.

The Trial

The date of the trial was set for May 20th.

The Tribunal's president received 19,300 signatures of lawyers wishing to defend me, from all over the country. Two days before the trial, trainloads of students began to arrive. Just as at Focsani the students from Iasi came 300 strong. Likewise the students from Bucharest, Cluj, Cernauti, came in large numbers. Among those who came, there was a Focsani delegation headed by the former jury foreman on March 14, Mihail Caras who now signed up as defender representing the jury from Focsani. Prosecution witnesses also arrived: the policemen of Iasi. The proceedings began in the National Theater, Counselor Varlam presiding. By my side, on the bench of the accused were: Mota, Tudose Popescu, Garneata, Corneliu Georgescu, Radu Mironovici. On the defense bench sat: Professor Cuza, Professor Gavanescul, Paul Iliescu, Professor Sumuleanu, Em. Vasiliu-Cluj, Nicusor Graur, the entire Turnul-Severin bar, etc.

The theater was full to capacity, and around it outside, over 10,000 people were waiting.

The jurors were picked. The following were drawn: N. Palea, G.N. Grigorescu, J. Caluda, I. Preoteasa, G.N. Grecescu, D.I. Bora, V.B. Jujescu, C. Vargatu, C. Surdulescu, Adolf Petayn, P. I. Zaharia, G.N. Boiangiu, I. Munteanu and G.N. lspas. They took the oath and gravely sat in their places. The indictment was read. The interrogation followed. I told things as they had happened. The other five replied to their questioning likewise, telling the truth, namely that they were not at all involved in the case being judged.

The prosecution witnesses were one Jew and the policemen from Iasi. During the proceedings they denied everything. Nothing was true. All beatings, all torturing—pure inventions. They even denied the medical certificates issued by Professor Bogdan, the pathologist.

Their attitude, considering they took an oath upon the cross to tell the truth and only the truth, provoked the indignation of the entire courtroom.

One of the witnesses, Commissar Vasiliu Spanchiu, whom I now saw metamorphosed into the most tender-hearted being, saw nothing, did nothing. Standing up, with the presiding judge's permission, I asked him loudly full of indignation:

"Are you not the one who struck me in the face with your fist, in Mrs. Ghica's garden?"

"I am not."

"Are you not the one who dipped the students' heads into pails of water while they, hung head down, had the soles of their feet whipped?"

"I was not there at the time. I was downtown."

On his face, in all his gestures, by his whole behavior, one could see he was lying; though he swore on the cross, he lied. The entire crowd in the theater was seething with indignation. Suddenly, as if the collective fury of the crowd willed it, a man in the audience jumped up, lifted the commissar up in his arms and bodily carried him out. It was Mr. Tilica Ioanid. We heard him shout as he pushed the commissar down the back steps:

"Get out of here, scoundrel, for we do not guarantee your life!" Returning, he told the other commissars from Iasi: "With your own hands you have savagely tortured these children. Had you done something like this here in Turnul-Severin people would have slaughtered you. Your presence in this town stains it; leave on the first train, otherwise misfortune will befall you."

As a matter of fact this gesture was welcome, for people were upset. It relaxed the whole tense atmosphere.

The torturers were humiliated, and now as they walked, they greeted people by bowing to the ground, begging for the minutest sign of attention from the most humble carrier of the tricolor band.

"As if we are not good Romanians! What were we to do? We received orders."

"No! Scoundrels! You had not the heart of a parent, nor the heart of a Romanian. You had no honor, nor respect for the law. You say you had orders? No! You had traitors' hearts." This is how people told them off on the streets.

Then for about two days followed depositions of defense witnesses among whom was the elderly Professor Ion Gavanescul of the University of Iasi, himself manhandled by Prefect Manciu at the Congress of the University Professors over which he presided; also officers of the Military Lycee and School of Infantry, my former superiors and teachers. Then victims and parents testified, re-enacting before the judges, and almost in tears, the painful scenes of humiliation to which they had been subjected.

The civilian observer was Mr. Costa-Foru, the head of a Masonic lodge in the capital.

Defense lawyers spoke in the following sequence: Paul Iliescu, Tache Policrat, Valer Roman, Valer Pop, Sandu Bacaloglu, Em. Vasiliu-Cluj, Cananau, Donca Manea, Mitulescu, Virgil Neta, Neagu Negrilesti, Henrietta Gavrilescu, Professor Dr. Sumuleanu, Professor Ion Gavanescul, and Professor A.C. Cuza.

Brief statements were then given by Mihail Caras, Col. Vasilescu Lascar, the old priest Dumitrescu from Bucharest, Col. Catuneanu; by Ion Sava, Dr. Istrate, I. Rob, Dragos, Ion Blanaru, and Camenita, representing the students of Iasi, Cluj, Cernauti, Bucharest, Falciu County, and Turnul-Severin respectively; Navy Capt. Manolescu, Alexandru Ventonic for the Christian merchants of Iasi; then Costica Ungureanu, Petru Vasiliu, Grecea, Capt. Peteu-Ploesti, war invalid, and M. Negru-Chisinau.

It was I who took the floor last. I said:

> "Gentlemen of the jury. Everything we have fought for was out of faith and love for our country and the Romanian people. We assume the obligation to fight to the end. This is my last word."

This was in the sixth day of my trial, May 26, 1925.

All six of us were taken to a room, there to await the verdict. We were not overly excited, but somewhat, just the same. Several minutes later we heard thunderous applause, shouting and hurrahs, coming from the large hall. We had no time to reflect upon this for the doors opened and the crowd took us into the meeting hall. When we appeared, carried on their shoulders, everybody stood in acclaim and fluttered their handkerchiefs.

Presiding Judge Varlam too, was seized by the wave of enthusiasm he could not resist. The jurors were all at their places, this time wearing tricolor lapel ribbons with swastikas.

As soon as the verdict of acquittal was read to us, I was carried on shoulders outside where there were over ten thousand people assembled. They all fell into a column carrying us on their shoulders along the streets while people on the sidewalks showered us with flowers. When we reached Mr. Tilica loanid's home I addressed the people from his balcony in a few words expressing my gratitute to the Romanians of Turnul-Severin for the great love they showed me during the trial.

Returning To Iasi

After I thanked several families in Turnul-Severin by visiting them, for the manner they adopted toward me, I boarded the next day a special train for Iasi. The special train was not for me, but for the over 300 Iasians who came to the trial, to which were hooked up the cars of the Focsanians, Barladians and Vasluians.

Thousands of people came to the station to see us off and decorate our train with flowers.

The train left. Behind, the multitude fluttered handkerchiefs expressing its love and wish to continue the fight by "hurrahs" that made the air reverberate. From my window I was watching that large crowd of people, none of whom I had known before, but that now parted from us with tears in their eyes as if they had known us for years. Inwardly I prayed, thanking the Lord for the victory He gave us.

It was only now, as I passed from car to car, that I could see again my comrades from Iasi, talking to each and rejoicing together that God made us victorious, saving us from the threat from which all our enemies thought I would not be able to escape.

In one compartment I encountered Professor Cuza, and Professor and Mrs. Sumuleanu. They were contented, being surrounded by our love.

All the compartments were beautifully bedecked with flowers and greenery. And at the first stop out of Turnul-Severin a new mountain of flowers was brought—to our great surprise—by peasants with their priests, by teachers with their school children, all of them dressed in national costumes.

There were many people in each railway station awaiting the arrival of the train. These were not like the cold, official receptions. It was neither duty, nor fear, nor self-interest that brought those people out.

I saw old folks at the edges of some crowds who cried. Wonder why? They knew no one on the train. It seemed that an unknown force compelled them to come, mysteriously whispering to them: "Go to the depot, for among all the trains that pass by, there is one that goes on the line of Romanian destiny. All the rest run for the interests of those riding them, save this one that runs on the people's course, for the people." Crowds sometimes establish contact with the soul of the people. A moment of vision. Multitudes see the nation, with its dead and all its past; feel all its glorious moments as well as those of defeat. They can feel the future seething. This touch with the whole immortal and collective soul of the nation is feverish, full of trembling. When this happens, crowds cry. This perhaps is the national mystique that some criticize because they do not know what it is and which others cannot define because they cannot experience it.

If Christian mystique aiming at ecstasy is man's contact with God, through a "jump from human nature into the divine one" (Crainic[3]), national mystique is nothing more than man's contact, or that of the multitude, with the soul of their people, through a jump outside of personal preoccupations into the eternal life of the people. Not intellectually, for this could be done by any historian, but living, with their souls.

When the train, all decked out with flags and greenery, stopped at Craiova, the station's platform was crowded by more than 10,000 people. We were carried on shoulders behind the depot where we were welcomed by one of the townsmen. Professor Cuza spoke. And myself, briefly.

We were received like that at all the stations, large and small, but especially in the towns of Piatra-Olt, Slatina and Pitesti. Though there were no nationalist organizations in most of these towns along the railway, and no one put out any flyers to call out people to the stations, the platforms were all full of thousands of people to greet us.

It was about 8 o'clock in the evening when we arrived in Bucharest. Again, I was lifted up, triumphantly carried on shoulders through the station to the front, where the whole square was a sea of heads that extended along Grivita Way, way beyond the Polytechnical School. There must have been over 50,000 people, showing an enthusiasm that could not be dampened by anything. Professor Cuza addressed them. Then I.

3 Nichifor Crainic (1889-1972), Romanian journalist, theologian, philosopher. (Tr.)

As a matter of fact throughout the entire country there prevailed such a powerful patriotic current that it could have led L.A.N.C. into power. But these propitious, tactical, politically great moments, which this movement would never see again, were not seized upon.

Professor Cuza did not know how to take advantage of a great tactical opportunity which is so rarely encountered by political movements.

In the eyes of any objective observer familiar with political clashes, L.A.N.C.'s fate was sealed at that moment.

We left. All night people met us at stops. There were over 1,000 in Focsani at 3 o'clock in the morning who had been waiting since 4 o'clock the previous afternoon. They wanted us to stop there for one day. But we kept on going.

A delegation made up of Hristache Solomon, Aristotel Gheorghiu, Georgica Niculescu and others, boarded the train. They told me: "Since we did not have the good fortune to host your trial in our town, you must have your wedding in Focsani. On June 14, early in the morning, you must be in Focsani. Everything will be taken care of." The delegation left the train at Marasesti after I promised that I'd be in Focsani as planned.

We arrived at Iasi in the morning, exceedingly tired. Students and townspeople were at the station. They carried us on their shoulders through the city to the university. There we were met by cordons of gendarmes. The crowd broke through and entered the university taking us into the amphitheater. There, Professor Cuza spoke, after which people dispersed peacefully. Everybody went to his home. I revisited the little house on Flowers St. that I had left eight months earlier. Next day I left for Husi, where my mother was expecting me, crying in the doorway.

Several days later, at the City Hall, my civil marriage was performed.

Corneliu Zelea Codreanu with his wife Elena Ilinoiu.

JUNE 1925 - JUNE 1926

My Wedding

Accompanied by my mother, father, brothers and sisters, the bride and in-laws, I left on June 13th for Focsani. There, we were guests in Gen. Macridescu's home. We were informed that evening by the wedding's organization committee which paid us a visit, that everything was ready and that already over 30,000 people had arrived from other towns who were all quartered, with more coming that night; that all inhabitants of Focsani received these guests with joy and happily put them up.

A horse was brought to me the next morning according to our old popular tradition—as called for in the program—and after I rode by the bride's house, I led a column to the Crang (Grove) outside of town.

On both sides of the road there were people, children in the trees even. Following behind me were the god-parents riding in ornate carriages: Professor Cuza and Gen. Macridescu, Hristache Solomon, Col. Cambureanu, Tudoroncescu, Georgica Niculescu, Maj. Bagulescu, and others. The bride's wagon came next, drawn by six oxen and bedecked with flowers, followed by the wagons of the guests, in all, there were a total of 2,300 wagons, carriages and cars all embellished with flowers and the people dressed in national costumes. I reached the Crang, better than four miles from Focsani, and the tail end of the column had not yet left Focsani.

The wedding ceremony took place on a platform, especially built for that purpose. There were between 80,000 to 100,000 people present. After the religious ceremony we danced the hora and other national dances, and the celebration continued with a banquet on the grass. The inhabitants of Focsani brought provisions for themselves and also for the out-of town guests.

The entire festivity with the great display of national costumes, bedecked wagons, with its dancing and enthusiasm, was filmed.

Corneliu Codreanu greeted by crowds for his wedding at Focsani 1925.

Several weeks later it was shown in movie houses in Bucharest, but only twice, because the Ministry of Internal Affairs confiscated the film and the one copy, and burned them.

The celebration ended toward evening in a general feeling of brotherhood and animation. Together with my wife and a few comrades I left for Baile Herculane that night, where we spent two weeks with a family of old friends, the S. Martalog's.

Mota, on his part, went to Iasi to commence digging the foundation of the Christian Cultural Home on the lot donated by engineer Grigore Bejan.

The Baptismal Ceremony At Ciorasti

On August 10 at Ciorasti near Focsani I stood as godfather at the baptism of 100 babies who were born that month in the county of Putna and vicinity.

The baptism was to take place in Focsani. But the government in order to prevent it decreed a state of siege there. After overcoming many obstacles we retreated to Ciorasti where we succeeded in performing the baptism of the infants under the shadow of bayonets.

After One Year, Work Resumes

I returned to Iasi to work by the side of my comrades to build our Home. We pursued the old plan of building as well as that of organizing the youth, which had been interrupted by fate for nearly one whole year.

Donations began to come in. The Moruzzi family of Dorohoi contributed 100,000 lei; Gen. Cantacuzino donated three freight cars of cement; the Romanians in America, through the paper *Libertatea* ("Liberty") contributed over 400,000 lei. Peasants from the remotest villages in Transylvania, Bucovina, Basarabia sent in some from their meager means to the "House in Iasi," as they affectionately called it.

All these contributions were pouring in by virtue of the sympathy our movement enjoyed at that time in all social strata. Pictures showing how students and coeds were building their own home stirred especially a great enthusiasm. This was something totally new, which had not been seen before either in our country or abroad. This activity generated so much sympathy in Iasi, that when office workers left work at the end of the day, they came to the building site, took off their coats and grabbed the shovel, pickaxe or the cement wheelbarrow. Students from Cluj, Basarabia and Bucovina, Bucharest, met there at this kind of work. Brotherhoods of the Cross had by now been organized in many cities under Mota's supervision so that young high school students were coming there from all over to work, returning home educated in our spirit.

Two years of student struggle, of agitation and suffering, common to all the youth of Romania, had brought about a great miracle: a re-establishment of the nation's spiritual unity which had been threatened by the incapacity of the old generation to fuse and become one with the great national community.

Now the youth, gathered from all parts of the country, was consolidating and sanctifying this unity of soul through its common efforts, in the school of work, for our country.

Dangers That Threaten A Political Movement

This current now throughout the whole country was formidable. I do not believe that a popular current as unanimous as this had existed in the country many times before. Yet, the League was not doing well, for lack of organization, lack of a plan of action. There existed, in addition, as a result of this great current, the threat that some compromising and dangerous elements might infiltrate the movement. A movement never dies under the blows of the enemy without, but because of the enemies within, like any human organism. Normally, only about one human being in a million dies of external causes (run over by a train or a car, shot to death, drowning, etc.); man succumbs to internal toxins, he dies poisoned.

As it was, in the wake of the Vacaresti, Focsani and Turnul-Severin trials, anyone who wished could join our ranks. Some joined to engage in swindling: collecting subscriptions, sales of brochures, loans, etc. and no matter where these characters appeared they invariably compromised the movement; others, who joined as political climbers, began fighting and telling on each other, each vying for the leadership position or for a seat in Parliament, etc. Others were of good faith but lacked discipline, refusing to obey orders from their superiors; these people interminably haggled over each directive, each acting on his own. Others, again having joined our ranks in good faith, were simply incapable of integrating themselves into our spirit.

There are many very good individuals possessed of such a moral structure that they just cannot merge into an organization like ours and therefore endanger its very existence from the inside. Some are intriguers by birth; whatever they join, they destroy by tale-bearing. Certain others have a fixed idea; they honestly believe they have found the key to all solutions, seeking to convince you of their worth. Others are ill, afflicted with the malady of journalism. They wish, at any price, to be newspaper directors or to see their name printed at the end of some article. There are others who act in such a way that no matter where they go they succeed in compromising the whole fight and in eroding the trust the organization enjoyed there. Finally, there are some who are specifically paid to engage in intrigue, in espionage, and will compromise any noble endeavor of the nationalist movement.

How much care, how much circumspection, then, must be

exercised by the head of a movement with respect to those wanting to come under his leadership! How much he must do to educate them and how much untiring supervision he must exercise over them! Without these precautions a movement is irremediably compromised. Regretfully, Professor Cuza was totally unaware of these imperatives. His slogan was: "In the League anyone can come in, but only he who is able stays in." And this attitude was to bring a real disaster. In fact several months later the League became a cauldron of intrigues, a real hell.

My belief at that time, which I still hold today, was that an organization must not permit "whoever wishes" to come in, but only whoever "deserves to join," and allow to remain in it only those—and only for as long as they are—correct, hard working, disciplined and faithful.

If signs of gangrene such as those mentioned above appear to be evident in an organization, they must be immediately isolated, then extirpated most energetically. If not, the infection spreads like a cancer throughout the entire organism of the movement, and the cause is lost. Its mission and future being compromised; it will either die, or drag out its days between life and death, incapable of accomplishing anything.

Our efforts to move Professor Cuza to remedy this situation failed, because, on the one hand he was totally unaware of these elementary principles of leading a movement, and on the other because the intrigues succeeded in isolating us, too, from him, and consequently began to paralyze any influence we might have had upon him.

We, the Vacarestians, realizing this, and seeing the desperate assaults, the waves of intrigue battering us, aimed at splitting us from Professor Cuza, went to his home, again swearing allegiance to him and asking him to trust us that we would do everything in our power to redress the state of affairs within the movement.

Our attempt proved futile, for he noticed that we saw things in an entirely different light both with respect to organization and to a plan of action, and even with respect to the fundamental doctrine of our movement. We started from the idea of man's moral worth, not as a numerical, electoral or democratic digit. But he was convinced that we maintained such an idea because we were the victims of some intriguers.

The Critique of the Leader

Who was responsible for this state of affairs? The leader of course. Such a movement has to have a great leader, not a brilliant doctrinaire who remains oblivious to the waves of the movement down below; an imposing leader, to dominate and control the movement.

Not everybody can fill this function. A professional is needed, a man possessing inborn qualities, a connoisseur not only of principles of organization, but also of development and fighting. It is not enough to be a renowned university professor to be in command of such a movement.

Here is needed a good helmsman, an accomplished skipper to lead us over the waves, a man to know the law and to be familiar with the secret of such leadership; who would know the winds and the depths of the sea, who should be familiar with dangerous reefs, who finally would hold the helm with a firm hand.

It is not enough that a man proving that Transylvania belongs to the Romanians is entitled therefore to assume command of the troops setting out to conquer it; just as the fact that he can theoretically demonstrate the existence of a Jewish peril is not sufficient for him to be entitled to take command of a popular political movement that proposes to solve this problem.

There are two levels of activity here, totally differing, levels demanding aptitudes and qualifications that are totally opposite in the involved individuals.

We can imagine the first level up high at 1,000 yards. The domain of theory, the abstract field of laws. There, the theoretician engages in researching truth and its theoretical formulation. He begins at the bottom from concrete realities, from the ground up climbing to formulate laws there in his creative domain.

The other level is down on the earth. Here, the man who is endowed with leadership qualities engages in the art of imposing truth by the play of forces. He reaches for the heights in order to be in harmony with the laws, but his place of accomplishment is down here on the battlefield, in the area of strategy and tactics.

The former creates ideals, delineates objectives; the latter realizes, fulfils them. By virtue of the natural principle of the division of labor, the exceptions in which the qualities of these two functions are found in a single individual are extremely rare.

Professor Cuza is above all else a theoretician. On the theoretical plane he shines like the sun. His work is the following:

a) Research and formulation of the truth of the law of nationality.

b) Discovery and perfect identification of the enemy of nationality: the Jew.

c) Postulating solutions to the Jewish problem.

That is all! However, this is a colossal accomplishment. For, though all scientific evidence is on his side, all men of science are against him, striking at him from all directions and trying to topple his findings. But he resists.

This first level does not require the use of men, of human forces; on the contrary, the man on the first plane shuns people.

But the second plane demands first of all, people. Just any people? Certainly not! But people whom the leader must change into human forces.

That means:

1. Knowing how to organize them according to certain rigid principles.

2. Giving them a technical and heroic education in order to augment their power, namely to change men into human power.

3. Leading these forces, now organized and educated, onto the strategic and tactical field of battle to fight other human forces, or nature itself in order to attain a useful aim.

If the doctrinaire is expected to master the science of researching and formulating truth, the leader of a political movement is expected to *master the science and the art of organization, education and leadership of men.*

Professor Cuza, excelling and unsurpassed on the first plane, when brought down on the practical one showed himself ignorant, awkward, naive as a child, incapable either of organizing or of technically and heroically educating his followers, incapable, in other words, of leading human forces.

A man who is illustrious on the theoretical plane will never be able to score a victory on the second plane. He will be vanquished or, at best, he will be content with small successes obtained for him by those around him.

Which are the characteristic spiritual traits that the leader of a political movement must possess? In my opinion they are:

1. *An inner power of attraction.* There are no independent, free people in the world. Just as in the solar system each star follows its own orbit on which it turns around a greater power of attraction, likewise people, particularly in the field of political action, gravitate around some attracting personalities. It is the same in the realm of thought. On the outside remain those who neither want to show an interest nor to think.

A leader must have such a power of attraction. Some have it over ten people, being thus leaders for them only; others over a whole village, a county; others over an entire province, country; and some even outside the boundaries of a single country. The individual's capacity to lead is limited by the extent of his inner power of attraction. It is sort of a magnetic force which if not possessed by a man, renders him incapable of leading.

2. *Capacity for love.* A leader must love all his comrades-in-arms. His love must penetrate to the edges of a movement's community.

3. *Knowledge and sense of organizing.* People attracted within the orbit of a movement must be organized.

4. *Knowledge of people.* While organizing, one must take into account the principle of the division of labor, using each in his place, according to his aptitudes and refusing to accept anyone lacking them.

5. *The power to educate and to inspire heroism.*

6. *Mastering the laws of leadership.* When a chief has an organized

and educated troop, he must know how to lead it into the political battlefield to compete with the other forces.

7. *A sense of timing.* A chief must have a special sense to indicate to him when to wage a battle. An inner intuition must tell him: Now! This minute, neither later nor sooner.

8. *Courage.* When a leader hears that inner command he must have the courage to draw out his sword.

9. *The conscience of just and moral objectives to be pursued by honest means.* In addition to all the virtues of a soldier that a leader must possess, spirit of sacrifice, resistance, devotion, etc., he must be animated by a spirit of high morality, for there is no lasting victory if it is not based on justice and legality.

A Case Of Conscience

In fact Professor Cuza was not responsible for the chaotic situation in which the League floundered. When he opposed our efforts to organize, he had, I believe, the clear conscience of his theoretical competence and of his lack of power on the political plane. It was we who were responsible and especially myself, for we forced him against his will to engage in an action in which he was weak. As a matter of fact he had been absent from all important events that took place during those two years of struggle. All the fights that had shaken the whole country and roused the Romanian masses, had been initiated without the help of Professor Cuza. In each of them he was of great help, certainly, but always toward the end—the initiative did not belong to him.

I had erred; and as there is no mistake that does not soon turn against those who committed it, my mistake too, will turn on us as on the movement. And this will happen when Professor Cuza, incapable of understanding us, will be working alone, without our support.

This year was a difficult one for him too. After 30 years of dedication at the University of Iasi, the government committed the unheard-of inequity of deposing him from his chair. When, at the summary investigation that was made he was accused of instigating the students, Professor Cuza replied:

"I am an instigator of the national energies."

A lifetime of fighting and of illustrious teaching in the service of the Romanian nation was ended by such a reward on the part of the people led by the Judeo-politicians.

To this low blow was added also the fact that being alone on the street he was provoked and struck in the face by a Jew's fist. When such outrageous daring became known, students went into all pubs, and struck in the same manner every Jew they met. On the occasion of that demonstration, ten students were arrested, Mota and Iulian Sarbu included, who were sentenced to one month in jail. They served it in Galata. Urziceanu, a student, took several shots at the individual suspected of being the moral instigator of the insulting act of violence.

In France, At School

The Departure and First Stage in Strasburg

On Sept. 23, 1925 we laid the cornerstone of our student home. The walls were about three feet up when, considering that I had given to our nationalist movement all that I could at my age, I thought it opportune to go abroad again in order to complete my education, the more so as my health was not in very good shape as a result of the difficult trials I had gone through.

I was prodded towards this decision also by the fact that I felt somewhat isolated in my opinions regarding the League's organization and plans of combat. I was telling myself: "It is possible that I am wrong and it would be better for me not to hinder the development of a point of view that might, after all, prove to be a good one," especially in view of the fact that lately the League had acquired new strength (1) by uniting with "Romanian Action" led by Professor Catuneanu, which brought to our side such eminent intellectuals from Transylvania as Valer Pop and Father Titus Malai; and (2) by joining forces with "The National Fascia" a smaller but healthy organization. Hopefully, the innocent shortcomings of the League's leadership would now be remedied by the presence of so many elite men, among which one could count: our lawyer Paul Iliescu from Bucharest with a notable following of intellectuals; Gen. Macridescu, heading another elite group from Focsani; the distinguished professor of sociology from the University of Cernauti, an old nationalist, Traian Braileanu; and the illustrious professor of pedagogy Ion Gavanescul from the University of Iasi, who up to now had not joined our movement though he too had been preaching the national idea for a lifetime from his chair of pedagogy.

Now with us also was the erudite professor of physiology Nicolae Paulescu at the University of Bucharest, connoisseur without equal of Judeo-Masonic manipulations, who illumined the national movement in the capital.

To these personalities who honored our movement and imparted to it an unsurpassed prestige was added the precious aid of *Libertatea* ("Liberty"), the most widely read and appreciated Romanian popular newspaper, edited by Father Mota.

My comrade Mota—Father Mota's son—who was expelled from the University of Cluj, only a sophomore, had decided to go abroad along with me to finish his law studies.

We both agreed to go to France to one of the smaller towns. We chose Grenoble. I had 60,000 lei from the sales of my pamphlet *Letters of An Imprisoned Student*, and from wedding presents; Mota had help from home, monthly.

After saying goodbye to our families at home, we paid our respects to Professor Cuza and to our comrades. Then we went up Rarau Mountain to the hermitage to pray, and began our trip. My wife and I left first. Mota followed two weeks later.

After a long journey through Czechoslovakia and Germany followed by several days' stay in Berlin and Jena, we entered France and stopped at Strasburg. What surprised me exceedingly was the fact that this city, contrary to all my expectations, had changed into a real wasps' nest of Jewish infection.

Stepping off the train I expected to see people of the Gallic race that with its unequalled bravery had marked history's centuries.

Instead, I saw the Jew with his aquiline nose, thirsty for profit, who pulled me by the sleeve to enter either his store or his restaurant, the majority of restaurants around the railway station being run by them. In the France of the assimilated Jew everything was kosher. We entered restaurant after restaurant in order to find a Christian one, but in each we saw the sign in Yiddish: "Kosher food." Finally we found a French restaurant, where we ate.

We found no difference between the Targul-Cucului Jews and those of Strasburg; the same figure, the same manners and jargon; the same Satanic eyes in which one read and discovered under the polite look, the avidity to jip one.

At Grenoble

One more night of travelling and we arrived at Grenoble in the morning. What wonders opened to our eyes! What scenery! A city situated for ages of time at the foot of the Alps. A huge rock advanced toward the center of the city as if to cut it in two. Gray, rugged and bold, it dominated the houses, which, though many-storied, seemed like little ant-hills by contrast.

Further away, but also near the city, there was another mountain full of old fortifications, trenches and parapets, that had been transformed into one immense fortress. Far away in the background, above all these, white as honor, the snow shone winter and summer over the imposing massive Alps.

Awed by what we saw, and walking as through an enchanted castle in some tale, I was telling myself: "This is the city of bravery." And sure enough, as I continued to walk, I was certain I was right, for stopping before a statue I read: "Bayard, chevalier sans peur et sans reproche." Bayard was a great epic warrior in the fifteenth century, who, after a lifetime of battles, was mortally wounded and lay dying, holding his sword whose handle now was transformed into a cross from which the brave old man was receiving in the hour of his death, the last benediction.

We rented a room in old Grenoble. There is also a new, modern Grenoble. But we liked the old section better.

Mota arrived a little later. We registered at the university. He, for his bachelor of law degree; I, as a candidate for the doctoral degree in economy. I began auditing freshman and sophomore courses, but I understood absolutely nothing. These were the first lessons. I could make out only isolated words. However, doggedly continuing to audit these courses, towards Christmas, I began to understand the lectures quite well. There were only eight doctoral candidates and that is why these classes developed a familiar character of close bond between student and professor. The professors, extremely conscientious, did only teaching, not politicking too. Meals for all three of us were prepared by my wife.

On holidays I began to make small excursions around the city. I was impressed by castle ruins and old towers. Wonder who lived in these of old? They must have been forgotten by everyone. Let me go pay them a visit. I entered such ruins and stood there for hours in undisturbed quiet, talking with the dead.

I visited a little old church on the edge of town dating back to the fourth century, St. Lawrence Church, and to my astonishment I saw on its blue tinted ceiling more than fifty swastikas.

In the city, on the Prefecture Building, the Palace of Justice and other institutions, one could see the Masonic star, the symbol of the absolute control of this Jewish hydra over France. That is why I retreated into the quarter of old Grenoble, where the churches with their crosses were darkened by age and forgetfulness. I turned my back on modern movie houses, theaters and cafes, finding enjoyment among ruins where I suspected Bayard may have lived. I sank myself into the past where, to my great happiness, I lived in the historic France, in Christian France, in nationalist France, not in the Judeo-Masonic, atheistic and cosmopolitan France but in that of Bayard! Not in Leon Blum's France!

The square "Marche des puces" as Frenchmen called it, was full of Jews, which accounted for her name. In fact the university too was overwhelmed by them. There were 50 Jewish students from Romania alone studying here, in addition to the five Romanians.

I also visited the ancient monastery, "Grande Chartreuse," whose 1,000 monks were chased out by the atheistic government. On various icons I could still see the marks of the stones thrown by the mob during the French Revolution (1789), when they mutilated the image of God.

It was not too long before material worries came over us. My money was getting low and I did not expect any from back home. In spite of all the severe economizing, we could not manage on what Mota alone received. We spent many hours thinking how we could earn some money without disrupting the schedules of our course work.

Realizing that needlework is appreciated and well paid in France, we decided to learn from my wife embroidering and then try to sell these Romanian embroideries.

We learned this trade in the course of several weeks. We embroidered in our free time, had our products exhibited in a store window and, adding the little we thus earned to what Mota received from home, we managed to live very modestly.

General Elections Back Home May 1926

Around Eastertime, letters and newspapers from back home that we regularly received brought news of the fall of the Liberals from power and the advent of Gen. Averescu. The new general elections were to take place around the middle of May.

For the League this was the opportunity to engage for the first time in a great battle. I was telling myself:

> "I must go home to take part in this fight. And then come back to my studies."

I wrote to Professor Cuza, asking him for fare money. Receiving no reply I then wrote to Mr. Hristache Solomon in Focsani. He sent me 10,000 lei out of which I left a portion with my wife. With the rest I left for home.

I arrived in Bucharest around the beginning of May during the full electoral campaign. I went immediately to Professor Cuza who did not appear very glad to see me there, telling me there was no need for me to come for the movement could do well, even without me. This hurt me a bit but I did not get angry. There is no room in a political organization for a member who gets angry for being admonished by the leader. The admonishing may or may not be justified, yet one should never get angry; this is the principle that must guide a man in any organization.

Then I left for the county of Dorohoi to assist Professor Sumuleanu. From there I went on into other counties, Campul-Lung, Iasi, Braila, etc.

Meanwhile, as a result of a letter I received from Professor Paulescu and at the further insistence of Gen. Macridescu, I decided to run myself in Focsani. There I was, in the most disgusting and by me unwanted predicament: to go out begging for votes for myself. Where?

Among the crowds, who, right at the time when they ought to have been inspired by the most sacred sentiments—for one dealt with his country and its future—is dazed by the abundantly-offered drinks by electoral agents, and is possessed by the passions unleashed by the evil spirit of the politicians. In these moments, over the serene and clean life into villages there descend the flood tides of political corruption. This hell spreads throughout the whole country and from it emerges the next leadership of the country for one, two, three or four years. It is from this heap of putrefaction that democracy — "holy" democracy — produces the leadership of a country!

I arrived at Focsani which had been under a state of siege ever since the Ciorasti baptisms. In order to be able to go on the campaign trail, one had to have a pass for free passage, issued by the garrison commander, which I requested and received. Around 10 o'clock in the morning, accompanied by Mr. Hristache Solomon and others, we left in two cars. But 500 yards outside of town we ran into a barricade of two wagons placed across the road, with nearby, several gendarmes. We stopped. The gendarmes came to us and told us we were not allowed to pass. I produced the general's order and showed it to them. They read it and then said:

"Even so, you cannot pass."

I ordered my companions to open the road. Following a brief scuffle, the road was passable. The cars started moving slowly. The gendarmes, several yards behind us, knelt, aimed and began firing. I said:

"Keep moving, they are shooting in the air."

One bullet hit a fender; another, close to us. We continued driving. But two bullets stopped us, one punctured the gas tank, the second a tire. We could not continue driving. We got out and walked back.

Again, we went to the general who had issued our free passage permit, and reported what happened, Gen. Macridescu also being present. He replied:

> "You are free to travel. I ordered no one to stop you. Perhaps it was the administrative authorities."

From there we went to the Prefecture together with Gen. Macridescu. The county prefect was Nitulescu, a surly and rough man. Very calm, we entered his office. Gen. Macridescu related the events. But the prefect, from the very first moment treated us in a very uncivil manner. He began to deliver an interminable speech from his lofty position.

"Gentlemen, the superior interests of the State demand..."

"There are laws in this country; we are within the laws. We have the right..." Gen. Macridescu tries to explain. But the prefect continued:

"The country demands in these difficult times..."

Gen. Macridescu tried again to explain. The prefect authoritatively:

"The will of the country is..."

"Listen here, Mr. Prefect," I broke in, quite upset. "I see that you do not wish to understand reasonable talk. Tomorrow morning, I shall leave on the campaign trail and if the gendarmes fire on us again, I will come back here into your office and I'll fire on you."

And without: waiting for a reply. I turned around, leaving the others behind. Several hours later I was summoned to the Council of War. I went. A royal commissar[1] interrogated me. I declared in writing exactly what happened. They arrested me. And I said:

"Well gentlemen, you do nothing to those who actually fired at me yet I, who only said I would fire, you arrest!"

So, there I was again, in an incarceration room of a regiment's barracks.

Three days later I was called in by the general. An officer led me into his office:

"Mr. Codreanu, you must leave the town of Focsani."

"Sir, I am a candidate here. Your ordering me to leave is against the law. Certainly, I shall not oppose this measure because I cannot do so, but I ask that you give me this order in writing."

"I cannot put it in writing."

1 Army officer who in Romanian military justice fulfills the role of an investigating judge or prosecutor in the Council of War. (Tr.)

"Then I shall leave for Bucharest to complain about this treatment."

The general let me go free asking for my word of honor that I would leave on the first train out. And I did leave for Bucharest on the first train.

Next day I presented myself to Mr. Octavian Goga, the Minister of Internal Affairs, who received me well. I related to him what happened to me and demanded justice.

He promised me he would send out an administrative inspector to investigate the case and asked me to come see him again the following day. I came. He put me off till the next day. But, as time was running out and the election day was drawing near, on the fourth day I left.

Again I took a free passage permit from the general and again we started out driving. There were only two days left before elections.

We reached the first village where there were a few villagers gathered together as on the eve of any election, but they seemed frightened by the prevailing general terror. The gendarmes showed up:

"You are permitted to talk to these people, but only for one minute. This is our order!"

I spoke for one minute and then we went on. It was the same in all the other villages only for a minute in each. Pity justice and legality in this country! One is given the privilege of voting, one is called upon to exercise this privilege; if you don't show up to vote, you are fined and if you do show up to vote, you are beaten. Romanian politicians, be they Liberals, supporters of Averescu, National-Peasants, are only a band of tyrants who behind slogans like: "Legality," "Freedom," "The rights of man," shamelessly and fearlessly trample underfoot a whole country with all its laws, all its freedoms, and all its rights. What possible recourse is left us, I wonder, for the future?

On election day our delegates were beaten, covered with blood and otherwise prevented from getting to polling places; whole villages could not get near polling stations. The result: I lost, though in the town of Focsani I won over all the political parties.

"No matter," I told myself. "Had I won, it would have disrupted my plans for continuing my studies."

Two days later I learned to my great joy the election result nationwide. The League totaled 120,000 votes and sent into Parliament ten deputies: Professors Cuza and Gavanescul from Iasi; Professor Sumuleanu from Dorohoi; my father from Radauti; Paul Iliescu from Campul-Lung; Professor Calan from Suceava; Dr. Haralamb Vasiliu from Botosani; Valer Pop from Satu-Mare; engineer Misu Florescu from Piatra-Neamt; and Iuniu Lecca from Bacau. Truly an elite corps of men had been elected who honored the nationalist movement, men whom people looked upon with a boundless love and lively hopes. Those 120,000 votes represented the best and purest in the Romanian nation. Voters overcame all threats, all enticements, all obstacles in order to reach the voting booths. But those who could not reach them were very numerous—more than those who made it. There were at least another 120,000 votes that had either been stopped or stolen from the ballot box.

I went back to France, satisfied with the results, but constantly haunted by the following question: How could we win if all administrations conducted elections in such a manner, using corruption, theft and the state's force against popular will?

In The Alps

Arrived in France, I was too late to take my exams in the June session. I was faced with a grave problem. Mota would have to return home to fulfill his military service in the fall. How were we going to make a living when from our embroidery work we could provide hardly enough for one individual, let alone for two souls... I tried to find some work in the city, anything at all. Impossible. Then I thought perhaps out in the country, near town, I might be able to secure something. Together with Mota I went in several directions in search of work; but in the evening we came back unsuccessful.

One day we took the tram to Uriage-les-Bains some six miles from Grenoble (There, streetcars run not only in the cities but outside as far as 12 miles in all directions, for there is abundant electrical energy generated by the waterfalls in the mountains).

From Uriage we followed some paths up the mountain. After about a half hour we got to Saint Martin, quite a large village with a well-paved road through it, well cared-for stone houses, several stores and a beautiful tall church. But we passed on. After another hour of walking, climbing constantly in heat that made us sweat, we arrived in a small hamlet, Pinet-d'Uriage.

We were at an altitude of approximately 2,600-2,700 feet. Above us the Alps offered our eyes an admirable prospect as they were covered with snow. It seemed that the snow started but a few miles from where we were. On our left, toward the Chateau de Vizille a beautiful valley stretched out; toward Grenoble to our right, another one; and along the valley the paved road meandering down shone like the water of a river bathed in the sun.

On the fields we could see the people working. We were wondering how there, on the slope of the mountain, but a few miles from perpetual snows, wheat could grow as tall as a man; or oats and barley, as well as all kinds of vegetables. Probably because of the milder climate and a rock-free soil. In fact their soil was of low fertility, even poor. But farmers continually used manure or fertilizer.

As we saw them working their fields we were faced with the same problem as in the other villages: how could we get into conversation with them to tell them we were looking for work. We passed them by not daring to talk to them. Further up there were some more houses, five or six. We went there. We got to the last one. Beyond it, no other human habitation appeared between us and the massive Beldona, except for tourist cabins. Nearby an old man was mowing. We had to speak to him. We greeted him and began talking. He realized we were foreigners, consequently asked us what we were. We told him we were Romanians, that we liked it here very much and we wanted to rent a room to spend several months in the clean air. The old man was boastful, and probably thinking he found somebody from whom he could learn many things, asked us to come and join him and sit at the outside table on which he placed a bottle of black, astringent wine and three glasses which he filled. Then he began questioning us, following our answers with great curiosity:

"So you say you are Romanians?"

"Yes, Romanians, Romanians from Romania."

"Is Romania far from here?"

"Almost 2,000 miles."

"Are there also peasants in your country as there are here?"

"There are many, Pere Truk," for this was his name.

"Does there also grow there hay-grass? Are there oxen there? Cows? Horses?"

Finally we answered all his questions, thus making friends with him quickly. But we did not tell him anything of what ailed us, because the old man realized that we were educated people, "gentlemen," and he would have lost all his illusions had we told him we were looking for work.

We only asked him if he knew of a room for rent somewhere. He gave us an address and insisted we tell the landlord that it was he, Pere Truk, who sent us.

As we left, we expressed our thanks and promised that we would come back to help with his mowing. We found the address he gave us several houses down the slope. It was the house of M. Chenevas Paul, a pensioner about 70 years old, well dressed, a former non-commissioned officer, now retired. He was proud to be the only pensioner in the village. He owned two houses side by side which he used all for himself, for he was alone. All of his relatives had died. He rented to us his smaller house comprising two rooms below, one large and one small, and another room above (all houses there had a second story). In the downstairs room there was a stove to cook on; in the one upstairs, simply furnished, there was a bed. All this conveyed the aspect of emptiness. It was apparent that for a long time no one had lived in it. We agreed on 400 francs till Christmas (that was for six months). In Grenoble we were paying 150 francs a month. We paid in advance for three months and said we would move in in a few days. Then we went back to the city in good spirits. I felt that now, having fulfilled my residence course work required in the doctoral program, I would study for the exams here, and would go down into Grenoble only to take them.

At Pinet-D'uriage Among French Peasants

Several days later we were climbing the same paths, belongings on our backs, my wife, Mota and I, to our new quarters. At last, we settled down. Mota took leave of us and left for Romania. We stayed behind with only a few francs in our pockets. A dire situation! How were we going to eat?

Next morning, rather depressed, I went to Pere Truk. I helped with the mowing and hay loading all day. He asked me to eat with him both at noon and at suppertime. Had I been able to take something to my wife also it would have been perfect, but I returned empty-handed. I went again the following morning. This time he had someone to work for him, a short man with red, unkempt hair, shiny restless eyes in which I could not divine any trace of goodness; he seemed to be a mean man. His name was Corbela. Probably Corbelle in the literary and official language. But the peasants of the region speak all "patois," namely a peasant dialect that differs much from the official language both in pronunciation and in the structure of words. This difference is so great that a city Frenchman can not understand a country Frenchman who speaks "patois." But the latter know also the official language.

The three of us were invited by a housewife, the old man's woman, to eat at her place at noon. She was an old woman just like old women back home. In France peasants do not eat an onion with a mound of cornmeal mush at noon as do our peasants; as a rule they have a vegetable dish, a meat course, then cheese and regularly a glass of wine. I thanked them for having invited me to partake of their meal but said I would not eat.

Considering that I felt embarrassed, they insisted. Then I told them that being Friday I fasted till evening. This was an old habit with me which for three years ever since I was imprisoned for the first time in Vacaresti prison I had faithfully kept.

When Corbela heard I was fasting, he asked me gruffly:

"But why do you fast?"

"Because I believe in God."

"How do you know there is a God? Did you see Jesus Christ?" continued he.

"No, I did not see Him, but this is how I am; I do not believe you telling me He does not exist, while I believe the innumerable martyrs who, when spiked on the cross, cried out: 'You may kill us, but we saw Him'."

"Ah, the priests! The charlatans! I crush them under my heel, pushing and turning it into the ground, like I would crush a worm."

Seeing him so aroused I broke off the discussion.

That evening I left for home with a basketful of potatoes and a piece of bacon the old man gave me: I worked likewise that Saturday. On Sunday I went to church. There were many people, probably the entire village. In a side pew, close to the altar, solemn as a saint, stood a man who resembled Corbela. I took another look. He followed the priest very closely. At a certain moment he approached the priest and very humbly assisted him. It was he, Corbela! Cantor, sacristan and bell-pealer.

Later as I made friends with the villagers I told them about my encounter with Corbela, all of us enjoying a good laugh.

> "We too, have our fools among us" I was told. "They listen to important people who hate the Church. But we, the French peasants, believe in God as we have learned from our parents."

The priest, a man of vast culture, a doctor in philosophy and theology, was living in great misery, receiving no salary from the atheistic state which persecuted priests as enemies. The latter live only on help received from the few villagers.

The following week I worked for someone else, harvesting potatoes, who gave me a larger quantity of potatoes, the basis of our existence for some time. I moved on to another peasant to help with sheaving wheat and threshing. In each village, people own a threshing machine in common which is used in turn by all. Yields are rich and beautiful as gold.

Every villager subscribes to some agricultural weekly which is full of advice for farming in general, vegetable gardening, raising cattle, apiculture, etc. They read these periodicals very attentively, cover to cover, trying as in a great contest to apply that advice as best they can and make use of most of it. Their stables are cared for as well as their homes. Cattle are well protected from cold and hunger, are brushed daily. That is why they look well, can be worked hard and produce much.

Frequently I saw a piece of cardboard in their stables on which I read:

"Love the animals, our partners in labor!"

After about a month the villagers began to get used to me. I was known as "le roumain" (The Romanian). They heard I was a doctoral student and we had talks in the evening. They were interested in questions of philosophy, politics, international relations, and in political economics, particularly in the subjects of pricing, law of supply and demand and other laws determining prices, as well as causes of price fluctuation and the right time for marketing their products. Peasants of the 25-40 years age group were well oriented in these topics and one could discuss with them even higher questions; they understood them perfectly.

After a while I began studying for my exams. Mota had taken his exams in June successfully. I worked days, and evenings and at night I studied as much as I could. In this first year I took four subjects: political economy, the history of economic doctrines, industrial legislation, and financial legislation. But in about two months I was beginning to lose my strength. Our nourishment proved inadequate. Lately we had been on a diet of boiled potatoes almost exclusively. Every two or three days a quart of milk, and meat but once weekly, occasionally cheese. This was all I could earn by working. But worse than me was my wife, who became anemic.

I took my exams in October. I flunked them, though in the main subject matter, political economy, I obtained the highest grade and in the other subjects, passing marks. In financial legislation I got a nine only, the passing grade for doctorate being ten. For the moment I was disoriented. I had never been a shining element when it came to studying, but up to now I had never flunked an exam as I was considered among the average students. This was a serious blow in view of our difficult economic predicament. The difficulty was that I could take my exams anew only three months later, and then, in all the subjects. I became stubborn and resolved to start all over. Farm work in the fields had ended. The ground was snow covered. The only work available was cutting firewood in the forest. My payment for work there was a wagonload of wood.

But we began getting financial help from back home from Father Mota who obtained a loan in my name.

We spent the winter months and Christmas holidays amongst the peasants, mainly with the Belmain-David family. I registered for my exams again in the February session for my first year of the doctorate and passed them all.

I began studying immediately for those of the second year: administrative law, the philosophy of law, the history of French law, and the civic international law. In the spring, I rented a patch of garden which I began to work on my own. But in May 1927 I received a desperate letter from Mota and others from Focsani as well, and from students, asking me to come back home right away because the League had broken into two, Mota and Hristache Solomon also sent me money for the trip. But I had another month before the exams. I saw the Dean of the Faculty informing him of the emergency demanding my return to Romania and requesting permission to take my exams ahead of the regular session. My petition was approved. On May 16 I took and passed my exams. On May 18 I left for Romania after taking leave of the inhabitants of Pinet among whom we had lived nearly a year. When we left, some of them, the old ones, cried. Others accompanied me to the Grenoble station.

I came to France with the worry that I would find an immoral, corrupt and decayed people, such as it was reported oftentimes throughout the world. But I reached the conclusion that the French people, whether peasant or townsman, is a people of a severe morality. The immoralities belong to spoiled foreigners, the rich of all nationalities attracted by Paris and other large cities.

The leading class, in my opinion, is however irremediably compromised, thinking, living and acting under the influence, and exclusively under the influence, of Judeo-Masonry and its bankers. Judeo-Masonry uses Paris as its world headquarters (London, with the Scottish Rite is but a subsidiary). This leading class has lost contact with French history and the French nation. That is why as I left France I was making a big differentiation between the French people and the French Masonic state.

For the French people I carried in my heart not only love but also the faith—that will never be shaken—in its resurrection and victory over the hydra that plagues it, darkening its reasoning, sucking its strength and compromising both its honor and its future.

At Bucharest The League of Christian National Defense Broken in Two

I arrived in Bucharest. It was a disaster. The League had broken into two. The hopes of this nation were crumbling. A whole people who strained to gather up its exhausted strength in a difficult moment of history, and fought the greatest peril ever to threaten its existence, was falling now to the ground, all its hopes shattered. Such a disaster, to the valiant hearts of thousands of fighters, all of them seeing in a moment all their past sacrifices and all their hopes crashing down, inspired a feeling of profound pain even in those who stood outside our movement. I had never before seen more widespread sorrow. All those waves of enthusiasm from Severin to Focsani, from Campul-Lung to Cluj, were now changed into waves of grief and despair.

I went to the Parliament to see Professor Cuza. To my great astonishment, in the midst of general grief he was the only joyful man. This man was Professor Cuza. I give here, with the greatest possible accuracy, our conversation:

"Welcome back dear Corneliu" he said, advancing toward me, arm outstretched. "You are a good fellow. Just keep on minding your business as you have done so far, and everything is going to be just fine."

"Sir, I am depressed to the bottom of my being by the misfortune that befell us."

"But no misfortune took place. The League is stronger than ever. Look, I returned from Braila yesterday. It was something fantastic. I was received there with bands, drums, unending hurrahs. You'll see the country's atmosphere. You do not know what it is like. The entire country is with us." We said a few more words and then left. Dumfounded, I wondered: "Could a leader, seeing his troop rent by grief, divided into two and possessed by despair, enjoy a perfect disposition and good humor? Not realize the disaster boiling under him? But perhaps he does realize it! If so, how, then, is it possible for him to be rejoicing?"

What Happened?

The parliamentary and extra-parliamentary activity of the League's ten deputies during their term, left quite a bit to be desired. Were they weak men? Decidedly not! Were they of bad faith? Decidedly not! They were of absolute good faith but they had small deficiencies, either as to knowledge of the Jewish problem because they were the newer League members, or because they were a little cumbersome and slow in action and in hitting the trail, being the older ones. But such deficiencies are inherent in all men gathered into an organization and they must be lovingly and tactfully corrected by the leader. Then, what were the real causes for this state of affairs?

In my opinion they were:

1. The lack of coordination of their parliamentary and extra-parliamentary activity.

2. The lack of spiritual unity, a unity absolutely indispensable to such an organization that is surrounded on all sides by enemies who try to take advantage of any internal dissension.

But these two drawbacks are basically the result of the true cause: the lack of leadership, the leader's errors. A leader must constantly expound his views to all the fighters around him, in order to reach a unity of thinking of his following; to elaborate a plan of action; to direct the action of his men; to be a permanent servant of the movement's unity, trying by his love, observations, reprimands, to smooth out misunderstandings and inherent discord within the organization; to be a constant example to his followers of fulfilling one's duty; to handle matters with justice, respecting the norms of leadership taken upon himself and on the basis of which he assembled his supporters.

But Professor Cuza has done none of these. He did not educate his men. He did not even consult with them.

> "Let us have a consultation, Sir," requested some of them, "so that we can know the attitude we should take, and how we should present ourselves, in Parliament."
>
> "We need hold no consultation because we are not a political party."

He never issued any directive to anyone. One can find valuable tomes, scores of pamphlets written by Professor Cuza, hundreds of articles. But I dare anyone to bring me ten circulars, or organizing or action orders given to the most troubled political organization from March 4, 1923, its founding, to May 20, 1927, the moment of its abolition. One will not find ten, nor five, not even three. Professor Cuza had urged others, but himself was not one to spur his followers to action; he punished others but when he did so, he caused a real disaster because he did not handle the matter wisely.

Meantime, certainly, in view of the situation thus presented, some of the deputies sensing that things were not running as they should, expressed their dissatisfaction. They saw that gradually the movement was heading toward ruin especially because, in addition to lack of directives from time to time, certain outbursts by Professor Cuza in Parliament had a devastating and disconcerting effect upon the entire movement. For instance, when, immediately following the opening of Parliament, one of the League's deputies protested against the state of siege imposed at Focsani and the unheard-of abuses, Professor Cuza stood up commending the government for having done so, even saying he would have done the same thing, because people were agitated on account of the Jews.

Another time, discussing the Royal message to Parliament, answering members of the National Peasant Party (in fact they were in the opposition at the time), he declared:

> "The People's Party could become a governing factor through a system of rotation with the Liberal Party if Gen. Averescu would adopt the doctrine of the League of Christian National Defense."

Such statements—thrown from the eminence of the parliamentary tribune just when thousands of men, beaten, tortured and wronged, were anxiously awaiting, as a weak succor for their suffering, a word condemning the government whose victims they were—disseminated instead an atmosphere of general discouragement. In the following I quote the Official Monitor regarding a passage from the discourse just mentioned:

> "There are then at the present time in the service of the state, two mature parties, parties of order, of the present day order, governmental parties, which complement each other and which assume the normal play of constitutional mechanism: the People's Party and the Liberal Party.
>
> "They both stand on solid foundations, relying on production interests which, though differing, are nevertheless general, real and permanent and assure their existence and the efficacy of their action. The new work of political and constitutional organization of the country is their work in which they collaborated, each to the extent of the responsibility and role they played as governing or opposition. The People's Party will continue this work by all the improvements that sincere practice and good faith shall indicate as necessary for the further consolidation of the state and the total unification of the country...
>
> "The Liberal Party is the exponent of Romanian bourgeoisie

interests, of financial, commercial and industrial legitimate interests, indispensable for the country's well-being.

"The People's Party, called to perfect the economic organization of the state, basing it on real foundations, preoccupied by everyone's needs within the superior interests of the country, relies particularly on the over-all, real and permanent interests of agricultural production, which is a preponderant factor of our economic life.

"The People's Party, which has the deepest and most extensive roots throughout the country, within social harmony.... wants to give the ploughmen, masters of their soil, the role they deserve in the state's economy in accordance with their labor and their numbers."

(Official Monitor, July 30, 1926, p. 395).

This attitude on the part of the leader of a national movement is unconscionable. To present such an eulogy of the political parties which the nationalist movement denounces as a calamity fallen over Romania and against which it has fought with grievous sacrifices in order to create a new fate for this country, differing from the one meant for it by the parties' politicians, is the same as sentencing to death your own movement.

To sing the praises of a rotational system represented by the Liberal and Averescan parties, denounced by you for a lifetime as enemies of the people, means to remove any chance for victory of the national movement you have led, at the same time proving that you yourself do not put any faith in it.

What would people say of the commandant of heroic troops who fight, make supreme sacrifices, believe in their victory, live and are ready to die for it, if he during a discourse in the course of the fight in front of thousands of wounded soldiers, would eulogize enemy troops and forecast their victory?

What would happen to the poor troop which instead of hearing a word of encouragement of its hopes in victory, would hear its own commanding officer speak of the wonderful victorious prospects of the enemy?

What would happen? The troop would scatter demoralized.

And this is exactly what did happen. Many fighters on the front of the national movement had left in despair.

Owing to this strange attitude, the League's deputies began showing their unhappiness. They were wrong, I think. They had no right to express their dissatisfaction except to the president and within the limited circle of the leadership. But they went out of bounds. Under such conditions each word haphazardly uttered means an additional misfortune over the one caused by the movement's president himself.

Gradually, the mistakes of one group and then another had led to coolness in their relations. Until one day, with no sufficient reason, with no advance consideration, thus without respecting the norms and laws of the organization, deputy Paul Iliescu was expelled from the League of Christian National Defense. And what is more, President Cuza informed none of the parliamentarians of his decision but purely and simply announced from his prestigious position the dismissal, demanding that the deputy be simultaneously thrown out of Parliament and his seat in Campul-Lung declared vacant.

This struck like a bolt of lightning over the heads of the poor deputies of the League. Two days later, Professor Sumuleanu, who in the meantime had hurried in from Iasi, presented a communication to the Chamber of Deputies signed also by the other deputies, Ion Zelea-Codreanu, Valer Pop, Dr. Haralamb Vasiliu, and Professor Carlan, in which they stated that Professor Cuza's declaration was certainly premature, because the League's statutes stipulate that exclusions are pronounced by the committee, which in this case was totally in the dark. It did not know of any guilt on the part of this man, yet it did not ask that he not be expelled, but only that he first be judged so he could defend himself; it demanded in other words that the League's by-laws be respected; that the law which all vowed to respect, be obeyed. At the same time Professor Cuza was approached with this same request.

The result of these interventions: *All signatories were expelled from the League,* Professor Sumuleanu and my father included, some of them having higher merits of labor and sacrifice in the formation of the League than Professor Cuza, Professor Sumuleanu being himself the League's Vice-President. All these, likewise were expelled without being judged; without being told a thing; without being approached.

In my opinion the procedure used by Professor Cuza in his capacity of president of the organization—whose duty it was to exercise the greatest concern for the well-being of the organization and the greatest care in any step that might endanger its existence—was fundamentally erroneous. In fact it was not only unjust but totally uncalled-for, particularly considering the individuals involved who represented the very group who were leading the League. They were the creators of this organization. The measure was unreasoned, for Professor Cuza did not foresee its consequences for the movement.

A special issue of *Apararea Nationala* ("The National Defense"), put out immediately following their expulsion, stated that these men, with Professor Sumuleanu and my father heading the list, had sold out to the Jews, thus spreading this insinuation throughout the country.

Professor Sumuleanu, Professor Cuza's constant friend for a quarter of a century, a man of exemplary correctitude, was horribly and unconscionably attacked in this special issue at the direction and under the advice of Mr. Cuza. He walked the streets overwhelmed with grief, having been accused of treason. Then he published a pamphlet in reply titled: "The Treachery of Some Friends." His riposte was only one consequence of the errors commited by Professor Cuza. In this case Professor Cuza, in my opinion, had been not only unjust but was more than unjust. Those who were expelled, on their part, erred by printing flyers containing equally unjust attacks, but their error followed in the wake of Professor Cuza's.

All these attacks and counter-attacks were unfolding to the great despair of Romanian fighters and the great satisfaction of and ridicule by Jewry. It was at this stage that I got back from France. The question as to whether the parliamentarians expelled from the League should be permitted to serve out their terms was being debated in Parliament.

I ask myself even now: "I wonder whether, when Professor Cuza took those steps, he was not the victim of some suggestions or intrigues, or did he persuade himself that this was the right thing to do?"

Several days later, several members of the League who were petrified by Professor Cuza's measures demanded their annulment and respect for statutes. This resulted in elimination of this group, among whom were: Gen. Macridescu, Professor Traian Braileanu, Hristache Solomon, Professor Catuneanu, etc.

At large, the rumor was systematically spread that all expellees sold out to the Jews. Among the active agents disseminating those rumors were Col. Neculcea and Liviu Sadoveanu, the right and left hand respectively of Professor Cuza. Those expelled then formed themselves into the Statutory League of Christian National Defense, thus indicating that they stood within the League's statutes. At this time Professor Cuza called for a great national assembly in Iasi, in the Bejan Hall to which about 1,000 people came. They ratified the expulsions on the false basis that the members expelled had sold out to the Jews.

I shall stop here, leaving out observations on what was printed either by one side or the other, considering that as much as I have put down on paper should be enough for understanding the situation of the movement at that time. I would only like to add that time (nine years have passed since) proved Professor Cuza to have erred, because neither Professor Sumuleanu, so grievously hurt in his honor, nor my father who received nearly mortal blows from the Judaic power—which Professor Cuza cannot boast of having suffered—nor Gen. Macridescu, Professor Gavanescul, Professor Traian Braileanu, Professor Catuneanu, Dr. Vasiliu, Professor Carlan, Father Mota, etc.—none of these had sold out to the Jews.

Years later, after this disaster had devastated the League, Professor Cuza came to his old friend, Professor Sumuleanu, whom he had struck down so cruelly, and said: "Dear Sumuleanu, I have nothing against you. Let us make peace!" But Professor Sumuleanu turned away and as he left, said: "It is too late."

Not because Professor Sumuleanu did not want to forgive the cruel blow he had received, but because down there one saw the ashes of a movement and of Romanian hopes.

My Reaction In the Face of this State of Affairs

When I arrived from France in the midst of this disaster that descended on the national movement, I intended to salvage what yet could be saved. I hastily convoked in Iasi the Vacaresti group and part of the leaders of student youth from the four university centers.

I hoped to localize the split, by forming a youth bloc; to prevent this atmosphere of hate that was dissipating the ranks of the older generation from enveloping the youth. As it was only natural I wanted to base this bloc first of all upon the awareness that disunity and hate among us meant death for the national movement.

Once this bloc was formed, I wanted to direct our efforts toward the burning ranks of the veterans, to apply determined pressures in order to re-establish the unity, save the situation. But my plan fell through. The youth was already enveloped by the consuming flames of hatred so that in Iasi in spite of all ties existing between the youth and myself, my proposition had found no response in their hearts. The student leadership in Iasi could at that time have given the signal of a saving initiative, but unfortunately a series of weak elements had assumed control of it, their negative tendencies precluding the acceptance of my proposals.

It was only the Vacaresti group, out of all the youth, that supported my point of view, to which I must add a few Iasian students, about 10 or 12, veterans among them being Ion Blanaru, Ion Sava, Ion Bordeianu, Victor Silaghi and the others, newcomers, a group of Transylvanians headed by Ion Banea, Emil Eremeiu, Misu Crisan. These were all that rallied around us out of all the youth of the country.

I pursued my plan.

We all left for Bucharest to see both sides. We went first to see the "Statutories, ' asking them to make any sacrifice needed in order to re-establish the movement's unity. After several hours of discussion they agreed conditionally, being even disposed to make sacrifices but insisting that statutes be respected in the future.

After that we went to see Professor Cuza. But he, following our pleading and argumentation refused. It is better for me not to reveal the discussion we had on that occasion.

We left. Despondency took over our souls. All that had been built all the movement's brightness of yesterday did not come as a gift of fortune. Everything grew out of fighting step by step, foot by foot. We had carried the burden of our grave decisions, faced innumerable perils, risks, physical and moral suffering some more heart-rending than others. We had given the health of our bodies, the blood of our hearts; we had fought and sacrificed day in and day out.

Now, all seemed turned into ashes.

THE LEGION OF MICHAEL THE ARCHANGEL

Faced by the situation mentioned above, I decided to go with neither side, not meaning to resign myself, but to organize the youth, assuming this responsibility according to my soul and brains and to continue the fight, not to capitulate. In the midst of these troubles and times at the crossroads I remembered the icon that protected us in the Vacaresti prison.

We decided to close our ranks and to pursue the fight under the protection of the same sacred icon. With this in mind, we brought it to our Home in Iasi from the altar of the St. Spiridon Church where it had been placed three years previously.

The Vacaresti group agreed immediately to my plans. Several days later I convoked in Iasi in my room on 20 Florilor St. for Friday, June 24, 1927, the Vacaresti group and the few students still with us.

Several minutes before the meeting was to begin I entered in a register the following order of the day:

> "Today, Friday, June 24th, 1927 (The feast of St. John the Baptist), at 10 o'clock in the evening, is founded under my leadership, 'The Legion of Michael the Archangel.'
>
> "Let anyone who believes without reservation, join our ranks.
>
> "Let him who has doubts remain on the sidelines.
>
> "I hereby nominate Radu Mironovici as leader of the guard of the icon."

Corneliu Zelea Codreanu

This first meeting lasted one minute, only long enough for me to read the above order. After this, those present left in order to ponder whether they felt sufficiently determined and courageous to join an organization like this, without a program other than the example of my life as a patriot up to then and that of my prison comrades.

Even to the Vacaresti group I had given time for reflection and search of their conscience for them to be sure whether they had any doubts or reservations, because once enrolled they had to unhesitatingly keep on going for the rest of their lives

Our intimate feelings from which the Legion was born were these: it did not interest us whether we would triumph or be conquered, or whether we would die. Our purpose was different: to advance united. Moving forward in a united front, with the help of God and the Romanian people's justice, no matter what destiny awaited us—that of being vanquished or that of death—it would be a blessed one and it would bear fruit for our people. Professor Nicolae Iorga once said: "There are defeats and deaths which can awaken a nation to life, just as there are triumphs of the kind which can put a nation to sleep."

During the same night, and entered into the same register, we edited a letter to Professor Cuza and one to Professor Sumuleanu. At 10 o'clock the next morning all the Vacarestians got together and went to the house of Professor Cuza, 3 Codrescu St.

After so many years of battles and difficult trials we were now going to see him to take our farewell, and to ask him to release us from the vows we took.

Professor Cuza received us in the same room in which he had stood for me 28 years earlier at my baptism. He was standing behind his desk; we in front. I read him the following letter:

"Sir,

"We are coming to you for the last time to say goodbye and to ask you to release us from all the vows we took.

"We can no longer follow you on the road you have taken for we no longer believe in it. To march by your side without faith is impossible, because it was faith that nourished our enthusiasm in battle.

"Begging you to release us from our vows we remain to fight alone in the best way our brains and hearts can guide us."

Professor Cuza then spoke to us in the following manner:

"My dear friends, I release you from your vows and advise you that, stepping into life on your own, do not make mistakes.

> Because, particularly in politics, mistakes are very costly. You have as an example the political errors of Petre Carp which had fatal consequences for him.
>
> "On my part I wish you the best in life."

Then he shook hands with all of us and we left.

We thought that it was correct on our part to proceed thus and that this was the honorable way our dignity as fighters obliged us to take.

From there we went to Professor Sumuleanu on Saulescu St. reading to him the other letter written approximately in the same terms, in which we informed him and his "Statutories" that we could not go along with them either and that we would carve for ourselves from now on our own path.

Leaving him we felt in our hearts how very much alone we were, alone as in a desert, and we were going to build our road in life through our own powers.

We gathered even closer to the icon. The more difficulties that might assail us and the more our compatriots' blows might be showered heavily on our heads, the more we would seek the protection of St. Michael the Archangel and the shadow of his sword. He was no longer for us an image on an icon, but very much alive. There at the icon, we took turns keeping watch, night and day, candle burning.

Matter Versus Spirit

When we gathered together in the room at our Home, the five of us plus some ten freshman and sophomore students, and when we wanted to write several letters announcing our decision to Mr. Hristache Solomon and others, only then did we realize how poor we were, for all of us put together lacked even the money for envelopes and postage. Up to then, any time we needed money we went to the older veterans and asked them for it. But now we had no one to turn to. To launch a political organization totally penniless! It was both a difficult thing to do and a daring one. In this century in which matter is all powerful, in which no one starts anything however small without first asking himself "how much money do I have?" God wanted to prove that in the legionary struggle and victory, matter played no role.

Through our daring gesture we turned our backs on a mentality that dominated everything. We killed in ourselves a world in order to raise another, high as the sky. The absolute rule of matter was overthrown so it could be replaced by the rule of the spirit, of moral values.

We were not denying and will never deny the existence, function and necessity of matter in the world, but did deny and forever will deny the right of its absolute domination. In other words, we were striking a blow at a mentality which placed the golden calf in the center and as the main purpose in life. We realized that, were we to go on this road of reversed relationship of values between spirit and matter, we would have exhausted in us all courage, strength, faith and hopes. During those first beginnings we found the only moral strength in the unshaken faith alone, that placing ourselves in life's original harmony, matter's subordination to the spirit, we could subdue the adversities and be victorious over the satanic forces coalesced with the purpose of destroying us.

Reason

Another characteristic of our beginning, in addition to the lack of money, was the lack of a program.

We had no program at all. And this fact will no doubt raise a big question mark. Whoever heard of a political organization lacking a program which stemmed from reason, from somebody's brains or those of several people?

It was not those of us who thought alike that banded together, but those of us who felt alike. Not those among us who reasoned in the same way, but those who had the same moral-emotional-spiritual construction.

This was a signal that the statue of another Goddess—Reason—was to be smashed; that which mankind raised against God, we—not intending to throw away or despise—should put in her proper place, in the service of God and of life's meaning.

If then we had neither money nor a program, we had, instead, God in our souls and He inspired us with the invincible power of faith.

Against Treachery

Our birth was greeted with a hurricane of hate and ridicule. The two camps of the League—Cuzists and Statutories—broke relations with us. All students in Iasi left us and the attacks of the Cuzists[1] up to now directed at the Statutories were from now on to be aimed at us, piercing like arrows into our hearts.

We would not be hurt by the arrows' wounds but we were going to be terrified by what we were to discover in people.

Briefly, we would be rewarded and honored with the weightiest insults for everything we had done before, and suffer blow after blow. We would not only feel the hate but would see lack of character and incorrectitude of soul in all their nakedness.

Soon we would become "exploiters of the national idea" for our personal benefit. We would not have believed that those who pounded their breasts with their fists a year earlier, claiming rewards for their pretended suffering, would now have the courage to throw into our faces the accusation just mentioned. Soon people would learn that we had.... "sold out to the Jews" and even articles full of insults were going to be written and there would be peasants who would believe it and men who would turn their backs on us. Unjustly! Insults the enemies never dared use against us before, out of fear, were coming now at us from our friends, fearlessly and without shame.

If it be true that we who had gone through such suffering and whose bodies had endured so much abuse, would be capable of such an infamy, namely to sell ourselves as a group to the enemy, then there would be nothing left anymore to do but set dynamite to this people and blow it up. A people which had given birth and had raised in its bosom such children deserves to live no longer. But if it be not true, those who invent such lies and disseminate them are scoundrels who drain away the trust of their nation in its own future and destiny. For such as these, no punishment from their country is great enough.

What confidence could this people have in victory and the future if in the midst of the tough fight it is waging it hears that we, its children, raised in its arms, in whom it placed its most sacred hopes, betrayed it?

---

1 Professor Cuza's party members. (Tr.)

I leave those days only in the memory of those of us who lived them. To them, my comrades of that time, witnesses of those hours, I said:

> "Do not be afraid of these pygmies, for whoever has such souls, cannot ever win. You will see them some day fail on their knees at your feet. Do not forgive them. Because they are not going to do it out of remorse for the committed transgression, but out of treachery. And now, even if hell with all its unclean ghosts should confront us, unmoved in our firm stand, we will vanquish it."

Up to that time I had known the beast in man. Now I saw the scoundrel in man. Guard yourselves and the children of today and tomorrow of the Romanian people and of any other people in the world of this frightening plague: treachery.

All the intelligence, all the learning, all talents, all education will be of no avail to us if we are going to be treacherous.

Teach your children not to use treachery either against a friend or against their greatest foe. Not only will they not win, but they will be more than defeated, they will be crushed. Nor should they use treachery against the treacherous person and his treacherous ways for if they should win, only the persons change. Treachery will remain unchanged. The treachery of the victor will be substituted for that of the defeated. In essence, the same treachery will rule the world. The darkness of treachery in the world cannot be replaced by another darkness but only by the light brought by the soul of the brave, full of character and honor.

And yet, at the very beginning of this barrage of hatred and treachery, came to us as to a refuge giving them hope: Hristache Solomon, that man of great honor and conscience, engineer Clime, engineer Blanaru, attorney Mille Lefter, Andrei C. Ionescu, Alexandru Ventonic, Dumitru Ifrim, Costachescu, Ion Butnaru, Hierodeacon Isihie Antohie, etc.

All these distinguished and veteran fighters in the League now gave me the impression of some ship-wrecked souls, whose ship sank in the middle of the sea, and they landed tired and troubled on our small island on which they could find inner peace and confidence in the future.

Gen. Macridescu told us:

> "Though I am old, I will go with you and I will help you, only on one condition: that you not shake the hands of these people who lack honor, for if you did this it would disgust me to no end and I would lose all my hopes in you."

Professor Ion Gavanescul began to show an interest in us and in what we were doing.

The Beginnings of Legionary Life

Four lines marked our small initial life:

1. *Faith in God.* All of us believed in God. None of us was an atheist. The more we were alone and surrounded, the more our preoccupations were directed to God and toward contact with our own dead and those of the nation. This gave us an invincible strength and a bright serenity in the face of all blows.

2. *Trust in our mission.* No one could be presented the smallest reason for our possible victory. We were so few in number, so young, so poor, so hated and detested by everyone, that all arguments not based on fact, pleaded against any chances of success. And yet we went ahead thanks only to the confidence in our purpose, an unlimited trust in our mission and in the destiny of our country.

3. *Our mutual love.* Some of us had known one another for some time, having formed close friendships, but others were youngsters, freshmen or sophomores in college, whom we had never met. From the very first days an ambience of affection between us all was established as if we were of the same family and had known each other since childhood.

The need for an inner equilibrium was obvious in order to be able to resist. Our common affection had to be of the same intensity and force to match the wave of hatred from outside. Our life in this nest was not cold, official life, with distance between chief and soldier, with theatrics, rhetorical statements and assumed airs of leadership. Our nest was warm. Relations between us were absolutely casual. One did not come in as into a cold barracks but as into his own house, among his own family. And one did not come here just to take orders, but one found here a ray of love, an hour of spiritual quiet, a word of encouragement, relief, help in misfortune or need.

The legionary was not asked so much for discipline, in the sense of barracks discipline—as for propriety, faith, devotion and zeal for work.

4. *The song.* Probably, because we had not started out on the road of reason by setting up programs, contradictory discussions, philosophical argumentations, lectures, our only possibility of expressing our inner feelings was through singing. We sang those songs in which our feelings found satisfaction.

"*There, High Up on a Black Rock,*" Stefan the Great's song, the melody of which, it was said, had remained unchanged from his time to this, from generation to generation. It is said that at the sound of this melody Stefan the Great triumphantly entered his fort at Suceava 500 years ago. When we were singing it we felt alive with those times of Romanian greatness and glory; we sank 500 years back into history and lived there for a few moments in touch with Stefan the Great and with his soldiers and archers.

"*Like a Globe of Gold,*" the song of Michael the Brave; Avram Iancu's song; "Let the Bugle Sound Again," the march of the Military School of Infantry in 1917; "Arise Romanians" written by Iustin Iliesu and Istrate, which we proclaimed as the Legion's hymn.

To be able to sing, one has to be in a certain state of spirit, an inner harmony. A person bent on robbing somebody cannot sing, nor can one who is about to commit some other wrong; nor he whose soul is consumed by envy and hate of his comrade; nor he whose soul is devoid of faith.

That is why you, legionaries of today and tomorrow, anytime you feel the need to orient yourselves in the legionary spirit, must return to these four lines of our beginning which constitute the basis of our movement. The song will be a guide to you. If you are not going to be able to sing you must know that a sickness gnaws at the depth of your spiritual being or that life has filled your innocent soul with sins; and if you cannot rid yourselves of these sins, you ought to step aside, leaving your place to those who can sing.

Pursuing our life on the above mentioned lines we set out to act from the first days. I designated leaders, who received and gave orders. We did not start out by engaging in some spectacular actions. As we were faced by some problem, we set out to solve it.

Our first action was fixing the room in our Home in which the icon of St. Michael the Archangel was kept. We whitewashed it, we scrubbed the floor. The legionary girls began sewing curtains. Then legionaries wrote down several maxims I collected either from the Gospels or from other writings. They embellished our walls. Here are some of them:

"God carries us on His victorious chariot."

"Whoever wins.... I shall be his God."

"He who does not have a sword, let him sell his cloak and buy one."

"Fight bravely for faith."

"Avoid carnal pleasures, for they kill the soul."

"Be vigilant."

"Do not destroy the hero that is in you."

"Brothers in fortune... as in misfortune."

"Whoever knows how to die, will never be a slave."

"I await the resurrection of my Fatherland and the destruction of the hordes of traitors," etc.

In a week's time our headquarters was set up.

Our second action was of a different nature: it pertained to what our attitude should be toward outside attacks. We decided not to respond to them; which was extremely difficult for us all. Our moral being was being ripped apart. But this was the time of heroic endurance.

Another action: no one is to try to convince anybody to become a legionary. The customary sleeve-pulling and fishing for members always displeased me. The system was and has remained contrary, even to this day, to the legionary spirit. We shall state our point of view, simply. Whoever wanted to join, would come. And will join, if he is accepted.

But who was coming? People of the same spiritual essence as ours. Many? Very few. In Iasi, one year later, there were only two or three more than the first day. In the rest of the country however, there were more who were joining as they learned about our existence.

All those approaching us were characterized by two distinct lines clearly visible:

1. A great correctitude of soul.
2. The lack of personal interest. Among us, one could profit by no benefits. No promising prospects opened up. Here everybody had only to give—soul, wealth, life, capacity for love, and trust.

Even if one who was an incorrect individual or was motivated by some interest joined, he could not remain with us, for he could not find here a propitious setting. He would automatically leave, a month, a year, two or three, retreating, deserting or betraying.

Our Program

This nest of youth was the first beginning of legionary life, the first cornerstone. It had to be laid on solid ground. That is why we did not say: "Let us go out to conquer Romania! Go through villages and shout: 'A new political organization has just been formed, come ye all and sign up!' "

We had written up no new political platform in addition to the ten existing ones in the country—all of them "perfect" in the eyes of their authors and supporters—and we did not send out legionaries to wave a program around in villages calling people to adhere to it in order to save the land.

In this point of view, again, we differed fundamentally from all the other political organizations, the Cuzists included. All of these believed that the country was dying because of lack of good programs; consequently they put together a perfectly jelled program with which they started out to assemble supporters. That is why everybody asks: "What is your program?"

This country is dying of lack of men, not of lack of programs; at least this is our opinion. That, in other words, it is not programs that we must have, but men, new men. For such as people are today, formed by politicians and infected by the Judaic influence, they will compromise the most brilliant political programs.

This kind of man who is alive today in Romanian politics we earlier met in history. Nations died under his rule and states collapsed.

The greatest wrong done to us by jews and the political system, the greatest national danger to which they exposed us, is neither the grabbing of the Romanian soil and subsoil, nor even the tragic annihilation of the Romanian middle class, nor the great number of Jews in our schools, professions, etc. and not even the influence they exercise over our political life—though each of these in itself is a mortal danger for our people. The greatest national peril is the fact that they have deformed, disfigured our Daco-Romanic racial structure, giving birth to this type of man, creating this human refuse, this moral failure: the politician who has nothing in common with the nobility of our race any more; who dishonors and kills us.

If this species of man continues to lead this country, the Romanian people will close its eyes forever and Romania will collapse, in spite of all the brilliant programs with which the "trickery" of this degenerate creature is able to dazzle the eyes of the unfortunate multitudes. From among all the pests brought to us by the Jewish invasion, this is the most frightening one!

All peoples with whom we Romanians came in contact and fought, from the barbarian invasions till today, have attacked us on a physical, economic or political level, leaving untouched our moral and spiritual patrimony, our conscience, from which sooner or later sprang forth our victory, the breaking of the foreign yoke—even when they came upon us in large numbers and took all our riches, even when they ruled us politically.

Now, for the first time in our history, Romanians face a people which attack us not with the sword but with the weapons that are specific to the Judaic race, with which they strike and paralyze first the moral instinct of peoples, then systematically spread all sorts of moral sickness, thus to destroy any possibilities of reacting. That is why our people feel disarmed and defeated.

As a consequence of seeing this state of affairs, the cornerstone on which the Legion stands is man, not the political program; man's reform, not that of the political programs. "The Legion of Michael the Archangel" will be, in other words, more a school and an army than a political party.

In these critical times, the Romanian nation has no need of a great politician as many wrongly believe, but of a great educator and leader who can defeat the powers of evil and crush the clique of evil-doers. But in order to do this he will first have to overcome the evil within himself and within his men.

From this legionary school a new man will have to emerge, a man with heroic qualities; a giant of our history to do battle and win over all the enemies of our Fatherland, his battle and victory having to extend even beyond the material world into the realm of invisible enemies, the powers of evil. Everything that our mind can imagine more beautiful spiritually; everything the proudest that our race can produce, greater, more just, more powerful, wiser, purer, more diligent and more heroic, this is what the legionary school must give us! A man in whom all the possibilities of human grandeur that are implanted by God in the blood of our people be developed to the maximum.

This hero, the product of legionary education, will also know how to elaborate programs; will also know how to solve the Jewish problem; will also know how to organize the state well; will also know how to convince the other Romanians; and if not, he will know how to win, for that is why he is a hero. This hero, this legionary of bravery, labor and justice, with the powers God implanted in his soul, will lead our Fatherland on the road of its glory.

A new political party, be it even a Cuzist one, at best can give us a new government and a new administration; a legionary school however, can give this country a great type of Romanian. It can produce something great we never had before, which could break in two our whole history, to lay foundations for the beginning of a different Romanian history to which this people is entitled. For our people by virtue of its millenary suffering and sufferance, by virtue of its purity and gallantry of soul, has been perhaps the only people in the world which, in all its history, never committed the sin of invading and subjugating other nations. We shall create an atmosphere, a moral medium in which the heroic man can be born and can grow.

This medium must be isolated from the rest of the world by the highest possible spiritual fortifications. It must be defended from all the dangerous winds of cowardice, corruption, licentiousness, and of all the passions which entomb nations and murder individuals.

Once the legionary will have developed in such a milieu, i.e. in the nest[2], work camp, in the legionary organization and family, he shall be sent into the world: to live, in order to learn how to be correct; to fight, in order to learn to be brave and strong; to work, in order to be diligent and love all those who work; to suffer, in order to steel

2 Basic unit of the legionary organization. (Tr.)

himself; to sacrifice, in order to get accustomed to overcoming his selfish interests, serving his Fatherland.

No matter where he goes he will create a new milieu of an identical nature. He will be an example; will turn others into legionaries. And people, in search of better days, will follow him.

The newly arrived will have to live by and respect the same norms of legionary life.

All of them together, in the same army, will make a force which will fight and will win.

This is what "The Legion of Michael the Archangel" is to be.

Aspects of Romanian Public Life

In what follows I present the general aspect of our public life in the midst of which and against which "The Legion of Michael the Archangel" was just forming.

The Averescu government had fallen about a month before. On July 7, 1927 the Liberals came to power. They staged new elections and, as usual, the government had the majority. Nevertheless, the administration had to overcome, by any means, the great popular current supporting the National-Peasant Party. The poor masses of the Romanian people ran from party to party, from promise to promise, attaching their sincerest hopes—with their centuries-long confidence—to each party in turn, but ending up cheated and dejected, all hopes shattered. And this will continue to be so, until they finally understand some day that they had fallen into the hands of robber gangs set on profit and loot.

There were three large parties, Liberal, Averescan, and National-Peasant and several smaller ones.

Fundamentally there was no distinction between them other than differences of form and personal interests—the same thing in different shapes. They did not even have the justification of differing opinions.

Their only real motivation was the religion of personal interest, with any desideratum and superior interests of the country left out.

That is why the spectacle of political fights was disgusting. The chase after money, personal situations, wealth and pleasures, loot, gave these fights an aspect of merciless hostility. Political parties appeared as real organized bands that hated and fought each other for the booty.

Only the struggle for the Fatherland or for an ideal that surpasses personal interests, egoism or lust, is calm, decent, noble, without blind unleashing of passions. One can put enthusiasm into it, but not base and blind passion. The hatred and baseness involved in these fights is sufficient proof that they were not waged in the realm of lofty and sacred ideals or based on principles, but in the sorry depth of the most shameless personal interests.

The politician's world unfolds in luxury and scandalous partying, in the most disgusting immorality, riding on the back of an increasingly demoralized country. Who is to devote any attention to its needs?

These politicians, with their families and their agents, need money, for partying and entertaining their political clientele, for purchasing votes and human consciences. One by one, they, in bands, descend upon the country to despoil her. This, in the last analysis, is what their governing amounts to. They drain dry the budgets of the state, the prefectures, the city halls.

They attach themselves like ticks to the boards of directors of all enterprises from which they will receive, without effort, salaries in the millions from the sweat and blood of the exhausted worker. They are included in the councils of the Jewish bankers from whom they collect honoraria of more millions as the price for betraying their country.

They originate scandalous business deals which stun their countrymen. Corruption spreads in public life like a plague, from the most humble servant up to cabinet ministers. They sell themselves to any and all; anyone with money can buy off these monsters and through them the whole country.

That is why, when the squeezed country can no longer give them money, they yield up to consortia of alien bankers, one by one, the riches of our land, and thus give away our national independence. A real plethora of men of business spreads over the whole of Romania, who do not work or produce anything, but suck the sap of the country. Such are the exploits of the politicians.

Misery, demoralization and despair spread among the lower level. Scores of thousands of children die, mowed down by illness and hunger, weakening thus the people's power of resistance in the fight it wages against the organized Jewish people which is supported by the alienated politicians and defended by the entire state apparatus.

The few honest politicians, several score perhaps, maybe even party leaders, are not able to do anything any more. They are like some poor puppets in the hand of the Jewish press, of the Jewish or foreign bankers and of their own fellow politicians.

This mess, this demoralization, this infection, is sustained step by step by the whole phalanx of Jews, interested in our destruction, in order to replace us in this country and thus steal our riches completely. Through their press, which usurped the role of our Romanian press, through hundreds of filthy sheets, through an immoral and atheistic literature, through movie houses and theaters which spread licentiousness, through banks, the Jews have become masters of our country.

Who could oppose them? Today, when they are the promoters of disaster and their appearance is the signal of our national death, who shall confront them?

The national movement lies prostrate on the ground.

In these last elections the League came out 70,000 votes less, totalling less than 50,000, less than two percent nation-wide. From the ten parliamentarians it had yesterday, today it has none. There must come a day when the legionary will know how to face this monster and how to tackle him in a life or death battle. He, alone.

Our Apprehensions Facing This World

Our small number, compared to the giant force of this all-powerful might, made us oftentimes pose questions such as these to ourselves:

What if we will be outlawed? If these hydrae realize what we plan, they will raise before us every possible obstacle and will try to crush us.

Their eyes are fixed upon us. They can provoke us. They did it once to us, when quietly and peacefully we started work at Ungheni; then they took us to the brink of the abyss with all our plans.

What are we going to do if they provoke us? Shall we again pull out our pistols and fire so that our bones may rot in prisons and our plans may fail? Faced with glimpses of such perspectives, the idea of retreating into the mountains sprouted in our minds—there, where the Romanian accepted fighting all the enemy hordes. The mountain has been close to us for a long time, to our life. It knows us. Rather than letting our bodies dry up and our blood dry out in our veins in the bleak and ugly prisons, better to end our life dying to the last man up in the mountains for our faith.

We reject thus the humiliation of finding ourselves again in chains.

We will attack from there, by incursions down into all the Jewish wasp nests. Up above, we will defend the life of the trees and the mountains from further devastation. Down below, we will spread death and mercy.

We will be sent for to be caught and killed. We will escape, hide; we will fight back; and in the end, certainly, we will be downed. For there will be but few of us, sought by Romanian battalions and regiments. Then we will receive death. The blood of all of us will flow.

This moment will be our biggest discourse addressed to the Romanian people, and the last one.

I called Mota, Garneata, Corneliu Georgescu and Radu Mironovici and shared with them these thoughts of mine. We had to think both about good and bad days ahead. We had to have solutions and be prepared for anything. Nothing ought to surprise us. We will follow the path of the country's laws, not provoking anyone, avoiding all provocations, not answering any provocation. But when we are no longer able to suffer, or when insurmountable obstacles are placed before us, our road must be toward the mountains.

It is not advisable to try a rebellion of the masses, for in this day they would be decimated by cannon and this would result in spreading only misfortune and sorrow. On the contrary we must work alone, in limited numbers and only on our own responsibility. They all agreed.

"It cannot be" they said, "that our blood, the blood of twenty youth, would not redeem the sins of this nation. It cannot be that this sacrifice of ours will not be understood by Romanians, that it would not make their souls and consciences tremble and that this will not constitute a starting point, a point of resurrection for Romanians."

Our death, in this fashion, could eventually bring this people more good than all the frustrated endeavors of our lifetime. Nor will the politicians who will kill us go unpunished.

There are others among our ranks who will avenge us. Not being able to win while alive, we will win dying. After that, we lived with the thought and determination of dying. We had the sure solution for victory, come what might. It gave us peace of mind and strength. It will make us smile in the face of any enemy and any attempt to destroy us.

The Stages of The Legion's Development

Pamantul Stramosesc (*"The Ancestral Land"*)

We were born on June 24, 1927. Several days later we occupied our headquarters. Now we felt we should have our own publication in order to enlarge our field of influence, formulate in it the norms of our life and through it direct the movement.

What should we call it? "The New Generation" was suggested; I did not like it. It sounded like a definition; it distinguished us from another generation, which will not do. "*The Ancestral Land*," Let this be its name. This title keeps us tied to our country's earth in which our ancestors rest; the land which must be defended. It plunges us deep into undefined realms; it will be more than a name, it will be a constant call to battle, the appeal to bravery, the stirring up of the warlike qualities of our race.

Moreover, in addition to those qualities mentioned several pages back, this title underscores another structural trait of the legionary's soul: bravery, without which a man is incomplete. For if a man is only just, correct, devoted, faithful, diligent, etc. but lacks heroic qualities which would enable him to fight unscrupulous, dishonest and incorrect enemies, he would perish at their hands.

Here we were now with the axis of our movement already fixed; one end rooted in the earth of our Fatherland, the other in the heavens: "*The Ancestral Land*" and Michael the Archangel.

But a paper costs money of which we had none. What are we going to do? We decided to write Father Mota asking him to print it for us on credit, in the old printing shop of *Libertatea* ("The Liberty") in Orastie. He accepted; he would print our paper and we would pay him from subscriptions and sales.

"The Ancestral Land" No. 1 was published on August 1, 1927 in a magazine format as a bi-monthly, having in the center of the cover the icon of St. Michael the Archangel. On the icon's left were reproduced the following words from St. Michael the Archangel's icon in the Church or the Coronation[3] in Aiba-Iulia:

"Towards the unclean hearts who come into the most pure House of the Lord, I mercilessly point my sword."

And on its right a stanza from Cosbuc's poem "Decebal to his People:"

> "Though we were descended from the Gods
> We still owe the debt of death
> Whether one dies young or a stooped old man
> Is just the same
> But it is not the same to die
> A lion or a dog in chains!"

Underneath, the map of Romania which showed in darkened spots the extent of the Jewish invasion.

The Contents of The First Issue

The leading article, entitled *"The Ancestral Land"* delves into the situation of the national movement following the conflict within the League and endeavors to explain our position. It ends with the entreaty: "Face to the enemy!" It is signed by Corneliu Z. Codreanu, Ion Mota, Ilie Garneata, Corneliu Georgescu and Radu Mironovici.

The second article is signed by me, "It is Your Hour, Come" a continuation of the same line of thought covered in the first article. The third one was signed by Ion Sava, a young talented fighter who took part in many a battle of the student movement, who attached himself to us, but did not become a legionary. Its title: "The Results of the Elections."

---

3 Popular name of the church in Alba-Iulia in which King Ferdinand and Queen Maria were crowned on October 15, 1922. (Tr.)

There follows a brief panegyric on the occasion of King Ferdinand's death, who had passed away a few days before. Above his picture, bordered in black, appeared the title "Our King has Died."

Then followed Mota's article which I reproduce here in part:

BY THE ICON

"It is from the Icon and the Altar that we started. Then we wandered for a while carried away by human waves and we reached no shores despite the purity of our impulses. Now, with heavy hearts, dispersed, torn, we gather in the shelter, to our only warmth and consolation, strength and comfort, giver of power, at the feet of Jesus Christ, on the threshold of the heavens' blinding brilliancy, at the Icon. We have not been engaged in politics, for not even one single day in our lives, ever. We have a religion, we are the slaves of a faith. We consume ourselves in its fire and, totally subjected to it, serve it to the limit of our strength. There is no defeat and disarming for ourselves, for the power whose tools we want to be, is eternally invincible.

"We cannot for the time being discuss in detail the causes of the old League's downfall. Let it only be said that, in these moments of new creation, we want to clearly and decidedly state, in order to imprint the character of the new system being born:

"Light of light...."

The article then continues giving some insights into the new organization, ending with an expression of faith in victory.

Extract from an article of Corneliu Georgescu:

LIGHT THE TORCH OF FAITH!

"Ancient chronicles tell us that the Gods had sent down a difficult trial on ancient Hellas for her sins. From the wastelands of Asia, large armies many hundredfold stronger than the Greeks swooped down like a tempest on the country's plains, ravaging her fields, demolishing her cities, devastating her temples and shattering her armies which, though valiant, were too small in number to put up a successful opposition. Meeting no further resistance, the victorious Medes penetrated into the heart of Greece at Delphi, the location of Apollo's most famous temple. The temple priests were trembling with fright that soon the enemy would be able to desecrate the sacred temple. The grand priest alone was not afraid. Full of confidence in divine power, he turned to his fellow priests and said: 'Do not fear, God has no need of armies. He will Himself defend us!'

"And the grand priest and all the others set out to pray, and their prayer accomplished miracles. As soon as the confident armies of the Persians approached within a stone's throw of the temple, Mount Parnassus shook and rolled rocks down its slopes with a deafening thunder over the enemy, crushing him. The lightning coming down as if from nowhere, completed their ruin, so that from the grand army of but a moment earlier, hardly a few remained to tell of this heavenly miracle...

"Fighters! Light anew in your souls the torch of faith that victory and triumph shall be ours."

Then follows a letter of Radu Mironovici to one of his brothers in the village back home. Knowing him to be discouraged he tells him:

"Certainly, we can be sad and grieved, but there is one right we do not have, that of losing our courage and laying down our weapon."

After which he explains to him the disunity in the League and the founding of the Legion, thus:

"Our house, that we all built with our own sweat, which was our shelter, has burned down...

"Only some smoke-blackened walls remain as a painful reminder of the little old house.

"What do you want us to do now? Rebel against God? This cannot be, for 'the Lord hath given, the Lord taketh away, blessed be the name of the Lord.'

"Shall we cross our arms and perish in misery, cold, rain and wind? No! But, with faith in God, we shall begin to work, and little by little, should build for ourselves a new home twice as beautiful. Here it is, 'the Legion,' for which we have laid a first cornerstone."

Garneata's article is next:

DISCORD AMONG BROTHERS—THE ENEMY'S JOY

"My heart full of chagrin, I take my pen in hand to share with others the torment of the disquieting thoughts that enveloped us in the face of our late troubles....

"The quarrel among brothers and the disagreements among leaders have become so evident that we can no longer hide them. Their consequences are likely going to discourage many, and the discouragement of those who placed their confidence in the League, is certainly a step backward, a step toward defeat.

"This is so obvious, because at no time in history was it ever evidenced that disunity led to anything else but misfortune, disaster....

"We shall know how to walk on the road we chose seven years ago, and just as determinedly. Our bones, accustomed to the harshness of prison days and misery, will feel good in battle-trenches, on position against the adversary.

"Let the Jews, who today rejoice believing the hour of their masterdom had arrived know that there is a corner in this country where, at any hour of the day or night, there is a troop watching, its face to the enemy."

Several items of information complete this first issue together with the article "Dreams, Hopes, Reality" by engineer Gheorghe Clime, former vice-president of L.A.N.C. in Moldavia, from which I extract the final part:

"What do we need in order to reach this final goal?

"A fighting army led by a capable leader surrounded by devoted helpers. In this question, as far as I am concerned, though much older, I follow the action group of the young Corneliu Z. Codreanu, Ion I. Mota...

"Obviously, the contribution of many, of all those today dispersed in demoralized camps, is needed.

"Consequently, if someone in some corner of Romania has opened a list of subscribers, whether authorized or not, let him enter there my name also, with what I can give—'my life'."

The Fundamental Principles of Legionary Ethics

The second issue of "*The Ancestral Land*" was published on August 15. In the lead article entitled "*The Legion of Michael the Archangel*" I try to formulate briefly the first ethical norms of legionary life which we mean to strictly respect and affirm, and around which should gather all those who prize them. Anyone who would come and grow in our midst will have to grow up respecting them,

I select from this statute-article the ideas in the order in which I wrote them at that time.

- The first idea: "Moral purity."
- The second: "Disinterestedness in battle."
- The third: "Enthusiasm."
- The fourth: "Faith, work, order, hierarchy, discipline."
- The fifth: "The Legion shall stimulate the energy and moral force of our nation without which there can never be any victory."
- The sixth: "Justice, (the Legion shall be the school of justice and of the energy to enthrone it)."
- The seventh: "Deeds, not words—You accomplish! Do not talk!"
- The eighth: "At the end of this school, a new Romania will emerge and the long-awaited resurrection of this Romanian people, the aim of all our efforts, suffering and sacrifices we make."

I want to elaborate upon some of them.

The Disinterestedness In Battle

Defeating personal interest is another fundamental virtue of the legionary. This is tn total opposition to the politician's position whose single motive of acting and fighting is his personal interest alone, with all its degenerate by-products— greed for enrichment, luxury, debauchery or arrogance.

That is why, dear comrades, from now on for as long as a legionary life shall exist, you ought to know that wherever you shall feel corning on, be it in the soul of some fighter or be it in your own soul, the snarl of this personal interest, there the Legion has ceased to exist. There, the legionary ends and the politician begins to show his fangs.

Look a newcomer right in the eye and if in his eyes you should detect a gleam of some small personal interest (either material, or ambition, passion, pride) know that he cannot become a legionary.

Nor shall donning the green shirt or adopting the legionary salute be enough for someone to become a legionary, not even if he "rationally" understands the legionary movement; but only if he leads a life in conformance with the norms of legionary life. For the Legion is not only a logical system, a chaining up of arguments; it is a "living faith." Just as someone is not a Christian if he "knows" and "understands" the Gospel but only if he conforms to the norms of life espoused in it, if he "lives the Gospel."

Discipline and Love

The entire social history of mankind is full of struggles, having at its base two great principles, one striving for a place to the detriment of the other: the principle of authority and the principle of liberty. Authority has striven to expand to the detriment of freedom, and the latter has endeavored to limit as much as possible the power of authority. These two, face to face, cannot but mean conflict.

To orient a movement after one or the other of these two principles means to continue the historical line of unrest and social warfare. It means to continue on one hand the line of tyranny, oppression and injustice, and on the other hand the line of bloody insurrection and of permanent conflict.

Therefore I want to call the attention of all legionaries and in particular that of newer ones that they should not deviate from the movement's line because of a misunderstanding. In many a case I noticed that as soon as a legionary received a rank he stiffened with all his being into "authority," breaking away from everything that bound him to his comrades till then, and felt compelled to "impress" others by the use of his authority. The legionary movement is based exclusively neither on the principle of authority nor on that of liberty. It has its foundations rooted in the principle of love. In it, both authority and freedom have their roots.

Love is the peace between the two principles: authority and liberty. Love is in the middle, between them and above them, embracing both of them in everything they have best and removing the conflicts between them.

Love can bring neither tyranny, oppression, injustice, bloody insurrection, nor social warfare. It can never mean conflict. There is also a hypocritical concept of the principle of love practiced by tyrants and Jews who, continuously and systematically appeal to the sentiment of love of their fellow men, behind which they continue to hate and oppress undisturbed.

Applied love means peace of soul in society and in the world. Peace no longer appears like the poor expression of a mechanical and cold equilibrium between the two principles: authority and liberty condemned to war eternally, namely to an impossibility of harmony.

Goodness and love are going to give us peace, not justice. For justice is very difficult to realize integrally. Even if an instrument of its perfect realization would be found, man, who is incapable of recognizing and appreciating it, would remain forever discontented.

Love is the key to peace which our Savior offered all nations of the world. In the end, nations, after they have wandered, searched and tried everything, will be convinced that except for that love which God implanted in man's soul as a synthesis of all human qualities and which He sent to us through Jesus Christ our Savior, Who placed it above all virtues, nothing exists which can give us quiet and peace.

Faith, labor, order, discipline too, have their roots in love.

How wonderfully and wisely speaks the Apostle Paul:

> "If I speak with the tongues of men and of angels, and I have not love, I am become as sounding brass, or a tinkling cymbal. And if I should have the gift of prophecy and should know all mysteries and all knowledge, and if I should have faith, so that I could remove mountains, and have not love, I am nothing.
>
> "And even if I should distribute all my wealth to feed the poor, and if I should deliver my body to be burned, and have not love, it profiteth me nothing.
>
> "Love is patient, is kind, it envieth not, dealeth not perversely; is not puffed up by pride,
>
> "Is not ambitious, seeketh not her own, is not provoked to anger, thinketh no evil,
>
> "Rejoiceth not in iniquity, but rejoiceth with the truth.

> "Beareth all things, believeth all things, hopeth all things, endureth all things.
>
> "Love never falleth away;
>
> "Prophecies shall be made void, tongues shall cease, knowledge shall be destroyed."
>
> (Corinthians I, 13, 1-8)

It is from here that our movement stems. I do not know how to urge you more to cultivate love, both you who lead and you under command. Love will give you unsuspected and unlimited possibilities for solving all the tough problems with which you will be confronted. Where there is no love, there is no legionary life. Look for one moment at this legionary life and you will understand what it is that binds us all one to another, the big to the small, the poor to those who are rich, those old to the youth.

But love does not abolish the obligation of being disciplined, just as it does not do away with the obligation of working or that of being orderly.

Discipline is a limitation we impose upon ourselves, either in order to conform to some ethical norms of life or to the will of a leader. In the first case we practice it in order to attain the heights of life; in the second to be successful in battle either against nature or enemies.

Though one hundred men may love each other like brothers, it is possible that, faced with need for some action, they may each have a different opinion. One hundred opinions will never win. Love alone will never make them win. Discipline is needed. In order to win, all of them must adopt a single opinion, that of the one among them who is most experienced, their leader. Discipline is the guarantee of success for it insures the unity of effort.

There are difficulties that only a united entire people, obeying a single command, can overcome. Who is the imbecile who in such an eventuality would refuse to join the rest of his people, when they, as one, will heed the same command—under the pretense that discipline would wound his personality?

In such cases, when your country is threatened and when the nature of things urges you to endanger life and limb, to break up your family, to risk the future of your children, to renounce everything you own on this earth in order to save your fatherland, it is at least ridiculous for one to talk of his "personality being hurt."

Discipline does not humiliate one, for it leads to victory. And if victories cannot be attained except by sacrifice, then the submission to discipline is the smallest of all sacrifices a man can make for the victory of his nation.

If discipline is a renunciation, a sacrifice, it does not humiliate anyone. For any sacrifice ennobles one, does not demean him.

As our people has to overcome tremendous difficulties, every Romanian should joyously accept the education of discipline and be thus aware of his contribution to the victory of tomorrow.

There is no victory without unity; and there is no unity without discipline. Therefore our nation should consider it a hostile act and condemn as dangerous to her victories and her very life any deviation from the school of discipline.

The Struggle For Maintaining Our Review

The struggle to assure the publication of our review was the second stage of our development. Lacking finances, our efforts took on the aspect of a real battle. In fact, "battle" is what we named it from the start.

We made use of two strategies:

1. Concentrating all our efforts on the same objective at the same time.
2. Stimulating our fighters during the battle by citations and distinctions.

You will encounter this principle in all our legionary activity. It embodies the following advantages:

The rapid accomplishment of the desired purpose.

The education of united action and of the disciplined effort of all workers.

The awakening to the consciousness of their own powers. Confidence in themselves and in their own powers.

The memory of economic defeats, particularly the unsuccessful endeavors, threw the Romanian people into resignation, lack of initiative and loss of confidence. We shall have to awaken his confidence in himself by substituting the painful memories with a tradition of success in his endeavors.

And finally, by stimulating our fighters, we shall be able to attain a screening of the zealous—of an elite cadre of fighters.

We launched an appeal in our review addressed to all our friends, to go on the offensive between September 1st and October 15th, in order that together we might get as large a number of new subscribers as possible.

As a result of this appeal a real ant-like campaign got underway in which one and all took active part: youth, old folks, peasants, intellectuals. Some brought in as many as 45 subscriptions (Constantin Ilinoiu).

The outcome of this first battle was printed in the November 1, 1927 issue. Here is what I wrote at the time:

> "At six o'clock in the evening on October 15, the number of subscribers reached 2,586. The Legion thanks all those who labored for its first victory."

All those who participated in this battle were mentioned in that issue. First of all we gave thanks to Father Mota who extended to us favorable publicity through *Libertatea* ("The Liberty").

I give again here the names of all as they were printed in "*The Ancestral Land*" Some of them did not become legionaries and some are no longer with us, having died in the legionary faith. And I give their names here because they were believers from the start; they are listed in the order in which they had distinguished themselves:

Mother Pamfilia Ciolac (Varatec), Octav Negut (Focsani), Arhimandrite Atariasie Popescu (Balti), Hieromonah Isihie Antohi (Neamt), Mihail Tanasache, Victor Silaghi, Ion Bordeianu, Radu Mironovici, Capt. V. Tuchel (Ivesti), Constantin Ilinoiu (Iasi), N. Grosu (Botosani), Ion Minodora (Husi), Grigorie

Balaci (Movilita-Putna), Andrei C. Ionescu (Barlad), Spiru Peceli (Galati), engineer Mihai Ittu (Bucharest), engineer Gh. Clime (Iasi), Ion T. Banea (Sibiu), Ilie Garneata (Iasi), Totu Nicolae, (Iasi), Coman Alexandru (Gauri-Putna), Decebal Codreanu (Husi), Mihail Marinescu (Galati), Traian Lelescu (Piatra-Neamt), Sebastian Erhan (Campul-Lung, Bucovina), N. Tecau (America), Elena Petcu (Vaslui), Dr. Socrate Divitari (Tecuci), Ion Plesea (Orhei), P.I. Morariu (Suraia-Putna), Nanu Gavril Raileanu (Orhei), Cotiga Traian (Focsani), Maria Mitea (Severin), I. Ciobanita (Belcesti), Carausu (Voinesti), Tinistei Neaga (Orhei), Zosim Bardas (Tarnava Mare), Ion Blanaru (Focsani), Iuliu Stanescu (Marsani-Dolj), Corneliu Georgescu (Poiana-Sibiului), Fanica Anastasescu (Bucharest), D. Ifrim (Iasi), I. Durac (P. Neamt), Pacuraru Gh. (Bucharest), Professor Isac Mocanu (Turda), Marius Popp (Cluj), N. Voinea (Panciu), N.B. Munceleanu (Roman), Grigorie Berciu (Varna), Corneliu Cristescu Basa (Comanesti), Angela Plesoianu (Severin), Emil Eremeiu (Nasaud).

Eight years later we established that from the 59 who took part in the first legionary battle:

- Four had left us, incapable of understanding us; in fact, they even attacked us.
- Eight, after one or two years, gave no sign of life whatever.
- Twenty-two received the highest ranks, becoming legionary commanders, commander-aides, or legionary senators.[4]
- Seven became legionaries, men of unshakable faith, defying all persecutions.
- Eighteen remained our friends, helping us to the present day.

As a result of this battle, publication of "*The Ancestral Land*" was assured for one year.

4 Members of the Legionary Senate. See page 326. (Tr.)

Other Names Encountered in the First Issues of our Review

Vasile State, merchant and C. Vasiliu, pensioner (Adjud), Gh. Oprea (San-Nicolaul Mare), Ion Schiopu (Prundul Bargaului), attorney Budescu P. (Banat), Adolf Greiter, Misu Stefanescu, Iosif Dumitru (the first subscriber to "*The Ancestral Land*"), Ile Berlinschi (Igesti-Bucovina), Dr. Elena Bratu, Mille Lefter (Galati), Ion Demian (Turda), Dr. Popescu (Vaslui), Teodorescu Craciun, Augustin Igna, Ivanovici, Adam Branzei, Sofron Robota (Dorna), Bacuta Boghiceanu (Husi), the brothers Balan (Soveja), C Gheorghiu Contar, Capt. Siancu, Gh. Postolache, Gheorghe Despa (Dorna), Luchian Cozan (Dorna), Dr. Crisan, engineer Camil Grossu, Chirulescu Victor, Iordache Nicoara, Ion and Alexandru Butnaru, Adriana and Teodora Ieseanu, Vasile Stan, Professor Razmerita, Craciunescu (Focsani), Ion Belgea, Gurita Stefaniu, Ghita Antonescu, Pantelimon Statache, Octav Pavelescu (Foscani), Gheorghe Potolea (Beresti), I. Gh. Teodosiu, Margareta Marcu, Gheorghe Marcu (Galati), Dan Tarnovschi, Simion Tonea, engineer Stoicoiu, Col. Paul Cambureanu, Amos Horatiu Pop (Ludos), Stefan Nicolau, Ileana Constantinescu, Elvira lonescu, Marioara Cidimdeleon, Gh. Amancei, Coca Tiron, Iulius Igna, Aristotel Gheorghiu (Rm.-Sarat), D. Bunduc, Valer Danieleanu, Constantin Ursescu, Vasile Tampau, C. Mierla, Octav Danieleanu, Stefan Manzat, Col. Blezu, Eufrosina Ciudin, Reverend Mother Zenaida Rachis, Gh. Liga, Ana Dragoi (Galati), Professor Matei Coriolan.

I cite these names, mentioned often in the paper, not in order to satisfy the reader's curiosity but because the people who helped us—particularly in our first tough hours—must always be remembered.

Some of these have died while some have turned into fighters braving all the persecutions to this day.

I hastened to list them now because I may not again have the opportunity to do so in the course of this book.

Our Action as Seen From the Outside

From the very first hour, we had the benefit of the Judeo-Masonic politician's hatred. But there were also people who received us into their hearts like a ray of hope.

Here are several letters from readers, which were printed in the first issue of "*The Ancestral Land*:"

"I shall not endeavor to express at great length my joy on the appearance of the review. I welcome it with our greeting of old: 'May God help them.' Nor shall I delve in these lines into the recent events, but I say: 'Onward, always forward, you, the new men. Long live the troop of Michael the Archangel. May the band of the wicked be swallowed by Belzebut's darkness.'

"St. Michael the Archangel will have to strike unhesitatingly and mercilessly. Such is the aim set forth in the pages of '*The Ancestral Land*.'

"Neither Satan nor his servants can answer the Archangel's call. Nor should they imagine that they can fool anyone by disguise. Traitors deserve a stiffer punishment than enemies.

"Show no indulgence to anyone, for nobody lacks the maturity to judge which is the decisive hour.

"I close my lines by wishing to see victory one hour sooner, the great victory."

Col. Blezu

"The bright sun of the swastika has not failed us this time either to pull us out of chaos. It gave us its beneficent light, for our salvation, 'The Legion of Michael the Archangel.' From now on the Romanian soul is again warmed by the faith that this holy movement shall not perish.

"The national idea will call us to duty.

"Those who will not understand us shall fall by the wayside. I am on your side."

M.I. Lefter, attorney President of L.A.N.C. for Galati

"You are the hopes of our future days. We place our future and that of our children at your feet.

"All of us wait impatiently to see yours a powerful organization and we are anxious to join the fight.

"And when I tell you this I am not telling just what I myself feel, but what I see in many others."

C.N. Paduraru Country accountant, Ruptura (Roman).

"I see and I feel Romanian hearts again being reborn. I do not only hope now that the victory will be ours, I am sure of it."

Ion Banea, student, Vurpar (Sibiu).

"It is my duty as a Christian student I feel, to send my congratulations and those of my friends in the Jiul's plains for the determination and energy you show in the struggle just begun."

Iuliu Gh. Stanescu, student.

"We, the Romanians of the village of Vulcani, workers in the Petrosani Co. carry even today in Greater Romania the yoke placed upon us by the company's functionaries, for all of them are aliens.

"I, Augustin Igna, contracted tuberculosis. Miner by profession, I can no longer work down in the mine for the polluted air hurts me.

"I forwarded a petition, co-signed by the doctor, requesting work of a lighter nature outside, not down under, because there, I would end my days in a few weeks. It was turned down. I now appeal to you for help for I have no one to turn to."

Igna Augustin

"Please stop sending me your review; my name is Axente Poenar, miner, Carteju de sus[5], because I do not have enough money to pay it even for three months, and I hate to send it back.

"And now let me explain to you why I do not have the money. It is fall here and everybody enjoys it because it is harvest time. That is, everybody but us miners, for we lack the clothing and the shoes that the oncoming winter demands; and our children must be sent to school. The little we save out of our bitter bread we must spend on these needs."

Axente Poenar, miner.

"Dear and beloved children of our people:

"Though I approach the sunset of my life, a new ray of hope penetrates my soul for the resurrection of our dear country,

5 We continued to keep his name on the subscriber's list.

seeing your pure and holy movement 'The Legion of Michael the Archangel,' the great celestial prince: I feel very much saddened that I will not live long enough to see the flowering of our people and to enjoy the labored yield wetted by the cold sweat, and maybe the blood, of those martyrs destined by God, who are and will yet be, for the fullfilment of the great plan that has been kneaded with so much suffering. It is quite late: the plague is spreading, our grave is being dug, the grave-diggers are ready to bury us forever; and we Romanians big or small, hesitate, barter and quarrel over ambitions, empty vainglory and perishable wealth.

"I keep quiet, for I am unschooled; you keep quiet because you are wily; he, because he is harnessed in a political party; they keep quiet because they are the administration; and so we all keep quiet; the darkness of our downfall envelops us gradually and the torch of our people goes out.

"I am a poor peasant ploughman, but I can handle the pen as well as I can the shovel or the scythe. I shall help you with my money, my pen, by deed and word, asking you to give me a little corner in our review '*The Ancestral Land.*' I shall write under the title 'Are we Romanians, or are we not, on the threshold of doom? And why?'

" 'Who are the guilty?

" 'Which is the cause of causes?

" 'What is being done and what must be done?

" 'What must each Romanian know and do?' "

V.I. Onofrei, ploughman,
Village of Tungujei (Vaslui)

Beyond Forms

As a matter of fact, *"The Ancestral Land"* is full of such letters; a contribution of our countrymen to the Legion's creation. For the Legion is more than an organization with members, books, and chiefs. It is a state of spirit, a unity of feeling and living to which all of us contribute. Members, chiefs, numbers, uniforms, program, etc. make up the visible Legion. The other one though, that one does not see, is the most important. The visible Legion without the invisible one, namely that state of spirit, of life, means nothing; it would be but a form devoid of any content.

We did not set ourselves up, with our review, like professors at their chairs, raising a barrier between us "the chiefs," "the teachers," who had their teachings and theories printed in the review, and the readership who has nothing to do but learn our teachings and conform to them. On one hand us, on the other they. No.

To make the Legion does not mean giving her a uniform, buttons, etc.; it does not mean to elaborate her system of organization. It does not even mean to formulate her legislation, leadership norms, logically enumerating the texts on paper. Just as to create a man does not mean making his clothes or fixing his principles of behavior or establishing his program of activity.

Neither statute, nor program nor doctrine make a movement. These could constitute its legislation, define its aims, system of organization, means of action, etc. but not be the movement itself.

These are concepts that even men of science confuse.

Creating only a "statute," "program," etc. then believing you created a "movement" is as if wanting to make a man, you would only make his clothing.

Creating a movement means first of all giving birth to a state of spirit, a gushing enthusiasm of the spirit, of the heart of a people which has nothing in common with the speculations of cold reasoning.

This is what constitutes the essential in the legionary movement.

I was not the one to create this state of spirit, it came to life by the convergence of our contribution of feeling with that of the other compatriots. The review *"The Ancestral Land"* was the meeting ground where our aspirations and later our thoughts fraternized with the feelings and thoughts of those Romanians who were attuned to us.

So then, the Legion in her essence, in that unseen state of spirit, which was felt by all of us, was not my creation. She was the fruit of a collaboration.

She was born by the fusion of the following contributions:

1. The feelings of the first legionaries.
2. The corresponding feelings of other Romanians.
3. The presence in the conscience of everybody of all our people's dead.
4. The urge of our Fatherland's soil.
5. God's blessing.

I would not want my thoughts to be wrongly interpreted by someone, as if I were saying:

> "I am not one of these legionaries in uniform, I am a legionary in spirit."

This cannot be.

On this spiritual foundation is created doctrine, program, statute, uniform, activity, all alike, not as accessories but as factors that fix the spiritual content of the movement, giving it a unified form and maintaining it alive in the people's conscience and carrying it toward accomplishment and victory.

The legionary movement is all of these together.

The uniforms that appeared in all contemporary movements, Fascism (the black shirt), National-Socialism (the brown shirt), etc., were not born from the leaders' imagination. They were born out of a necessity of expressing this state of spirit. The expression of the unity of feeling. They are the visible face of an unseen reality.

The National Movements and Dictatorship

Anytime there is talk about a national movement, tendencies toward a dictatorship are systematically attributed to it.

I do not wish to make a critique of dictatorships in this chapter, but I want to show that Europe's present day national movements such as the legionary movement, Fascism, National-Socialism, etc., are neither dictatorships nor democracies.

Those who fight us by shouting: "Down with Fascist dictatorship!", "Fight against dictatorship!", "Defend yourselves against dictatorship!" do not hit us. They are shooting off-target. They can only hit the notorious "dictatorship of the proletariat."

Dictatorship presupposes the will of a single man forcibly imposed upon the will of the other subjects in a state. In other words, two opposing wills: that of the dictator or a group of men on one hand, and that of the people on the other.

When this will imposes itself by constraint and cruelty, then the dictatorship is tyranny. But when a nation with a majority of 98 percent, in indescribable enthusiasm, a nation of 60 million or one of 40 million souls, approves and deliriously applauds the chief's measures, it means that there is a perfect accord between the chief's will and that of the people. Moreover, they mesh so perfectly that there no longer exist two wills. There is only one: the will of the nation, the expression of which is the chief. Between the will of the nation and the leader's will exists then only one relationship: a perfect rapport between them.

To claim that the unanimity obtained under the regimes of national movements is due to "terror" and "inquisitorial methods" is absolutely ludicrous, because the people among whom such movements arose have a highly developed civic awareness. They fought, bled, and left thousands who died for freedom; they never submitted, either to the enemy without or to the tyrant within. Why should they not fight and bleed also today, if faced by such terror? And then, one can draw votes or even majorities forcibly, by terror; one can draw tears or sighs; but it has never been heard nor will it ever be heard that one can produce enthusiasm and fervor by force. Not even within the most retarded nation in the world.

Because the national movement is not dictatorial in its essence we ask ourselves then: What is it?

Is it a democracy? Not at all, because the leader is not voted in by the electorate, and democracy is based on the eligibility principle. Or, in national regimes, no leader is selected by voting. He is acquiesced to.

If these regimes be not dictatorships or democracies, what then are they? Without defining them one must admit that they represent a new form of government, sui generis, in the modern states. It has not been encountered up to now and I do not know what name it will be given.

I believe that it has at its basis that state of spirit, that state of elevated national conscience which, sooner or later, spreads to the outskirts of the national organism.

It is a state of inner revelation. That which of old was the people's instinctive repository is reflected in these moments in the people's conscience, creating a state of unanimous illumination which is encountered only in the great religious revivals. This phenomenon could rightly be called a state of national oecumenicity.

A people in its entirety reaches an awareness of self, of its purpose and destiny in the world. During past history only flashes of such awareness have been noticed, but today we are faced with some permanent such phenomena.

In such a case the leader is no longer a "master," a "dictator," who does as he "pleases," who leads "according to his whims."

He is the incarnation of this unseen state of spirit, the symbol of this state of consciousness. He no longer does "as he pleases," he does what he "must" do. And he is guided not by individual or collective interests, but by the interests of the immortal nation which have penetrated the conscience of the peoples, it is only within the framework of these interests and only in that framework that personal and collective interests find their maximum of normal satisfaction.

The First Beginnings Of Organization

The organization of cadres constitutes a new developmental stage in the legionary movement.

Any movement, in order not to remain chaotic, must be cast into moulds of organization. The entire legionary system of organization is based on the idea of "the nest," namely a group varying between 3 and 13 men under the command of a leader. We have no "members" in the sense of isolated individuals. There is only the nest and the individual member is part of a nest. The legionary organization is not formed from a number of members, but a number of nests. This system has not varied much in its essence, from the beginnings to the present day. It occasionally received needed improvements, for an organization must consider realities; it is like a child constantly growing, whose clothing must constantly be fitted as it develops.

It is wrong for those who imagine how the organization should be in its final stage, to proceed by cutting for it from the start a vestment that will not fit it except in that final stage of development; just as it is wrong for some to proceed with cutting a tight fit at the beginning, then discounting later on the movement's growth, thus compelling it to struggle in forms no longer fitting.

I shall not insist here too much on "the nest" because I treated that question extensively in "*The Nest Leader's Manual*." However, what led me to choose this system? First of all, the needs of the movement.

There is a world of difference between the time when the League was founded, when one system was used, and that when the Legion was founded, when we adopted another system.

At the time the League was founded there existed a very widespread current of support. It had to be urgently tapped. While when the Legion came into being there was no such current of support for us, but only sparse, isolated men, scattered in towns and villages. I could not get started by founding county committees because we lacked people. Nor could I take some man and name him county head, for it did not make any sense if he was barely able to organize one small village.

The leader of a movement must take reality into account in greatest earnestness. My basic reality was "the single man"—a poor peasant in some village, crying; an unfortunate sick workingman, an uprooted intellectual.

And then I gave each of these the opportunity to gather around him a group, according to his abilities, with himself as leader. That was the nest with its leader.

It was not I naming him the nest's leader; it was his merits that put him there. He did not become a leader because I "wanted" him to be one, but only if he could gather a group, inspire it and lead it. In time—in contrast to all other parties where chiefs are often nominated on the basis of gifts—I succeeded in having a corps of small leaders "born" not "made," in whom leader's traits were obvious. That is why the leader of a legionary nest is a reality on which one can depend. The network of these nest leaders forms the whole skeleton of the legionary movement. The pillar of the legionary organization is the nest's leader. When these nests multiply they are grouped under village, district, county, provincial commands.

How did I acquire leaders over the larger units? I nominated no leader for village, district or county. I told them: "Conquer and organize! And, as much as you can organize, you will be chief over." I just confirmed them leaders in the positions to which their power, qualities and aptitudes elevated them. We started with the nest's leader and progressively he grew to village leader, district, the town and county leader, and only in 1934, that is seven years later, to the regional leader.

The nest's system also presents the following advantages:

a) It activates, puts to work the entire membership of a movement. In the other parties, where there are committees and members by village or county, it is only several committee members who work; the rest, 1,000, 2,000, 10,000, are inactive.

In our system, thanks to the wide initiative the nest leaders have, within prescribed norms, and thanks to the obligation of each nest to write as glorious a page as possible in its record, as there are no separate members as such outside of the nest, everybody, absolutely every single legionary, works.

b) *Solves all local problems.* There are a host of items which a single man is unable to cope with and a whole organization is too large to look into them, e.g. the digging of a small well in a village, the repairing of a little bridge, etc. A single man cannot do these by himself; an organization cannot busy itself with them; the nest however, of 6, 8 or 10 men is the most suitable unit to execute them.

c) *The nest is easily changeable.* From a fighting unit into a working one, or vice-versa.

d) *It creates a large number of cadres,* consequently developing men specialized in the art of leading,

e) *The effect of a defection or a betrayal remains localized,*

f) Finally, the nest is the best place for one to receive his legionary education. That is because men of the same age meet there, men of identical comprehensiveness and of like spiritual constitution. There, all are friends. A man who could not confess his troubles, bare his soul, before a youngster—either because of embarrassment or because he is reluctant to make him aware too early of the difficulties and worries of life—here in the nest among friends, he can do it. Just as he can take a reprimand or even a punishment. The nest is a small legionary family having love as its foundation. In "*The Nest Leader's Manual*" I laid down the six laws by which this family should be guided (page 4, point 3). This family should not be governed according to the leaders's whim; this would be dictatorship, but by laws.

1. *The law of discipline:* Legionary! Be disciplined! For only thus you can win. Follow your leader through thick and thin.

2. *The law of work:* Work! Work every day. Put your heart into it. Let your reward be, not gain, but the satisfaction that you have laid another brick to the building of the Legion and the flourishing of Romania.

3. *The law of silence:* Speak little. Say only what you must. Speak only when necessary. Your oratory should be deeds, not words. You accomplish: let others talk.

4. *The law of education*: You must become another person. A hero. In the nest become completely educated. Get to know the Legion well.

5. *The law of reciprocal help*: Help your brother who fell into misfortune. Do not abandon him.

6. *The law of honor*: Go along only on the paths of honor. Fight, and never be a coward. Leave the path of infamy to others. Better to fall in an honorable fight than win by infamy.

But I want to emphasize once again, dear legionaries, and I call your attention to an essential thing: the meeting of a nest is incomplete if a cold atmosphere prevails; "What have we accomplished?," "What else is there to be accomplished?," "Let us do this or that." "Good-bye!"

Give free rein to your souls. Reserve for them a place in the meeting. Proceed with warmth. Give everyone the chance to open up his heart, unload his difficulties, anxieties, worries, with which life has burdened him. Let him share his joys. Let your nest be a place of consolation and of sharing joys. A nest meeting is successful when a man returns home after unloading there the burdens of his soul and is full of faith in his people. If in "*The Nest Leader's Manual*" I have not sufficiendy stressed this point, I do it now.

Also in connection with the activity of education in the nest, I reproduce from "*The Nest Leader's Manual*" point 54: Prayer as a decisive element for victory. Appeal to our ancestors:

> "The legionary believes in God and prays for the victory of the Legion.
>
> "It should not be forgotten that we are here on this earth by God's will and the blessing of the Christian Church. Before the altars of our churches, the entire Romanian Nation on this earth has assembled, times without number, in periods of flight and persecution—women and children and old people—aware that that is the last possible place of refuge. And today too, we are ready to assemble—we, the Romanian people—round the altars as in former times of great danger and to kneel to receive God's blessing.
>
> "Wars were won by those who knew how to summon the mysterious powers of the unseen world from above and to ensure their help. These mysterious powers are the souls of the dead, the souls of our ancestors who too were once attached to this land, to our furrows, and who died in the defense of this land, and who today also are attached to it by the memory of their life here, and through us — their children, grand-children and great-great-grandchildren. But above all the souls of the dead stands God.

"When these powers are summoned, they come to our aid and encourage us, to give us strength of will and everything necessary to help us to achieve victory. They introduce panic and terror into the hearts of the enemy and paralyze their actions. In the last analysis, victory does not depend on material preparation, on the material strength of the belligerents, but on their capacity to ensure the support of the spiritual powers. This is the explanation—in our history—of miraculous victories even when our material weapons were decidedly inferior.

"How can we make sure that we have the support of these forces?

"1. By the justness and morality of your action, and

"2. By appealing fervently and insistently to these powers. Invoke them, attract them by the strength of your soul and they will come.

"The power of attraction is the greater when the appeal, the prayer, is made by many people assembled together.

"Therefore,—at the nest meetings which take place throughout the entire country every Saturday evening—prayers will be raised and all legionaries exhorted to attend church next day—Sunday.

"Our Patron Saint is the Archangel Michael. We ought to have his icon in our homes, and in difficult times we should ask his help and he will never fail us."

These nests are then grouped in units, either by age or sex, as follows:

1. The Brotherhoods of the Cross[6]

   a) assembling youngsters up to 14 years of age: the little brothers of the cross.

   b) assembling young men between 14 and 19 years of age: the brothers of the cross.

2. The legionaries in the making,

6 The "brothers of the cross," a literary translation of the Romanian "*frati de cruce*," are the young men who, according to a native popular traditional ritual, take a vow to each other on the cross, for eternal friendship, reciprocal help and faithfulness. The legionary movement was inspired by this Romanian popular institution to name the young legionary aspirants "brothers of the cross." The "Brotherhoods of the Cross" are then groupings of the "brothers of the cross."

3. The sworn-in legionaries,

4. The citadels, grouping girls and married women, or by administrative criteria, village, town, county, with their respective leaders who guide their activity, thus assuring unity. All these matters were treated extensively in "*The Nest Leader's Manual.*"

This system of nests could have a disadvantage; it would seem that it breaks, grinding down by its fragmentation the movement's unity. But this is only an apparent threat, for it is removed by the mutual love and the large dose of discipline which is poured into legionary education.

The Vow of the First Legionaries

November 8th, 1927, the feast day of Sts. Michael and Gabriel the Archangels was approaching. That day we were to take our first vow. We searched and found a symbol which could be a faithful expression of the character of our movement, of our union with the earth of our ancestors, our dead and the heavens. We collected a small quantity of earth from all the glorious spots of Romanian history for 2,000 years back, which we then mixed well. Small leather sacks were then filled with it and tightly tied with laces. These were to be received by legionaries upon taking the vow and were to be worn close to their hearts.

Here is the description of this solemnity, reproduced from the No. 8, November 1927 issue of "*The Ancestral Land:*"

> "On the morning of the 8th November, 1927, all the legionaries in Iasi met in our headquarters, and several others who took the trouble to come from other places.
>
> "Few in number, but strong through our unflinching faith in God and confident of His aid; strong in our decision and stubborn obstinacy to remain unflinching in the face of any storm; strong in our complete detachment from everything earthy—a fact which can be seen from our desire, our pleasure to bravely break away from material things and serve the cause of the Romanian Nation and the Cross.
>
> "This was the state of spirit of those who were impatiently awaiting the hour to take their vow, so as to joyfully form the Legion's first

wave of assault. And everyone can be sure that no other attitude is possible when, in our midst, clothed in white as in the hour of wrath, were united: Ion I. Mota, Ilie Garneata, Radu Mironovici, Corneliu Georgescu—those who, from prison to prison, had carried the whole weight of the nationalist movement on their shoulders for the last five years.

"The prayer.

"At ten o'clock, we all set off for the Church of St. Spiridon, dressed in national costume with caciula[7] and the swastika over our hearts, marching in columns. There, Stefan the Great, ruler of Moldavia; of Michael the Brave; of Mircea Ion Voda; of Horea, Closca and Crisan; Avram Iancu; Domnul Tudor; King Ferdinand; and for 'the memory of all rulers and soldiers who fell on the fields of battle in defense of the Romanian land against enemy invaders.'

"The solemnity of taking the vow

"We returned to our Home, marching and singing the Legion's Hymn There, the touching solemnity of the vow made by the first legionaries took place.

"The ancestral land.

"This solemnity began by mixing the earth brought from the tomb of Michael the Brave from Turda, with that from Moldavia—from Razboeni—where Stefan the Great fought his greatest battle, and from every other place where our ancestors' blood was soaked by the earth in ferocious battles, thus blessing it. When the packets of earth were opened, and before they were emptied out onto the table, the letters were read of those who had brought, or sent them."

The following took their vow:

Corneliu Zelea-Codreanu, Ion I. Mota, Ilie Garneata, Corneliu Georgescu, Radu Mironovici, Hristache Solomon who presided at this solemnity, G. Clime, Mille Lefter, Ion Banea, Victor Silaghi, Nicolae Totu, Alexandru Ventonic, Dumitru Ifrim, Pantelimon Statache, Ghita Antonescu, Emil Eremeiu, Ion Bordeianu, M. Ciobanu, Marius Pop, Misu Crisan, Popa, Butnaru, Budeiu, I.

7 Pelt cap made of curly lamb. (Tr.)

Tanasache, Stefan Budeciu, Traian Cotiga, and Mihail Stelescu, a high school student.

A New Battle

In the December 1, 1927 issue of *"The Ancestral Land"* we opened a new drive to seek funds for the purchase of a Light panel truck to use in our travels. Again, we used the same system of general effort. Legionaries began organizing festive shows, conferences, Christmas choirs, and to contribute their mite.

"The Vrancea Brotherhood of the Cross" of Focsani distinguished itself by collecting the sum of 50,000 lei as a result of a festive show sponsored by Gen. Macridescu. It was at that time that I changed its name of "Vrancea" to "Victory Brotherhood of the Cross" under which it is known to this day.

On February 19, 1928, that is in ten weeks, this drive was successful. We bought a new panel truck in Bucharest for 240,000 lei of which we put down 100,000 lei, the balance of 140,000 lei to be paid in twelve monthly instalments.

We left Bucharest for Iasi, with Stefan Nicolau driving "The Doe"[8], as the boys baptised her, and Banea, Bordeianu and Mironovici. The legionaries and our friends expected us at the edge of the city and we were welcomed upon our arrival amidst general joy.

In order to meet our monthly instalments we formed a Committee of 100 whose members were to contribute 100 lei per month for one year. This committee reached a membership of 50 within two months, poor people most of them, small employees, workingmen, or peasants who, parting with 100 lei per month were making a real sacrifice.

The girls of the Iasi "Citadels" and in particular those of "The Iulia Hasdeu Citadel" of Galati, began to do embroidery work and sell it to collect money.

---

8 Endearing name given by legionaries to their first panel truck. (Tr.)

Problems of a Material Kind

For its small needs, the movement was moving along fine from a material point of view. From the work and the contributions of poor people, enough was being collected for us to live on and support activities.

Absolutely all sums contributed were published in *"The Ancestral Land"*

The journal is full of those who gave 10 or 5 lei. Those who gave 50 or 60 lei were rarely found. And our bankers were those who could contribute 100 lei per month, the Committee of 100 members.

Let us take at random from this committee:

#16. Nicolae Voinea from Panciu, a family with five children living off a two acre vineyard.

#17. D. Popescu, a retired sub-lieutenant.

#18. Ion Blanaru, till yesterday a student; now an engineer making 4,000 lei per month.

#19. Ion Butnaru, clerk at the Romanian Railways.

#20. Nistor M. Tilinca, salesman in a cooperative.

#21. Corneliu Georgescu, help from parents.

#22. Radu Mironovici, help from parents.

#23. Ionescu M. Traian, engineer in forestry.

From the economy these contributors imposed upon their spending for food and clothing, enough was being collected for the organization, which by judicious use of the money, managed to stay alive and develop normally.

But the Jewish press was yelling: "With what money do these gentlemen buy panel trucks? [The Jew, always in bad faith, made several trucks out of the one we owned]. Who finances this movement?"

Oh! Gentlemen, no one has "financed" it. No one, but the infinite faith of Romanians who, for the most part, are poor as Job. Not only were we not "financed" by capitalists, but I counsel anyone who leads a movement based on sane principles to refuse all offers of financing if he wishes his movement to survive. Because a political movement must be constituted so as to be able to produce alone, out of the faith and sacrifice of its members, exactly as much as it needs to live and grow.

For a normal and healthy development a movement has the right to consume only as much as its members can provide; and its membership can only provide to the extent of their capacity for faith, that is, for sacrifice. It does not provide sufficient funds? Do not resort to outside financing but go about increasing the faith of the membership. In fact, insufficient contributions on the membership's part is an indication of little faith. It does not provide any funds? The organization is dead and it will soon collapse. Lacking faith it will be vanquished by those that have it.

A leader who accepts the outside financing of his movement is like the man who accustoms his body to live on medication. To the extent an organism is administered medication, to the same extent it is condemned to being unable to react on its own. Moreover, when it is deprived of the medication, it dies; it is at the mercy of the pharmacist! Likewise, a political movement is at the mercy of those who finance it. These could cease their financing at any given moment and the movement, unaccustomed to living on its own, dies.

A movement, just like an individual, in fact may sometimes need a larger amount of money. It then may borrow and repay the loan in time, but only if the certainty of being able to do so exists.

Consequently, gentlemen leaders of movements—and saying this I address myself to those who shall come after us—turn down those well-intentioned who offer to finance your movement, naturally, if you should encounter this species in the future; though I think they won't exist in Romania, where even today they seem to be vanishing. All those who can and do finance are the Jewish bankers, the very rich Jews, the big Jewish grain dealers, the great Jewish industrialists and merchants. They finance the political parties in order to exterminate the Romanians in their own country.

Pretty soon there will be no one to engage in financing—this word reeks of banker, of prey, of injustice and indecency!—no one. Neither Romanians nor, least of all, Jews. For this caste of bankers and tycoons, of businessmen enriched as a result of business coups, these birds of prey who greedily stalk human society, are going to be exterminated. Well-to-do people, rich people, to the limits of decency, there will be, but they will not be capable of financing but only of helping a movement from their savings. This obligation to help, to help their nation in hard times rests upon every Romanian and it will so rest forever; and such aid is and will always be welcome. But my own material situation, as well as that of my comrades, was becoming worse and worse, more pressing.

I had become the burden of my poor father-in-law, who not counting me, from his small salary could hardly feed and clothe his five children. With my wife we occupied one room while the other seven members of the family shared the other two rooms. Understanding my predicament, thanks to his great love for me and for the Romanian cause, he never said a word to me though I saw as time passed that he was bending ever more under the weight of difficulties.

Then we decided that I would devote full time to the movement and Mota with the other three comrades of Vacaresti prison would set up a law practice to make their living as well as to help me. They would commence shortly but they would meet with tremendous hardships. I looked back. Registered in the university ten years earlier, we had fought side by side with all student classes as they came along. And by and by, all of them had found placements, creating for themselves a small situation by which they managed to live; only we remained alone on the fringes of society, like some madmen lost in the middle of the world's ways.

Although capable lawyers, my comrades would be able to eke out but a meager existence. They could not be hired by the railways, city hall or the state; such places are reserved for those who desert the ranks of the national movement and cross over to the political parties—an encouragement to those lacking character. The honor of our lives dictated that they take no Jewish case to defend. Romanians would shun them. It would be only the poor who would come into their offices.

The road was tough for us, we being ostracized in our own country and thus placed in the position where it was next to impossible to make a living.

The Summer of 1928

The entire winter we spent in organizing nests. Spring saw the resumption of work in the Ungheni brickyard and the garden of Mrs. Ghica. We worked in these two places making bricks and raising vegetables. We wanted to build ourselves another Home, for we were not sure we could stay in the old one because a lawsuit was initiated to evict us.

In this hard work we became closer to one another, feeling ever closer to those who work with their hands and ever more distant from those who live by the labor of others.

This work was completing our education more than the lectures of some university professor. There we learned how to overcome hardships; we steeled our will; we strengthened our bodies and became accustomed to a tough and severe way of life in which no pleasure found place save that of spiritual satisfaction. It was then that "The Brotherhood of the Cross" from Galati with Tocu, Savin, Costea, came to help, as well as other brotherhoods.

Radu Mironovici learned to drive our panel truck very well and, helped by Eremeiu, carried paying passengers between Iasi, Varatec, Agapia, and Neamt monasteries. Yet, because of the summer, which is always poorer, I had to seek a loan from the Albina Bank of Husi, mortgaging my father's house for 110,000 lei, which I divided, part for the brickyard, part for the panel truck's monthly instalments and part for the legionary publications. Unable to repay this loan even to this day, my indebtedness reached the sum of 300,000 lei.

During that summer we also entered the field of commerce in order to make some money for the Legion.

The Jews have control over the vegetable marketing in nearly all markets in Moldavia.

Three teams of legionary students were charged with marketing vegetables. These teams were buying merchandise on the Iasi market, loading 600 to 800 lbs. onto the panel truck, then descending like a plague upon the Jews, lowering prices to half. August 1, 1928 was the first anniversary of our review's publication. Here is what I wrote then:

"On August 1, '*The Ancestral Land*' celebrates one year of regular publication.

"This is not much. Several days ago, between 13 and 30 of July the town of Carcassonne (a fort in France) celebrated 2,000 years of existence. It may be that the Legion too, will have 2,000 years ahead of us! But the hardest of those is the first year when one has to break virgin soil, to plow the first furrow. During these early days a lot of difficulties came upon us, but our journal—sometimes richer, sometimes poorer—yet always great, stood firm, overcoming them.

"When a year ago, starting penniless, in the most critical moment of the national movement, we placed St. Michael the Archangel's icon on the cover, we knew that our review would survive."

Fighting Misery

Towards fall, personal material difficulties became oppressive. We no longer had any decent shoes or clothing, my wife and I; my wife was wearing four-year-old shoes. We could no longer expect anything from my father because there were six other children besides myself, all in schools, and the fights he fought left him overwhelmed with debts. Only several thousand lei were left out of his salary to feed and clothe a large family.

I then gathered all my strength and decided that I too, would commence law practice, intending at the same time to lead the movement. I opened my office in Ungheni, working together with my secretary, Ernest Comanescu. As a result I was able to realize a small, very small, income with which I managed to take care of our needs and the few modest indulgences of our lives. Six years had passed since we had limited our existence to only the strict necessities of life. For six years I had not entered a theater, movie, beer hall, ballroom or gone to a party. And now as I write, it has been 14 years since I have been to any of them. I do not regret it. What I do regret is, that after a life of such restrictions some individuals have accused me of leading a leisurely existence.

In this misery that lasted years, as in the tough trials in which my fate has put me, I had the steady support of my wife who faithfully took care of me. She shared my numerous blows, experienced privations and endured even hunger, in order to help me fight on. I will forever be grateful to her.

Professor Gavanescul Receives the Sack of Earth

There is a soul who has watched us closely, step by step, having been interested in us. He has been studying us, perhaps. I speak of the old imposing figure of Ion Gavanescul, professor of pedagogy at the University of Iasi since 1880. Once he told us: "I wish so much that I too could have a little sack of earth!"

We invited him to our house on December 10, 1928 where, in the midst of the group of legionaries I presented him with our gift—the most precious gift we could give him—the little sack of earth.

The old white-haired and white-browed professor opened wide his eyes as in a moment of the gravest solemnity. Then, following a moment of silence he said:

> "Gentlemen, I am not worthy to receive this talisman except on my knees."

He took it then, slowly knelt and prayed. We all knelt around him.

The Liberal Party fell that fall of 1928 as a result of the relentless assaults of the National-Peasants who threatened "violence" and "revolution."

The National-Peasant Party succeeded them in power after eight years of political opposition. But they soon proved to be a great disappointment to the whole country. They would begin to steal, just as the Liberals did; they would engage in "scandalous business deals" just like Liberals; they would use the gendarmerie to "terrorize" and even shoot down their adversaries or those who would express dissatisfaction, just like Liberals; they would set up their own bankers, just like Liberals,

But particularly they would fall under the continual influence of international finance, to which they began yielding up little by little, for years, for decades, the riches of Romania, in exchange for ruinous loans.

The First Assembly of Nest Leaders and The Forming of the Legionary Senate

I convoked at Iasi on January 3-4, 1929, the first national meeting of nest leaders. Forty to fifty participated. The meetings were held in the house of Gen. Ion Tarnoschi who on this occasion, during a touching ceremony, with tears in his eyes, was now receiving the little sack of earth which included the blood of his own soldiers and officers.

"How I wish God gave me enough days to live to see the hour of Romanian deliverance. But I do not think that I shall live that long," he told us.

On this occasion another series of legionaries took their vow. They were: Spiru Peceli, war invalid, Gheorghe Potolea, invalid since the charge at Prunaru, Nicolae Voinea, and others.

From the discussions we had and from reports each of those present made as representatives of all regions, we became convinced that the system of "nests," unused in our country up to then, could catch on and give good results. Certainly, there are problems and awkwardnesses that are inherent in any endeavor. However, it was enough for me to find out that in one year's time without any other education but only on the basis of appeals and directives given in our review, isolated nests had been formed, active nests, in all regions and social strata. I told myself: "The system passed the exam. It works."

This meeting of January 3-4 proved the correctness of my principles of organization. Consequently, what we had to do now was to continue steadily along the same lines.

I realized at the same time that the movement was catching on particularly among youthful ranks; that the system of dynamic education—education in parallel with action—is much superior to the static one.

Therefore we should continue this system for another year, not yet trying to reach out to the masses, and dismissing the idea of an electoral campaign.

It was also then that the Legion's Senate was set up: a forum made up of men over 50 years of age, intellectuals, peasants or workingmen, who had led a life of great correctitude, had showed great faith in the legionary future, and great wisdom. They would be convened at difficult times any time it was felt that their advice was needed. They were not to be elected but designated by the head of the Legion, and later passed on by the rest of the Senate. The title of Senator was the highest honor to which a legionary could aspire.

The Senate then was formed by Hristache Solomon, Gen. Dr. Macridescu, Gen. Ion Tarnoschi, Spiru Peceli, Col. Cambureanu, and Ion Butnaru. Several months after its constitution, the illustrious university Professor Traian Braileanu—who five years later in his journal, "Sociological Essays," was to explain in the highest scientific terms the legionary phenomenon—took his place in the Senate.

TOWARDS THE POPULAR MASSES

Among the Moti

The Moti still live in the mountains of central Transylvania. Old as those mountains, they have lived for centuries the same existence always dominated by two characteristics: poverty—they are the only Romanians, perhaps the only people on earth, who have never known throughout their history a single day of happiness and plenty—and the struggle for liberty. Their whole life has been a struggle for liberty. They gave us Horea, Closca and Crisan, and they supported the revolution of 1784; they gave us Avram Iancu, and fought in 1848. History has recorded over 40 uprisings in their mountains against Hungarian domination; all of them drowned ultimately in their own blood. Yet, their steadfastness could never be broken.

Lately the tribune voices of Amos Francu and Capt. Emil Siancu, Moti themselves, ring out in vain like a cry of alarm. There are gold mines in their mountains. One by one their exploiters were getting rich, while they remained unclad and without bread:

> "Gold lies in our mountains' core
> While we beg from door to door."

The gray rock is bare. Nothing grows on it; neither wheat nor corn. The only wealth there is, is the gold in the exploiter's hands, and the only possibility of making a living is in the timber of the forests.

The calvary of alien domination lasted one thousand years. One thousand years of endurance, hoping that some day Greater Romania would be born to save them, to finally look after them and their children, to redress the long and killing injustice, to come and reward them for their millenary patience, suffering and struggles.

Only those who are motherless know not consolation. Only those who do not have a fatherland know neither consolation nor recompense. The fatherland always rewards its children, those who have been awaiting its justice and believed in it, and those who have fought and suffered for it. It was inconceivable that the Moti would not be recompensed for their immense patience, suffering and bravery!

But after the war every man, especially every politician, busied himself with his own "self," his own material, electoral, political situation. So that the Moti were forgotten. Whoever busies himself with his own "self" cannot busy himself with "others." And whoever is surrounded by present worries cannot place himself, his thoughts and feelings, in history so that working in the name of his fatherland he would see to it that the great redress and historical rewards which are owed its brave men are given.

Not only were they forgotten but they were delivered as prey to the Jewish usurers who, in their race for profit, infiltrated their mountains where the alien's feet could never trespass, and stole their only livelihood by building mills high up in the mountains and felling their forests, leaving them the bare rock.

"O Iancu, why don't you come back from the dead
To see our mountains bared?"

In their song of despair they call out to Iancu their hero, to see his mountains despoiled, his forests "shaved" by the bands of "little Jews;" this, during an administration of Greater Romania, in the days of the people's long-awaited victory.

Verily, what frightening tragedy, to resist for ten centuries against all iniquities, and now to die of misery and hunger in Greater Romania you had awaited for a millenium!

It is she you have expected. She was the only moral support that sustained you. Now this hope too, falls to the ground. You did not have any bread but yet you hoped. For this population Greater Romania did not turn out to be an invigoration, a triumph, a coronation following a thousand years of suffering, with joyous reward from all their people. For this, someone with a soul like Stefan the Great was needed, not the pygmy soul of the Romanian politician. Greater Romania meant a collapse into mortal despair for the Moti people.

These politicians stain the face of our nation. For a nation, over and above any other interest, has the duty to fulfill certain moral obligations. If that nation does not meet them, its face remains stained.

Touched by the letter of a teacher from Bistra, near Campeni, I boarded a train in order to go there and examine the state of affairs for myself.

Riding a small mountain train I was coursing with shrinking heart through the valleys of the Apuseni Mountains where death had frolicked in scores of battles and where the ghosts of Horea and Iancu wander.

I approached a peasant Moti man in a railway station. He had at least twenty patches on his coat, an evidence of unparalleled poverty. He was selling wooden barrel hoops he had made—for a pittance. His eyes were sunken, his cheeks drawn in. A gentle physiognomy. His look was shy; one could read no particular thoughts on his face, but in his eyes was pain and I saw not only a hungry man but one tortured by hunger.

No interest for living could be seen in these gentle eyes that inspired pity, no preoccupation; they were just blank.

"How do you manage in these parts?" I asked him.

"Well! Well, thank you."

"Can you raise corn, potatoes here?"

"Yes, we can."

"Do you have everything you need, food,..?"

"Yes, we have...we have..."
"Then, you don't have it too bad ..?"

"No!...No!..."

He sized me up several times, showed himself very little disposed to conversation—for who knows on what shores of despair his mind was wandering—and in his inherited racial nobility he did not wish to explain to a stranger.

Finally I arrived at Bistra. I called on the teacher in the village who had written me. I only stayed a day. In the poor homes of the Moti that I visited, I saw their many little cold children huddled together—awaiting for two, three weeks, or sometimes a month or more, the return of their parents who had gone on the road with horse and wagon to bring back to them a sack of corn meal in exchange for the wooden hoops and barrels they make, then sell hundreds of miles away in other parts of the country to which God had been more generous.

It is only for a few months of the year that the Moti stay at home; the rest of the time they are on the road.

The teacher told me:

> "Not even during the Hungarian domination could the foreigner settle here. But nowadays, a lumber mill has been set up, owned by a Jewish company in Oradea which grabbed our forests and cut them down. Throughout their poor lives, the Moti have eked out a livelihood by making barrels and barrel hoops. But from now on they will be deprived of this. They are condemned to die.
>
> "Hunger and other necessities force them to work for the Jews, felling their own trees for a 20 lei daily wage, a trifle. That is all that is left to them out of all that richness which is extracted from their mountains and taken down their valleys in long trainloads. And when the timber is all cut down, that will be the end of us too. But there is something that is even sadder. We have lived a life of virtue for hundreds of years. The Jews brought in with them the sins of debauchery. There are over 30 Jews employed at this lumber mill. And Saturday evening when they get their wages, they take the girls and women of the Moti and dishonor them in night-long orgies. Moral and physical illnesses consume our villages in addition to poverty.
>
> "And one cannot say anything. No protest can be attempted because these Jews are on such good terms with all the politicians that they are virtually all-powerful masters. Local authorities are at their bidding, from gendarmes all the way to the top.
>
> "If you try to say something you are immediately accused of "urging" one part of the citizenry to "hatred" against the other citizens; that you "disturb social harmony" and "the brotherhood" in which the Romanians have always lived with the "peaceful Jewish population;" that we are not good "Christians" for Jesus Christ said: "Love your neighbor even him who wrongs you..." etc.
>
> "If you utter one single word, you are arrested as an "enemy of the State's security" and as an inciter to "civil war." You are insulted and even beaten. They control the authorities and you must keep quiet and watch the whole tragedy of your people. It would be better for God to blind us so we would no longer see with our own eyes; so we would know nothing."

My blood was boiling in my veins and the idea occurred to me anew of grabbing a weapon, going into the mountains and mercilessly starting to shoot into the bands of enemies and traitors, if the Romanian authorities and laws of Greater Romania can condone such crimes against the Romanian nation, her honor and her future, and if these laws and sold-out authorities have stripped her of any hopes for justice and for salvation.

I returned to Iasi with an aching heart, borne down by the burden this people carries. How terrible is the alienation of the leading class of a people, of its political and cultural class!

Literati and writers consecrate their efforts to all kinds of irrelevant topics. Books and books are published which fill the bookstores' shop windows. What shall the future's verdict be regarding these men, if for such a historical tragedy as that of the Moti, unfolding under their very eyes, they found not a single word of protest which could also serve as an alarm signal to the people dazed by all the scandalous literature that puts it to sleep and clouds its future road and life?

In what light shall the nation look at these writers and literati, whose mission, the most sacred one, is precisely that of denouncing the dangers that threaten its moral and physical being, and of lighting the way for its future? And how will this leading political class of "orators" in Parliament or anywhere else be looked upon, which has deserted its most elementary obligation to watch over the nation's life and honor?

As I was going down on the little train from Bistra toward Turda, the director of the sawmill in Bistra also entered the same compartment; a fat Jew hardly contained by his clothing who gave the impression of a life abundantly lived. I do not believe that one like him ever knew hunger in his life, even once.

A young man approximately of my age also entered the compartment at the next stop. From the very first I realized they were friends on very good terms and that the young man was Romanian.

The Jew poured himself some coffee out of a thermos bottle and took out some slices of cake from a packet. He began to eat; I observed a wolf's appetite. He began gulping before realizing he had not invited his friend to partake, so immediately did so. The young man took a slice of cake and a cup of coffee and began eating somewhat timidly, showing himself grateful and respectful to the rich Jew for the "attention" accorded him.

It was about five o'clock in the morning, not quite light yet, on the Friday before Easter: Passion Friday. Saddened, I asked myself: "Who, I wonder, is this scoundrel of a young Romanian who, on this day when the whole Christian world fasts, eats cake side by side with the Jew, the torturer of Romanians?"

From their talk I learned he was a forestry engineer. The Jew showed a compulsive inclination to talk. He talked and joked continuously.

Then he produced a record player and began playing records, everything on them most indecent. I sat in a corner of the compartment and listened without a word, looking out the window. The day was beginning to break and I could see, on the road paralleling the railroad, a long line of horse-drawn wagons, and at the head of each, a Moti man, trudging quiet and sad. Loaded with charcoal, they were headed for the market of Turda, a 40 mile drive, to sell it and buy, not new clothes or toys, but a few pounds of cornmeal to take home to their children, for it was Easter time. This is the only joy they could bring their children.

My heart groans with pain and anxiety. It is not enough that these robbers take their bread; they also desecrate, insult, on this Passion Friday, their poverty and faith. They pass by singing and insulting, on these roads of millenary suffering on which—out of respect for human suffering and pain—no man should tread except in the deepest quiet and decency, heads uncovered before the hungry and ragged people who walk heavily under the sentence of their merciless fate.

When it was daylight our eyes met, the young man's and mine. I could see that he recognized me. Uneasy, he lost his composure. I too, recognized him. Back in 1923 I had seen him as a Christian nationalist student. He was in the front lines of a demonstrating student group, singing:

> "And we shall crush the Jews under our heels
> Or else shall gloriously die," etc.

I reflected, full of bitterness: "If all the youth who fight will get to be like this tomorrow, then this people of ours must perish; through Jewish conquest, floods, earthquake, or dynamite—it does not matter which—but perish it must."

The Summer of 1929

Two marches were organized this summer, one with the young men in the Galati and Focsani "Brotherhoods of the Cross" and one with legionaries. I wanted to take them on the roads I had so often trod, to spend with them as much time as possible, in order to observe and study them as well as to show them the beauties of our country.

This time, as in all future marches that I shall make, I shall seek to develop in the young legionaries first of all their will: by long marches in which everyone will carry heavy loads through rain, wind, heat or mud; in formation and in step, with talking forbidden for hours; through a Spartan life, sleeping in forests, eating simple fare; through the obligation of being severe with themselves in all respects, beginning with their bearing and gestures; through creating for them obstacles they would have to overcome, such as climbing over huge rocks, getting across streams.

I was trying to turn them into men of strong will, who were to look straight at and behave in manly fashion under any difficulty. Therefore I never permitted the circumvention of an obstacle; it had to be overcome.

In lieu of the weak and defeated man, who bends with any passing wind, a type now predominating in both political life and the professions—we must create for this people a conqueror, unbending and undaunted.

By instructing them in common, I shall seek, on the other hand, to develop an esprit de corps, a sense of unity. I have noticed that the instruction in common has a great influence upon a man's intellect and psyche, rendering order and cadence to his disorderly mind and anarchic feeling.

By imposing punitive measures I shall seek to develop, in fine, the sense of responsibility and the courage to assume that responsibility for his acts. There is nothing more disgusting than the man who lies and shuns his responsibility.

I punished regularly, without exception, any infraction. I punished a youth in Vatra-Dornei for having caused a disturbance in a public park.

Something of a more serious nature happened at Dorna-Cozanesti, not so much in itself, as an indication of the state of spirit the case revealed. Four youths went to a Jewish tavern, ordering sardines, bread and wine, and after they ate well, they stood up. Instead of paying their bill, one of them heroically brandished a revolver threatening the life of the Jew if he should squeal, for—he added—they were from Corneliu Codreanu's group.

I punished him. Had I not done so, it would have been this youth—not the Jew from whom a can of sardines had been stolen—who would have morally destroyed himself. As a matter of fact, among legionaries, punishment cannot cause resentment, for all of us are fallible. In our concept, punishment means a man of honor has to make good on his error. Once the punishment is fulfilled, man is free of its burden as if nothing had happened.

In most of the cases this punishment takes the form of some work. Not because labor would be in the nature of a condemnation, but because it offers the chance of amending through a good deed the wrong that has been committed. That is why the legionary will receive and carry out punishment with serenity.

The Decision to go to the Masses
November 8, 1929

More than two years had passed since the Legion came into being. Our nests had multiplied all over the country. The need was now felt to strengthen the movement by using and stimulating these small nuclei to work. The only legal way to bring about nationwide measures for the solving of the Jewish problem was through political avenues. This presupposed a contact with the masses at large. Whether good or bad, this was the method that the law placed at our disposal, and which sooner or later we had to follow. With Lefter and Potolea we fixed the first legionary public meeting in Tg. Beresti in the northern Covurlui county on December 15. The decision was taken on November 8, when a new series of legionaries from various parts of the country took their vow on the anniversary of the Legion's patron saint.

At the same time I sent Totu into Turda county where, together with Amos Horatiu Pop, he was to intensify the legionary propaganda and also organize a meeting.

December 15, 1929

On the evening of December 14 I was in Beresti. Lefter, Potolea, Tanase Antohi and others were expecting me at the depot. The market town of Beresti is a real wasp's nest of Jews; houses and shops crowded together. The only street runs through the middle of town, with the mud ankle-deep, and along the sides, some boardwalks. I was to stay at Potolea's. Next morning the Galati prosecutor and a gendarme major came to tell me that I was not permitted to hold the meeting. I told them:

"The interdiction you confront me with is neither right nor legal. Anyone has the right to hold meetings in this country, Germans, Hungarians, Turks, Tartars, Bulgarians, Jews. Is it only I who do not have this right? Your measure is an arbitrary one; being illegal I shall not obey it. I shall hold the meeting at any cost."

Finally, after some discussion, they approved my holding the meeting on the condition that we not cause any disturbance

What was I to do? What kind of disturbance? Break into people's homes? This was my first public meeting. Was I not fully determined to keep it in perfect order and thus retain the privilege of holding others?

At the determined hour a very small number of people gathered, hardly one hundred. I learned from them that a lot more people had wanted to come but they were prevented from leaving their villages.

The whole meeting lasted only five minutes. Lefter spoke one minute, Potolea another, and I the rest, I said: "We came to hold a rally, but authorities forcibly prevent our men from coming. Against all orders I shall hold ten rallies! Let someone bring me a horse and I will ride from village to village throughout the whole district of Horincea."

In fact through all that mud the only means of locomotion was the horse. Two hours later a horse was brought and I started off. After me on foot came Lefter with four other legionaries. We reached the first village, Meria. There, in the church yard, in a matter of minutes, everybody was gathered—men, women and children. I said but a few words and I outlined no political program:

"Let us all unite, men and women, to carve for ourselves and for our people another destiny. The hour of Romanian resurrection and deliverance is approaching. He who believes, he who will fight and suffer, will be rewarded and blessed by this people. New times knock at our gates! A world, with an infertile and dry soul is dying and another one is being born, belonging to those who are full of faith.

"In this new world everyone will have his place, not based on his schooling, intelligence, or knowledge, but above all in accordance with his faith and character."

Then we went on. Less than three miles away we came to Slivna. It was getting dark. Yet people were expecting me with lighted candles. A nest of legionaries headed by Teodosiu came out to meet me at the edge of the village. I spoke here too. Then I headed for Comanesti, the Slivna nest of legionaries leading the way. These were roads I had never traveled before.

Here too, people were expecting me with lanterns and candles, while the young men sang.

People were receiving me joyously no matter to what party they belonged. We were strangers, yet it seemed we had been friends for ages. Enmities melted. We were all one soul, one people.

Next morning I resumed my ride. But this time I was not alone. Three other riders asked me if they could come along. On the edge of the neighboring village, Ganesti, we stopped at Dumitru Cristian's. He was a man about 40 years old with a bearing of haiduc and a pair of eyes hidden under dense brows. He had been a fierce nationalist fighter since early student battles. Now, on the instant, he unhitched his horses from the wagon, put the saddle on one of them and came with us. Soon our number grew larger with Dumitru and Vasile Popa, Hasan and Chiculita.

As we rode from village to village the number of riders increased to twenty. Most were between 25 and 30 years of age, a few being 35 or 40, the oldest, Chiculita from Cavadinesti, was about 45. When our numbers had so increased, we felt the need for a distinctive insignia, a uniform. For lack of something better, all of us placed turkey feathers in our hats. And so we entered villages singing. It seemed—as we went singing, our horses trotting along the hills' crests near the river Pruth where so often long ago had passed and fought our ancestors—that we were the shadows of those who of old had defended Moldavia's territory. The live ones in the present indentified with the dead of the past, we were the same soul, the same great unity of Romanianism carried by the wind over the crests of the hills. The news of my arrival, carried by word of mouth, had spread through all the villages. Villagers were expecting us everywhere. Everyone we met on the road was inquiring: "When are you going to come to us too? People had waited for you yesterday well into the night."

In those villages, as I sang and spoke to the people, I felt how I was penetrating into those undefined depths of soul where the politicians with their borrowed platforms could never descend. There, into those depths, I plunged the roots of the legionary movement. No one will ever be able to pull them out.

Thursday was market day in Beresti. At 10 o'clock in the morning about 50 of us riders appeared on the top of the hill above the market town. From there we descended into the town in formation, singing.

Townsfolk received us with great enthusiasm. Romanians came out of Christian homes pouring pailfuls of water across our path—an old custom wishing us in our travel the fulfillment of all our hopes. Again we went into the yard of Nicu Balan where the first rally was supposed to take place. There were over 3,000 people this time. We did not hold a meeting. I gave some of the riders souvenirs.

I gave my cigarette holder to Nicu Balan; it was made in the prison of Vacaresti. Chiculita received a swastika. Lefter and Potolea were named members of the Legion's Supreme Council, and Nicu Balan to the county of Covurlui's general staff; and Dumitru Cristian as leader of the legionaries in the Horincea Valley.

This Horincea Valley, with its places and people, remained dear to me. After Focsani, it was to remain the second strongest pillar of the legionary movement.

In Transylvania, At Ludosul-D-Emures

We left for Ludos on the Friday before Christmas, at 5 o'clock in the evening. There were four of us in the panel truck: Radu Mironovici driving, Emil Eremeiu, an acquaintance, and I. Extremely cold weather had forced train cancellations. That night we almost froze to death, although we filled our panel truck with straw and covered ourselves with it. We traveled the route, Iasi, Piatra-Neamt, Valea Bistritei, and at 4 o'clock in the morning we reached the crest of the Carpathian Mountains.

We arrived in Ludosul-de Mures at 11 o'clock that Christmas Eve after more than 24 hours of driving. Here we had a good rest at Amos's house. We went to church Christmas morning, then visited the little town. It was larger than Tg. Beresti; situated about 28 miles east of

Turda, the county's capital. This town too, is full of Jews, though not reaching the Beresti percentage. Here too, Judas, settled in the market place, spread his web like a spider over the whole Romanian region. The poor peasants will be caught in this web, twirled around and dazed, then sucked dry of all their possessions.

On the morning after Christmas we got started, the panel truck carrying ten legionaries up ahead, then I with some twenty riders on horseback—Amos, Nichita, Colceriu, Professor Mattei and others, all of us wearing turkey feathers in our hats.

On the road we were looked upon curiously as the people we met were not aware of our purpose. But we were riding as if we were invested with the greatest authority, for we felt we were coming in the name of the Romanian people who ordered us to do so.

In Gheta, Gligoresti and Gura-Ariesului, people were gathered in as large numbers as in the Horincea Valley. Here too, we outlined no political program. We just told them we came from Moldavia to stir to life again the suffering soul of Romanians, for one thousand years of slavery, injustice and entombment had been long enough.

Greater Romania had been realized with much sacrifice, but it seems that the alien domination and the old injustice had extended even this side of the Greater Romania's birth. Ten years of Romanian administrations had not succeeded in healing our painful wounds nor had they corrected the injustices of centuries. They had given us a semblance of unity but the Romanian soul still was split into as many pieces as there were political parties.

The resurrection of this people is seething underground and it will soon erupt, lighting with its light our whole future and the dark past. He who believes shall conquer!

Again I had the feeling that I was descending into their hearts.

Although I was hundreds of miles away from Moldavia, in regions that had been for centuries separated from us by borders, there too I had found the same soul, exactly the same as in the Horincea Valley near Pruth. The same soul of the nation, over which I understood that no man-made frontier whatever had ever been drawn, for the same breath flowed from one end of the nation to another, from Dniester to the Tisa in total disregard of man-made frontiers, just as the underground water flows without regard to any obstacles man has raised on the surface. There, in the depth I found no political parties, no enmity or clashes, of interest, no "blind disunity" of fratricidal fights, but only unity and harmony.

On the second day after Christmas we again took to the road. We had stopped at a church on our way to say a prayer in remembrance of Michael the Brave[1], Horea and his men, and Iancu, so they would know too that we were treading today on the paths on which, out of their love for our people, their bodies had been tortured and ripped apart. It was the feast of St. Stefan; therefore I lighted a candle for the repose of Stefan the Great's soul; through him our people reached the greatest glory. I consider him equal in rank with Napoleon, Julius Caesar and Alexander of Macedon.

No matter where my steps are going to carry me or into what battles I shall engage, if above me I feel the shadow of St. Michael the Archangel and below me those of our twenty beloved martyrs of the family of the legionary movement, on my right I shall also feel the soul of Stefan the Great and his sword.

In Basarabia

On January 20, 1930 I sent Totu, Cranganu, and Eremeiu, with a team, in the panel truck, into the county of Tecuci, while I myself on January 25 was again in the Horincea Valley in the midst of my riders. On the evening of the 26th after passing through Rogojeni, we entered Oancea. In both villages we were received warmly and with high expectations. We were lodged in Oances by the Antachi family. The next day, a Monday, it was market day in Cahul, on the left bank of the Pruth.

Therefore we decided to go into Basarabia where the Jews were more numerous and provocative. In Cahul, as in the other Basarabian market towns, Jewry is communistic; not because of "love for the people" but because of hatred for the Romanian state which only through the triumph of Communism could be toppled and placed under the heel of total Jewish domination. Communism's triumph coincides with Judaism's dream of ruling and exploiting the Christian nations by virtue of their theory of the "chosen people" which is at the base of the Jewish religion.

1 It was on the plains of Turda that the Hungarians had assassinated Michael the Brave, Prince of Wallachia in 1601. He was the first ruler to accomplish the temporary unification of Wallachia, Moldavia and Transylvania. (Tr.)

We made some white cloth crosses that evening, about eight inches high which were sewed on the riders' coats. I was given a wooden cross to carry.

At ten o'clock the next morning I cross the Pruth at the head of 30 riders, carrying the cross against the heathen power that was strangling Christian Basarabia. After covering close to three miles we entered the town. The Christians came out of their houses and followed us. They did not know us, but saw the white crosses on our coats and the feathers in our hats. We rode along the streets singing. "Awake, awake, ye Romanian!"

We stopped in the public square. Over 7,000 peasants gathered around us in no time at all. None among them knew who we were and what we wanted, but all of them had the premonition we had come to save them. I began to talk to them in the same vein I used in the Horincea Valley and Turda. But two minutes later, Popov, a policeman, accompanied by local authorities, made his way through the crowd and stopped me:

"You are not allowed to hold a public meeting in this square..."

"The Romanian people are allowed to do that anywhere."

The authorities wanted to prevent us from talking; the people wanted to listen to us.

"My good people"—I said to them—"this is the way it is - the law forbids us from holding meetings in public squares. Let us go to the edge of town or into someone's courtyard."

I signaled the riders and we started for the edge of town. An army cordon stopped the crowd. Several minutes later I was confronted by a soldiers' detachment with bayonets, headed by a colonel, Col. Cornea. He drew his revolver and pointed it at me:

"Halt, or I fire!" he said.

I stopped.

"Colonel, why should you shoot me? I have done no wrong. I too, carry a revolver, but I did not come here to fight anybody, least of all the Romanian army."

I argued with him for almost an hour, but all that proved futile. I stayed there an hour, taking all possible insult and ridicule. I could have replied to him in the same tone of voice, or fought him, but I had to muster an iron will, for otherwise I would have fallen into a sadder predicament, that is, with myself, a Romanian nationalist, fighting the army of my own country and being watched by communist Jews.

The colonel began hitting us and our horses with his saber and the soldiers pricked us with their bayonets; then the prefect arrived. I dismounted and accompanied him to the Prefecture. He was a civilized man. The colonel came also.

I told him:

> "I respect your rank; that is why I did not answer you. But it does not matter. We will see you again next Monday at the same place."

Then I left. A sergeant brought my horse. Cristian and Chiculita were expecting me at the gate, on foot. They then brought their horses and we returned the same way we came, chased from behind by police and accompanied by the insulting glares of the Jews. At the edge of town we met the rest of the saddened riders, dejected by the defeat we suffered. A bit further out a few peasants who sneaked out of town asked us who we were.

> "Go back and tell the people that we will be back again, next Monday. All the Christians in the county should come to Cahul."

We took a beating. We were in no mood for singing. We were going back and no one said a word. When we got back to Oancea we made ten posters announcing that Monday, February 10, we would again come to Cahul. These were sent by horse riders into several points of the county. Then we returned to Ganesti to Cristian's home where we arrived around midnight after a hard trip, a night so dark we could not see two paces ahead, whipped from in front by a cold rain lashing our faces and from behind by the recollection of our stinging defeat. I spent the night at Cristian's and in the morning I left for Beresti. There I issued a directive to the legionaries in the Horincea Valley, Galati, Iasi, Bucharest, Focsani and Turda, informing them of our defeat at Cahul and saying that, since this is now a matter of honor, all of us must go back there and win; they must report there in the greatest possible numbers. The meeting place—Oancea, where they should arrive no later than Sunday evening, February 9. At the same time I so informed the team of Totu, Cranganu, and Eremeiu, who at the time were in the county of Tecuci. I also wrote a letter to my father in which I asked him to come give us a hand. The legionaries put some money together for me and I left for Bucharest to see Mr. Ioanitescu, Under-Secretary of the Ministry of Internal Affairs.

I told him what had happened at Cahul and requested permission to hold another rally there — a legal request — assuming the responsibility for conducting this rally in perfect order, provided the authorities did not provoke us. After some additional clarifications he demanded of me, our rally was approved. We needed no approval for such a rally, as it was not required by law, but I wanted to be covered by official permission, thus to parry any possible tendentious interpretation of my action.

Sunday morning I was in Oancea once more. Lefter went to Cahul in order to determine the meeting place with the authorities. There was much excitement in Cahul as news had come to the authorities that thousands of peasants from all parts of the county were headed for Cahul for the rally.

Two truckloads arrived during the day from Focsani, the groups led by Hristache Solomon and Blanaru; from Turda, Moga and Nichita; from Iasi, the legionaries with Banea, Ifrim and Father Isihie; from Galati, Stelescu with the Brotherhood; a student delegate from Bucharest; and Pralea with the nests from Foltesti. Then came on foot, or with wagons and riding horses, those from Beresti, and the legionaries from the Horincea Valley.

My father too, came. By evening, over 300 legionaries had arrived; they were lodged in Oancea. And more kept coming. Being concerned lest the pontoon bridge over the Pruth might be unhooked by authorities in order to prevent our crossing, I dispatched overnight 30 legionaries to occupy both ends of the bridge.

On Monday at 8 o'clock in the morning I sent into Cahul a team of 50 legionaries under the command of Potolea, to police the rally. In the meantime new interventions were attempted in order to prevent us from going ahead with the rally. This was an impossibility. At 10 o'clock we formed a column and started out:

In the first group, 100 riders carrying a flag, all with feathers in their hats, many wearing green shirts. Each had a white cloth cross sewn on his coat. We looked like some crusaders who marched in the name of the Cross, against a heathen enemy, to free the Romanians. In the second group came over 100 pedestrians in a marching column with their flag. In the third group there followed about 80 wagons, 4 to 5 men in each, the greatest part people from Oancea, also carrying a flag. We seemed like an army ready for battle.

When we approached the edge of Cahul a sea of uncovered heads welcomed us, with no hurrahs or music, in an impressive church-like silence. We rode through this crowd of peasants. Some of them were crying.

The Basarabian peasant population, too, since the unification of Romania at the end of the First World War, had felt no improvement in its lot. For, though delivered from Russian occupation, it fell under the domination of the Jews. It was purely and simply prey to the Jews.

For 12 years it had been exploited and bled by the communist Jews in worse manner than the most tyrannical regime known in history had ever exploited any human society.

The Basarabian cities and market towns are real colonies of leeches clinging onto the exhausted body of the peasantry.

And, the epitomy of shamelessness, these leeches dared disguise themselves as fighters against people's exploitation, against the terror oppressing the people. These then are Basarabia's and Romania's communists.

Moreover, these leeches, bloated by the sucked blood of Romanians, keep up in their press, of which *Adevarul* ("The Truth") and *Dimineata* ("The Morning") are the main papers, the following style:

> "We have lived (the leeches!) in the best brotherhood and harmony with the Romanian people,"
>
> "Only some enemies of the people, of the country, some right-wing extremists, want to spoil this harmony."

There were over 20,000 peasants at the rally. Certainly this was the greatest assemblage of people this town had ever seen since the beginning, and all without any manifestoes or newspapers to publicize it. The rally was conducted very solemnly. On one side the riders were placed in a row; on the other, the column of pedestrian legionaries.

The peasantry listened with heads uncovered. There was not one word, not one gesture to disturb this solemnity. This time Col. Cornea did not keep the rendezvous we promised him.

I told this Basarabian peasantry—which, I saw, was expecting a word of consolation, and which came to this rally in such overwhelming numbers, not urged by me but by its great suffering: "That we would not abandon it to the Jewish slavery now oppressing it; that it would be free, master of the fruit of its labor, master over its land and its country; that the dawn of a new day for the people was approaching; that in this fight we have begun, all we expect the peasants to give would be faith—faith to the death—and in exchange they would receive justice and glory."

Then spoke Lefter, Potolea, Banea, Ifrim, Father lsihie, Victor Moga, Tarziu, Hristache Solomon. My father spoke for two hours at the end unsurpassed in style and depth, and in the people's language.

When speeches were over, I advised the peasantry to return to their villages in perfect order and quiet, calling it to their attention that if we were to end this imposing assembly with the slightest disorder, we would render a great service to the Jews.

People wanted us to go with them. From all sides they wished us:

"May God help you!"

Accompanied by the affection of these peasants we left for Oancea where we parted ways. From that moment of the rally in Cahul my father entered into the legionary movement.

Everyone went home in perfect order. Our victory was great, particularly by virtue of the peaceful and orderly manner in which the rally progressed and ended. But the Jews of Cahul needed a scandal, a disturbance, a disorder at any cost in order to compromise our movement and initiate governmental steps against us.

Seeing though that people left for their homes in a peaceful manner, two Jews, surely set up by their rabbi, broke the windows of a store, their own. Had the local authorities and some people not caught them in the act and taken them to police headquarters, the Sarindar St.[2] Jewish press, *Dimineata* ("The Morning") and *Adevarul* ("The Truth") would have printed such headlines as: "Great devastation at Cahul," "How much the country loses in the eyes of the people abroad!" etc.

I have given this case, seemingly of minor significance in itself, because of its immense importance for those who wish to understand and know the Jews' devilish system of fighting. They are capable of setting a whole city on fire in order, by throwing the blame on their

2 Sarindar St. in Bucharest is where the Jewish press offices and presses are located. (Tr.)

adversaries, to compromise an action which otherwise would lead to the ultimate solving of the Jewish problem.

Therefore, I warn the legionaries not to permit themselves to be provoked, for we will win only by maintaining the most perfect order. Disorder, for us, does not mean a conflict with the Jews but with the state. But it is exactly into this that the Jews want to push us, into a permanent conflict with the state. That is why, as the state is stronger than we, if we were to be lulled or pushed into conflict with the state, we would be crushed; and they would continue to remain impartial on-lookers.

My dog Fragu welcomed me at the gate upon my return to Iasi; I had him since 1924, a witness to all my trials and fights ever since.

In Iasi I took care of all current questions of organization, correspondence with nests, which Banea—the head of the legionary correspondence—presented to me in perfect order. Banea had begun to grasp my way of seeing things very well in the two years of correspondence, so that he could himself handle many questions during this period when I rarely came to Iasi.

In Basarabia Again

I could stay at home only for a week because the Basarabian peasants sent delegates, letters and telegrams, asking that I come to them. One cannot imagine the hopes they put in this movement of ours, and their faith.

During two weeks following the rally in Cahul, the news about the legionaries spread like lightning among all Christian people of southern Basarabia; from village to village all the way to the banks of the Dniester; that is, news of a beginning of deliverance from the Jewish slavery had inflamed the hearts of the poor peasants.

Up to then they had placed their hopes in the Peasant Party, believing that when this party would come to power, they, the peasants, would receive justice. But after eight years of hardships, battles, hopes in this party, they discovered something frightening for their souls: that they had been betrayed, cheated; that behind the name of the Peasant Party, Jewish interests lurked; the party of "The Romanian Peasant with Jewish earlocks"[3] as Professor Cuza baptized it.

3 Sideburns extended into long corkscrew curls. (Tr.)

One was seized by anguish upon seeing the faith in their hearts crushed that way, when after eight years they could see that their good faith had been betrayed.

I went back to Beresti again and from there by car to Rogojeni on the banks of the Pruth, where I was expected by over 200 riders headed by Stefan Moraru and Mos Cosa. They came from all the surrounding villages.

"Let us march all the way to the Dniester" said one of them. "Yes! We will march" I replied.

It was then that the notion struck me to stage a grand expedition over the whole of southern Basarabia from Tighina to Cetatea-Alba.

Back in Iasi the thought troubled me constantly as to how could we cross Basarabia all the way to the Dniester? There existed one great difficulty: how best to proceed so that the authorities would not oppose us, to avoid fighting the state, the army? It *occurred* to me that if I launched a new national organization for combating Jewish Communism, an organization inclusive of "The Legion of Michael the Archangel" and any other youth groups not affiliated with any political party, we might succeed in getting into Basarabia.

What name should we give this new organization? I debated this question with legionaries, in the lobby of our Home. Some said: "The Anti-Communist Falange," others proposed other names. Cranganu said: "THE IRON GUARD!"

"Let this be it!"

Now we began preparing this anti-communist action backed also by workers. Actually, by "anti-communist action" I do not mean an "anti-workers" action; when I say "communists" I mean Jews.

In order to obtain authorization for entering Basarabia and thus avoid any possible trouble with local authorities, I had an audience several days later with Mr. Vaida-Voevod, at that time Minister of Internal Affairs. He was the second politician of high rank whom I consulted. Ionel Bratianu had been the first. He kept me there for three hours. I realized he was erroneously informed both with regard to our movement and to the Jewish problem which he did not know in its true light.

He took us for some rambunctious youth inclined to solve the Jewish problem by breaking windows. I explained to him then how we saw the Jewish problem; how we consider it a life and death problem for all Romanians; how their number is overwhelming and inadmissible; how they destroyed the middle class and Romanian towns, I told him what the proportion between Christians and Jews was in Balti, Chisinau, Cernauti, Iasi; the danger they represent in our schools, threatening the alienation of the Romanian leading class and the falsification of our culture. I also explained to him the manner in which we see the solving of this problem. He understood from the very beginning what I was talking about. But, though a man of his stature readily understood the gist of the matter, yet, I believe he will never be able to completely understand us, for such is the nature of things; the eyes of 1890 no longer see as do those of 1930.

There are calls, urgings, mute commands which only the youth hear and grasp because they address themselves only to it. Each generation has its own mission in life. That is why, perhaps, he will not trust us completely.

I obtained approval for our march into Basarabia, after, naturally, assuming responsibility for maintaining complete order. Several days later I put out a manifesto addressed to all the youth of the country.

Troubles in Maramures

Meanwhile great turmoil erupted in Maramures. This is another corner of Romanian soil over which death had spread its wings. There, Jewry had invaded villages, imposed its control over fields, mountains and sheep corrals. Romanians, in a state of virtual slavery, retreat step by step before this Jewish invasion and gradually perish, leaving the estates they had inherited from Dragos Voda in the hands of the invaders. No government shows an interest in them any longer, no law protects them.

It was early in June 1930 that a wagon drawn by two horses stopped at the gate of my house in Iasi. From it descended two priests, a peasant and a young man.

I asked them to come in. They introduced themselves, Orthodox priest Ion Dumitrescu, Greek-Catholic priest Andrei Berinde, and the peasant Nicoara.

"We come by wagon from Maramures. We have been on the road for two weeks; we are both priests in Borsa, one Greek-Catholic, the other Orthodox. We can no longer bear to see the misfortune of the Romanians of Maramures. We wrote memorandum after memorandum which we sent all over, to Parliament, the government, cabinet ministers, the Regency, with no reply from any of them. We do not know what else to do. We came by wagon here to Iasi to ask Romanian studentry not to abandon us to our fate. We speak in the name of thousands of peasants from Maramures who have grown desperate. We are their priests. We cannot close our eyes to what we see. Our people are dying and our hearts are breaking with pity."

I hosted them for a few days and told them:

> "The only solution I see is to organize them and try to boost their morale. They should know that they are not waging this battle by themselves, that we are behind them, fight for them and that their fate depends on our victory."

Finally, I sent Totu and Eremeiu to organize them; and later Savin and Dumitrescu-Zapada. Thousands of peasants from Borsa and all mountain valleys were enrolling in our organization. The Jews, realizing the danger of a Romanian rebirth, started provoking people. Seeing that their tactics failed, they resorted to an infernal means. They set fire to Borsa, blaming Romanians for it. Jewish newspapers immediately began yelling, demanding energetic measures be taken against the Romanians who, they were saying, were preparing pogroms.

Both priests were attacked by Jews, insulted, struck, then chased several miles and stoned. To cap it off, they were both arrested as "agitators" and thrown into jail in Sighetul Marmatiei. Also arrested were Savin and Dumitrescu-Zapada and several score of leading peasants. Totu and Eremeiu, were arrested in Dorna and locked up in the Campul-Lung prison. *Adevarul* ("The Truth") and *Dimineata* ("The Morning") set off a real cannonade of lies and calumnies heaped upon the priests and the others arrested.

All the protests, telegrams, memoranda, etc. remained fruitless, as they were drowned by the Jewish yells, noise and pressures.

The March into Basarabia is Forbidden

In view of the march we were to make I issued an "order of the march" which I printed in *"The Ancestral Land"* I extract from it:

"COMRADES,

"1. We shall cross the Pruth to the tune of the old Romanian hymn of unity: 'Come, let us join hands together, those of Romanian heart.'

"2. The march will last one month.

"3. We will form seven powerful columns, 14 miles apart.

"4. The crossing of the Pruth will be done at seven points, the right flank column aiming to reach Cetatea-Alba; the left flank column, Tighina.

"5. The mode of advancement will be marching on foot from the Pruth to the Dniester.

"6. The date of departure, July 20 in the morning. The crossing of the Pruth at an hour to be announced."

When Jewry learned about our plan to enter Basarabia in order to awaken the conscience of Romanians, the Jewish press launched against us a hurricane of attacks. Calumnies, lies, incitations, came upon our heads unremittingly for a whole month.

These attacks were directed in the same measure against Mr. Vaida. The Jews were demanding that Mr. Vaida be forthwith demoted in the Ministry of Internal Affairs, in fact "thrown overboard" because he dared consent that we, Romanian youth, enter Basarabia in order to take to our parents and brothers across the Pruth a Romanian word of consolation and hope.

Basarabia has been delivered over economically and politically to absolute domination by the Jews. Any effort for Romanian emancipation, any mention of this black rule was considered a crime. Under the pressure of attacks and intrigues in the Jewish press, the march into Basarabia was forbidden just the day the legionaries from all parts set out toward the Pruth.

I wrote on that occasion the following protest which I had distributed throughout the capital:

The Legion of Michael the Archangel "The Iron Guard"

An Appeal and a Warning

ROMANIANS OF THE CAPITAL,

"The march of 'The Iron Guard' which was to take place in Basarabia was stopped. The enemies of a healthy and powerful Romania have triumphed. For a full month the Sarindar St. little Jews from *Lupta* ("The Fight"), *Adevarul* ("The Truth"), *Dimineata* ("The Morning"), these poisoners of the Romanian soul, have threatened, insulted, slapped our souls, here in our own land.

"From ticks hooking into the bosom of this nation, they became the only ones who could understand the superior interests of our Fatherland, and turned themselves into uninvited censors of all its administrative acts.

"At Turda, they demanded the government stop our demonstration, claiming that Transylvania was being set afire; at Cahul, that revolution was being started in Basarabia; at Galati, that slaughterings and pogroms were going to begin.

"They turned out to be contemptible provocateurs in each case, for the Legion kept perfect order and discipline everywhere.

"We were headed today towards the Dniester in order to turn Basarabia's face toward Bucharest.

"But this did not please these mercenaries of Communism.

"Basarabia must continue to remain prey to Bolshevism and look to Moscow so that they can continue to terrorize, through the province between the Pruth and the Dniester, Romania's entire political life.

ROMANIANS,

"The venal and perverse political system, this puss infecting our lives, aids and abets them—out of selfish petty electoral interest and out of a demeaning spirit of servility—in their work of dismembering our country and alienating our ancestral land. It was this selfish interest and this spirit which have been putting Romania for the last 60 years into the hands of foreigners.

"Look!,.. Today the martyrs of Maramures and Bucovina are beginning to stir! They cry out along their roads about the bitterness of slavery into which they were pitched by the treachery of all the country's leaders; not that they had been forgotten by them, but that they had been sold out.

"Does it not seem to you at least strange that no voice has been found in this country to come to them with a word of consolation? And does it not seem to you to be at least a shamelessness to reduce the entire affair in Maramures to the 'instigators' Nicolae Totu and Eremeiu? Are they the ones who are guilty? What about the politicians who for 12 years have daily been cheating these Maramures peasants, are they not guilty? What about the hundreds of thousands of roving Jews who descended upon them like locusts to take away the land they inherited from their ancestors and to enslave them, are these not instigators and provocateurs? What about the gentlemen from Sarindar St. who ridicule our pride in being masters in our own country, are they not provocateurs?

ROMANIANS,

"Here is a typical example from which one can see the real cause of the 'disorders' in Bucovina and Maramures.

"Universul ("The Universe") of July 17, 1930 published the following statistic: 'At Cernauti: children of school age in the elementary schools: 12,277, of which 3,378 only are Romanians (boys and girls) while the rest are foreigners.' What other proof of the domination of the Romanian element in the northern part of Romania do you need? Where do you want the soul of the Romanian people to run from this huge and murderous invasion? You denigrate, slander, offend it by saying it rises up for a slice of bread due to its 'precarious economic situation' when in fact it daringly rises up to defend its own being on the northern borders. Why is it that no politician has come out to tell His Majesty the truth?

YOUR HIGHNESS

"These unfortunate people do not ask bread. They demand justice! They demand deliverance for the Romanian soul on the verge of dying because it is being suffocated both in Maramures and Bucovina. They demand that measures be taken against the hundreds of thousands of Jews, gorged, rotund and white as worms, who defy them daily in their poverty, being protected by all Romanian local authorities.

GENTLEMEN JOURNALISTS FROM SARINDAR STREET

"Certainly, the Romanians know all too well that such a problem will not be solved by violent demonstrations; but, having reached the limit of their endurance, they wish to impose a Romanian leadership for Romania; to force Romanian legislation, laws for the protection of the Romanian element in Romania.

"Perhaps you wish that, through your continuous insults with which you wound our Romanian souls, you will see me some day at the head of the holy rebels from Maramures? You had better know that at that instant your last hour has struck!

"In any case, if you consider the existing laws inadequate to simmer you down, I declare to you that I have enough power to put you in your place and make you understand in which country you live. If you do not quiet down, I shall call up against you all that is alive in this country, determined to fight with all the weapons that my mind can call up.

ROMANIANS,

"A *New* Romania cannot be born from the back rooms of political parties, just as *Greater Romania* was not born from the calculations of politicians, but on the battlefields of Marasesti and the deep valleys on which cannon rained steel.

"A New Romania cannot be born except by battle; from the sacrifice of its sons.

"That is why I do not address myself to politicians but to you, Soldier! Rise up. History calls you again! As you are. With your broken arm. With your fractured leg. With your bullet-riddled chest. Let the powerless and the imbecile tremble. You, engage courageously in the battle

"Soon 'The Iron Guard" will be calling you to a great rally in Bucharest for the defense of Maramuresans, the children of Dragos-Voda and of the Bucovinans, the sons of Stefan the Great and the Saint.

"Write on your banners: *'The foreigners have invaded us.' 'The alienated press poisons us.' 'The political system kills us.'*

"Blow your trumpets in alarm. Blow them with all your power.

"At this moment, when the enemy invades us and the politicians betray us, Romanians, shout with trepidation as of old on mountain paths in hours of storm:

"FATHERLAND! FATHERLAND! FATHERLAND!

"Corneliu Zelea-Codreanu "Head of the Legion"

The Attempt on the Life of Minister Anghelescu

On the evening of the day my manifesto was posted, I was at the student center talking with several students. The young Beza appeared. All of a sudden he ripped off his insignia of the "Vlad Tepes"[4] organization to which he belonged, pitched it away and said: "Henceforth I shall have nothing to do with 'Vlad Tepes' anymore; I resign."

This gesture on his part did not impress me. First, because the "Vlad Tepes" League seemed to lack earnestness, more especially the youth in that league, whose existence I doubted from the start. A resignation from such a youth group left me completely cold.

Several minutes later, this youth again joined our discussion saying he would like to become a legionary, if I had no objection. My vague reply avoided a direct refusal. Legionary dogma imposes reserve toward anyone new seeking to join the Legion, and this applied particularly in the present case.

Several weeks earlier I had seen Beza in a small restaurant where he asked me whether it would not be advisable to shoot Stere[5]. Then too, I did not take him seriously.

Upon leaving, he asked me to spend the night at his place. I refused. Instead, I spent the night with the medical students. Next day around

4 Grigore Filipescu had given his party the name of "The Vlad Tepes League" to indicate he was to follow the practice of Vlad "the Impaler," a Wallachian ruler of the 16th century who impaled thieves and dishonest subjects. (Tr.)

5 C. Stere, Romanian politician from Basarabia who in 1914 had advocated Romania's alliance with the Central Powers against the Allies. (Tr.)

noon I heard the newspaper street vendors: "An attempt on the life of Minister Anghelescu!" Who? Beza. How? He fired several shots, superficially hitting his victim.

Why? I did not know. Inquiring I learned that a conflict arose between Macedonians and Anghelescu around the Law of New Dobrogea[6] which infringed upon Romanian interests in that province. I had never met Anghelescu. Two days later I was summoned before the judge preparing the case. "Iron Guard" manifestoes have been found on Beza. I declared that I had no knowledge whatever of and no connection with this attempt, nor did I know his motive.

I was released. As I left I was pondering how easily misfortune can befall a man. Had I accepted Beza's invitation to sleep at his place I would have become the moral author of his crime. Any argument presented to defend myself would have been dismissed. Particularly in view of the fact that this attempt coincided with the denial of our march into Basarabia.

To my great astonishment the next day I read the half-page headline in *Dimineata* ("The Morning"): "Corneliu Codreanu brands Beza's act." I was dumfounded. Consequently I went to see the judge who had interrogated me the day before.

"Your Honor, I am very astonished that such incorrect information could originate with your office from a secret interrogation. I did not brand Beza's act. It is not for me to do so!"

"I have released no such information. This is an invention of the press."

Then I said to myself: "Should I let myself be insulted by the Jewish press? Even if I knew Beza for such a short time, though I had no connection of any kind with him, no one can compel me to be such a scoundrel as to jump on him, in such a case as this, to condemn him. I do not want to do it. Let anyone else but me do it, because I do not know what the matter is and because of my past in which I had worn the same shoes precludes me from condemning others. I shall write another warning.

The same day I printed a manifesto which I distributed throughout the capital:

---

6 Romanian province between the Danube and the Black Sea. (Tr.)

THE SECOND WARNING

"Because the press dared again becloud the truth, claiming I 'branded' Beza's gesture, I insist on giving the following clarification:

"If Minister Anghelescu might have reason to be defended, I believe that the youth Beza has as many reasons at least, both in the courts and before the conscience of his countrymen.

"I declare that I am not going to defend the former by branding the latter, but that I will defend the young Beza and his cause with all my heart and all my power.

"As for you, gentlemen from Sarindar St., write on the list of settlements to come, this second warning."

Corneliu Zelea-Codreanu

As a consequence of these two warnings my relationship with Mr. Vaida was ended. Mr. Vaida became angry with me. But I could not proceed otherwise than as my conscience dictated.

Summoned again before the same judge, I was arrested. So there I was again in the Black Maria headed for the Vacaresti prison. There were seven other youths in the same van, to whom I introduced myself: Papanace, Caranica, Pihu, Mamali, Anton Ciumeti, Ficata and Ghetea. They issued a declaration of solidarity with Beza. I walked again under the same gates as seven years earlier with my old comrades, and by coincidence I was placed in the same cell I occupied then. I entered the church the next day to view St. Michael's icon from which we started but children seven years before.

There in prison I got to know well these Aromanians[7] who came from the mountains of Pind. They exhibited a high culture, sound moral health, were good patriots, built to be fighters and heroes and willing to sacrifice.

There I came to know better the great tragedy of the Macedo-Romanians, this Romanian branch which for thousands of years, alone and isolated in its mountains, has defended—weapons in hand—its language, nationality and Freedom.

7 The Aromanians or Macedo-Romanians of Macedonia (Greece) are Romanian-speaking populations. (Tr.)

It was then that I met Sterie Ciumeti[8] whom God has chosen for his good soul, pure as dew, to become through his tragic torture and death, the greatest martyr of the legionary movement, of legionary Romania.

There, our thought and hearts united forever. Henceforth we would fight together for our whole people from Pind to beyond the Dniester.

No amount of complaining, petitioning or intervening before an administration which has been deaf to all Romanian problems here and abroad, will ever solve Romanian problems anywhere without a strong Romanian nation being in control of her own house. At that time, these Romanians, scattered outside our borders shall be brought back into Romania. For the blood of all is needed here where Romanians are faced by death. And it is well to note that in this struggle the governments that opened the country's gates to thousands of Jews, at the same time did not permit Romanians from abroad to come in.

All the occult forces were at work, bearing down on Justice in order to secure my conviction.

My recent arrest and incarceration in Vacaresti caused great rejoicing among the Jewish ranks. Every impertinent little Jew was attacking and insulting me in every paper. To please the Jews, even Romanian newspapers run by the political parties, attacked me.

The date of my appearance in court had been set. I began the necessary preparations. I was waiting for Nelu Ionescu, who had been defending me in every trial since 1920, to arrive from Iasi. My defense was joined also by Mr. Mihail Mora, upon the insistence of students.

My trial, as always, was a Judaic attack trying to secure my conviction, no matter how small—demanded the Jews from *Adevarul* ("The

8 Arrested on the night of December 30, 1933, Sterie Ciumeti, although innocent of the shooting of Prime Minister I.G. Duca, was assassinated by three police commissars, then thrown into the icy waters of Dambovita by orders of the responsible authorities in the Ministry of Internal Affairs. Fished out, he was secretly buried, later to be disinterred clandestinely and again buried in sinister circumstances by "unidentified" representatives of the public order. This ignoble crime remained unpunished, after having caused before the Court of Appeals in Bucharest a scandalous trial where occult as well as obvious pressures by the Liberal government and the police apparatus were exercised, even within the hall of justice, upon the jurors (among whom was Dr. Gheorghiu, the rector of the University of Bucharest, the jury's foreman), Ciumeti's widow and the attorneys. (Tr.)

Truth")—so they could say that the movement I lead is anarchical because it uses illegal means of action.

The halls of the Ministry of Justice were full of Jews running to and fro with intercessions of all kinds.

However, Romanian justice, inflexible and undaunted, acquitted me. But the prosecutor appealed; therefore I continued to be kept in prison.

This time the pressures and the interventions of the Judaic power were increased. Again I was taken to the Court of Appeals. To please the Jews, Prosecutor Praporgescu placed me in the same box with embezzlers, horse thieves and pickpockets. For three hours, while their cases were judged, I was the object of ironical and defiant glares from scores of Jews. My case was the last to be considered and, as earlier, it was Mr. Mihail Mora and Nelu Ionescu who pleaded it. The verdict on the appeal was a new acquittal. After close to one month and a half of imprisonment, I was released. I left for home.

Following all this, together with Nelu Ionescu, Garneata, Mota and Ibraileanu, I left by our panel truck for Sighetul Marmatiei to look into the fate of the two priests who were locked up in frightening misery. No one was coming to see them, even to bring them food. Father Dumitrescu's wife was sick; he had two small children. Their home was a breadless, moneyless, medicineless home; they lived on charity. The fate of Christian priests, sworn to defend the cross, the church and their people! The lot of the other ten imprisoned peasant leaders was just as bad.

On the outside, Jewry was jubilating. Money was being collected both at home and abroad; the government gave money for the "unfortunate Jews" of Borsa so they could build for themselves new two-story stone homes, while the poor Romanian peasants were eating bread made from sawdust meal mixed with oatmeal.

I, who then saw this Romanian Maramures groaning and writhing in the throes of death, cannot but urge every politician, every member of the teaching corps, every priest, all university students and secondary school students, and every preacher of humanitarianism—all who come here to censure our political life— "Go all of you and observe Maramures. Name anyone in the world as an arbiter to tell us if it is tolerable that in Romania something like that happening in Maramures, can happen to Romanians."

At the end of four months, the priests were transferred to the prison in Satu Mare where the trial was held in which some 50 peasants and peasant women with children in their arms were involved, as well as 20 Jews.

Professor Catuneanu, Ion Mota, a local attorney and myself, formed the defense of the accused Romanians. The 20 Jews were represented by four Jewish attorneys. After eight days of proceedings, all were acquitted, for all charges levelled at them were proven false.

Dissolution of The Iron Guard and the Legion of Michael The Archangel January 11, 1931

Meanwhile, Mr. Vaida, under pressures of Jewish attacks, was dismissed from the Ministry of Internal Affairs, being replaced by Mr. Mihalache, who, as his late attitude indicated, let it be known that he would not hesitate to use against us "strong arm" methods. This moment had arrived.

The youth Dumitrescu-Zapada, who had been arrested in Sighet, exasperated by the lies, attacks, insults of the Jewish press, without asking or telling anyone one word, grabbed a revolver he happened to find, went to Bucharest, entered Socor's office and fired one shot. But the revolver was defective; it could not be fired the second time.

This happened around Christmas time. It had been a year in which I had not spent even a month at home. I wanted to spend the holidays with my family. I was at Focsani preparing to leave for home when I read in the papers what happened in Bucharest. Immediately I was summoned to come before Judge Papadopol at the Tribunal. It was proven I had no connection at all with the shooting. I could go my way. I returned to Focsani where by orders from Mr. Mihalache, for no reason, I was surrounded by police in Hristache Solomon's house and kept incommunicado for eight days.

Mr. Mihalache dissolved the Iron Guard and the Legion through a decree of the Council of Ministers. Searches were made of all our headquarters; all our records were seized; all our offices sealed. At home in Iasi, as well as in Husi, even my pillows and mattresses were ransacked. For the fifth time, my house was rifled, everything connected with the movement being taken away, down to the smallest notes I had. Sackfuls of documents, letters, papers, were confiscated from our homes and taken to Bucharest. But what could they find in our homes that could be illegal or compromising? We had been working in broad daylight and anything we had to say was said out loud. We confessed our faith strongly before the whole world.

On January 9, I was taken by agents from Focsani to Bucharest, and there, following a 12-hour interrogatory, I was placed under arrest and sent again to Vacaresti.

The second day were brought in the following legionaries from the counties in which we were most active: Lefter, from Cahul; Banea, from Iasi; Stelescu, from Galati; Amos Pop, from Turda; Totu and Danila.

This was another hard blow to the top of the head of a Romanian organization which had done nothing illegal, but only was trying to lift its brow against the Judaic hydra. A new attempt on the part of this people to rise up through its youth, from its slavery, was going down under the blows of a Romanian Minister of Internal Affairs, with the unanimous applause of Jewry both at home and abroad.

This time too, the fury to destroy us had been mercilessly unleashed. No means were spared to annihilate us; no infamy. And we were guilty of nothing. The Jewish papers in which we were violently attacked, ridiculing us and the truth, reached us in prison, and we could do nothing, we could answer in no way.

With arms crossed, within the four prison walls, we watched how insults and all kinds of accusations were hurled at us.

It is sufficient to give one example showing the extent of the infamy of the Jewish press at that time from the many attempts made with the intention of setting public opinion against us to force our condemnation. I call the attention of the reader to the fact that I never planned, wrote or signed such an order[9]. No word in it belongs to me.

9 It is on the basis of such false documents, notably on a letter that Corneliu Z, Codreanu allegedly had written to Adolf Hitler, that the military judges acting as servile instruments of interested individuals — later convicted the chief of the Iron Guard to ten years at hard labor for "crime of treason and incitation to social revolution." This letter "uncovered" by the Siguranta, in which Codreanu requested help from Adolf Hitler for preparing the "social revolution" was categorically declared false by Corneliu Z. Codreanu both at the preliminary hearing and in court. Not only was he denied the required

It is wholly invented by Jewry.

Here I reproduce in full the contemptible lie as printed in *Dimineata* ("The Morning"), which was then copied and commented on by the other papers:

An Edifying Document

"With regard to the aims and means used by the 'Archangel Michael' organization, we are in position to publish a sensational document issued by the Legion in Iasi.

"The matter pertains to a circular sent to Campul-Lung and Ludosul Mare by the Legion 'Archangel Michael' in the capital of Moldavia:

The Legion 'Archangel Michael'
Headquarters Iasi (Rapa Galbena)
The Cultural Christian Home
245/930 ad circulandum

Copy

Address your reply to Corneliu Zelea Codreanu
20 Florilor St., Iasi
— in code —
To

Second Battalion, Campul-Lung
Third Battalion, Ludosul de Mures

We have the honor to bring to your attention the following:

Considering that both civil and military authorities have relaxed their vigilance because we had intervened with some highly placed officials—both in the Ministry of Internal Affairs and in...

---

handwriting expert advice and the witnesses for the defense, but more, under the pretext that public discussion of the case would hurt the "superior interests of the State," the proceedings regarding this point took place behind closed doors so as to remove from Codreanu, infamously accused, the possibility of defense before national and world opinion. The truth is that this vile staging which had to justify the sentencing to ten years at hard labor and the imprisonment of the innocent Codreanu was but the preparatory phase to his assassination, premeditated by His Majesty King Carol II of Romania, carried out by the order of His Majesty's government on the night of November 29-30, 1938. (Tr.)

(another highly placed individual, N.R. is mentioned here)—we must take advantage of this opportunity to double our propaganda and instigation efforts, for this favorable situation may one day be reversed. Consequently, with no further hesitation or loss of time, you shall do the following:

1. Make lists of all legionaries who have taken their vow, by companies and platoons. These lists should be of defense before national and world opinion forwarded to the Legion by November 1 of this year to be totaled by regions.

2. The Second Battalion shall convoke in Campul-Lung the important leaders: Robota, Popescu, Serban, Despa, and in total secrecy Commissar Nubert of Vatra-Domei and the chief of the gendarmes post of Poiana Stampii, Paduraru Gheorghe. You shall inform them that the Legion took the decision to change the plan of action.

Henceforth we shall work conspiratorially in absolute secrecy; you shall no longer hold public meetings or engage in propaganda,—you shall get in touch with all legionaries who are nest leaders — instructing them to sustain the present state of revolt among the peasantry. The decisive coup will be delivered this fall on the occasion of the Mironeseu government change.

3. Third Battalion shall convoke Professor Matei, Moga Victor, Moga Tanase and the platoon chief of Grindeni—and from Urea you shall call only the merchant Moldovan. Secretly you shall call the gendarme instructor Sgt. Constantin of the Ludos post—inform them... (as in the Second Battalion).

4. You shall take out for exercises the legionary youth twice each week—on the village grazing grounds or elsewhere—preparing it and explaining our noble aim, encouraging it.

5. The chief of the Third Battalion's Staff shall terminate the mission he was charged with both verbally and by secret order No. 7/1930 to carry out as soon as possible; if the quantity of dynamite sent is insufficient he is to demand more from the individual in question.

6. You shall also tell the above, by letter, to Dr. Iosif Ghizdaru of Sighisoara and also send him a detailed report on the activity in Ludos. A Fourth Battalion shall come into being in Sighisoara under the command of Dr. Ghizdaru. This order is to be burnt immediately after being read. Be careful, an army of Jewish spies

is on our tracks; do not talk to anyone or see anyone who does not show you my signature.

Courage; long live the Legion and with God, forward!

Iasi, October 7, 1930, Commander of the Legion
(SS) Corneliu Zelea-Codreanu
Chief of General Staff and Secretary
(ss) Garneata

"It is obvious from this circular that the Legion 'Archangel Michael' has prepared criminal actions, supported by a certain number of public officials.

Though late, the authorities have the duty to identify absolutely all these public officials who place themselves in the service of this criminal action of the Legion 'Archangel Michael' and apply the most severe penalties."

Arrest Warrant

I realized that the situation was difficult; our organization dissolved, headquarters padlocked, searches everywhere. The public, completely dazed as a result of Jewish outcries and stupified by their accusations heaped upon us, was inclined to take as real all these odious frame-ups. Moreover, in prison we were living in misery, cold, dampness, lack of air and light, lack of blankets. It was due only to insistent interventions on our behalf that some straw was issued to us to stuff our mattresses with and some mats to cover the dampness of the walls.

We began 1931 in prison under a rain of Jewish lies, insults and blows.

This time too, I took my new prison comrades, who were sharing this trial with me, to see the icon and all the places which for me were full of memories.

Certainly the situation was difficult for them too. But they had to answer only for themselves, and this responsibility was much smaller. The enemy who had to be shattered and destroyed, was I. I felt that black clouds were gathering anew over our heads, that an enemy world was coming down on us anew with even more determination to annihilate us.

The only support in the midst of all these infemal machinations and gigantic assaults, was to be found in God. We began to fast each Friday, total fast; and to read each midnight the Akathist of Virgin Mary. Outside, legionaries in the capital, headed by Andrei Ionescu, Ion Belgea, Iordache, Doru Belimace, Victor Chirulescu, Cotiga, Horia Sima, Nicolae Petrascu Iancu Caranica, Virgil Radulescu, Sandu Valeriu, were dong their utmost to enlighten public opinion which was misled by the Sarindar St. press

At the same tme, the devoted and undaunted Fanica Anastasescu—always present at my side in all the trials I had to go through—tried to improve our material prison lot. Here is the accusation levelled at me in

Arrest Warrant No. 194

"...Whereas the acts of criminal procedure drawn up against Corneliu Zelea Codreanu, attorney in Iasi, aged 31, warned that he committed the act of trying to engage in an action directed against the form of government established by the Constitution and tried an instigation from which a danger for public safety could have resulted by organizing an association 'The Legion of Michael the Archangel'--'The Iron Guard, having the aim of setting up a dictatorial regime which was to have been imposed at a given moment wished by him, by violent means, toward which his partisans were prepared and urged through quasi-military drills, orders, directives and speeches, as well as through publications, posters, emblems, discourses during organized or public meetings;

"Whereas, this act is specified by Art. 11, Paragraph 2 of the Law for the suppression of some new infractions against public order, as punishable by imprisonment of from six months to five years and a fine of from 10,000 to 100,000 lei and with loss of civil rights;

"Considering that from the investigation conducted, serious charges and grave indications of guilt result against Corneliu Zelea Codreanu; and that in order to prevent the above named to communicate with the informers and witnesses which are to be questioned; as well as in the interest, of public safety; it is important for the preparation of this case that the accused, until further disposition, be placed in detention;

"After listening to Prosecutor Al. Procop Dumitrescu's conclusions and in conformity to the terms of Art. 93 of the penal procedure;

"For these reasons:

"We mandate all agents of the public force, that in conformance to the law, they arrest and lead to the arrest house of the Vacaresti prison, said Comeliu Zelea Codreanu...

"Given in our office today January 30, 1931. "Investigating Judge Stefan Mihaescu.. "

(Dossier No. 10-1931)

The Trial - Friday, 27 February 1931

This rain of accusations continued uninterruptedly for 57 days, disseminated daily in millions of newspapers through villages and towns. We had no chance whatever of responding. No ray of hope from anywhere. No one had the capability of coming to our defense and to denounce the Jewish conspiracy for seeking our condemnation and burial and that of our movement.

We watched how the authorities, prosecutors, the Siguranta and this gentleman named Mihalache, Minister of Internal Affairs, who—though all knew from the investigations they made that we were guilty of nothing; that no munitions, weapons, dynamite deposits were found, etc.—still persisted in their infamous attitude, leaving prey to Jewish insults and ridicule some arrested men unable to defend themselves.

Because state security was involved, they should have heeded their elementary duty to quiet public opinion by issuing a communique denying the discovery of caches of munitions, the country was on the brink of civil war, etc.

It was under these inauspicious circumstances that our trial date was set for Friday, February 27.

Some of the defense attorneys felt that introducing a motion for the postponement of the trial was advisable in view of the agitated atmosphere; that in the meantime we call to the witness stand officials of security units to compel them to tell the truth under oath.

We turned down this proposition; we would go to trial without witnesses.

Counselor Buicliu presided, assisted by Judges G. Solomonescu and I. Costin; the prosecutor was Procop Dumitrescu.

We were defended by Professor Nolica Antonescu; attorneys Mihail Mora, Nelu lonescu, Vasiliu-Cluj, Mota, Garneata, Corneliu Georgescu, Ibraileanu.

Both the audience and the magistrates expected to see some proofs against us: bombs, munition deposits, dynamite, weapons. But nothing, absolutely nothing was produced in evidence. Half an hour after our testimony was completed, all the infamous farce collapsed.

Finally, we could speak, full of the indignation which for two months had been building up within us, hour upon hour. All that barrage of lies was broken in the face of truth. All the chains with which they shackled us came apart: our lawyers defended us brilliantly. Though the trial continued into the second day, sentencing was delayed for several days.

At the appointed time for the verdict to be handed down, we were again taken to the Tribunal. The verdict of unanimous acquittal was read to us (Penal sentence No. 800).

Here are the terms of this verdict of acquittal, detailing the actions on the basis of which "The Legion of Michael the Archangel" already dissolved, had been brought before the law:

> "Considering that the chief prosecutor's investigation results in the fact in the dossier that the adherents of the Legion had indeed been recruited only from among determined people: peasants, students and high school youth; that, for instance, the dossier speaks of nests of legionaries or 'white vultures;' it speaks of a probationary status, vow or oath, five fundamental laws, one of which is a law of secrecy; that the Legion is militarily organized with a uniform, baldrick, scarves, programs of physical education and military drills, signaling exercises and Morse code, etc., still, it has not been established that recruiters and recruited have engaged in any action against the present form of government established by the Constitution, or in an action which might result in some danger to state security. That the fact alone of being constituted into such an organization cannot be construed as an infraction, even if it might in someone's conception be considered such a danger. For, as long as the organization was not an occult one, administrative authorities could have stepped in either to stop it or to dissolve it.

That even in the supposition that it would have been established that the organization had copied the Fascist system as a form of make-up, even then its members could not be considered liable to the penalty stipulated by the text of the law on the basis of which the accused have been brought to trial; because no matter what its form, an organization in its static stage does not present any danger to state security; it could at most be the object of preoccupations of preventive measures on the part of administrative authorities, but not of any repressive measures which are in order only when such organization initiates some action, (excepting such cases as when the law specifically prohibits its form of organization).

"Furthermore, it cannot be said that just because several legionaries had gone through villages in order to seek adherents, advising the people to organize, to trust the Legion's movement, etc. one can produce proof that they intended to endanger state security—propaganda being a means for forming and replenishing the cadres of a political organization such as this; or that the inception of so-called nests of high school students—formations outside the organization proper—meant any threat to state security, if one considers that in the organization's program one recognized the awakening of national conscience together with precepts of physical and moral education befitting a school program, as long as there was no undue agitation.

"Considering that the accused cannot be blamed for having sought to change by their action the present form of government— for, from the dossier, this fact not denied even by the representative of the Public Ministry,—it is obvious that both the accused Corneliu Z. Codreanu and the others, as well as all the members of the organization, preached the need for a strong government to replace the parasitic political parties, and recognized the king's authority who was spoken of with all due respect and whose collaborators—as attested by their manifestoes— they wished to become.

"Also, as long as one speaks of collaboration with the head of the state, one cannot talk of toppling a form of government that the sovereign had not sanctioned....

"Whereas, for these considerations the subversive action (which as a matter of fact has not been proven from any angle as being subversive) of which the defendants are accused does not fall within the dispositions of Art. 11....

"Whereas the march the organization had planned to make into Basarabia had not taken place; that it would not have taken place if the authorities had not consented—consent that the accused as a matter of fact claim was obtained but later rescinded; that in such circumstances it is superfluous to retain the claims of the accused that they intended first to test the resistance of legionaries and second to awaken the national conscience of the populace penetrated by foreign elements...

"Whereas it was also claimed that all the acts of the accused have to be looked at in the light of their antecedents....

"Whereas as long as the fact for which the accused were brought to trial cannot be established, one cannot speak of the acts of Corneliu Zelea Codreanu, Danila, etc. as determining the degree of guilt, because the antecedents are of interest in establishing the degree of punishment and not in forcing a condemnation...

"That such being the case, the accused are innocent of the allegations brought against them and in consequence they are to be acquitted."

We returned joyously to prison, there to pack our bags and await the order to be released. We waited; 8 o'clock in the evening came, 9, 10, 11, o'clock; we jumped at each step we heard outside in the yard. Finally, we went to sleep with our bags still made up.

Next day, again we waited. Only on the third day did we learn that the prosecutor appealed and therefore we would have to stay in prison until the appeal was considered. Once more, days began to drag slowly.

The new date was set for Friday March 27, 1931 at the Court of. Appeals. The days passed slower and slower. Finally they took us by van to the Palace of Justice, Section II of the Court of Appeals presided over by Mr. Ernest Ceaur Aslan. The same defenders did their duty combating successfully the thesis of Prosecutor Gica lonescu who laced the indictment with insulting outbursts full of hatred.

Sentencing was postponed for several days. Back to Vacaresti where we waited. Recalled, we were told of a new acquittal, unanimous. After 87 days of imprisonment we were finally released because we were found to be innocent. Who, I wondered, was going to punish our detractors? Who, I wondered, will avenge all the injustices, blows and suffering we had undergone?

But the prosecutor took the case even higher, to the Supreme Court of Appeals. Later, when the case came up for consideration, this court too, unanimously upheld the acquittal of the lower courts.

Here we were, with two decisions: one, that of Mr. Mihalache, by which "The Legion of Michael the Archangel" and "The Iron Guard" were dissolved as subversive organizations dangerous to the existence of the Romanian State; the other, that of the whole of the Romanian juridical system, Tribunal, Court of Appeals, and Supreme Court of Appeals, which unanimously declared these youth to be innocent, and that the Legion and the Guard did not represent any threat to public order or state security. Despite all this, our headquarters continued to remain padlocked.

Jewry, which was again beaten, lay low, preparing in the shadows other lies, other attacks, other infamies.

Oh Lord! Oh Lord! How come this people does not see that we, its children are left prey to the enemy blows that fall upon us one after the other?

Oh Lord! Oh Lord! When will it wake up and understand the great storm and the cabal directed against it with so much hatred determined to stun it and slay it?

The Legionary Movement in the First Elections June 1931

The National-Peasant administration fell in April. The Iorga-Argetoianu government came to power. As the Legion had been dissolved, I registered my movement with the central electoral commission under the name of "The Corneliu Z. Codreanu Group" choosing as its electoral symbol the iron grid:

But the new designation, as expected, did not catch on. People, press, enemy, government, continued to call it "The Iron Guard." We had to take part in the elections so as to avoid the imputation of being different from the rest of the people, or that we did not take advantage of legal channels.

June 1 was election day. With great material efforts, with borrowing, we succeeded in registering lists of county candidates. The campaign had started; on our part the most legal and most delicate campaign. In the two counties in which the candidacy of the Minister of War and that of the country's Prime Minister were announced, we did not come up with any lists; thus, of the few counties which we could have counted on carrying, we had to abandon two, Focsani and Radauti.

On top of this, government, local authorities and their hit men continued to set upon us. Our propaganda had been stopped; in the end even some of our votes were stolen from the ballot box. Yet we obtained, after a tough fight, 34,000 votes. Cahul came in first with nearly 5,000 votes; then Turda with 4,000; Covurlui with its three sections, Beresti, Ganesti, Oancea, with nearly 4,000; Ismail with 6,000; etc.

Since December 15, 1929 when I went to the first rally in Beresti until now, June 1931, I have been in continuous battle and imprisonment; I do not believe I spent two months at home, were I to add up the brief stops there.

The Campaign of Neamt August 31, 1931

Twenty days after the elections I learned that a seat in Parliament had been declared vacant in the county of Neamt.

After I looked over the situation I decided to enter the battle.

We had only 1,200 votes in this county in the previous elections. This time, the Liberals, the National-Peasants making common front with the Averescans, and the Georgists,[10] were entering candidates for this vacancy.

The press intended to confer particular significance on this election because the battle promised to be a fierce one and its outcome would indicate the succession to power.

One noticed concentration of forces, people even ventured prognostications. Some gave the victory to Liberals, others to National-Peasants. In the midst of battle some would place bets. Naturally, no one spoke at all about us. No one dreamed of placing bets on our victory.

On July 25 I issued my order for mobilization. But we were exhausted; we even lacked the money to pay the registration fees for our list. The Iesanu family took care of that and the cost of printing electoral flyers.

On July 30 I was in Piatra-Neamt awaiting the arrival of our campaigners. Everyone came as best he could, on foot, by train, by wagon. It was at this time that elements formed within the Brotherhoods of the Cross entered more seriously into battle, forming teams under the command of veteran legionaries,

I assigned each team to a certain sector. Altogether we had 100 campaigners. They left on foot, in boundless faith, though they knew no one, not what they would eat or where they would sleep from then on. God would provide for them; and the need would teach them. The Brosteni team was made up of Banica, Professor Matei and Cosma, to be joined later by those from Campul-Lung; to Rapciuni went Tocu's team; to Bicaz, Crangarnu's; to Targul-Neamt, Victor

10 The "Georgists" were the members of the party that George Bratianu, Ion Bratianu's son, founded -- following the death of his father, head of the Liberal Party — which he named "The National-Liberal Party." (Tr.)

Silaghi, Jorjoaia, Stelescu; to Baltatesti, Banea, Ventonic, Ifrim, Mihail David; to Roznov, Popovici; to Buhusi, Paduraru with the Romascanu family, Hristache Solomon and engineer Blanaru; to Cracaoani, Doru Belimace and Ratoiu; to Razboeni, Valeriu Stefanescu, the Mihai Craciun family and Stelian Teodorescu. In addition to these, Professor Ion Z. Codreanu was holding meetings in various parts of the county.

There were also, here and there, legionary nests led by Herghelegiu, Tarata, Platon, Loghin, David, Nuta, Mihai Bicleanu, Ungureanu, Olaru V. Ambrozie, Macovei, etc.

These teams were working as day laborers on farms in order to earn their keep. Soon they became endeared to the peasants.

The National-Peasants came into the county by many carloads. There were seven former cabinet members who came into the county to campaign on their behalf. Likewise the Liberals came in great numbers.

Of all social categories, the priest showed us the least understanding. In a country in which the crosses on church steeples have been falling down before the politicians' masterdom, atheistic and Jewized, in a battle in which we were the only ones coming in the name of the cross—our chests bared before the pagan monster—the county's priests, excepting three or four, were against us.

During the last week I had to organize my forces in preparation for the final battle. We had now six strong sectors and ten weak ones. Discussing this with my team leaders, they opined that since we have six strong sectors we could transfer our teams into the ten weak sectors to strengthen them. I thought this was an erroneous opinion which could lead to losing the battle.

I proceeded on exactly the opposite course, concentrating more forces in our strong points and leaving in the others only small harassing units.

Our adversaries committed the error I had avoided; they concentrated their effort in the points where we were stronger. So that we fought in our strongest points whereas they fought in their weakest ones.

They were annihilated. I took in 1,000 votes in each of the six sectors, while they had 200 to 300 maximum. At the same time their strongest sectors, left with an inadequate defense, were halved by our teams.

Corneliu Codreanu at an "Iron Guard" parade.

On voting day, beginning early in the morning, accompanied by Totu in a powerful auto I covered 15 out of 16 voting sections.

At 12 o'clock that night we learned the results of the election, in the great enthusiasm of peasant masses and the teams of legionaries and in the indescribable depression of politicians and Jews. The Guard: 11,300 votes; the Liberals, 7,000; National-Peasants with Averescans, 6,000 between them; the others, even fewer.

And so, in our first battle, in an open field against the coalesced forces of the politicians, legionaries, though small in number with incomparably smaller means at their disposal, succeeded in winning the victory, spreading panic among all our adversaries.

DEMOCRACY AGAINST THE NATION

Remarks on Democracy Versus the Nation

In Parliament

As a result of this election I entered Parliament; I was alone in the midst of an enemy world. I lacked the experience of this parliamentary life and the talent of democratic oratory which is full of empty, but pompous, shiny phraseology, of mirror-studied gestures and a large dose of impertinence. The characteristics which help one to succeed, to rise, God had not endowed me with—perhaps in order to prevent my being tempted to climb the political ladder.

All the time that I stayed in Parliament I never exceeded the laws of propriety and respect for those older than myself, be they even my greatest enemy. I had not ridiculed, sworn at, laughed at, or offended anyone, which meant I could not become a part of that life. I remained isolated, not only due to the fact that I was one against the others, but altogether isolated from that kind of life.

One evening, rather late, when deliberations were nearing the end and benches were almost empty, I was granted the floor.

I tried to show that our country had been invaded by Jewry; that where the invasion is the greatest, human misery is most frightening: in Maramures; that the beginning of Jewish existence on our soil, foreshadowed the death of Romanians; that as their numbers increased, we would die; that finally, the leaders of the Romanian nation, the men of the century of democracy and of political parties, have betrayed their people in this fight by placing themselves at the service of great national or international finance.

I showed that in the portfolio of the Marmorosch Blank Bank, that Judaic nest of conspiracy and corruption, figure a great many politicians to whom this bank "lent" money; Mr. Brandsch, Undersecretary of state 111,000 lei; Banca Taraneasca of Mr. Davilla, 4,677,000 lei; Mr. Iunian 407,000 lei; Mr. Madgearu 401,000 lei; Mr. Filipescu 1,265,000 lei; Mr. Raducanu 3,450,000 lei; The Raducanu

Bank 10,000,000 lei; Mr. Pangal (the head of the Scottish Rite Masonry in Romania) 3,800,000 lei; Mr. Titulescu 19,000,000 lei—all of them leaders in Romanian public life. In addition to these, there are others, very many, but I could not get my hands on the list of them. Someone interrupted me saying:

"This is borrowed money, it will be repaid."

I answered: "Whether this will be repaid or not, I do not know. But I tell you one thing: when someone borrows money from such a financial source, he is under an obligation when he comes to power, to satisfy it, or even if he is not in power, to support it, but in any case, not to expose it when is should be exposed."

I read then a list from which I showed, removing any possibility of denial, how since the war the Romanian state had been defrauded of some 50 billion lei under democracy, the most honored and most perfect form of government of the "people by the people"! The leadership of "democracy" having the basic idea of the permanent "control" of the people in which the people, the great controller had been robbed during 15 years of government of the fabulous sum of 50 billion lei.

Then I made several critical observations regarding democracy. In the end I made seven demands:

1. We demand the introduction of the death penalty for the fraudulent manipulators of public funds.

At this point I was interrupted by Mr. Ispir, professor at the Faculty of Theology:

"Mr. Codreanu, you call yourself a Christian, a propagator of Christian ideals. I remind you that the idea just put forward by you is anti-Christian."

I replied:

"Professor, when it is a question of choosing between the death of my country and that of the thief, I prefer the death of the thief, and I think I am a better Christian if I do not permit the thief to ruin my country and to destroy it."

2. We demand the investigation and confiscation of the wealth of those who have bled our poor country.

3. We demand that all politicians who may be proved guilty of having worked against the interests of our country by supporting shady private speculations or in any other fashion, be brought to justice.
4. We demand that in the future, politicians be barred from the administrative boards of the various banks and financial enterprises.
5. We demand the expulsion of the hordes of pitiless exploiters who have come here to drain the riches from our soil and exploit the work of our hands.
6. We demand that the territory of Romania be declared the inalienable and indefeasible property of the Romanian Nation.
7. We demand that all campaigning agents be sent to work and that a single command be established, which will inspire the whole Romanian Nation with one heart and one mind.

These were the first efforts to publicly formulate several political measures that I considered most urgent. They were not the result of some prolonged thinking or ideological search, but the result of momentary reflections over what the Romanian people needed then, without delay.

Six months later, several quite popular movements appeared which had in their program my three initial points: 1. The death penalty, 2. The investigation of wealth, and 3. The prevention of politicians from getting on administrative boards—which meant that others also observed them to be necessary.

Several Observations Regarding Democracy

I wish, in the pages that follow, to present several conclusions of my daily experience in such a manner that they can be understood by any young legionary or workingman.

We live in the clothing, the forms of democracy. Are they, I wonder, good? We do not yet know. But one thing we do see: we know precisely that part of the greater and more civilized European nations discarded these clothes and put on some new ones. Did they shed them because they were good? Other nations too, make strong efforts to shed them and change them. Why? Could it be that all nations went mad? That only Romanian politicians remained the wisest men in the whole world? It seems, I cannot quite believe that.

Certainly, those who changed them or who wish to do so, have their own reasons. But why should we be concerned with somebody else's reasons? Let us better be concerned with the reasons which would make us Romanians shed these clothes of democracy.

If we have no reasons for discarding them, if for us they are suitable, then we should keep them, even if all Europe should discard them.

However, they are not good for us either, because:

1. *Democracy breaks the unity* of the Romanian people, dividing it into parties, stirring it up, and so, disunited, exposing it to face the united block of the Judaic power in a difficult moment of its history.

This argument alone is so grave for our existence that it would constitute sufficient reason for us to change this democracy for anything that could guarantee our unity: namely our life; for our disunity means death.

2. *Democracy transforms the millions of Jews into Romanian citizens*, by making them the equal of Romanians and giving them equal rights in the state. Equality? On what basis? We have lived here for thousands of years; with the plow and with the weapon; with our labor and our blood.

Why should we be equal to those who have been here for hardly 100, 10, or 5 years? Looking at the past, it was we who created this state. Looking at the future, it is we Romanians who hold the entire historical responsibility for Greater Romania's existence; they have none. How could Jews be made responsible before history for the disappearance of the Romanian State?

To sum up: they have neither equality in the labor, sacrifice and fighting that created the state, nor equality of responsibility for its future. Equality? According to an ancient maxim, equality means treating unequal things unequally. On what basis do the Jews demand equal treatment, political rights equal to those of Romanians?

3. *Democracy is incapable of continuity in effort.*

Divided into parties that govern one, two or three years, it is incapable of conceiving and accomplishing a long range plan. One party nullifies the plans and the efforts of another. What was conceived and built by one today is demolished next by another.

In a country in need of construction, whose historical moment is that very construction, this drawback of democracy constitutes a threat. It is as if on a farm the owners would change yearly, each coming with different plans, doing away with what the predecessors did, their work only to be done away with by the next owner coming tomorrow.

4. *Democracy makes it impossible for the politician to do his duty to his nation.*

A politician of the greatest good will becomes, in a democracy, the slave of his supporters; he either satisfies their personal appetites or they destroy his backing. The politician lives under the tyranny and permanent threat of the electoral agent.

He is placed in the position of choosing either the renunciation of his lifetime's labor or the satisfaction of his supporters. And then the politician satisfies their appetites; not out of his pocket, but out of the country's pocket. He creates jobs, positions, missions, commissions, sinecures, all of them loading down the national budget which burdens more and more the ever more bowed backs of the people.

5. *Democracy is incapable of authority.*

It lacks the power of sanction. A party, for fear of losing its supporters, does not apply sanctions against those who live through scandalous business deals running into the millions, through thievery or embezzlement; nor does it apply any sanctions against political adversaries lest they expose its own shady deals and incorrectitudes.

6. *Democracy is in the service of great finance.*

Because of the expensive system and the competition among various groups, democracy needs a lot of money. As a natural consequence it becomes the slave of the great Jewish international finance which subjugates it by subvention.

In this fashion the fate of a people is given into the hands of a caste of bankers.

Election, Selection, Heredity

A people is not led according to its will: the democratic formula; nor according to the will of one individual: the dictatorial formula. But according to laws. I do not talk here of man-made laws. There are norms, natural laws of life; and there are norms, natural laws of death. Laws of life and laws of death. A nation is headed for life or death according to its respect for one or the other of these laws.

There remains one question to be answered: Who, in a nation, can understand or know intuitively these norms? People? The multitude? If this were the case I believe that too much is expected. Multitudes do not understand much simpler laws. These must be explained to them by repeated insistence in order to be understood—yes, even by punishment if need be.

Here are a few examples of laws that are imperatively necessary to the life of the people, which multitudes understand only with difficulty: that in case of contagious illness, the sick must be isolated and a general disinfection is needed; that sunlight must enter homes, therefore a house should have large windows; that if cattle are better fed and cared for they yield more for man's nutrition, etc.

If the multitude does not understand or understands only with difficulty several laws that are immediately necessary to its life, how can it be imagined by someone that it could understand the most difficult natural laws; or that it would know intuitively the most subtle and imperceptible norms of human leadership, norms that project beyond itself, its life, its life's necessities, or which do not apply directly to it but to a more superior entity, the nation?

For making bread, shoes, ploughs, farming, running a streetcar, one must be specialized. Is there no need for specialization when it comes to the most demanding leadership, that of a nation? Does one not have to possess certain qualities?

The conclusion: A people is not capable of governing itself. It ought to be governed by its elite. Namely, through that category of men born within its bosom who possess certain aptitudes and specialties. Just as the bees raise their "queen" a people must raise its elite.

The multitude likewise, in its needs, appeals to its elite, the wise of the state.

Who chooses this elite—the multitude?

Supporters could be found for any "ideas," or votes for anyone running for public office. But this does not depend on the people's understanding of those "ideas," "laws" or "candidates" but on something entirely different: on the adroitness of individuals to win the goodwill of the multitudes. There is nothing more capricious and unstable in opinions than the multitude. Since the war, this multitude was, in turn, Averescan, Liberal, Nationalistic, National-Peasant, Iorgan, etc. hailing each, only to spit on each a year later, thus recognizing its own error, disorientation and incapacity. Its criterion for selection is: "Let us try some others." Thus, the choosing is done not according to judgement and knowledge, but haphazardly and trusting to luck.

Here are two opposite ideas, one containing truth, the other the lie. Truth—of which there can be but one—is sought. The question is put to a vote. One idea polls 10,000 votes, the other 10,050. Is it possible that 50 votes more or less determine or deny truth? Truth depends neither on majority nor minority; it has its own laws and it succeeds, as has been seen, against all majorities, even though they be crushing.

Finding truth cannot be entrusted to majorities, just as in geometry Pythagoras' theorem cannot be put to the multitude's vote in order to determine or deny its validity; or just as a chemist making ammonia does not turn to multitudes to put the amounts of nitrogen and hydrogen to a vote; or as an agronomist, who studied agriculture and its laws for years, does not have to turn to a multitude trying to convince himself of their validity by their vote.

Can the people choose its elite?

Why then do soldiers not choose the best general?
In order to choose, this collective jury would have to know very well;

a) The laws of strategy, tactics, organization etc. and
b) To what extent the individual in question conforms through aptitudes and knowledge to these laws.

No one can choose wisely without this knowledge. If the multitude wishes to choose its elite, it must necessarily know the national organism's laws of leadership and the extent candidates to this leadership conform by qualifications and knowledge to said laws.

However, the multitude can know neither these laws nor the candidates. That is why we believe that the leading elite of a country cannot be chosen by the multitude. To try to select this elite is like determining by majority vote who the poets, writers, mechanics, aviators or athletes of a country ought to be.

Thus democracy, based on the principle of election, choosing its elite itself, commits a fundamental error from which evolves the entire state of wrong, disorder and misery in our villages. We touch here upon a capital point, because it is from the error of democratic conception that we could say all the other errors originate.

When the masses are called to choose their elite they are not only incapable of discovering and choosing one but choose moreover, with few exceptions, the worst within a nation.

Not only does democracy remove the national elite, but it replaces it with the worst within a nation. Democracy elects men totally lacking in scruples, without any morals; those who will pay better, thus those with a higher power of corruption; magicians, charlatans, demagogues, who will excel in their fields during the electoral campaign. Several good men would be able to slip through among them, even politicians of good faith. But they would be the slaves of the former. The real elite of a nation would be defeated, removed, because it would refuse to compete on that basis; it would retreat and stay hidden.

Hence, the fatal consequences for the state.

When a state is led by a so-called "elite" made up of the worst, most corrupt, most unhealthy it has, is it not permitted a person to ask why the state is headed for ruin?

Here then is the cause of all other evils.. immorality, corruption and lust throughout the country; thievery and spoliation in the state's wealth; bloody exploitation of the people; poverty and misery in its hoites; lack of the sense of duty in all functions; disorder and disorganization in the state; the invasion from all directions of foreigners with money, as coming to buy bankrupt stores whose wares are being sold for a pittance. The country is auctioned off.

"Who pays higher?" In the last analysis this is where democracy is going to take us.

In Romania, particularly since the war, democracy has created for us, through this system of elections, a "national elite" of Romano-Jews, based not on bravery, nor love of country, nor sacrifice, but on betrayal of country, the satisfaction of personal interest, the bribe, the traffic of influence, the enrichment through exploitation and embezzlement, thievery, cowardice, and intrigue to knock down any adversary.

This "national elite," if it continues to lead this country, will bring about the destruction of the Romanian state, Therefore, in the last analysis, the problem facing the Romanian people today, on which all others depend, is the substitution of this fake elite with a real national one based on virtue, love and sacrifice for country, justice and love for the people, honesty, work, order, discipline, honest dealing, and honor.

Who is to make this substitution? Who is to place this real elite in its place of leadership? I answer: anyone but the multitude. I admit any system except "democracy," which I see killing the Romanian people.

The new Romanian elite, as well as any other elite in the world, must be based on the principle of social selection. In other words, a category of people endowed with certain qualities which they then cultivate, is naturally selected from the nation's body, namely from the large healthy mass of peasantry and workingmen, which is permanently bound to the land and the country. This category of people becomes the national elite meant to lead our nation.

When can a multitude be consulted, and when must it be? It ought to be consulted before the great decisions that affect its future, in order to say its word whether it can or cannot, whether it is spiritually prepared or not, to follow a certain path. It ought to be consulted on matters affecting its fate. This is what is meant by the consultation of the people; it does not mean the election of an elite by the people.

But I repeat my question: "Who indicates everyone's place within an elite and who sizes up everyone? Wbo establishes the selection and consecrates the members of the new elite?" I answer: "The previous elite."

The latter does not choose or name, but consecrates each in his place to which he elevated himself through his capacity and moral worth. The consecration is made by the elite's chief in consultation with his

Front row : Radu Mironovici, Corneliu Zelea Codreanu, Ilie Garneata
Back row : Corneliu Georgescu, Tudose Popescu, Ion Mota

elite. Thus a national elite must see to it that it leaves an inheriting elite to take its place, an elite not based, however, on the principle of heredity but only on that of social selection applied with the greatest strictness. The principle of heredity is not sufficient in itself. According to the principle of social selection, continually refreshed by elements from within the nation's depths, an elite keeps itself always vigorous. The main historical mistake has been that where an elite was created on the basis of the principle of selection, it dropped next day the very principle which gave it birth, replacing it with the principle of heredity thus consecrating the unjust and condemned system of privileges through birth. It was as a protest against this mistake; for the removal of a degenerated elite; and for the abolition of privilege through birth, that democracy was born. The abandonment of the principle of selection led to a false and degenerate elite which in turn led to the aberration of democracy.

The principle of selection removes alike both the principle of election and that of heredity, They cancel each other out. There is a conflict between them; for, either there is a principle of selection and in that case the opinion and vote of the multitude do not matter, or the latter votes in certain candidates and in that case selection no longer operates.

Likewise, if the principle of social selection is adopted, heredity plays no part. These two principles cannot go together unless the heir corresponds to the laws of selection.

And if a nation has no real elite—a first one to designate the second? I answer by a single phrase which contains an indisputable truth:

In that case, the real elite is born out of a war with the degenerate elite, the false one. And that, also on the principle of selection.

Therefore, summing it up, the role of an elite is:

a) To lead a nation according to the life laws of a people.

b) To leave behind an inheriting elite based not on the principle of heredity but on that of selection, because only an elite knows life's laws and can judge to what extent people conform by aptitudes and knowledge to these laws.

It is like a gardener who works his garden and sees to it that before he dies he has an inheritor, a replacement, for he alone can say who among those working with him is best to take his place and continue his work.

On what must an elite be founded?

a) Purity of soul, b) Capacity of work and creativity, c) Bravery, d) Tough living and permanent warring against difficulties facing the nation, e) Poverty, namely voluntary renunciation of amassing a fortune, f) Faith in God. g) Love.

I have been asked whether our activity so far has followed along the same lines as those of the Christian Church. I answer:

We make a great distinction between the line we follow and that of the Christian Chruch. The Church dominates us from on high. It reaches perfection and the sublime. We cannot lower this plane in order to explain our acts.

We, through our action, through all our acts and thoughts, tend toward this line, raising ourselves up toward it as much as the weight of our sins of the flesh and our fall through original sin permit. It remains to be seen how much we can elevate ourselves toward this line through our worldly efforts.

Individual, National Collectivity, Nation

"Human rights" are not limited only by the rights of other humans but also by other rights. There are three distinct entities:

1. The individual.

2. The present national collectivity, that is, the totality of all the individuals of the same nation, living in a state at a given moment.

3. The nation, that historical entity whose life extends over centuries, its roots imbedded deep in the mists of time, and with an infinite future.

A new great error of democracy based on "human rights" is that of recognizing and showing an interest in only one of these three entities, the individual; it neglects the second or ridicules it, and denies the third.

All of them have their rights and their duties, the right to live and the duty of not infringing on the right to life of the other two.

Democracy takes care of assuring only the rights of the individual. That is why in democracy we witness a formidable upset. The individual believes he can encroach, with his unlimited rights, on the rights of the whole collectivity, which he thinks he can trample and rob; hence, in democracy, one witnesses this rending scene, this anarchy in which the individual recognizes nothing outside his personal interest.

In its turn, national collectivity exhibits a permanent tendency to sacrifice the future—the rights of the nation—for its present interests. That is why we witness the pitiless exploitation and the alienation of our forests, mines, oil reserves, forgetting that there are hundreds of Romanian generations, our children's children to come after us, who likewise expect to live and carry on the life of our nation.

This upheaval, this breach of relationship brought about by democracy constitutes veritable anarchy, an upsetting of the natural order, and is one of the principal causes of the state of unrest in today's society.

Harmony can be re-established only by the reinstatement of natural order. The individual must be subordinated to the superior entity, the national collectivity, which in turn must be subordinated to the nation. "Human rights" are no longer unlimited, but limited by the rights of national collectivity, these in turn being limited by those of the nation.

Finally, it would seem that in a democracy at least the individual enjoying so many rights lives wonderfully. But in reality, and this is democracy's ultimate tragedy, the individual has no right, for where is the freedom of assembly in our country, the freedom to write, the freedom of conscience? The individual lives under terror, a state of siege, censorship; thousands of people are arrested, some being killed for their faith, as under the most tyrannical leaders.

Where is "the right of the sovereign multitude" to decide its fate, when meetings are forbidden and when thousands of people are prevented from voting, maltreated, threatened with death, killed?

You will say: "Yes, but these people want to change the Constitution, limit our liberties, enthrone another form of government!"

I ask: "Can democracy claim that a people is not free to decide its own destiny, to change its Constitution, its form of government, as it pleases; to live with greater or fewer freedoms as it chooses?"

This is the ultimate tragedy.

In reality man has no rights in a democracy. He did not lose them for the benefit of either the national collectivity or the nation, but in favor of a politico-financier caste of bankers and electoral agents.

Finally, the last beneficence to the individual. Masonic democracy through an unparalleled perfidy masquerades as an apostle for peace on this earth while at the same time proclaiming war between man and God.

Peace among men and warring against God.

The perfidy consists in using the words of our Savior "Peace among men," in order to pose as an apostle for "peace," while condemning Him and showing Him as mankind's enemy. And more, this perfidy consists also in that they pretend to want to save people's lives while in fact they lead them to their death; feigning to save their lives from war, condemn them—devilishly—to eternal damnation.

The Nation

When we say the Romanian nation, we mean not only all Romanians living in the same territory, sharing the same past and the same future, the same dress, but all Romanians, alive and dead, who have lived on this land from the beginning of history and will live here also in the future.

The nation includes:

1. All the Romanians presently alive.
2. All the souls of our dead and the tombs of our ancestors.
3. All those who will be born Romanians.

A people becomes conscious of itself when it attains the consciousness of this whole, not only of its own aims. The nation possesses:

1. *A physical, biological patrimony*—her flesh and blood,
2. *A material patrimony*—the soil of her country and its riches.
3. *A spiritual patrimony* which contains:

a) *Her concept of God*, the world and life. This concept forms a domain, a spiritual property. The frontiers of this domain are determined by the horizons to which the brightness of her concept reaches. There exists a country of the national spirit, a country of its visions obtained by revelation or by her own efforts.

b) Her honor which shines to the extent that the nation has conformed during her history to the norms stemming from her concept of God, the world and life.

c) Her culture, the yield of her existence resulting from her own efforts in the domain of arts and thought. This culture is not international, it is the expression of national genius, of the blood. Culture is international as far as its luminescence may reach, but national in origin. Someone made a beautiful comparison; both bread and wheat can be international as consumption items, but they carry everywhere the stamp of the earth in which they grew.

Each of these three patrimonies has its importance. A people must defend all three. *The most important however is its spiritual patrimony, for only it carries the stamp of eternity, it alone endures through all the centuries.*

The ancient Greeks are not remembered because of their physique—nothing but ashes is left of that—nor their material riches, had they had any, but because of their culture.

A people lives in eternity through its outlook, its concept of honor, and its culture. That is why the nations' leaders must reason and act, not only according to the physical or material interests of the people, but also by taking into account its historic honor, its eternal interests. In other words, not bread, but honor at any price.

The Final Aim of the Nation

Is it life?

If it be life, then the means people use to assure life does not matter; even the worst is good. Therefore the question must be raised: Which are the principles guiding nations in their relationship with other nations? Should they be guided by the animal instinct, the tiger in them, as fish behave in the sea or beasts in the forest?

The final aim is not life but resurrection. The resurrection of peoples in the name of the Savior Jesus Christ. Creation, culture, are but a means, not a purpose as it has been believed, of obtaining this resurrection. It is the fruit of the talent God planted in our people for which we have to account. There will come a time when all the peoples of the earth shall be resurrected, with all their dead and all their kings and emperors, each people having its place before God's throne. This final moment, "the resurrection from the dead," is the noblest and most sublime one toward which a people can rise.

The nation then is an entity which prolongs her existence even beyond this earth. Peoples are realities even in the nether world, not only in this one.

St. John narrating what he saw beyond the earth, says: "And the city has no need of the sun, nor of the moon, to shine in it; for the glory of God has enlightened it, and the Lamb is the lamp thereof.

"And the nations shall walk in the light of it and the kings of the earth shall bring their glory and honor into it."

(Apocalypse, 21, 23-24).

And again:

"Who shall not fear Thee, Oh Lord, and magnify Thy name? For Thou only art holy; for all nations shall come and shall adore in Thy sight, because Thy judgements are manifest."

(Apocalypse 15, 4).

To us Romanians, to our people, as to any other people in the world, God has given a mission, a historic destiny. The first law that a person must follow is that of going on the path of this destiny, accomplishing its entrusted mission.

Our people has never laid down its arms or deserted its mission, no matter how difficult or lengthy was its Golgotha Way. Even now, obstacles high as mountains appear before us.

Shall we be, I wonder, the weak and cowardly generation to drop from our hands, under pressures of threats, the line of Romanian destiny and abandon our mission as a people in this world?

Monarchy and the Law of Monarchy

At the head of peoples, above the elite, one finds the monarchy.

I reject the republic.

One has met some monarchs that were good, some very good, others weak or bad. Some enjoyed honors and the love of their people to the end of their lives, others were beheaded. Therefore, not all of the monarchs were good. Monarchy itself, however, has been always good. One must not confuse the man with the institution and draw false conclusions.

There can be bad priests; but can we, because of this, conclude that the Church must be abolished and God stoned to death?

There are weak and bad monarchs certainly, but we cannot renounce monarchy because of this.

In farming, there is occasionally a bad year following a good one, or one good and two bad; even so, it occurred to no one in the world to quit farming.

Does a monarch do as he pleases, whether he be great or small, good or bad? A monarch does not do what he wants. He is small when he does as he pleases and great when he does what he must.

To each nation God has traced a line of destiny. A monarch is great and good when he stays on that line; he is small or bad, to the extent that he wanders away from this line of destiny or opposes it. This then, is, the law of monarchy. There are also other lines that may tempt a monarch: the line of personal interest or that of a class of people or group; the line of alien interests (domestic or foreign). He must avoid all these lines and follow that of his people.

Stefan the Great has shone in history for 500 years and Romanians remember him because he identified himself perfectly with the destiny of his people.

King Ferdinand, in spite of pressure from outside interests and influences, placed himself on the line of the nation's destiny, he suffered with her, sacrificed side by side with her, and won with her. It is by virtue of this that he is great and immortal.

The Battle of Tutova
April 17, 1932

Only four months had passed since the election in Neamt and the young legionary army engaged in a new battle. At the beginning of January 1932, a congressman's seat was declared vacant in Tutova[1]. I had weighed the situation. In the previous general elections, we got only 500 votes there. The county was weak; but it was framed in by the stronger counties of Covurlui, Cahul and Tecuci, so that we could easily bring in legionaries.

It seemed to me that we could possibly win. I was thinking of the impact an echo of a new victory would have. Two consecutive victories of the youngest generation against all political parties would have considerably enhanced its prestige in the eyes of the country. I decided that my father should run, as he was most necessary for me in the movement, both in Parliament and out of it for organization and propaganda. The election had been fixed for March 17.

---

1 County of Tutova with Barlad as its county seat .(Tr.)

On January 9 I sent out a manifesto to the whole county. My father with a first electoral team arrived on January 10. Then came the teams from Iasi, Tecuci, Beresti and Cahul.

During the first three weeks, the speed and the bravery of the small legionary forces had set off a current of sympathy in our favor throughout the whole county. In a bad winter with heavy snows and cold weather, the political parties could not go out. They waited for better weather. But during this time, over hills, through waist-deep snows, through blizzards, legionaries traveled from village to village.

Around the beginning of February, fighting the enemy became more difficult. A coalition of Liberals, National-Peasants, Lupists[2] and Cuzists was facing us with a fierceness we had never met before. The government resorted to truly terroristic measures and the Jewish press attacked us vehemently. I felt the need of new reinforcements, so I sent the last reserves from Iasi, led by Totu. I had none others except in Bucharest and these could not be secured for lack of funds. So I convoked a meeting of the legionaries and proposed a heroic step: that they start off on foot from Bucharest to Barlad, a distance of nearly 200 miles, explaining to them that this march would mean more for our victory than 100,000 manifestoes. It alone would constitute a great heroic discourse addressed by legionaries to the Romanians of Tutova.

The legionaries received my suggestion enthusiastically. A week later a team of about 25, led by Stelescu, Caratanase and Doru Belimace left Bucharest on foot for Tutova. At the end of a ten-day march through stormy weather, they arrived at Barlad where they were warmly welcomed by the whole populace. But the persecution had escalated to nerve-shattering tenseness. Mr. Argetoianu, Minister of Internal Affairs, sent out the gendarmes of Col. Ignat, with large forces, and orders to carry the legionaries out of Tutova county on stretchers. It was impossible for small teams to advance further. So I formed two strong teams under the command of Victor Silaghi and Stelescu which, supporting one another, should advance on the Puesti-Dragomiresti line, supporting my father. I sent another smaller team in the direction of Bacani. These two were the only two routes that remained uncanvassed. They constituted the north-east half of the county. The other half, the south, had been adequately worked by my father, Mr. D. Popescu the county head, Victor Silaghi, Teodor Tilea and Ion Antoniu, with the first teams.

2 Dr. Lupu's party members. (Tr.)

The two teams in the North advanced nearly 30 miles, fighting the bitter cold and ending up with several wounded, Tocu among others. In the northern part of the county they were met by large contingents of gendarmes. The teams barricaded themselves in the attic of an abandoned house where they resisted for 48 hours without heat, food or water In the end they were able to retreat through a difficult overnight march, executed in conditions truly heroic, only because of Victor Silaghi's stubborn persistence in encouraging the exhausted, starved and frozen legionaries to the last possible resistance. This orphan child, son of the Romanian priest Silaghi from Careii Mari who was murdered by Hungarians in 1918 under tragic conditions fought with bravery.

Finally, these teams were surrounded by superior forces, captured and brought to Barlad. My father was arrested and locked up in a regimental prison.

The third team was completely decimated in the battle of Bacani. There, in a valley before entering the village in the evening, it was attacked by a large contingent of gendarmes. The team's leader, legionary Lascar Popescu, struck over the head with a rifle, was the first to fall unconscious in a pool of blood. The other legionaries refused to retreat. They counterattacked with bare chests, nothing in their hands, trying to get into the village. One by one they all fell unconscious. The last one standing, attacked alone. Under blows, he fell on his knees, got up, attacked again. He fell near his comrades. The entire team lay unconscious in a pool of blood. From there they were dragged through the snow by the gendarmes, for better than a mile to the gendarmes post in the village. At 1 o'clock that night, a rider brought the news to Barlad of what happened at Bacani. The team from Iasi led by Totu, which arrived in Barlad that midnight, left immediately on foot to aid their wounded comrades. Following a battle from 3:30 to 5 o'clock in the morning, during which the gendarmes fired all their arms, the legionaries occupied the gendarmes' post, finding inside, still unconscious and lying on the ground, their comrades fallen in the battle of Bacani. They carried them to the hospital in Barlad.

But things did not rest here. Jewry launched a mammoth press campaign, attacking us with revolting cynicism and injustice. A wave of lies, insults, calumnies, came our way. All the political groupings coalesced to put us out of the battle.

The Second Dissolution of the Guard
March 1932

Kicked by the gendarmes, attacked by the Jewish press, we were hit by a new dissolution of the Guard ordered through a simple ministerial decision.

Although we were within the framework of perfect legality, the Iorga-Argetoianu government, in defiance of laws and Constitution, dissolved the Guard arbitrarily. Our headquarters all over the country were again taken over and padlocked, the Iasi print shop closed down. Attacked in the press, we were placed in the impossible position of not being able to defend ourselves as all our publications had been suspended. In Parliament I tried to speak, but I was prevented by the din of the majority, who did not permit me to defend myself.

However, the candidacy in Tutova could not be stopped.

The team from Bucharest was expelled from the county. Likewise the others, one by one. Our Iasi team of about 30, under Totu's command, as it was being taken to the depot for the same evacuation operation, broke the cordons and occupied the waiting room in which, barricaded, it resisted for 24 hours, until it was gassed out. In the end it was loaded on the train and taken out of the county.

Only Ibraileanu, Nutu Esanu, and my father who was arrested, remained in town. The persecution was then switched to the villages. Peasants, school teachers and priests were arrested and beaten; their homes broken into. The election was postponed one month, until April 17.

My father was released. The elderly legionaries then came into town to step into the battle: Hristache Solomon, Col. Cambureanu, Ventonic, Ifrim, Father Isihie, Peceli, Potolea, etc. I assigned them to various sectors. Each slipped to his post under the cover of night. Our teams from the neighboring counties again entered Tutova at several points. Gh. Costea's team crossed the Barlad river, water up to their necks, for all roads were patrolled; they arrived at the polling station dripping wet.

April 17 in the morning the voting began, continuing into the night. April 18, at 5 o'clock in the morning, the legionary victory was announced: 5,600 votes; Liberals: 5,200; National-Peasants: 4,000; the other groups, less than 2,000; Cuzists: 500 votes.

This second legionary victory, against the coalition of all the Romanian politicians, won through the dauntlessness and the iron will of the legionaries, through their heroism and blood, defying obstacles, insults, blows and persecution, had stirred up throughout the country an indescribable enthusiasm.

New General Elections July 1932

My father was validated the last day of the parliamentary session. But our rest lasted only one week, for the lorga government had fallen. A National-Peasant government was formed, headed by Mr. Vaida.

Exhausted both physically and financially, we went into a new battle. That was June 1932. Ever since December 15, 1929 we had been in a constant fight: December 1929 - April 1930, the campaigns in Covurlui, Cahul, Turda, Tecuci; the summer of 1930, the preparation, then interdiction of the march in Basarabia, followed by my imprisonment until that fall; in October and November we were in Maramures—that winter imprisoned again; the spring of 1931, battle preceding general elections; summer of 1931, elections in Neamt; winter 1932, elections in Tutova; and now we were again about to come to the general elections.

In spite of all these fights, we continued the organizational work in the rest of the country. The year before, we entered electoral lists in 17 counties, this year we entered 36,

All political parties engaged in the same quarrels, full of intrigues, for the naming of their candidates. This lasted a whole week. But I, alone, in one night fixed all our candidate lists in 36 counties. No one among legionaries fights over his place on the list; if anything, he asks to be put last.

The difficult problem for us is money matters. Most of the counties have been able to meet their own expenses out of legionary contributions. Others have not. I needed 50,000 lei only to cover electoral taxes. I walked as in a daze till the last day. I tried one, I tried another. Nothing.

I went to see Mr. Nichifor Crainic, the director of *Calendarul* ("The Calendar") in the hope he might have money. But in vain. With his journal, which had been published for five months, he supported our struggle, following the bravery of our legionary teams step by step; however, he could not help us financially. Finally, I borrowed from Pihu and Caranica, who, by running to all the Macedonians, found the necessary sum. Several counties were supported by the county of Focsani and Hristache Solomon.

The campaign commenced. A new persecution befell our ranks. Being spread over a large front, our thin ranks were everywhere violently attacked. Legionaries Savin and Popescu were wounded at Tighina. At Barlad scores of teachers and priests were dragged into cellars and maltreated by orders of Mr. Georgescu-Barlad. At Vaslui our small teams were wounded. Likewise at Podul-Iloaiei and throughout Iasi county.

At Focsani, the aged Hristache Solomon, engineer Blanaru, and ten others were attacked on orders of attorney Neagu by armed bands of National-Peasants in the village of Vulturul. Legionaries fell to the ground wounded by bludgeons and knives. One only remained on his feet like a mountain, Hristache Solomon, whom no one dared touch up to then. He fiercely defended himself, but in the end, fell in the middle of the road, overwhelmed by blows. There on the ground he was bludgeoned over the head by these beasts who always made an issue—then as they do now—of legality, civilized methods, freedom, etc.

The Guard obtained 70,000 votes, double that of the previous year. The counties of Cahul, Neamt, Covurlui and Tutova where my father ran, came out strongest. Then followed Campul-Lung with Mota; then Turda, Focsani, Ismail, Tighina. We won five seats, and now we must make our choices to fill them. I stayed in Cahul, in order to let Nutu Esanu enter Parliament. I decided that my father should remain in Barlad in order to let Stelescu, a 25 year old student, enter Parliament; I wanted thus to give the youth of the country encouragement and a stimulus.

The trust and love I showed this youth, however, was not returned to me.[3]

---

3 The author refers here to Stelescu's future betrayal of his legionary comrades. (Tr.)

In Parliament For The Second Time

All the time in Parliament I fought against the government and its measures which I considered contrary to the well-being of the Romanian people, as in fact I had fought also all the former administrations that took turns at the state's helm. The country had nothing to expect from all these governments. Nothing of any sanity for the future of our people was being forged there. All measures and laws were but some palliatives that prolonged from day to day the bitter and sad existence of our country. When at Grivita, Romanian workers were shot by orders of the Ministry of Internal Affairs, sickened to the bottom of my heart by the attitude of the pro-communists within the National-Peasant Party who were applauding the government's step, I took the platform and deemed it my duty to speak as follows:

> "It is bad that the unfortunate workers went out into the street, but it would be worse if they and our people, faced with the injustice that cries out to heaven, would not go out, but resignedly bend their heads under the yoke, leaving the country in the hands of some exploiting politicians...[4]

I quote here from the Official Minutes of this session.

> "Mr. Corneliu Zelea Codrednu: Mr. President, fellow congressmen! In the name of the group to which I belong, I demand that in addition to the investigation which is normally made by competent authorities, another parliamentary investigation be conducted, composed of representatives of various political groups in this Parliament. I demand this because I doubt the veracity of Mr. Minister of Internal Affairs' statement; I doubt that for a very good reason. On January 24, when Romanian students, nationalist and Christian, went to the tomb of the unknown soldier to place a cross, the State Securitate had leaked the information to a newspaper in Bucharest that that action was engineered and financed by Moscow.
>
> "If the information you have, regarding the Grivita affair also comes from such a source, then I understand very well how right you are in taking steps of this nature as you did yesterday and today (Applause from the benches of 'The Iron Guard' and those of the National Party of Dr. Lupu).

---

4 The author speaks here of the workers' strike at the Grivita Railway Works in Bucharest on February 4, 1933 under the National-Peasant administration. (Tr.)

"Secondly, I wish to state that I, as well as all people of common sense in this country, am not afraid of Communism or Bolshevism. We are afraid of something else, of the fact that those workers have nothing to eat; they are hungry. (Applause from the benches of 'The Iron Guard' and those of the Peasant Party of Dr. Lupu).

"Some of those workers make only 1,100 lei a month and have 5, 6, 7, children.

"Dr. N. Lupu: It is true.

"Mr. Corneliu Zelea Codreanu: Having 5, 6, 7, children, such wages are not enough even for their daily bread.

"I, on the other hand, am also afraid of something else: of their thirst for justice.

"Dr. N. Lupu: Very good!

"Mr. Corneliu Zelea Codreanu: Therefore, you will have to satisfy these two needs: hunger, and thirst for justice. (Applause from the benches of 'The Iron Guard' and those of the Peasant Party of Dr. Lupu), and this country will enjoy complete order."

(Meeting of Thursday, February 16, 1933.
Official Monitor 41.
of February 23, 1933)

One of the hardships putting the brakes on parliamentary activity is the thousands of demands to the ministries for intercessions of some kind. This constitutes a real punishment for us from our constituency, (1) because parliamentarians have to waste most of their time satisfying these demands. This system is dangerous to the life of an organization, for it paralyzes its entire activity; it can lose the whole battle. You have to abandon the fate of your country in order to serve your supporters. After a while I noticed that there were no legionaries among those coming to me with such demands. All were either professional beggars or specially sent adversaries seeking to paralyze us. (2) This system placed us in the touchy position of going before, and seeking favors from, the men we were fighting. For these reasons I personally refused to intervene for anyone. During all my serving in Parliament, I asked nothing of any minister.

Another category was made up of those coming to ask us for money. Out of the hundreds knocking on our doors daily, there were no legionaries. Some were truly sick or fallen into misfortune, but some turned this system into a real profession.

Finally our group was a small organization, in formation, on the move, in constant battle. This demanded particularly from me uninterrupted attention to all enemy moves; it involved the uncovering and parrying of enemy plans, the winning and organizing of new positions, in other words, a permanent survey, day and night, of the battlefields nation-wide. But before anything else came the supervision of legionary education so as not to wake up and find ourselves being gradually changed into a political category of moral infection from which we would not be able to extricate ourselves and in which the legionary spirit would die.

Parliament took away from me the time I really needed for leadership.

The Condition of the Legionary Organization in 1932-1933

In the fall of 1932 and the winter of 1933 legionaries could breathe. Three and one half years of fighting were over. These youth now deserved their rest.

It had been almost two years since I set up residence in Bucharest. In Iasi to take my place, Banea, aided by Totu, Cranganu, Tasca and Stelian Teodorescu, stayed to handle questions relating to students, print shop, our Home, etc. The legionary student group increased, comprising now more than half of the militant students. In Cluj, a healthy start toward organization was accomplished by Banica Dobre; likewise in Cernauti with Lauric where legionary life was budding nicely under the spiritual guidance of Professor Traian Braileanu around whom Professor Toppa and others gathered. In the whole of Bucovina the legionary current and organization were growing under the able command of the veteran and distinguished nationalist Vasile Iasinschi. In Chisinau Tudorache and Serghie Florescu were working; In Oradea Mare, Iosif Bozantan.

The youth raised in the Brotherhoods of the Cross were prepared by the time they entered university.

A nationalist newspaper of great courage and excellent direction had started publication in Bucharest, *Calendarul* ("The Calendar") under the directorship of Mr. Nichifor Crainic and with the collaboration of a handful of intellectuals headed by Professor Dragos Protopopescu. This paper was cutting, courageously, a new and wide path in the

Romanian intellectual world, along the Christian and nationalist line. Mr. Crainic's articles particularly were real cannon fire which caused devastation within enemy ranks.

Within the student movement in the capital, legionaries occupied the first lines. Traian Cotiga held the presidency of the student center, having a legionary committee.

A turnabout was felt among the intellectual youth of the capital. Their consciences were preoccupied with the great problems affecting the life of our nation. A talented group gravitating around the new review *Axa* ("The Axis") with Polichroniade, Vojen, Constant, joined the legionary ranks, while other eminent youth such as Professor Vasile Cristescu, Vasile Marin, Professor Vladimir Dumitrescu, engineer Virgil Ionescu, Professor Radu Gyr, attorney Popov, painters Basarab and Zlotescu, all very talented and enthusiastic, worked along the lines of legionary ideology.

The healthy Macedonian youth, pure as a tear, and brave, came ever closer to us. However, we thought it unwise that the mass of Macedonians in the Quadrilateral[5] be received into the Guard, because, so recently resettled in the country, we would expose it to too many persecutions. The Macedonian university youth however, in its entirety, joined the legionary movement. At the head of these Macedonian youth were three distinguished men of culture: Papanace, Caranica, and Sterie Ciumeti.

With the first two I consulted often, both of whom had admirable judgment supported by irreproachable purity and sincerety, great love and courage.

I do not believe that since 1931 there has passed a day without meeting with them. During this time of persecution, we discussed for hours blow after blow, injustice after injustice, treachery after treachery. Each bit of news of a new torture of a legionary was a knife piercing our hearts. The pain we suffered for all maltreated legionaries tormented our souls; and particularly the impossibility of seeing ahead any hope for justice.

Sterie Ciumeti was living with me day and night. He was a young man

5 Several counties in southern Dobrogea annexed by Romania at the end of the Balkan War in 1913. (Tr.)

of great righteousness and dog-like faithfulness. He became the chief treasurer of the Guard. All his days—as many as he will have—he will think only of the Guard, will be concerned and will act only for the Guard, will not live his life for anything else but for the Guard.

In various points of the country appeared other valuable elements: Dr. Pantelimon, Father Ionescu Duminica, Dr. Augustin Bidian at Sibiu; Father Georgescu-Edineti, the students' spiritual confessor, a veteran fighter, Capt. Ciulei at Bacau, Aristotel Gheorghiu, also a veteran, who commanded at Ramnicul-Sarat; at Braila, Ion Iliescu; at Constanta, Seitan; Father Doara and Victor Barbulescu at Valcea; Professors Vintan, Ghenadie and Duma at Timisoara; and the veteran legionaries, Professors Nicolae Petrascu, Horia Sima, attorney Iosif Costea, Colhon and others, who now have command posts in various parts of the country.

Bucharest is divided into sectors[6] and we began to organize within them. There were two good men in the Green and Blue sectors, Nicolae Constantinescu and Doru Belimace, two strong characters, two solid brains, Doru Belimace being one of the most distinguished students at the Faculty of Letters; Nicolae Constantinescu possessing an eminent economic background, was a student at the Commercial Academy. Soon, both of them would prove to have imposing qualities of legionary faith and bravery.

During this period also, was created the first legionary rank by the following order of the day of December 10, 1932:

"A) The first superior rank, named Legionary Commandant, is established in legionary hierarchy.

"In view of their sacrifice, work, heroism, faith, capacity and seniority, the following legionaries are advanced in rank, alphabetically:

"Banea Ion, doctoral candidate in medicine; Belgea Ion; Blanaru Ion, engineer; Dumitrescu Ion, priest; Ionescu Andrei; Silaghi Victor, attorney; Stelescu Mihail, congressman; Totu Nicolae, student; Traian Cotiga, student; Tanase Antohi, craftsman.

"B) All legionaries of the 1927 and 1928 series who took their vow and

---

6 Each of the five large sectors bears the name of a color: Green, Yellow, Red, Blue, and Black. (Tr.)

are still in the active ranks of the Legion, are hereby promoted to the rank of Legionary Commandant Aide.

Signed: Corneliu Zelea Codreanu."

The others, more advanced in years, were moved into the Legion's Senate and the Legionary Superior Council.

THE OFFENSIVE OF CALUMNIES

“Anarchic and Terroristic Movement”

The legionary movement was visibly growing, especially among the high school and university youth, and among peasants in all the Romanian provinces. It grew more slowly, however, in towns where the Romanian element was state-employed and thus prevented from expressing their views, or economically enslaved by Jews.

The same muted persecution that we have known since we started this fight, back in 1922, increasingly haunted us, all the fighters and their families. If you were a young graduate you could not get a state job unless you reneged on your conscience and your faith. Hundreds of youth were sought out to be lured with money, promises, honors, positions. The state got to be a school of treason in which men of character were murdered while treason was abundantly rewarded. If you were a Romanian merchant, the only one among Jewish merchants and you happened to believe in the Legion, everyone, from street officer to mayor and prefect, turned into your enemy. They harassed you day and night; taxed you more than they did the Jews; fines were continually levied against you; you received blow after blow until they destroyed you.

If you were a peasant, you were handcuffed and taken on foot from one village gendarmes post to the next, and the next, and the next, for scores of miles, being beaten every day at each gendarmes section. You went hungry 4 to 5 days; they looked at you like savage beasts and everyone slapped you in the face. If you were a workingman, they threw you out like a piece of used rag from every factory and enterprise.

Because, in this country, a man holding our beliefs must starve to death, together with all his children. All of us are considered enemies of our people and country.

But we have maintained ourselves within the most perfect order and legality, so that no trouble could be imputed to us. But this does not mean a thing. The reasoning of our governments is: "We cannot destroy you because you broke the laws? No matter, we will break them and will destroy you! You do not want to act illegally, well, we will act so!" So that, in this fashion, we have entered into a truly Talmudic system; on one hand we were accused through the press and by all political agencies of "illegality," and on the other, staying perfectly within the law, we were ground down by the most odious and illegal procedures by all governmental and state representatives, themselves in the most flagrant illegality.

Dragged before tribunals, juridical decree after juridical decree throughout the country confirmed the movement's line of legality and order. There was not one decree condemning us. Yet the basic argument of the politicians and the Jewish press remained invariably: "A movement of disorder," "anarchy," "lawlessness," "terroristic."

The Jewish press constantly incited politicians against us, for them to lunge at us to rip us apart, annihilate us.

"The Iron Guard In the Service of Foreigners"

After a while, at a loss for new accusations, the Jewish press stated that we were taking money from Mussolini; that we pretended to be nationalists but in fact our purpose was to squeeze money from anyone we met. Now, we found Mussolini, whom we were squeezing.

One by one, we learned with astonishment that:

"We were in the service of 'the Hungarians who were awakening',...

"We were in Moscow's service....

"We receive money from the Jews.... "

As ridiculous as the last accusation is, it was not spared us. Here I quote a significant passage from the Jewish newspaper Politica ("Politics") of August 10, 1934, in an article titled: "Max Auschnitt and The Iron Guard:"

"In our country too, then, the phenomenon had been verified exactly as it is a known fact to anybody, that the most important movement of Romanian Fascism, the Iron Guard, was created and financed by the big capitalists. And here comes the not-at-all sensational sensation:

the Jew Max Auschnitt has supported and financed the Iron Guard directly. This fact was stated by two quite serious and responsible people, Mr. Minister Victor Iamandi and the known publicist Scarlat Calimachi.

"According to these explanations, the fact appears as very natural.

"Who does not yet know that Hitler too, was financed by the great Jewish capitalists of Germany?"

"The Iron Guard in the Pay of the Hitlerites"

Lately in Germany Hitler won against the Judeo-Masonic hydra of the entire world. The German people, with an extraordinary determination and unity, fought and put down the Judaic power.

The Jews print lie upon lie in their press, seeking to confuse the minds of the people:

1. Adolf Hitler is a painter, stupid, incapable. Who is going to fall for him in a civilized country like Germany? But Hitler moves ahead.
2. Adolf Hider is not going to win because the German communists are going to oppose him. But Adolf Hitler gets closer to power.
3. Hitlerism has broken into two, three. Great dissatisfaction within the party, etc. But Hitler is not phased.
4. Adolf Hitler went crazy. He went into the mountains, etc. But Adolf Hider is in good health and gets ever closer to victory.
5. Should he win, the second day after, Germany will have a revolution. Communism will start a general uprising and Hitler will fall. But Hitler wins power and the revolution dreamed of by the Jews does not erupt. He will go from majorities to unanimity never before encountered in history.
6. All countries will economically boycott Germany and Hitlerism will fall. But Adolf Hitler moves ahead victorious.
7. "Dictatorship," "Hitlerist terror" throughout Germany. "The vote is snatched by terror." But the German people march on behind him enthusiastically.
8. Hitler wants to take our Transylvania. And we, all Romanian nationalists, who wish to rid ourselves of the Jewish calamity, are,

neither more nor less, "Hitlerites," namely, we want to give our Transylvania to the Germans.

But we answer:

"Let us presuppose that Hitler wants to make war on us to take our Transylvania. In order for us Romanians to be able to defend Transylvania against the Germans, we must get rid of the Jews; we, too, must solve this Jewish problem, must strengthen the position of our people squeezed by Jewry and sucked of its strength until it has been made quite unable to defend itself. Saddled by the Jewry which poisons our souls and sucks our blood, we will have neither weapons, nor soul, nor meat on our bones."

Finally, we "receive money," are financed, are "in the pay" of the Nazis. We answer: "A.C. Cuza has been fighting the Jews since 1890; we, since 1919, 1920, 1921, 1922, when we had not even heard of Adolf Hitler. Venomous snakes!"

"Printing Counterfeit Banknotes in Rasinari"

Before much time had gone by, a new politico-Jewish campaign was launched against us. Not wanting us to be content with money from Mussolini, Hitler, Moscow and Auschnitt, our enemy found for us a new financial source in the printing of counterfeit banknotes of Rasinari. The sensational discovery filled the columns of Jewish and party newspapers.

We give below, out of that period, several, passages meant to illustrate the system of perfidies which attempted our annihilation in the eyes of the nation.

The newspaper *Patria* ("The Fatherland") of July 22, published:

THE IRON GUARD AND THE PRINTING PLANT OF
COUNTERFEIT MONEY FROM RASINARI
SOURCE OF PROPAGANDA FUNDS

"Cluj, July 21—At Rasinari, a village near Sibiu, a sensational discovery was made, of a kind which presents an entire political organization in the ugliest light and against which the government now has in hand the most damaging proof to proceed with all severity.

"A PRESS FOR COUNTERFEIT MONEY
OF THE IRON GUARD.

"Specifically in the village of Rasinari, one of the many plants of counterfeit money was discovered. From the investigation made it was established however, to everybody's astonishment that this time we are not talking about a band of Gypsies or misfits who defy the rigour of the law in the hope of a quick enrichment, but of the Iron Guard, Mr. Corneliu Zelea Codreanu's political organization, which lately has indulged in the most abusive campaign against our government and generally against all political parties in Romania.

"THE IRON GUARD AND ITS PROPAGANDA IN VILLAGES

"But for those who know the activity of the Iron Guard a little better, with its bands of guardists which cover the whole country from one end to the other, this thing seems very natural. For in such circumstances money is needed first of all. In fact it has been known that the Iron

Guard propagandists lately had large funds, which permitted their travel through the villages as well as the printing of newspapers and the arming of its devoted members with everything necessary to copy the system 'a la Hitler.'

"HOW THE COUNTERFEITING WAS DISCOVERED

"The Ministry of Internal Affairs had for a long time been informed that some of the Transylvanian leaders of the Iron Guard, particularly those in Brasov and Sibiu, had at their disposal large sums which they then distributed to local organizations throughout the country. At the beginning it was suspected that the money was supplied by who knows what similar foreign organization, but as a result of surveillance, it was established that the suspicion was unfounded. The discovery of the money printing press at Rasinari supplied the police authorities with a new lead, and the result of the investigations was most startling.

"SIBIU FINANCES THE ENTIRE ORGANIZATION

"Immediately the Bucharest authorities delegated Investigating Judge I. Stanescu of Bucharest to begin the customary investigation. Accompanied by Chief-Prosecutor Radu Pascu and Prosecutor

Mardarie, he left for Sibiu, making his first search at the home of attorney Bidianu who headed the guardist organization, where sensational compromising material was discovered from which it was evident that the money press served exclusively the political and subversive aims of the Iron Guard. Among the confiscated correspondence, letters of various local organizations were found, particularly from the Iasi organization in which Mr. Banea was asking for a large sum of money in order to buy a panel truck and to intensify propaganda in Moldavia.

"The police effected a series of arrests and confiscated all compromising material together with the equipment used in counterfeiting.

"Investigations continue assiduously and an attempt is being made to establish the ties between the press and guardist organizations, and in particular the amount of funds distributed to the latter.

"THE MORAL VALUE OF THE IRON GUARD

"When the Iron Guard's organization, which succeeded in creating nuclei over the whole country, was so shamefully caught red-handed, it made a profound impression throughout our country and caused real consternation within the Guard's ranks of partisans. It was known that agitation in villages was done in the name of justice, honor, decency, respect for the law, etc., nothing but claims now proving to have been only empty words of the Iron Guard, when, in fact, it sought only unscrupulous power when it came to the means used.

"In view of these discoveries the government seems disposed to proceed with all severity. Mr. V.V. Tilea, Undersecretary of State, declared to an intimate circle, that in view of the gravity of the acts committed by some members, the Iron Guard will have to be dissolved.

In *Chemarea Romanilor* ("The Romanians' Call") of August 6, 1933, one can read the following:

LOVE OF MONEY
AND THE COUNTERFEITING OF MONEY

"Newspapers have reported these past days how lackeys of the Iron Guard were caught by the authorities counterfeiting money. We know that these kinds of men began lately to go through all our villages promising people all kinds of things and demanding the death penalty for lawbreakers. We are young men who have waited for quite a while to learn for ourselves what the aims and purposes of these people are. Preaching with ardor, love of country, its wise administration and the extirpation of foreigners, for a while we thought they were well-meaning. When we read in the papers that they began working to the country's detriment by counterfeiting money, we began to realize that we had been mistaken and that now we have come to know them. They are part of the clique of professional pillagers of our country and, for the great lawlessness they committed, we would not advise the government to do anything but to judge them according to the manner in which they demanded the judgement for such deeds: the death penalty. To the gallows with the counterfeiters!"

In *Dreptatea* ("The Justice") of July 22, 1933, the official paper of the National-Peasant Party we read:

THE GUARD OF COUNTERFEITERS

'If a definitive proof were needed for the appraisal of the individuals who form the so-called nationalist wing of our political right, here we have it in the resounding case of the money counterfeiters of Rasinari.

"Everywhere and always the parties of the extreme right—which are actually composed of bands of hooligans and bullies—have used the most abominable, base and unconscionable means in the propagandizing work on the naive multitudes.

"For, in the right's 'conception' (sic) and 'doctrine' (sic) the aim, which is reduced to grabbing power, justifies the dirtiness of the means.

"There cannot exist nobility in procedure, tactics, method and behavior, where there exists no nobility in ideal or purpose in the objective sought. Who could affirm that—let us say—the ideal of the extreme right hides the least bit of nobility? The cult of brute force in the coarse scorning of elementary rights will never constitute an ideal and a superiority! The ideal whose rays warm mankind's soul is a different one, an ideal of justice, peace and constructive work, for the ever higher elevation on the intellectual ladder of national collectivity, and through this, of all humanity.

"However, this is not the ideal of right-wing extremism, which is embraced by the basest human exemplars with the vain thought of their gaining dictatorial powers. Right-wing extremism substitutes for intelligence the power of the fist (that does not distinguish between an intellectual and a common lawbreaker); for justice, arbitrariness; for the noble ideal of peace and cooperation among states and peoples, the obtuse dogma of hatred among nations.

"No intellectual can approve of right-wing extremism.

"If it succeeded in catching several men, then this was only because they did it in the name of an odiously exploited faith, the nationalistic faith.

"This is how the association of conspirators called 'The Iron Guard' proceeded. It pretends to act in the name of nationalism.

"In the name of nationalism? This hypocrisy must be unmasked before public opinion. There is no need for nationalism to be served through occult organizations, secret associations, and in particular it has no need for methods as practiced by 'The Iron Guard.' Nationalism is a faith that defends itself in broad daylight, openly, honestly, sincerely.

"In any case, one does not serve nationalism by secret orders to... 'nests' (?!?), to invisible 'battalions' and occult 'cells'; and particularly by counterfeiting money like some contemptible infractors.

" 'The Iron Guard' is nothing but a handful of adventurers, clandestinely grouped for the violent conquest of power in the state through the most shameless and deceitful demagoguery. This, in the name of the nationalist idea.

"In the name of the nationalist idea? This faith, that belongs to all the sons of this land, does not tolerate such means as those used by 'The Iron Guard;' does not admit counterfeiting.

"The discovery of the band of Rasinari places 'The Iron Guard' in its true light.

"People were asking themselves: where do these fellows get money from? So much money for propaganda? For organizing and purchase of consciences? For travel, living, cars? Where from?

"The discovery of Rasinari reveals the source: counterfeiting of money!

"This is how 'The Iron Guard' works. 'The Iron Guard's pioneers are individuals who fall under the laws of the penal code. They want to make a political party by counterfeiting money.

"What moral authority do they now have to demand the approval of the masses? And yet at the same time in the name of the nationalist idea?

" 'The Iron Guard' is a guard of counterfeiters. And a guard of counterfeiters cannot speak in the name of nationalism!"

And finally, in order not to excessively prolong this quotation, we give from *Patria* ("The Fatherland") of Saturday, July 22, 1933, the following extract:

"THE GUARDISTS" AND THE COUNTERFEITERS

"The discovery of Rasinari has a truly sensational side. It goes beyond the usual, the banal, and the ordinary, placing into full breadth and bloody crudity the entire decomposition, dissolution and moral elasticity of those who pretend to regenerate the over-credulous masses seeking a new creed. And we say: 'truly sensational' because, if newspapers lately got us used to learning that in various corners of the country small clandestine mints appear, never have the ingenious and little chivalrous patrons of this inflationary institution, at odds with the penal code, proved themselves to be members of a somewhat higher social situation. At Rasinari the heroes are no longer Gypsies after petty thievery, nor only some people at odds with justice seeking an easy and underhanded kill, or one of those heroes who consider as aesthetic the enjoyment of a fruitful adventure with great risks. But one speaks of the head—note well—the Chief of 'The Iron Guard' in Sibiu. We quote from an objective newspaper which many a time took under its disinterested protection the movement of Codreanu's faithful:

'The Sibiu authorities, searching the home of attorney Bidian, head of 'The Iron Guard' organization in this town, uncovered sensational material from which it is obvious that the plant of counterfeit money of Rasinari was set up in order to support 'The Iron Guards.' Among other documents was also a letter of the

> president of the Iasi organization, Mr. Banea, asking money for the purchase of a panel truck and for the intensification of propaganda for 'The Iron Guard'.'
>
> "It is clear, is it not? A mint for the support of a party proclaiming itself a regenerator of politics and mores! Known as unscrupulous agitators, scandalmongers and bullies, now they come to be known also as counterfeiters, an attribute as disgraceful as the former but perhaps more culpable. Someone may claim to find here a curious and grave sign of our times; and a cross-word puzzle lover would find that for a guardist even if he be of iron, it is a bit too much to turn into a counterfeiter. No matter how one looks at it, the Rasinari case is extremely serious. It throws a strong light on the resources with which these adventurers pose now as bully-boys, now as martyrs, and maintain an agitated and ambulatory existence. Right in these columns, we have asked, amazed and curious, whence do these gentlemen get their money? Let us sincerely confess it, we did not expect that the answer would come so promptly, so frighteningly, and right from — Rasinari!
>
> Dr."

This odious campaign lasted three weeks. It was in vain that Caranica, Sterie Ciumeti and Papanace, the three elite legionaries desperately knocked at newspaper offices to obtain a denial. These young men, ever since 1931, in view of their qualities of clear judgement and great sincerity, have lived with me daily, sharing with me the same tormenting worries and helping me step by step in the difficult burden of leading an organization on the battlefield.

Futile efforts, for all these infamies thrown against us were ordered.

They will have only one effect: that of amassing in our souls injustice after injustice, calumny after calumny, blow after blow, pain after pain.

Our youth has stood them all, burying them in its soul. Now, so many years later, if I wanted to give the world advice, I would shout: Beware of those who endure it for too long!

The Death Team

But in the face of these obstacles, blows, intrigues and persecutions, assaulting us from every direction, having this terrible feeling of aloneness, having nowhere to turn,—we opposed all this with a firm determination to die.

"The death team" is the expression of these inner feelings of the legionary youth throughout the whole country, to receive death; its determination to go forward, through death.

At the beginning of May 1933, a team was formed, consisting of Father Ion Dumitrescu, Nicolae Constantinescu, Sterie Ciumeti, Petru Tocu, Constantin Savin, Bulhac, Constantin Popescu, Rusu Cristofor, Adochitei, Iovin, Traian Clime, Iosif Bozantan, Gogu Serafim, Isac Mihai, Professor Papuc, Radoiu...

Before setting out to travel through half of the country, they dubbed themselves "The death team." *Caprioara* ("The Doe") was driven down from Iasi for their use. They had to cover the route of Bucharest, Pitesti, Ramnicul-Valcea, Targul-Jiu, Turnul-Severin, Oravita, and Resita. So far they were to be accompanied also by Father Duminica lonescu. Then to Timisoara, Arad, and back to Bucharest. They were on the threshold of the biggest legionary expedition and they left with only 3,000 lei in their pockets for gasoline; for the rest they trusted in God and in what people on their way would give them. They took along a code of the country's laws in their hands. They would stay within legality but would defend themselves against illegal measures.

At Tg. Jiu, Turnul-Severin, Bozovici, they were followed by police and gendarmes and attacked. They knelt in front of the truck to protect the tires, baring their chests to the revolvers.

On the outskirts of Oravita they were met by machine guns, then arrested. A day later, Prosecutor Popovici, released them, finding them innocent; for they were not doing anything, were not giving speeches, were not holding meetings. They were just traveling and singing—that was all.

But people understood, and greeted them with flowers. They were given food and gasoline for their panel truck. Wherever they went, a trace of enthusiasm remained.

At Resita I came out to meet them. There we decided to hold a public rally. It was within our rights to do so. Since I was a member of Parliament and had entered a legionary list of candidates in the county of Caras, winning 2,000 votes, I was coming to get in touch with our supporters in order to give them a report on our activity in Parliament. It is legal. It is perfectly legal. But when it comes to us, laws no longer exist.

Not even during the war did Resita see so much military might. It was brought in from nearby towns to occupy the town and encircle it. I realized the government was setting a trap for me. It would have liked for me to try an irrational move; to lose my temper in order to occasion a reason for repression.

> "That is why we stop these gentlemen. That is why they must be abolished. Wherever they pass, they rouse the populace against our measures of order, against the military and the authorities. They want to bring on a revolution."

Such an error on our part would have been exploited by the government and the Jewish press. For this reason I did not give them this opportunity, but by drowning all rebellion within myself I avoided any clash. It would have been exactly in just such a clash that they would have scored a victory. We preferred to give up our rally.

The team went on, passed through Timis-Torontal county and entered the county of Arad. There, in the village of Chier, the gendarmes together with the Jews, stirred up the peasants shouting that the red bands from Hungary crossed over into Romania.

The peasants, armed with pitchforks, axes and bludgeons, fell upon the legionaries who had no time to identify themselves. The blows covered them with blood. Ciumeti's right hand was broken and he fell down at the edge of the road, unconscious. Adochitei was lying by him. All of them were wounded. Then they were arrested, transported to Arad and put in separate cells in the city jail. They were brought to trial for rebellion ten days later.

Our lawyers from Arad; Mota, Vasile Marin and myself defended them and they were all acquitted.

The Romanian populace of Arad gave them a warm demonstration of sympathy.

As a consequence of this incident, I decided to go along with them. Part of the team went on by panel truck, while I, accompanied by four of them and the peasant Fratila, left on foot, going through all the villages clear to the tomb of Avram Iancu in the mountains, some 80 miles. Peasants received me joyously everywhere.

In Tebea we parted ways. They continued their route through Hunedoara County and I left for Teius.

At Teius

My father was scheduled to deliver a speech here. As I arrived that evening I found my father in the home of a peasant; he was covered with blood. A large number of gendarmes entered the hall where the people were assembled and began using their rifle butts on everybody. My father was hit over the head. Legality! Legality!

A Romanian parliamentarian, enjoying guaranteed immunity and rights, goes to deliver a speech and the representatives of public force enter the hall cracking his head with rifle butts. Peasants, teachers, priests are all shocked. I decided then and there that we would hold a protest meeting two weeks later in the same place.

On the eve of the meeting "The Death Team" arrived in Teius as well as legionaries from Cluj and Bucharest, but the meeting could not be held.

An infantry regiment and a gendarmes battalion surrounded Teius, preventing the peasants from entering. It was the same as in Resita. I tried to avoid a confrontation, deciding that my father and all the legionaries should leave town but me; because the presence of a number of men, however few, could generate a conflict, while the presence of a single man before such large forces could not cause a rebellion; nor a glory for the many, should they bear down on him.

Yet the peasants of Mihalt and surroundings tried to forcibly cross the bridge already occupied by the army.

"We, the peasants of Mihalt conquered this bridge from the Hungarians in heavy battles. We do not admit that today Romanian gendarmes prevent us from crossing over it" were saying these brave and undaunted peasants from Mihalt.

A battle ensued which lasted over two hours. Shots were fired. One peasant was killed, and from "The Death Team," Tocu, Constantinescu and Adochitei were seriously wounded for the second time.

The entire "Death Team" and other students, a total of 50, were brought back by the authorities to Teius during the day. They were told that they would be put on the train, but as they did not have train tickets, they had to go to Alba-Iulia to get them.

But there, instead of getting their tickets, they found themselves thrown, without any arrest warrants, into the famous prison where Horea had been thrown.

All their protests were futile. They protested in vain that their detention was illegal; that no detainee may be imprisoned without an arrest warrant; that the authority who threw them there was committing an illegal act. At 2 o'clock that night they broke down the prison gate, formed a column and went to the prosecutor's home. They reported events to him. There they stayed in the yard till the next morning when together with the prosecutor, they returned to the prison. This time arrest warrants were issued for "having forced the prison's gate."

In the trial that followed they were acquitted because, lacking arrest warrants in the first place, they were being detained illegally. They conformed to legal dispositions. By informing the prosecutor they were just following regulations.

Once again it was proved in court that those who provoked disorders were not the legionaries but the very authorities who instead of upholding the laws, broke them with sovereign disdain.

"The Death Team" returned to Bucharest after two months of campaigning. Its fights, the suffering to which it was subjected, its wounds, stirred the soul of the whole of Transylvania.

Now, at this moment, we can say that the legionary movement had spread throughout the country, despite all opposition of authorities, in spite of all persecution.

Beginning now, we will stop, we said. We will begin to deepen legionary education by life in work camps. Who could be disturbed by this silent activity, particularly when it was outside the political framework?

The Dam of Visani
July 10, 1933

Yet during the previous winter the pharmacist Aristotel Gheorghiu, legionary leader of Ramnicul-Sarat, forwarded to me a report in which he described the situation of the village of Visani where the Buzau river each year flooded the fields of farmers over an area of several thousand hectares. And he was saying that the entire village were begging us to come help them by building a protective dam. I approved this request and took all necessary steps by sending out specialized engineers, making plans, and issuing an order that all legionaries in that region were to be present at Visani on July 10, 1933 when the work camp was to be opened. Here is that order:

TO ALL NEST AND LEGIONARY UNIT LEADERS
IN THE COUNTRY

COMRADES,

"Never has the problem of light been raised more than in the instant in which man has lost his sight. Likewise the problem of construction is posed in a particularly pressing fashion at the moment mankind comes to clearly realize that everything around it is breaking down.

"When everything is slowly turning to ruin, the human soul heads in an opposite direction, in an attempt to a counterattack by manifesting a formidable drive to build from foundations, to erect through labor, to construct.

"Never has this problem of construction been raised in Europe as it is today when the war period has left us in ruins and when the post war period has augmented our ruinous state day by day.

"In our country, following 15 years of public discourse, pompous but sterile, which have left nothing behind but ruins, our soul is disgusted with words and seeks action. We too, want to build; from a broken bridge to a road and the tapping of a waterfall and its change into energy; from a new peasant homestead to a new type of Romanian village. Romanian town, Romanian state.

"This is the historic call of our generation, that on today's ruins we build a new and beautiful country. In our country today the Romanian people cannot fulfill its mission in the world, that of creating its own culture and civilization in Eastern Europe.

LEGIONARIES,

"These truths have urged me to call you to the middle of the country, on the shore of the Buzau river, in order to raise with your own arms that huge dam which should carry your name for decades. I asked you so that you can tell the other Romanians that you are those who will build the new Romania.

"This new Romania cannot be born in clubs, cafes, cabarets, or from the heels worn on city streets in promenades and amusements of the various Don Juans. She will be born out of the heroism of your labor.

EXPLANATIONS AND INDICATIONS

"1. The dam will rise near the village of Visani in the southern part of the county of Ramnicul-Sarat, four miles north of the Faurei depot on the Buzau-Braila line.

"2. Meeting place, the village of Visani. All teams will be under local command as soon as they arrive.

"3. Dates of arrival in Visani: July 8 and 9, 1933.

"4. The project is going to be executed in two stages of 30 days each.

"First stage: July 10 - August 10, 1933.

"Second stage: August 10 - September 10, 1933.

"Each team will be 500 strong.

"General command will be in the hands of the legionary commander of Ramnicul-Sarat county, Aristotel Gheorghiu who will organize:

- provisioning,
- lodging,
- tooling,
- all other questions pertaining to the general direction of the project.

"Under his command are to be placed: 1. The project site chief, a legionary to be personally named by me at the beginning of work, 2. The chief of lodging and provisioning, and 3. The legionary commandant of the team. Together they will establish all services that will be needed (provisions, etc.).

“The first team will be made up of legionaries from Braila, Buzau, Ramnicul-Sarat, Focsani, Tecuci, Bucharest, Ploesti, Ialomita, Dambovita, Muscel, Arges, Vlasca, Oltenia. The legionaries from Basarabia will come on July 15, in other words 5 days later. They will leave Chisinau on foot, passing through Gradiste, Comrat, Congaz, Cahul, Colibasi, Reni, Galati, The legionaries from Cahul, Tighina, Ismail and Cetatea-Alba will join this group.

“The Brotherhoods of the Cross from through out the country will be part of the first team. The second team will be made up of the legionaries from the rest of the country. Legionaries will try to have working clothes, spare linen changes, a spade, a blanket.

“The other teams shall march or take the train, taking advantage of 75% reduction for group excursions. Five dependable legionaries from Braila are to report 5 days earlier, on July 5, in order to prepare the groundwork and receive their comrades; these will be named by the Braila legionary commander Ion Iliescu and will immediately get in touch with the legionary commander of Ramnicul-Sarat, Aristotel Gheorghiu.

“General headquarters where departures and arrivals are to be announced: Aristotel Gheorghiu, pharmacist, Ramnicul-Sarat.

I RECOMMEND:

“a) Complete order all the way. If you should be provoked I forbid you to react. Reaching your destination is paramount. “I wish that all localities through which you pass, villages or towns, to be impressed by the discipline, correctitude, fully dignified attitude and decency of the legionaries at all times. The teams’ leaders have all the responsibility.

“b) I call your attention to the fact, that in Visani and environs you must show exemplary behavior in all respects; friendly towards the people and, in particular, heroic in labor and endurance.

“c) In the event that dubious elements manage to slip in among legionaries, they will be sent home at their first attempt to stray from the straight path and this should be reported to me personally.

“In fact each leader is responsible for his men.

“d) I will arrive Monday morning July 10, following the rally in Suceava.

Legionaries building the dam at Visani, 1933.

"At daybreak, before starting work you will attend the religious service celebrated by all the priests in the area.

COMRADES,

"You are on the eve of writing a new page in the history book of legionary battles. The country will be looking upon you as upon heroes once again, as it has seen you so many times before. Head then, your hearts full of enthusiasm, towards the field where a difficult job is waiting for you, but through which you will make a new, sacrifice, thus a new step towards our victory, the legionary Romania. I expect therefore, all of you on our new field of battle."

Bucharest, June 23, 1933.

Corneliu Zelea-Codreanu
Chief of the Legion

Over 200 young legionaries gathered at Visani on July 10, coming on foot from Galati, Focsani, Bucharest, Buzau, Tecuci, Iasi, Braila, under the leadership of Stelian Teodorescu, Nicolae Constantinescu, Pavaluta, Dom Belimace, Stoenescu and Bruma.

But instead of being joyfully received and given something to eat and a resting place, tired and hungry as they were on arrival, they were surrounded by several gendarmes companies, attacked with the brutality of savage beasts and knocked to the ground under the blows.

The gendarmes were so instructed by their officers, by orders from the Ministry of Internal Affairs—where Mr. Armand Calinescu[1], according to his own statements, held a major role in the measures for our torture and suppression—that they rained their blows upon these young Romanians with as much hatred as if they were striking the greatest enemies of the Romanian people.

Among those wounded and humiliated to the last limit of humiliation were legionaries Stelian Teodorescu, Bruma, Doru Belimace, Father Ion Dumitrescu, Stoenescu, Pavaluta, and Nicolae Constantinescu, gravely wounded for the fourth time in two months.

The news of this unheard-of cruelty against some young people coming to do a good deed, and of all the indignities to which they were subjected, has spread like a black veil over the crushed and worried hearts of all our youth, who, for their faith and their love of country, felt betrayed by the politicians of the country to their alien enemy. I understood then, that all avenues were closed to us, and that from then on we must prepare for death.

We experienced a state of general depression in which we felt that all our reserves of patience and self control were at the breaking point. I realized that everything around me was cracking and that, over everything else, if one single slap in the face would occur, it would lead to irreparable misfortune. I felt like crying out from the depths of my soul: We can no longer stand it!

In this depressing atmosphere I addressed myself to the Prime Minister in the following letter which was published in the newspaper *Calendarul* ("The Calendar") of July 20, 1933:

---

1 Armand Calinescu, then Undersecretary of State at the Ministry of Internal Affairs, has just begun his series of persecutions of the Iron Guard. He left the National-Peasant Party in February 1938 and became — by virtue of his personal hatred of Corneliu Z. Codreanu — Minister of Internal Affairs and right arm of King Carol II of Romania. Since then, the star of this sorry hero of Judeo-Masonry kept rising until it reached its zenith the day when, by orders of his august sovereign, he had the chief of the Iron Guard assassinated; then to boast among his peers, in the technical language of a hangman, that he had "decapitated the Iron Guard," In fact Calinescu was only a sadistic rogue; the honor for this "deed of arms" goes entirely to the king. (Tr.)

The Persecution of the Iron Guard

The Letter to Prime-Minister Alexandru Vaida-Voevod

"Mr. Prime Minister,

"Following the incidents in Visani, of such moral gravity that they make my heart bleed, I decided to write you the lines that follow:

"I am moved to do this neither by momentary impulsiveness nor by any wish to see my letter published in newspapers in order for my friends to applaud, or in order to easily meet the customary formal obligation of 'protesting' the infamy perpetrated in Ramnicul-Sarat.

"I am urged to address this letter to you by my troubled conscience telling me that this path, onto which with so much ease you pushed us, is—for any man of honor—the path of fatal misfortunes which can no longer be avoided.

"Mr. Prime Minister.

"I shall not be able to describe to you here in a few lines our martyrdom during the last ten years, in our own country, for our Romanian and Christian faith.

"I shall only tell you that for ten years, Romanian governments have grown tired striking us. There was the Liberal administration which crushed us under blows; there followed Mr. Goga, and he too crushed us in 1926; then Mr. Mihalache, who likewise gloried, along with the alien masters, in barbarously hitting us, in exterminating us; there was then the Iorga-Argetoianu administration which anew struck us till it tired; finally, you came to power, continuing the blows.

"None among these has asked himself, Mr. Prime-Minister, whether we could support the unending moral and physical tortures which many times tended to surpass our powers of resistance.

"During all this time we have supported everything with great strength. We are full of wounds, but we never bent our heads.

"We bore them because no matter how trying our torture might be, at least our sentiment of human dignity and our honor were respected.

However, lately, under your administration, our persecution and tortures have entered the toughest phase.

"What happened at Teius where my father was hit and bloodied, and what happened particularly at Visani, are incomparably graver than all our suffering up to now. These abuses attack our very honor.

"I will not present to you too long an account.

"You certainly remember that two months ago—when I came to ask you what wrong had we done to deserve the persecution that you began—you told me:

'Why do you not start something constructive?'

'Mr. Prime Minister' I replied, 'I decided to build a dam on Buzau's shore. Do you have any objections?'

'No. Very well. Very nice.'

"I presented a petition to the Ministry of Public Works one month before anything was to get underway; I consulted the most distinguished professional engineers in the field and on July 10 work was to begin.

"This was not to be only some youth recreation; it was the call of our youth in the service of the great need for healthy accomplishment; it was to be the education of 1,000 young men in a constructive direction.

"It was to be an example for other scores of thousands of youth.

"It was to be a school for the great popular masses who for years had gone along with their bridges and roads in disrepair, waiting for the state to come fix them, when in a single day their work in common could have repaired them.

It was an encouragement for the whole country and an example for those who mistakenly imagine that a strong Romania could emerge out of someone's pity and not from the labor of us all.

"Several days before work was to begin I sent to Visani three distinquished young men to prepare the lodging and the provisioning for those to come. But they were picked up on July 8, transported to

Ramnicul-Sarat, then chained together by their handcuffs and sent home like the lowliest of thieves in this state of ridicule, demeaning to their human dignity.

"Two other youth from the University of Bucharest, spotted in the town of Ramnicul-Sarat, where they arrived to enthusiastically work, were picked up, taken to police, trivially insulted and slapped by the town's police chief and two police commissars — brothers Ionescu — then, with hands tied behind their backs, they were walked through the middle of town to the depot, and by train taken back home.

"Finally, on Monday, July 10, 200 youth arrived in Visani, most of them students.

"There, instead of being welcomed with open arms for their good intentions, they were met by the county prefect, the prosecutor, gendarmes Col. Ignat, Gen. Cepleanu, gendarmes Lieut. Fotea, several hundred gendarmes with weapons at the ready, an infantry company with machine guns set up, and they were called on to immediately leave the locality in a tone of unjustified insulting aggressiveness.

"Faced with such a predicament of threats, the 200 youth lay down in the six-inch mud and in that humble position began singing 'God is With Us.'

"The gendarmes were ordered to swoop down on them. Several hundreds rushed at them, trampling them, crushing with their boots their chests and heads; the youth endured this whole calvary in a martyr-like silence, offering no resistance.

"At the head of those kicking the students were Prosecutor Rachieru and Col. Ignat who with his own hand pulled out the hair of student Bruma, and Lieut. Fotea, who rained blows with his fists on the cheeks of the innocent youth.

"At the end, rope was brought; the hands of the 200 youth were barbarously tied behind their backs after which they were kept thus in the rain for half a day.

"In the meantime Father Dumitrescu arrived and the prosecutor asked him:

" 'What are you doing here?'

" 'I am a priest. I came to say Mass before work starts.'

" 'You are not a priest. You are an ass, replied the prosecutor. 'Tie his hands behind his back right away.'

"The priest's hands were tied just like the others and then all of them, in this humiliating position, were marched to Ramnicul-Sarat and locked up at the gendarmerie, where again they were insulted and horribly tortured by the prosecutor, gendarmes and policemen.

"Some, taken out of those torture chambers or the cellars in which they had been thrown, then beaten with ox-vein whips, fainted.

"Following four days of such an ordeal they were freed, for there was nothing of which they could be accused.

"Others, apprehended on their way to Visani, were locked up at Buzau and Braila whence, hands tied, they were sent home. There are 15 more who, up to today, Saturday, have not yet arrived. They were taken on foot from Buzau to Bucharest, from gendarme post to gendarme post, for four days unfed, insulted, slapped.

"Mr. Prime Minister,

"These are not isolated events, but, by the government's order reaching any place in the country.

"For two weeks, without any guilt—and the incontestable proof of this is all the decisions of justice handed down—we have been struck and insulted at each step; at Bucharest, at Arad, at Teius, at Piatra-Neamt, and at Suceava.

"Mr. Prime Minister,

"I call your attention in the most respectful manner, that we, who know history and the sacrifices made by each people when it wished to attain a better lot, we, Romania's present day youth, do not refuse this sacrifice.

"We are not cowards, to avoid the sacrifice due a new Romania.

"But, I again call it to your attention, that I taught these young men the sentiment of human dignity and that of honor.

"We know how to die, if need be, as we shall prove. You may lock us up; our bones can rot in the prison's depths. We may be shot to death. But we may not be slapped, we may not be sworn at and we may not have our hands tied behind our backs.

"We do not remember that our people—during our sad but proud Romanian history—at any time tolerated being dishonored.

"Our fields are full of the dead, but not of cowards.

"Today we are free men with the consciousness of our rights. Slaves we are not and never were.

"We receive death, but not humiliation.

"Rest assured, Mr. Prime Minister, that we cannot support these days of humiliation and indignity.

"Rest assured, I beg you, that after ten years of suffering we have sufficient moral strength left to find an honorable exit from a life we cannot support without honor and dignity.

"Please accept my sentiments.

Corneliu Zelea-Codreanu"

The Liberal Party Assumes Responsibility for Exterminating The Iron Guard

Yet, the torments of this youth were not to end. Before our eyes the horizon grew ever darker. Other trials, even greater, were being prepared for us. Hardly was the torture of Visani ended when I heard that I.G. Duca, the head of the Liberal Party, left for Paris. We were astonished to read in Parisian newspapers the declarations he made; that "The Iron Guard" is in the pay of Hitlerites; that the Vaida government is weak because it does not destroy us; and that he, I.G. Duca and his party have assumed the responsibility for preparing our death, for exterminating us. At home, *Viitorul* ("The Future") the party's official paper will bear down on us on the basis of the same arguments: "anarchical movement," "subversive movement," "a movement in the pay of the Hitlerites," and on the Vaida administration accusing it of "weakness" and "tolerance" toward our movement, and of "flirting" with our "anarchical" and "sold-to-the-Nazis" movement.

As a nation we will fall down these days to the lowest levels of humiliation. Two Romanian statesmen, I.G. Duca and N. Titulescu will arrange with the Romanian political front of the Paris Jewish bankers' trusts—interested on one hand in the merciless exploitation of our country's riches and on the other in assuring as happy as possible a situation for their co-religionists in Romania—the coming to power of the Liberal Party. This, on the formal condition, the obligation, to exterminate the legionary movement by any means. A young, strong, proud Romanian legionary nation to spew them out of the country with all their preying capital does not set well with the foreign bankers.

And thus, as a completion of our more than a decade of suffering, without being guilty of anything, our crown of death is prepared for us.

Be it permitted me that, at the end of this series of battles, I turn my thought toward my mother, whose soul has followed me year in and year out and hour by hour, trembling at each blow struck at me and shuddering at each threat thrown at me by fate.

Search after search conducted by brutal and indecent prosecutors and police commissars disrupted each year the tranquility of her home, from which any trace of joy and peace had long since disappeared. What a reward from a people debased by its politicians, to a mother who, in the bitterest privation, raised seven children in the love of their country!

Let these few words be a tribute to all mothers whose children have fought, suffered or died for the Romanian nation!

COMRADES,

With these last narratives concluding this volume, my youth, and that of many among you, has ended. We will never again traverse its paths.

If these last 14 years of our youth have not been too full of good times and joys, a great satisfaction lights my conscience now: a legionary Romania has thrust its roots, like those of a tree, into the flesh of our hearts. It grows from pain and sacrifice, and our hungry eyes watch it bloom, lighting the horizons and the future centuries with its splendor and majesty. This majesty overwhelmingly rewards, not only our small sacrifices, but any human suffering, be it most terrible.

DEAR COMRADES,

To you, who have been struck, maligned or martyred, I can bring the news, which I wish, to carry more than the frail value of a casual rhetorical phrase: soon we shall win.

Before your columns, all our oppressors will fall. Forgive those who struck you for personal reasons. Those who have tortured you for your faith in the Romanian people, you will not forgive. Do not confuse the Christian right and duty of forgiving those who wronged you, with the right and duty of our people to punish those who have betrayed it and assumed for themselves the responsibility to oppose its destiny. Do not forget that the swords you have put on belong to the nation. You carry them in her name. In her name you will use them for punishment—unforgiving and unmerciful.

Thus, and only thus, will you be preparing a healthy future for this nation.

At Carmen Sylva, April 5, 1936

APPENDICES

The Murder of Corneliu Codreanu

The testimony of gendarme Sarbu before the investigative commission of the Romanian Court of Cassation in Bucharest, in November 1940, follows:

We left Bucharest that night [November 29 to November 30] in two police vans from the police prefecture. We were accompanied by the gendarme majors, Dinulescu and Macoveanu.

Arrived in Ramnicul-Sarat we pulled in at the Gendarmerie where Majors Dinulescu and Macoveanu made contact with Major Scarlat Rosianu, of Jewish origin, commander of the Legion of Gendarmes at Ramnicul-Sarat.

Not having received a precise order, the gendarmes did not take the legionaries into custody. All of us were ordered to get back into the vans. We started back toward Bucharest. On the way, however, we were overtaken by Major Dinulescu who barked out: "Back to Ramnicul-Sarat!"

We turned around, but stopped in the village of Baltati, several kilometers this side of Ramnicul-Sarat, where we were quartered overnight. Here, we were given wine to drink, expensive cigarettes and fancy food.

Early next day we headed for Ramnicul-Sarat.

Arrived at the prison, all of us went into one of the cells where Majors Dinulescu and Macoveanu instructed us as to how we were to execute the legionaries.

Placing the driver of our van in a kneeling position, they threw a rope around his neck from behind, showing us how easily one can be thus executed. Everything was over in a few minutes. Then the gendarmes stepped out one by one in the prison yard and each received a legionary in custody.

I got one who was stronger and taller than the others, I learned later that he was the Captain, Comeliu Zelea Codreanu.

We then took them to the vans. There, the legionaries' hands were tied to the bench behind them and their legs to the lower part of the bench in front of them, in such a way that they could not move in either direction.

Ten of them were thus bound in the first van and four in the second.

I was in the first van with the ten, behind the Captain; each gendarme was seated behind the legionary in his charge.

In our hands we held the ropes. Then we left.

Major Dinulescu was in my van, Major Macoveanu in the other.

A tomb-like silence was kept for we were not permitted to speak, either among ourselves or the legionaries to one another.

When we reached the Tancabesti woods, Major Dinulescu, who was to give the code signal for the moment of execution, turned his flashlight on and off three times.

This was the moment for the execution, but, I don't know why, none of us moved. Then Major Dinulescu stopped the van, got out, and went back to the one behind.

There, Major Macoveanu was more authoritative; the legionaries had already been strangled.

The Captain turned his head slightly toward me and whispered: "Comrade, permit me to talk to my comrades." But at that very moment, even before he had finished his plea, Major Dinulescu stepped onto the van's running board, and stepping inside, revolver in hand, rasped out, "Execute!"

Upon this the gendarmes threw their ropes...

With drawn curtains the vans continued on their way to Jilava.

When we got there, it was seven o'clock in the morning. There, we were expected by Colonel Zeciu; Dan Pascu, the prison's commandant;

Colonel Gherovici, the legal medic; Lt.-Colonel Ionescu, and others.

The grave was already dug.

Pulled out of vans the corpses of the legionaries were then laid on the ground face down and shot in the back to thus simulate being shot while trying to escape.

Then we were gathered into a room of the Jilava prison where the colonel gave us a talk, saying: "You did your duty; you are not ordinary assassins."

Several days later I was summoned into Colonel Gherovici's office, who, seeing me, said: "You are mighty strong; you could have killed three at the same time.' He then handed me a piece of paper to be signed by me, stating that I received the sum of 20,000 lei as medical help. I told him: "I am not ill, Colonel." He answered: "Listen here Sarbu! Don't you see how bad you look? And keep your mouth shut, for, if you don't, I'll fill it up with dirt," pointing to a Mauser pistol on bis desk. Then I, as were the other gendarmes, was sent on furlough.

Prime Minister Ion Antonescu and Legionnaire Horia Sima
at the funeral of Corneliu Codreanu.

Representatives of the "Iron Guard" follow the funeral cortège.

HISTORICAL OVERVIEW

The Iron Guard: Its Origins, History, and Legacy

by

LUCIAN TUDOR

What is now commonly referred to as the "Iron Guard," more properly called the "Legionary Movement," was a unique Romanian nationalist political group founded by Corneliu Zelea Codreanu in the early twentieth century. Within Romania, the Legionary Movement has, despite failing to regain its original status after the fall of Communism, embedded itself into the nation's memory as an essentially positive force which aimed to create a better Romania. Its influence among the Romanian masses had been so significant that even many notable cultural and historical figures, including historians, clergymen and church leaders, philosophers and poets, had been associated with it. In addition, one may find the Movement or its founder referenced in numerous now well-known Romanian songs, poems, and writings from throughout the entire twentieth century since its founding.

Thus, while many foreigners from outside Romania see the Legionary Movement as merely a passing political phenomenon between the two world wars, were they to study the Movement more closely, they would find that in actuality "the Legionary spirit persists, invisible but tenacious, anchored in the depths of the Romanian soul."[1]

The Movement and its ideas have also had a certain level of influence among European nationalists even outside of Romania, and in more recent decades it is becoming better known outside of Europe as well. However, excluding Romania, the Iron Guard is not very well-known outside of the "Right," and even within the Right it is generally not well-understood. As Alexander Ronnett and Faust Bradescu pointed

1 Alexander E. Ronnett and Faust Bradescu, "The Legionary Movement in Romania," *The Journal of Historical Review* 7, no. 2 (Summer 1986): 193–228, 195.

out, "all possible defects are imputed to them [the Legionaries],"[2] and both the Legionary Movement's doctrine and history are oftentimes distorted, misrepresented, or discussed only superficially, even in scholarly works. How can one understand this movement or learn from its history when one cannot gain an adequate understanding of its ideas and history even from generally available academic sources?

The present essay is written for the purpose of contributing towards the establishment of a clearer understanding of the Legionary Movement; that is, a concise presentation of the Movement's origins, doctrine, history, legacy, and its role in the Right. We should make it clear that our intention here is not directly a political one; it is rather to spread an enlightenment and awareness of this Movement and its history.

For the Right of the present day, it is probably not possible to revive the Iron Guard and all of its particular ideas and methods. On the other hand, it is possible, and perhaps also desirable, to learn from its history and to take inspiration from its determination and spirit. The story of Codreanu and his Movement is an important one today, for like them, those of European ancestry on the Right today must struggle to protect European ethnic identity, culture, and tradition from the decay of corrosive foreign influences and ethnic decomposition, and from the corrupt politicians whose decisions led to our current situation in the West.

The story of the Iron Guard will be deeply inspiring to those who would attempt to further the cause of ethnic nationalism. The main protagonists endured constant struggles, imprisonment, torture, and death on behalf of their cause. In an age where so many Europeans devote their lives to entertainment and pleasure-seeking of various types, their story is a reminder that the struggles ahead will be difficult and not for the faint of heart.

---

2 *Ibid.*, 227.

Background And Historical Origins

The Legionary Movement (or Iron Guard) emerged out of the particular social, economic, and political conditions of early twentieth-century Romania, and thus its existence can only be understood within a specific context, just as any other political movement has its own particular context.

During the late nineteenth century, ethnic nationalism – the idea that ethnicity or nationality is a key source of identity and that each ethnicity or nation should live under its own independent state – spread throughout the Balkans. As a result of Russia's victory over the Ottoman Empire in 1879, certain Balkan states had achieved independence from the Ottomans, one of which was Romania. In order to be recognized as an independent state by other European powers, Romania submitted to the requirements of the Treaty of Berlin.[3]

Previously, Romania had refused to grant Romanian citizenship to non-Christians, including Jews, but the Treaty of Berlin demanded that Jews be given the opportunity to become citizens. The Romanian parliament granted Jews this possibility through new laws, but made the conditions for citizenship difficult due their hostility towards the Jews.[4] The reasons as to why this hostility existed, even among Romania's foremost political leaders, are particularly important to understand in order to comprehend the events of the time. Anti-Semitism in Romania was extremely common, and cannot be understood as simply hatred and xenophobia, for it was not without some justification, although that is how it has often been portrayed by Jewish academics. For example, in *Esau's Tears*, Albert S. Lindemann describes historian Howard Morley Sachar's chapter on Romanian anti-Semitism as "a tirade, without the slightest effort at balance."[5]

The Jews in Romania had for the most part strongly rejected assimilation and insisted on remaining separate from Romanians, culturally and religiously. Among Romanians, who were very much aware of their unique ethnic identity in relation to other ethnic

3 See Charles Jelavich and Barbara Jelavich, *The Establishment of the Balkan National States, 1804–1920* (Seattle: University of Washington Press, 1977), 141ff.

4 *Ibid.*, 178-79.

5 Albert S. Lindemann, *Esau's Tears: Modern Anti-Semitism and the Rise of the Jews* (New York: Cambridge University Press, 1997), 308.

groups, this created an awareness of the alien character of the Jewish population, especially since many Jews were unfriendly towards Romanians. A significant portion of the Jewish population, although not a majority, was wealthy and economically influential.[6]

By the late nineteenth century and early twentieth century, the presence of Jews in the fields of law, business, finance, journalism, and eventually politics would increase. This increase of Jews in important areas of culture caused the majority of average Romanians, who were largely of the lower classes, to feel as though a caste of foreigners was living off of their labor. In the early twentieth century, suspicions that Jews were slowly transforming Romanian culture and Romanian thinking by introducing Jewish elements into Romanian thought and education also increased. Romanians essentially felt that an alien and generally hostile people now constituted a threat to their ethno-cultural integrity.[7]

Albert S. Lindemann describes the context of Romanian anti-Semitism during this period, often noted to be the most extreme in Europe:

> It is a moot point whether Romanian anti-Semitism was the worst in Europe; certainly nowhere else did hatred of Jews become so prominently a part of national identity or one that so obsessed the intellectual classes.... Romania suffered from crushing poverty, lack of industrial development, widespread illiteracy, and competing, usually xenophobic identities—ethnic, religious, and national. Tensions between peasants and large landowners were even worse than in Russia; landholdings were grossly unequal, and the peasantry was brutally exploited. As in the Pale of Settlement, Jews in Romania served as agents for the large landowners, and were described as alien, parasitic, and contemptuous of the non-Jewish people among whom they lived. And even more than in the Pale, such judgments were both plausible and widely accepted as accurate, even by Jewish observers. Zionists often cited Romania as a place where hatred of Jews was justified, the clearest example of "objective anti-Semitism" in Europe.... Even Romanian moderates,

---

6 For an explanation of the cultural and economic disparities between Jews and native populations in Eastern Europe, see "Themes of Anti-Semitism," chapter 2 of Kevin MacDonald, *Separation and Its Discontents: Toward an Evolutionary Theory of Anti-Semitism* (Westport, CT: Praeger, 1998).

7 The particular attitude towards the Jews held by Romanians in that time period was explained well by Horia Sima in the first section of his *The History of the Legionary Movement* (Liss, England: Legionary Press, 1995).

> almost without exception, described Jews as alien and exploitative. The consensus, from conservative to liberal among Romanian nationalists, was that hostility to Jews was an integral part of Romanian national feeling. If the concept of anti-Semitism as an *Integrationsideologie* made any sense anywhere, it was in Romania, as Trotsky suggested. . . .
>
> As Prince Carol stated the matter, paralleling the views of the Slavophiles, Jews were a people whose superior industry and inferior morals allowed them to exploit and take advantage of the simple and good-natured Romanian people. It was a perspective shared by most Romanian nationalists. . . . Jewish belittlement of Romanian culture particularly incensed the spokesmen for Romanian nationalism.[8]

In 1879, in protest to the demands of the Treaty of Berlin, a number of significant Romanian nationalist intellectuals and politicians, including Vasile Conta, Vasile Alecsandri, Mihail Kogălniceanu, Mihai Eminescu, Bogdan Hasdeu, and A. D. Xenopol, spoke out against the Jews and declared them a threat to the cultural integrity of Romania. In later years, particularly in the early twentieth century, university professors such as Alexandru C. Cuza, Nicolae Iorga, Nicolae Paulescu, Ion Găvănescul, and Nichifor Crainic began producing literature describing the racial and cultural separateness of Jews from Europeans and also involved themselves in anti-Semitic political parties. They also warned Romanians of the rapid increase of the numbers of Jews in schools and universities in proportion to Romanian students, which meant that Jews would become increasingly overrepresented in the next generations of intellectual, economic, and political leadership. This meant not only that most Romanians would hold inferior positions in comparison to the Jews, but also that the latter would constitute an even more serious threat to Romanian culture in the future.[9]

These same intellectuals also generally held the view that the wealth and influence of the Jews was the result of an organized conspiracy on the part of important Jews, one which extended to an international level due to the bond between Jews across national borders. One may

8 Lindemann, *Esau's Tears*, 307, 312.

9 For excerpts from the works of these intellectuals and an overview of their position, see "The Jewish Problem" in Corneliu Zelea Codreanu, *For My Legionaries: The Iron Guard* (York, SC: Liberty Bell Publications, 2003), 58ff.

regard these conspiracy theories as unrealistic, but it is necessary to realize that because such notable intellectuals emerged to support these concepts, they began to appear increasingly justified to many average Romanians.

Furthermore, Jewish power and influence was a reality, even if the intellectual theories of the time were in some cases inaccurate in describing it. Alongside the issue of the Jews, the problem of the increasing infection of political corruption and ineffectiveness in the Romanian polity caused many Romanians to recognize the Legionary Movement as one of the few organizations that could offer a serious solution to the economic, political, and social problems of the early twentieth century in Romania. It was under these circumstances that anti-Semitic and nationalist political parties, and later the Iron Guard, became increasingly popular in Romania during the early twentieth century.

Codreanu's Early Life

Corneliu Zelea Codreanu was born in Huşi, a town in the region of Moldavia, on September 13, 1899, and was educated at the local schools. From age 11 to 16, he was sent to a military academy in Manastirea Dealului ("Cloister on the Hill") where, according to his autobiography, military virtues such as respect for authority and hierarchy, discipline, and a dislike of verbosity were ingrained into him.[10]

After serving as an underage volunteer in the Romanian army during World War I, Codreanu graduated from high school in 1919 and moved on to attend the University of Iasi as a law student. There he found that the majority of professors and a large portion of the students had converted to Communism. He also found that a large number of Romanian workers had become Communists, with Marxist intellectuals and propagandists attacking nationalism, the monarchy (at this time, Romania was a constitutional monarchy), and Christianity. Codreanu was alarmed not only by the spread of

10 Codreanu, *For My Legionaries*, 4. This book, first published in Romanian as *Pentru Legionari* (Sibiu: Editura Totul pentru Ţară, 1936) and translated into several languages, is one of the most important resources in any language about Codreanu's life. Also significant is Horia Sima's *History of the Legionary Movement*, which details the movement's history from its beginnings up to the year 1937. For further documentation from a source critical of the Legionaries, see Cristian Sandache, *Istorie şi biografie: cazul Corneliu Zelea Codreanu* (Bucharest: Editura Mica Valahie, 2005).

Communism, but also by the fact that a large number of Communist leaders were Jews, which led him and many other nationalists to conclude that Jews were conspiring to use a Communist revolution as a way of achieving dictatorial power.[11] Codreanu described his reaction in the following way:

> I could not describe how I entered this fight. Perhaps as a man who, walking down the street with his worries and thoughts, surprised by the fire which consumes a house, takes off his coat, jumping to the aid of those engulfed by the flames.
>
> I, with the mind of a youth of 19-20 years of age, understood from all that I saw that we were losing our country, that we were no longer going to have a country, that by the unconscious collaboration of the poor Romanian workingmen, impoverished and exploited, the ruling and devastating Jewish horde would engulf us.[12]

He decided to join the Guard of National Conscience, a small anti-Communist organization led by Constantin Pancu, which organized rallies as well as engaged in physical fights with Communists. The organization offered the program of "National Christian Socialism" as its response to Communism. This was a form of nationalistic and non-Marxist socialism which they formulated because they realized that nationalists must also "fight for the rights of the workers" and "against the oligarchic parties, creating national workers' organizations which can gain their rights within the framework of the state and not against the state," for they realized that their nation's future depended on liberating the workers and peasants from the poverty which the corrupt politicians of the time put them in.[13]

A decisive event in the downfall of the popularity of Communism occurred in 1920, after the Guard marched in to intervene in a strike by Marxist workers at the Nicolina railway works, with members of the Guard removing Red flags and replacing them with the Romanian tricolors. After Codreanu courageously and singlehandedly climbed to the roof of a factory and replaced the Red flag, the workers were so impressed with the efforts of the Guard's members that they let them leave without a battle.[14]

---

11 Codreanu, *For My Legionaries*, 6-10.

12 *Ibid.*, 47.

13 *Ibid.*, 15.

14 *Ibid.*, 10-17.

During the academic year of 1920-21, Codreanu and his friends among the nationalist students managed to end a Communist student strike in the university, wrecked the presses of Jewish-Communist publishers in response to Marxist propaganda in their newspapers, and even beat up the editors of *Opinia* ("Opinion"). In response, the University Senate expelled Codreanu from the University of Iasi, but dissidents led by A. C. Cuza, Dean of the Council of the Law Faculty, refused to recognize the Senate's decision and allowed Codreanu to remain. During that time, Codreanu participated in anti-Semitic and nationalist student organizations, meetings, and communications across multiple universities in order to spread an awareness of the Jewish Problem.[15]

By 1922, Codreanu obtained a degree in law and decided to continue his studies in Germany at the University of Berlin and later Jena, where he contacted local anti-Jewish nationalists and first learned of Adolf Hitler's party. There Codreanu also became aware of Mussolini's March on Rome, and wrote of the news that "I rejoiced as much as if it were my own country's victory. There is, among all those in various parts of the world who serve their people, a kinship of sympathy, as there is such a kinship among those who labor for the destruction of peoples."[16]

In December of 1922, Codreanu's studies in Jena were suddenly interrupted because student demonstrations had erupted all across Romania on a massive scale, calling for the improvement of conditions in universities and for quotas restricting the swelling numbers of Jewish students. Codreanu felt that he had to return to Romania to join the activities because it was a crucial moment in the student movement's history. During a rally on March 3, 1923, Codreanu and Cuza established an organization to unite the students: the League of Christian National Defense (LANC). The organization used the swastika as its symbol, which was most likely adopted as a result of inspiration from Hitler's NSDAP, although the LANC's goals and ideas differed from those of German National Socialism despite the relationship.[17] It should also be noted that Cuza had been an advocate of the expulsion of the Jews and been involved in anti-Semitic nationalist organizations, both political and intellectual, since the late nineteenth century.[18]

15 *Ibid.*, 30ff.

16 *Ibid.*, 52.

17 *Ibid.*, 54–55, 74–81.

18 See Gabriel Asandului, *A. C. Cuza: Politică și cultură* (Iasi: Editura Fides,

The LANC soon became the largest of the nationalist student organizations. A few weeks after its founding, the Liberal government of the time modified the Romanian constitution to grant all Jews then present in Romania citizenship and political rights to all Jews then living in Romania. Members of the LANC reacted by distributing pamphlets, collecting signatures for petitions, and making speeches criticizing the government. After Codreanu organized a student rally in Iasi, which resulted in a violent battle because a massive police force was brought in to stop it, he was arrested for the first time and spent a week in prison.[19]

Nationalist students across the nation went on a general strike in an attempt to keep universities closed in protest to the government, but the government responded by deploying the army to ensure that the protestors would be resisted. After repeated clashes with the authorities by students engaging in demonstrations as well as a failure to change the situation, Codreanu and a small group of friends established a plot in October of 1923 to assassinate key Romanian politicians, whom they regarded as corrupt, as well as the top rabbis and Jewish bankers, whom they believed influenced political decisions. However, they were betrayed by a member of the group and arrested. Upon being interrogated, Codreanu decided to "to tell the truth. And not timidly or remorsefully, but courageously."[20]

All members of the plot were held in prison for two months while awaiting trial. During that time, they were given permission to visit a local church where they were impressed by an icon of Saint Michael the Archangel, which gave them "the feeling that the Archangel was alive."[21] It also encouraged them to choose the name "Michael the Archangel" for a youth organization they planned to create in the future. Later, it was discovered that Vernichescu was the traitor. Ion Mota, another member of the plot, pulled Vernichescu aside as the group was led to the prison office, managed to acquire a gun, and shot him. The next day, during the trial for the assassination plot in Bucharest, all members (except Mota) were acquitted by the jury, which was sympathetic to their cause.[22]

2007).

19 Codreanu, *For My Legionaries*, 87-91.

20 *Ibid.*, 121.

21 *Ibid.*, 126.

22 *Ibid.*, 126ff.

Codreanu returned to Iasi in May 1924 and rejoined the LANC. Due to the fact that the Brotherhood of the Cross, the youth wing of the LANC, was low on finances and resources and was barred from holding meetings in universities, meetings were held in an old barracks in Ungheni. Its members later decided to build their own "Christian cultural home," doing physical labor themselves with the help of local brickmakers, with whom they shared their ideas for a new Romania. Their work was interrupted several times when policemen brutally attacked them without any legal justification.

The series of beatings by policemen culminated in the unwarranted arrest of Codreanu and some of his friends, after which the police prefect Constantin Manciu forcibly kept them in the police station and tortured them. They were only released by the intervention of Cuza and other important figures in Iasi, but Manciu was not punished but instead promoted by the authorities, and the local Jews rewarded him by buying him a car. On October 23, 1924, while Codreanu served as a lawyer for a student who had been tortured by Manciu, policemen led by Manciu burst into the courtroom, disrupting the proceedings. Refusing to be beaten or tortured once again, Codreanu fired at Manciu and two other policemen with his pistol: "The first to fall was Manciu. The second, Inspector Clos; the third, a man much less guilty, Commissar Husanu."[23]

After being held in various prisons with a number of his friends for months, Codreanu was brought to trial on May 20, 1925. He was acquitted once again because the locals, although far from the location of the original incident, were nevertheless aware of what had truly occurred despite the denials of the policemen.[24] It is worth noting here that, as Michel Sturdza pointed out, certain biased historians have attempted to portray Codreanu's killing of Manciu as criminal, but in reality Codreanu was arguably justified in his actions considering Manciu's criminal and gangster-like nature. However, Sturdza had also claimed that "those who knew Codreanu knew also that he never justified to himself the shooting of Manciu, whose death left an ineradicable shadow upon his thoughts."[25]

---

23 *Ibid.*, 159.

24 *Ibid.*, 160ff.

25 Michel Sturdza, *The Suicide of Europe: Memoirs of Prince Michael Sturdza, Former Foreign Minister of Rumania* (Boston: Western Islands Publishers, 1968), 34. On this matter, see also Sandache, *Istorie și biografie*, 77.

Corneliu Codreanu returned to Iasi and, after visiting friends and family members, went to Focşani on June 13, 1925, where he married Elena Ilinoiu. During the following months he noticed an increase in infighting and intrigue within the LANC, with Cuza doing little to correct the situation, causing Codreanu to question Cuza's leadership abilities. By September Codreanu decided that he would travel to France with his wife to continue his studies at the University of Grenoble. He temporarily broke off his studies to return to Romania during May of 1926 in order to assist the LANC in the general elections. During that time he encountered difficulties with certain authorities and with police who were illegally interfering with their campaigning. Nevertheless, ten deputies of the LANC (including Cuza and Codreanu's father) were successfully elected into the Parliament. Codreanu then returned to France to complete his studies, where he finally passed his exams for the second year of his doctorate early on May 16, 1927.

He returned to Romania quickly because he received word that the LANC had split into two factions, resulting in "waves of grief and despair" among its members.[26] When he met with Professor Cuza, the latter was apparently the only content person and also confident that the situation was generally good. He had also seen that Cuza was disseminating vicious propaganda against the other faction which had split from the League, which was led by Professor Corneliu Sumuleanu and included Codreanu's father. At this point, Codreanu decided that Cuza was an undesirable leader, incapable of bringing unity or properly coordinating activities; while Cuza as a doctrinaire was "excelling and unsurpassed," on the plane of political leadership he was "ignorant, awkward... incapable... of leading human forces."[27]

Codreanu was also disappointed by the political compromises Cuza had made with other parties, including the Liberal Party, while a member of the Parliament. After seeing that there was no way to reunite the two factions, which were embittered with each other, Codreanu decided that he and some friends would leave the LANC to create their own independent organization: the Legion of Michael the Archangel.[28]

---

26 Codreanu, *For My Legionaries*, 203.

27 *Ibid.*, 187.

28 *Ibid.*, 203-10.

The Doctrine Of The Legion

Before discussing the history of the Legionary Movement, it is important to clarify what it taught its members and what its basic aims were. One cannot understand the character of the Movement if one does not understand its doctrine (which is sometimes referred to as "Legionarism"), which is often misunderstood because many of its opponents, whether Liberals, Communists, or persons of other political persuasions, often make false claims about its ideas or goals. It has been typical to claim, for example, that Legionarism was simply the Romanian version of either National Socialism or Fascism, but it was in fact very much distinct from those two ideological groups when one examines the details. Even the term "nationalist" has been somewhat problematic as a description, even though the Legionaries themselves used it, because of confusions over its various meanings and implications. The following sections outline and attempt to clarify the principles of Legionarism.

1. Nation

The Legionaries, like their ideological precursors, believed that humans are constituted as nationalities or ethnicities (the two terms are equivalent in this context), which possess their own unique character. Humans have never been simply individuals, nor is there simply an undifferentiated "humanity" where the distinctions between peoples have no consequence or importance. The nation is a collective entity bonding a population of individuals who share a common history and destiny, a particular language, and a particular type of culture and tradition. As Codreanu wrote, a nation's "culture is not international. It is the expression of national genius, of the blood. Culture is international as far as its luminescence may reach, but national in origin."[29] Against the internationalism of Communism and Liberalism, which he saw flourishing after World War I, Horia Sima, an associate of Codreanu and a leader of the Iron Guard, also warned that internationalist policies "tend to erase the ethnic diversity of the masses, which is the very source of their possibilities for renewal."[30]

Legionarism also held that each nation had its own territory, a particular land on which it dwelled and with which it developed a

29 *Ibid.*, 314.

30 Horia Sima, *Menirea Nationalismului* (Salamanca: Editura Asociației Culturale Hispano-Române, 1951), 149. Note that this work was published in French as *Destinée du nationalisme* (Paris: P. E. G., 1951).

bond, and which it also had a duty to protect from foreign peoples who desired to seize it from them:

> We are bound to it [the land] not only by the bread and existence it furnishes us as we toil on it, but also by all the bones of our ancestors who sleep in its ground. All our parents are here. All our memories, all our war-like glory, all our history here, in this land lies buried.... We are bound to this land by millions of tombs and millions of unseen threads that only our soul feels, and *woe* unto those who shall try to snatch us from it.[31]

A nation is not solely the creation of historical chance and geographical conditions, but the creation of God, and is endowed with certain duties. Each nation has the goal of Resurrection in the afterlife, and those nations which betray their purpose and commit sins are those which will ultimately meet destruction—meaning that each nation has to respect the right to existence of other nations and refrain from imperialism.[32] As Horia Sima wrote:

> Nations and individuals have the same supernatural origin. The same Divine principle gives breath to both of them, and their ultimate goals do not differ. The final goal of the nation like that of the individual is resurrection from death.... Nations must affirm themselves "within the framework and in service to the laws of God," meaning that their historical existence must strive to fulfill the Divine plan.[33]

2. Race

A number of accusations have been made against the Legionary Movement claiming that the Legionaries had "racist" (i.e., racial supremacist) views similar to the National Socialists, or that they otherwise believed in the inferiority of Jews, Gypsies, or Hungarians. As a response to these accusations, and also due to the stigma that "racism" has received after World War II, many post-war pro-Legionary authors have denied that the Legionary Movement had any concern with the issue of race.[34] It is true that the Legionaries were not "racist"

31 Codreanu, *For My Legionaries*, 63–64.

32 On this matter, see also Alexandru Cantacuzino, *Opere Complete* (Munich: Colecția Omul Nou, 1969), 45ff.

33 Horia Sima, *Doctrina legionară* (Bucharest: Majadahonda, 1995), 86–87.

34 See, for example, Radu Mihai Crisan, *Istoria Interzisă* (Bucharest: Editura Tibo, 2008), 51–52. Alexander E. Ronnett also makes such claims in his *Romanian Nationalism: The Legionary Movement*, 2nd ed. (Chicago:

or "chauvinist" in that they clearly did not believe that other ethnic or racial groups were inferior to Romanians.

However, at the same time the Legionary doctrine held that biological race was real and important, which is evidenced by Codreanu's statements in *For My Legionaries* where he approvingly quotes Vasile Conta's racial separatist arguments and also by the fact that the Legionary Movement's key ideological precursor, A. C. Cuza, made racialist arguments against the Jews, arguments with which Codreanu expressed no disagreement.[35] Horia Sima himself had also affirmed that race was real, although he criticized National Socialism for its "biological materialism" and explained that "races represent only the raw material of peoples."[36]

The Legionaries believed that nationality (i.e., ethnicity) and not race is the essential category of human types, but they recognized that because race is still a significant factor in nationality, when a nation's racial type and solidarity is destroyed through excessive miscegenation, the biological background of the nation is eliminated and thus the nation is harmed and endangered. It is crucial to grasp this concept in order to understand what race means in the Legionary doctrine, and also to avoid common misunderstandings regarding the Legionaries' view of race.

3. The Jewish Problem

Like their intellectual predecessors and the great majority of common Romanian people, Codreanu and the Legionaries saw the presence of the Jews in Romania as a menace to the Romanian people because of the negative influence Jews had on the nation. The most basic and essential point is that Jews were a culturally, ethnically, and racially alien people on Romanian territory; they were seen as having no right to occupy Romanian land or interfere in Romanian cultural and intellectual affairs.

The Legionaries furthermore observed that Jews were connected to

---

Romanian-American National Congress, 1995), 6. We should note that on some issues (such as this one) regarding the Legionary doctrine Ronnett is untruthful, but his work is otherwise an invaluable resource concerning the history of the Movement, especially in terms of chronological details.

35 See Codreanu, *For My Legionaries*, 92, and A. C. Cuza, *Naționalitatea în artă* (Bucharest: Cartea Romaneasca, 1905).

36 Sima, *Menirea Nationalismului*, 71.

attacks on the Christian religion, that a large number of Jews were supporters of Communism, that many Jews became wealthy and thus influential in economic or financial matters, and that Jews were ethnocentric and did not appear to have any concern for the well-being of Romanians. Legionaries also believed that Jews worked conspiratorially to achieve greater political power and worked to control politicians through their financial power.

Considering these perceptions, for which there is a substantial factual basis, it should be unsurprising that the Legionary Movement was hostile to and often came into conflict with the Jews. Some authors have, however, objected to the description of the Legion as "anti-Semitic." While the Legionary Movement did not accuse all Jews of behavior and attitudes inimical to Romanians, it is true that it was indeed anti-Semitic in the sense that it opposed the presence of Jews in Romania.

Furthermore, the Legionaries did not aim to exterminate the Jewish population, as some authors dishonestly claim, but rather to deport the Jews to another location. Nowhere in Codreanu's works is there any statement declaring an intention to exterminate Jews, and in fact, he made it clear in *The Nest Leader's Manual* that he intended to deport them to Palestine.[37] Michel Sturdza also asserted that "Codreanu never tolerated the slightest physical violence against Jews or Jewish properties."[38]

4. Moral And Religious Character

The Legionaries, like the majority of Romanians of their time, believed that Christianity was the religion which represented a revealed divine truth, and therefore desired a Romania composed solely of Christians. To join the Legion of Michael the Archangel one had to be a believing Christian and to share in the experience of Christian mysticism; Christianity thus formed the basis of the Legion's moral values. The Legion aimed to transform its members, and later the entire nation, through education and training which would make each individual into a "New Man," that is, a person more honest, moral, industrious,

37 See Corneliu Zelea Codreanu, *The Nest Leader's Manual* (Atlanta, GA: CZC Books, 2005), 103.

38 Sturdza, *The Suicide of Europe*, 54. It should be remembered, however, that while Codreanu did not normally tolerate anti-Jewish violence, there were likely cases where such violence was committed by certain Legionaries without his knowledge.

courageous, and willing to sacrifice. Codreanu described the New Man as

> a giant of our history to do battle and win over all the enemies of our Fatherland, his battle and victory having to extend even beyond the material world into the realm of invisible enemies, the powers of evil. Everything that our mind can imagine more beautiful spiritually; everything the proudest that our race can produce, greater, more just, more powerful, wiser, purer, more diligent and more heroic, this is what the Legionary school must give us! A man in whom all the possibilities of human grandeur that are implanted by God in the blood of our people be developed to the maximum.... This hero, this Legionary of bravery, labor and justice, with the powers God implanted in his soul, will lead our Fatherland on the road of its glory.[39]

The Legionaries intended to create a new society in which people would be devoted to their nation, would have a brotherly bond with their fellow countrymen, and would be free of all moral materialism. Codreanu declared that "through our daring gesture we turned our backs on a mentality that dominated everything. We killed in ourselves a world in order to raise another, high as the sky. The absolute rule of matter was overthrown so it could be replaced by the rule of the spirit, of moral values."[40]

This transformation in consciousness was, according to Codreanu, absolutely necessary to establish in the people before any political change could occur, for political programs alone would never achieve anything lasting if the mentality of the people remained corrupted: "It is not programs that we must have, but men, new men, For such as people are today, formed by politicians and infected by the Judaic influence, they will compromise even the most brilliant political programs."[41]

5. Politics And Structure

The Legion was designed as a hierarchical structure of units and leadership, the most basic being the "nest," which was made up of a small number of members, and from there proceeding to larger levels from town to region, with the highest being the "Captain," the leader

39 Codreanu, *For My Legionaries*, 221.

40 *Ibid.*, 213-14.

41 *Ibid.*, 220.

of the Legion.[42] Leaders in the Legionary system were selected by other high-ranking leaders based on demonstrated qualities of character and leadership. This same model of choosing leaders was to be applied, upon the Legion achieving political power, on a national level.

Corneliu Codreanu, unlike most of his precursors, rejected democracy (i.e., the republic) as a system of government because of his bad experiences with it and because he did not believe it guaranteed good leadership.[43] As Codreanu saw it, democracy had the following defects: it destroyed the unity of the people by creating factionalism; it did not grant good leaders a proper authority nor could it guarantee their election into power; it gave rise to demagogues who publicly appealed to the masses but only served themselves; it was manipulated by wealthy or economically powerful people; it did not guarantee lasting accomplishments or responsibility because of constant change in leadership; and it risked the destruction of the ethnic makeup of the country, as evidenced by the granting of citizenship to Jews.[44]

However, Codreanu also rejected dictatorship as a form of government, for "a people is not led according to its will: the democratic formula; nor according to the will of one individual: the dictatorial formula."[45] Horia Sima attempted to clarify the issue by explaining that while the Legionary Movement rejected what was commonly known as democracy, it was not necessarily undemocratic, for "respect for the will of the people emanated from the spiritual structure of the Movement, based on love, conviction and inner freedom."[46]

Codreanu also intended to support the continuation of the monarchy, for although some monarchs were bad, he felt no reason to renounce monarchy. However, the king's power would not be unlimited, for "a monarch does not do what he wants. He is small when he does as he pleases and great when he does what he must."[47] Furthermore, the monarch would be assisted in governing the nation by the Legionary elite, an elite whose members would, by law, be placed into power neither by election nor by their origin of birth. Rather, members of the elite

42 See Codreanu, *For My Legionaries*, 244-46, and *The Nest Leader's Manual*, 41ff.

43 Cuza, for example, supported the use of democratic or electoral government.

44 See Codreanu, *For My Legionaries*, 302ff.

45 *Ibid.*, 306.

46 Sima, *Doctrina legionară*, 213.

47 Codreanu, *For My Legionaries*, 316.

would be selected for positions of authority by the previous elite based on their character and ability, and would be "guided not by individual or collective interests, but by the interests of the immortal nation which have penetrated the consciousness of the people."[48] The rights of the individual and those of the masses would be subordinated to the rights of the "eternal nation," the nation in its past, present, and future.

6. Economics And Labor

The Legionary Movement, due to the fact that it struggled in poverty from its very beginnings, as well as the fact that it desired to remain independent of the influence of the wealthy or financiers, aimed to support itself by its own labor, resources, and money (which could also be supplemented by donations from sympathizers). Furthermore, the Legionaries set up a system of work camps by which they would either construct their own buildings or voluntarily assist impoverished fellow Romanians by repairing houses and other structures, helping with farm work, etc. The latter, acts of charity which were expected of Legionaries, who were taught to be hard-working, often gained the Legion more supporters and members.

The Legion rejected both capitalism and communism as economic systems, the former because it led to exploitation of workers by the wealthy and the latter because it was atheistic and resulted in dictatorship. Instead, the Legionaries aimed for a third position – generally a type of corporatist system in which commerce would be combined with socialistic practices.[49] In 1935, Codreanu attempted to establish a Legionary trading system: "Legionary commerce signifies a new phase in the history of commerce which has been stained by the Jewish spirit. It is called: Christian commerce – based on the love of people and not on robbing them; commerce based on honor."[50] Around the same time, the "Corps of Legionary Workers" was established to work towards fairer conditions for workers.[51]

7. Violence And Martyrdom

Corneliu Codreanu taught the Legionaries to refrain from violence; the Legionary Movement was to be a peaceful and legal one. At the

48 *Ibid.*, 243.

49 See Sima, *Doctrina legionară*, 227ff.

50 Codreanu as quoted in Ronnett, *Romanian Nationalism*, 96.

51 See Ronnett, *Romanian Nationalism*, 97.

beginnings of the movement, he declared that "we will follow the path of the country laws, not provoking anyone, avoiding all provocations, not answering any provocation."[52] He also taught the Legionaries that each of them must be willing to make sacrifices, even of their own lives, for the salvation of their nation. For this reason, the Legionary Movement produced countless martyrs throughout its history who were honored in songs. After their names were called out at rituals or gatherings, the Legionaries attending the event would shout "Present!" They believed that the souls of these martyrs and the Romanian dead would be present with them in future battles and "come to our aid and encourage us, to give us strength of will and everything necessary to help us to achieve victory."[53]

However, the Legionary Movement existed in an inherently violent and turbulent era in Romanian history in which the extreme criminal actions of their enemies often pushed some Legionaries to commit violent and seemingly extreme actions of their own. Codreanu himself had warned that if the government placed "insurmountable obstacles... before us" the Legionaries would be forced to turn to violence as a last resort in the hopes that others would later take up their cause.[54] The violence later committed by Legionaries is also not entirely foreign to Christianity, for in accordance with a traditional Christian approach which distinguished between public and private enemies,[55] Codreanu taught that Legionaries had the Christian duty to forgive those who wronged them for personal reasons, but

> those who have tortured you for your faith in the Romanian people, you will not forgive. Do not confuse the Christian right and duty of forgiving those who wronged you, with the right and duty of our people to punish those who have betrayed it and assumed for themselves the responsibility to oppose its destiny. Do not forget that the swords you have put on belong to the nation. You carry them in her name. In her name you will use them for punishment - unforgiving and unmerciful.
>
> Thus and only thus, will you be preparing a healthy future for this nation.[56]

52 Codreanu, *For My Legionaries*, 225.

53 *Ibid.*, 247.

54 *Ibid.*, 225.

55 See Carl Schmitt, *The Concept of the Political: Expanded Edition*, trans. George Schwab (Chicago: University of Chicago Press, 2007), 28-29.

56 Codreanu, *For My Legionaries*, 350.

The History of The Legion Under Codreanu

On June 24, 1927, Corneliu Codreanu, Ion Mota, Ilie Gărneață, Corneliu Georgescu, and Radu Mironovici met and created the Legion of Michael the Archangel as an independent organization. On January 4, 1929, the Legionary Senate, a group of elite Legionaries just under Codreanu in rank, was established. The members were: Hristache Solomon, General Ion Macridescu, General Ion Tamoschi, Spiru Pecieli, Colonel Paul Cambureanu, Professor Ion Butaru, and Professor Traian Braileanu.[57]

The Legionaries began their public rallies and activities during December of 1929 and the early months of 1930, during many of which policemen attempted to prevent or disrupt their meetings without any legal reason. Despite this, and despite the spreading of deceitful propaganda against them from the press, the Legion rapidly grew in size, drawing thousands of members. The Legionaries eventually were also forced to engage in battles with members of the *Lancieri*, the paramilitary branch of the LANC which was created by Cuza, who regarded the Legionaries as enemies.[58]

As part of a planned march across the region of Basarabia during June of 1930, Codreanu decided to create a new organization under which the Legionaries would be united with members of other nationalist youth groups in order to combat Communist propaganda. The new organization was named the "Iron Guard." Although Alexandru Vaida-Voevod, the Minister of Internal Affairs, had initially given them permission for the march, he had forbidden it later due to pressure from the press.[59]

Later, in December of 1930, a Legionary named Dumitrescu-Zapada, without informing anyone, attempted (and failed) to assassinate Emanoil Socor, the Communist director of the newspaper *Dimineața* ("Morning"). On January 9, 1931, Codreanu and other Legionary leaders were arrested because of the incident and on January 11, Ion Mihalache, the Minister of the Interior, dissolved both the Legion of

57 See Codreanu, *For My Legionaries*, 211, 258, and Ronnett, *Romanian Nationalism*, 86-87.

58 Nicholas M. Nagy-Talavera, *The Green Shirts and the Others: A History of Fascism in Hungary and Rumania* (Stanford, CA: Hoover Institution Press/ Stanford University Press, 1970), 289-96.

59 Codreanu, *For My Legionaries*, 276ff.; Ronnett, *Romanian Nationalism*, 88-89.

Michael the Archangel and the Iron Guard. Codreanu and the other Legionaries were acquitted and released by March 31, 1931.[60]

During June of 1931, Codreanu established a new organization called "The Corneliu Z. Codreanu Group" as a replacement for the Legion, but the press and common people continued to refer to them as the "Iron Guard." The organization entered elections and struggled with a number of difficulties, achieving about 34,000 votes but obtaining no seats. During July, they proceeded to campaign in the county of Neamț, where a seat had been declared empty, and managed to win. Codreanu himself was proclaimed a deputy on August 31 and received his first position in Parliament. By December 31, 1931, Codreanu gave his first speech to the Parliament, where he declared his intentions for the future of Romania, including the punishment of death for those who manipulated public funds, and the expulsion of foreign exploiters.[61]

During January of 1932, Codreanu's followers entered a new electoral campaign in Tutova where their opponents fought against them physically "with a fierceness we had never met before"; the "government resorted to truly terroristic measures," and the press vehemently attacked them.[62] During these battles, numerous Legionaries were severely beaten and imprisoned, and during March of 1932 the Iorga-Argetoianu government, "in defiance of laws and Constitution," dissolved Codreanu's organization.[63] By April 17, 1932, the "Iron Guard" still managed to win elections at Tutova, and Codreanu's father entered Parliament as a deputy; by July 17, the Iron Guard won five seats in Parliament in the general elections.[64] By May of 1933, a small number of Legionaries formed a group named the "Death Team" to spread the message of the Legion by traveling across the country. They were determined to act in an entirely legal manner and, if attacked by the police, to willingly receive death. They were beaten and attacked numerous times throughout their journey and by June of 1933, they were arrested and put on trial for rebellion. They were acquitted in two separate trials because they had committed no illegal actions.[65]

60 Codreanu, *For My Legionaries*, 288-92; Ronnett, *Romanian Nationalism*, 89.

61 Codreanu, *For My Legionaries*, 298ff.

62 *Ibid.*, 317.

63 *Ibid.*, 319.

64 Codreanu, *For My Legionaries*, 320-21; Ronnett, *Romanian Nationalism*, 91.

65 Codreanu, *For My Legionaries*, 336ff.; Ronnett, *Romanian Nationalism*,

Nearly a month later, on July 10, 1933, the government of Vaida-Voevod forbade the initiation of a work camp in Vasani, where Legionaries planned to build a dam, and an encounter with the police resulted in the beating and humiliation of the Legionaries. It was at this point that Codreanu warned Prime Minister Vaida-Voevod that "we receive death, but not humiliation.... Rest assured, I beg you, that after ten years of suffering we have sufficient moral strength left to find an honorable exit from a life we cannot support without honor and dignity."[66]

Throughout late July and August, the press launched a campaign of slander against the Legionaries, where they were accused of counterfeiting, of being subversive anarchists and terrorists, and of being financed by the Third Reich, Fascist Italy, and the Soviet Union.[67] During this time the head of the Liberal Party, I. G. Duca, repeated the false claims of the press in his speeches and further declared that he would destroy the "Iron Guard." Codreanu wrote of the situation that "the torments of this youth were not to end. Before our eyes the horizon grew ever darker."[68]

On November 15, 1933, Duca became Prime Minister and his government initiated an "unheard of terror against the legal activity of the Iron Guard: arrests, prohibition of placarding and meeting, suspension of the Legionary press, etc."[69] Throughout November and early December, the Duca government was responsible for the torture and assassination of certain Legionaries, and on December 10, Duca had the "Corneliu Z. Codreanu Group" (the official name of the Legion at that point) dissolved illegally specifically in order to prevent its engagement in elections. About 18,000 Legionaries were arrested and imprisoned as a result. Afterward, on December 29, three Legionaries named Nicolae Constantinescu, Doro Belimace, and Ion Caranica (a group later named the *Nicadori*) assassinated Duca in revenge, after which they turned themselves in to the police.[70]

The assassination of Duca resulted in a vicious reaction on the part of the government, which initiated a series of killings of certain Legionaries.

91-92.

66 Codreanu, *For My Legionaries*, 347-48.

67 See Codreanu, *For My Legionaries*, 327ff.

68 Codreanu, *For My Legionaries*, 348.

69 Ronnett, *Romanian Nationalism*, 92.

70 Ronnett, *Romanian Nationalism*, 92. On the issue of Duca, see also Sturdza, *The Suicide of Europe*, 35-37, 55-56.

On December 30, the Legionary Sterie Ciumetti was murdered after being severely tortured for refusing to inform the police of where Codreanu was hiding. On the same day, the newspapers *Calendarul* ("The Calendar") and *Cuvântul* ("The Word") were shut down and their directors, professors Nichifor Crainic and Nae Ionescu, were imprisoned for supporting the Legion. On March 14, 1934, Codreanu willingly went to a military court to be judged, and on April 5 the court acquitted all Legionaries except the three responsible for Duca's death. Afterwards, public support for the Legionary Movement increased greatly and their work camps multiplied.[71]

On September 5, 1934, certain Legionaries had discovered a scheme to murder Codreanu by poison by the Legionary Mihai Stelescu and his friends, who had made contact with certain politicians hostile to Codreanu. Upon being questioned, one of the conspirators, Vasile Cotea, admitted the plot. On September 25, 1934, a council made up of Legionary commanders found Stelescu guilty and expelled him from the Legion.[72] A short time after his expulsion, Stelescu, with funding from certain political figures, established his own group and newspaper called *Cruciada Romanismului* ("Crusade of Romanianism") in which he slandered Codreanu. Meanwhile, on March 20, 1935, Codreanu established the organization *Totul Pentru Țară* ("Everything for the Country"), a party led by General Gheorghe Cantacuzino to participate in elections, and on September 19, 1935, Codreanu announced the idea of Legionary Christian commerce. Later, however, the Legion took another violent turn, as on July 16, 1936, in response to Stelescu's propaganda campaign against Codreanu, and perhaps also out of fear that Stelescu might again attempt to murder Codreanu, ten Legionaries called the *Decemviri* ("The Ten Men") assassinated Stelescu.[73]

On November 24, a team of seven Legionary leaders – Ion Mota, Vasile Marin, Gheorghe Clime, Neculai Totu, Alexandru Cantacuzino, Banica Dobre, and Father Ion Dumitrescu-Borsa – left to join Franco in the Spanish Civil War in a symbolic act of support.[74] According to Ion Mota, their purpose was to support the Christian nationalist

71 Ronnett, *Romanian Nationalism*, 93-94.

72 Ronnett, *Romanian Nationalism*, 94-95, and Gabriel Stanescu, *Corneliu Zelea Codreanu și epoca sa: crestomație* (Norcross, GA: Criterion Publishing, 2001), 78-79.

73 Ronnett, *Romanian Nationalism*, 95-99, and Nagy-Talavera, *The Green Shirts and the Others*, 292.

74 Ronnett, *Romanian Nationalism*, 98.

battle against Communism, for the Legionaries were aware that it was not just Romania that needed to be defended, but all of European Christian civilization: "They were machine-gunning into Christ's face! The world's Christian civilization was shaking! Could we remain indifferent?"[75] Once in Spain, Mota wrote a famous last letter to Codreanu in which he made a statement that would later be immortalized: "Corneliu, make out of our country a country as beautiful as the sun, powerful and obedient to God!"[76] Aware that he would at some point become a martyr, Mota also once exclaimed:

> We, all of us, have the most formidable dynamite, the most advanced weapon of war, more powerful than tanks and machine guns: it is our own ashes! Every power in the world is destined to collapse, whilst it remains with the ashes of brave fighters, fallen for Justice and for God.[77]

On January 13, 1937, both Mota and Marin died on a Spanish battlefield at Majadahonda. The bodies of Mota and Marin were brought across Europe to Bucharest by train, receiving decorations from various nationalist groups along the way.[78] And by February 12, Codreanu and a selection of Legionary elites took the "Oath of Ranking Legionaries" before the bodies in Saint Gorgani Church, in which Codreanu declared:

> That is why you are going to swear that you understand that being a Legionary elite in our terms means not only to fight and win, but it also means above all a permanent sacrifice of oneself to the service of the Nation; that the idea of an elite is tied to the ideas of sacrifice, poverty, and a hard, bitter life; that where self-sacrifice ends, there also ends the Legionary elite.[79]

On February 13, a large nationwide funeral took place, with hundreds of thousands of people attending. Later, on January 30, 1938, in memory of Mota and Marin, a unit was created within the Legion named the "Mota-Marin Corps," with its motto being "Ready to Die!"[80]

---

75 Ion Mota as quoted in Jianu Dianieleau, "An Interview: The Iron Guard," *Liberty Bell* 13, no. 4 (December 1985): 39.

76 Mota as quoted in Dianieleau, "An Interview," 42.

77 Ion Mota as quoted in Michael Rienzi, "Mota's Ashes: Requiem for a Legionary," *Miscarea Legionara – Pagina României Nationaliste*, n.d. http://miscarea.net/mota-ashes.htm

78 See Sturdza, *The Suicide of Europe*, 100.

79 Codreanu as quoted in Ronnett, *Romanian Nationalism*, 98.

80 *Ibid.*

Due to the massive increase in public support for the Legionary Movement, the press renewed its attacks on the group, and the government of Tătărescu persecuted the Movement by closing all universities, ensuring that all cases against Legionary students end in sentences, and shutting down Legionary work camps.[81]

By October 9, 1937, Cantacuzino died and Gheorghe Clime took his place as leader of the party "Everything for the Country." On December 20, general elections took place and the Legionaries gained 66 seats in the Romanian Parliament despite violent resistance against their campaigning efforts from authorities. After Tătărescu resigned on December 28, Octavian Goga, leader of the National Christian Party (a party with which Cuza had earlier joined), was appointed by King Carol II to the position of Prime Minister.[82]

During the Cuza-Goga government, the Legionary Movement was slandered by the press and several Legionaries were killed by policemen during their election campaign. In order to prevent any further damage or casualties, Codreanu declared that he would withdraw his party from electoral activities on February 8. On February 9, Codreanu met privately with Goga to discuss their conflict and the two came to an agreement, establishing an alliance. However, on February 10, as Sturdza was about to suggest to Goga the possibility of carrying out a *coup d'état*, Goga informed him that he was forced to resign from his position as Prime Minister after King Carol discovered his agreement with Codreanu.[83]

By February 12, King Carol appointed the patriarch of the Romanian Orthodox Church, Miron Cristea, to the position of Prime Minister and created a new constitution in which he (Carol) possessed the ultimate power. The new constitution also eliminated party activities and elections; it was the beginning of what was later known as the "Royal Dictatorship."[84] On February 21, in order to prevent the exposure of the Legionaries to more intense persecution, Codreanu dissolved the party "Everything for the Country" and halted all Legionary activities. Subsequently, on March 5, the government removed all Legionaries

81 *Ibid.*

82 Sturdza, *The Suicide of Europe*, 102-3.

83 *Ibid.*, 104-6.

84 One additional significant resource dealing specifically with Carol's reign is Horia Sima's *Sfârşitul unei domnii sângeroase* (Madrid: Editura Miscării Legionare, 1977).

from their positions of leadership in various institutions, including government and educational posts.[85] Also, soon after, on March 6, due to the death of Cristea, Armand Calinescu (formerly Minister of the Interior) was assigned to the role of Prime Minister.[86]

On March 25, 1938, in response to Nicolae Iorga's slanderous statements against the Legionary Movement in his newspaper *Neamul Românesc* ("The Romanian People"), Codreanu sent a letter to Iorga declaring to him that "you are a spiritually dishonest being who has without reason mistreated our innocent souls."[87] Iorga published an article replying to Codreanu's letter in *Neamul Românesc* but did not publish the text of Codreanu's letter, which prompted Codreanu to send another letter on March 29 denouncing Iorga's behavior. The next day, instead of replying, Iorga took advantage of his recent appointment as a royal counselor to file a lawsuit against Codreanu for "insult and injury."[88] According to Sturdza, the only explanation for why Iorga took this decision, knowing that it would condemn Codreanu to a long prison sentence, was envy for Codreanu's popularity.[89]

As a result of Iorga's lawsuit, Codreanu was arrested on April 17 and thousands of Legionaries were subsequently arrested and imprisoned. On April 19, at a special court set up by Carol in Bucharest, Codreanu was sentenced to six months in prison, and on May 23, a second trial was initiated against Codreanu at a similar court closed to the public and controlled by the government. During this trial, on the charges of being a traitor and preparing a revolution, Codreanu was sentenced to ten years in prison, although no credible evidence whatsoever was produced to support the charges against him.[90]

During the next few months, leadership of the Legion was repeatedly reorganized due to arrests and simultaneously thousands of more Legionaries were placed into concentration camps, with hundreds of others being hunted, tortured, and executed. During his time in prison, Codreanu wrote his now famous *Prison Notes*, where he wrote, in his anguish, "God receive my suffering, for the good, for the

85 Ronnett, *Romanian Nationalism*, 101. See also Sturdza, *The Suicide of Europe*, 108ff.

86 Sturdza, *The Suicide of Europe*, xlvii.

87 Codreanu, as quoted in Ronnett, *Romanian Nationalism*, 102.

88 *Ibid.*

89 Sturdza, *The Suicide of Europe*, 113.

90 Ronnett, *Romanian Nationalism*, 103; Sturdza, *The Suicide of Europe*, 114.

flowering of our People. Pain by pain, torment by torment, suffering by suffering, wound by wound, in bodies and souls, tomb by tomb: so we will win."[91] On November 30, 1938, the date known in Romanian folklore as the "Night of the Vampires,"[92] by the orders of Armand Calinescu, the *Nicadori*, the *Decemviri*, and Codreanu himself were removed from prison and murdered in the forest of Tancabesti by the police. Their bodies were covered with acid before being buried and the government later officially claimed in the press that they were killed while trying to escape.[93]

The Movement After Codreanu

During the months of December, January, and February, groups of Legionaries successively fled Romania into Poland, Hungary, and Germany to escape the terror and death initiated by Carol's government. On February 8, 1939, a team of Legionaries preparing to assassinate Calinescu was arrested and shot immediately. Yet later, on September 21, a team of nine Legionaries named the *Răsbunătorii* ("The Avengers") managed to assassinate Calinescu, after which they declared the execution publicly on radio, stating that: "The Captain has been avenged!"[94] After they turned themselves in, they were tortured and executed by the police without trial and their bodies placed on public display.[95]

On September 21 and 22, 1939, the government of General Georghe Argeşanu carried out the execution of all Legionary leaders held in prisons and concentration camps. A total of 252 were killed, and hundreds more would die across the next few months. During January of 1940, leadership of the Legionary Movement fell to Horia Sima and Constantin Papanace, both of whom were refugees in Berlin. After months of sending delegations to negotiate with King Carol II for a detente, Horia Sima left Germany with a group of Legionaries on May 5 and was captured in Romania on May 19, but was set free on June 13.

91 Corneliu Zelea Codreanu, *Însemnări de la Jilava* (Munich: Europa, 1995), 35. See also the English translation of this work: *The Prison Notes* (USA: Reconquista Press, 2011).

92 Stanley G. Payne, *A History of Fascism, 1914–1945* (Madison: University of Wisconsin Press, 1996), 289.

93 Ronnett, *Romanian Nationalism*, 103–4; Sturdza, *The Suicide of Europe*, 118ff.

94 Quoted in Sturdza, *The Suicide of Europe*, 119.

95 Ronnett, *Romanian Nationalism*, 105.

On June 23, Sima was given an audience with Carol, at which the two came to certain agreements.[96]

On June 26, Carol was forced to surrender the province of Basarabia to the Soviet Union. Due to this loss, and because he was aware of the military conquests of the Third Reich, Carol decided to allow Horia Sima and other Legionaries to take part in a new government led by Prime Minister Ion Gigurtu. However, Sima resigned from his position on July 7 after seeing that no preparations were being made to confront the Soviet threat. On August 16, the Legionary leaders Horia Sima, Traian Braileanu, Corneliu Georgescu, and Radu Mironovici met with Carol but could not come to an acceptable agreement. Afterwards, on September 1, Horia Sima demanded the abdication of King Carol, and two days later large demonstrations occurred in the cities against Carol. The protests escalated to the point where Legionaries surrounded Carol's palace, but General Dimitru Coroamă was unwilling to carry out Carol's orders to shoot them. Thus, on September 4, General Ion Antonescu was chosen by Carol to create a new government and the next day, after the Constitution of 1938 was abolished by Carol himself, Antonescu was given complete power.[97]

On September 6, due to pressure from the Legionary Movement, and to the great joy of the nation, Carol surrendered and was forced to leave Romania. The Legionaries came to an agreement with Antonescu to create a new government. That same day, Horia Sima was formally declared the leader of the Legion and the successor of Codreanu by other Legionary leaders. On September 14, 1940, the National Legionary State of Romania was officially formed, with Ion Antonescu as Leader and Horia Sima as Vice President; a state which, during its brief existence, would enjoy the enthusiastic support of most of the Romanian populace.[98] According to Sima,

> rarely in our people's history has there been experienced a moment of collective exaltation of as impressive enthusiasm as that of the popular masses after the expulsion of King Carol from the country. You cannot even compare the intensity of national sentiment with

96 *Ibid.*, 106.

97 Ronnett, *Romanian Nationalism*, 107; Sturdza, *The Suicide of Europe*, lv, 158-59, 162-63.

98 Ronnett, *Romanian Nationalism*, 107-8; Sturdza, *The Suicide of Europe*, 163-64.

> that rush of joy in the annexed provinces, when the Union of 1918[99] was formed.... People from all classes celebrated victory against the odious regime.... The national mysticism, of which the Captain spoke, was now set to march, to assert the rights of our people.[100]

The Legionary State initiated the removal of Jews and corrupt Romanians from their various political, economic, legal, and educational positions, replacing them with trustworthy Romanians, mostly Legionaries. Although the living standards for Jews obviously declined as a result, their conditions under the Legionary State were not as harsh as some authors have claimed.[101]

On November 23, 1940, Legionary Romania entered the Tripartite Pact and thus became a member of the Axis Powers. Around the same time, on November 25, Legionaries initiated the work to unearth the bodies of Codreanu, the *Nicadori*, and the *Decemviri*. In that same prison the state was simultaneously holding 64 politicians who had been responsible for the tortures and deaths of Legionaries in the past so that they would eventually be put on trial, although it should be noted that, at the time, Antonescu desired many more arrests. On November 27, the group of Legionaries at Jilava experienced an outburst of emotion and rage upon seeing the bodily remains of Codreanu and the others, and, unable to control themselves, killed the 64 prisoners held at Jilava.[102] Later, the state held a massive funeral for Codreanu on November 30, the anniversary of his death.[103]

The Jilava executions would later be used as propaganda to denounce the Legionary State as "criminal" and "terrorist." However, a sober analysis of the situation shows that not only were the Legionaries justified in carrying out the deaths of these politicians, who would have inevitably been executed by the state later, but the Legionary

---

99 The "Union of 1918" refers to the unification of the regions populated largely by Romanians (which were, prior to 1918, not owned by Romania) under the state of Romania at the end of World War I.

100 Horia Sima, *Era Libertății: Statul national Legionar* (Madrid: Editura Miscării Legionare, 1982), 1:1.

101 For extensive details on the activities and policies of the National Legionary State, see Horia Sima's two-volume work, *Era Libertății: Statul național-Legionar* (Madrid: Editura Miscării Legionare, 1982–90).

102 Ronnett, *Romanian Nationalism*, 108.

103 László Péter and Martyn C. Rady, *Resistance, Rebellion and Revolution in Hungary and Central Europe: Commemorating 1956* (London: University College London, School of Slavonic and East European Studies, 2008), 139.

leadership, particularly Horia Sima, actually disapproved of these premature executions.[104] Furthermore, Sturdza (who was at the time Minister of Foreign Affairs) pointed out that this mass execution was entirely in conflict with both the interests and the principles of the Legionary Movement. He also speculated that the death of two additional figures along with those killed at Jilava – Nicolae Iorga and Virgil Madgearu (a former minister of the National Peasant Party) – was the work of agents provocateurs within the Legion:

> This... could only be the work of instigators, enemies of the Movement. Those two murders were indeed scientifically calculated to do as much harm as possible to the Legion: they provoked the indignation of European opinion, Professor Iorga having been a universally admired historian, and they might have caused Iuliu Maniu, chief of the National Peasant Party, the only important politician who had shown any sympathy for the Captain and the Movement, to turn against us.[105]

By November of 1940, Ion Antonescu had become increasingly paranoid about a (actually nonexistent) Legionary conspiracy to assassinate him and simultaneously grew ambitious to attain full state power without having to share it with the Legionaries.[106] On January 13, Horia Sima was informed of a message from Berlin requesting that he take part in a personal meeting which Antonescu had arranged with Adolf Hitler. Sima, in accordance with the opinion of other Legionaries, declined to join because he was informed of the meeting only at the last moment. At the meeting on January 14, Antonescu made an agreement with Hitler that Romania would assist Germany in a potential war against the Soviet Union only under certain conditions, one of which was "neutrality in case of a settling of accounts between him and the Legionary Movement."[107] Antonescu also assured Hitler that the Romanian military was entirely obedient to him.

Upon his return on January 15, 1941, Antonescu did not inform Sima of the nature of his discussions with Hitler and recalled the Romanian

104 Eugen Weber, an anti-Legionary historian, admitted of the Jilava "butchery" that "more would probably have died but for Antonescu's intervention and that of the horrified and embarrassed Sima." See Eugen Weber, "Romania," in *The European Right: A Historical Profile*, ed. Eugen Weber and Hans Rogger (Berkeley: University of California Press, 1965), 563.

105 Sturdza, *The Suicide of Europe*, 202-3.

106 On Antonescu's motivations for turning against the Legionaries, see Sturdza, *The Suicide of Europe*, 207ff.; Ronnett, *Romanian Nationalism*, 173ff.; Ronnett and Bradescu, "The Legionary Movement in Romania," 217ff.

107 Ronnett, *Romanian Nationalism*, 174.

Minister to Berlin, Constantin Greceanu, in order to ensure that no Legionary official in Berlin could protest his later actions. The next day, an enemy of the Legionaries, the German ambassador Wilhelm Fabricius, along with Antonescu, spread false claims to Germany and to the Romanian press that Legionaries were engaging in fights with the Romanian army and that they were undisciplined and disruptive in order to discredit them. On January 19, Antonescu dismissed all the Commissioners of Romanianization (who were all Legionaries) and the following day dismissed General Constantin Petrovicescu from his position as Minister of the Interior. Shortly afterward, on January 21, Antonescu summoned all Legionary Prefects to Bucharest for a meeting, covertly assigned new Prefects to their positions, and then arrested all the former Legionary Prefects at the meeting. This was the key event in Antonescu's coup against the Legionary State.[108]

On January 22, large numbers of Legionaries protesting against Antonescu barricaded themselves in buildings as they were attacked by military forces, and meanwhile Horia Sima made an agreement with the Germans to end the battles. The next day, Antonescu ordered the use of artillery against the buildings occupied by Legionaries as well as the massacre of a crowd of civilians in Bucharest by his soldiers. On that day, Sima ordered the Legionaries to cease fighting and turn over the buildings to the German army, which then had a presence in Romania. However, Antonescu disregarded the pact made between the Legionaries and the Germans and gave an order that the Legionaries be repressed. "The enactment of that repression registered several hundred killed and tens of thousands arrested."[109]

Ion Antonescu's repression, along with the complicity of the German forces with his actions, resulted in the end of the National Legionary State and the successful takeover of power by Antonescu. It should be noted at this point that a number of highly biased academic works, which are apparently far more concerned with condemning the Legionary Movement than with accurately describing the situation, attempt to claim that what actually occurred on January 21-23 was a "Legionary rebellion that was meant to transfer full governing power into their hands."[110] However, as even the anti-Legionary historian

108 *Ibid.*, 175.

109 *Ibid.*, 179.

110 Constantin Iordachi, "Charisma, Religion and Ideology: Romania's Interwar Legion of the Archangel Michael," in *Ideologies and National Identities: The Case of Twentieth-Century Southeastern Europe*, ed. John R. Lampe and Mark Mazower (Budapest: Central European University Press, 2004), 40.

Eugen Weber admitted, "the Legion's 'rebellion' was actually its resistance to a coup by its governmental partner to eliminate it from power."[111]

A further mention should be made of the claim that the Legionaries were responsible for a "pogrom" in Bucharest which took place during January 21-23, during the clashes between the Legionaries and the army. The pogrom, in which 125 Jews died, is oftentimes blamed directly and solely on the Legionaries, although it is not clear who was involved and it is usually said that it involved a mixture of policemen, civilians, and Legionaries.[112] However, it is clear that the event "was not a pogrom in the sense that it was a concerted and organized plan of attack on Jews and Jewish homes, businesses, and temples. It was a spontaneous, disorganized case."[113] In reality, this pogrom was not even supported by most Legionaries, who were in principle against such behavior, nor was it as destructive as some have claimed.[114] In fact, it should be noted that it is typical for anti-Legionary authors to look for cases of anti-Semitic violence where only a select number of Legionaries were involved and then incorrectly attribute the event to the Legionary Movement as a whole.[115]

This work may be taken as an example of the works which we refer to.

111 Weber, "Romania," in *The European Right*, 566. See also the references in note 106.

112 Liesbeth van de Grift, *Securing the Communist State: The Reconstruction of Coercive Institutions in the Soviet Zone of Germany and Romania, 1944–1948* (Lanham, MD: Lexington Books, 2011), 25. For an example of a source that blames the pogrom entirely on the Legionaries, see Nagy-Talavera, *The Green Shirts and the Others*, 326.

113 Gerald J. Bobango, *Religion and Politics: Bishop Valerian Trifa and His Times* (Boulder, CO: East European Monographs, 1981), 172.

114 See Sturdza, *The Suicide of Europe*, 215-16. Regarding the alleged killing and hanging of Jews on meat hooks in a Bucharest slaughterhouse during the larger pogrom, there is little evidence as to who committed the act or whether it even occurred because studies showed that the photographs of the bodies were most likely forged and the employees themselves denied that the event occurred. See Charles Krafft, "To the Abattoir: Investigating the Legionary Rebellion of January 21-23, 1941," *Smith's Report*, no. 190 (March 2012): 9-11. See also Răzvan Codrescu, *În Căutarea Legiunii Pierdute* (Bucharest: Editura Vremea, 2001), 15.

115 Another example of this is the case of the pogrom which occurred in Oradea on December 9, 1927, after a large student congress met there. Some sources claim that the Legionaries themselves organized this congress as well as the pogrom; see, for example, William I. Brustein, *Roots of Hate: Anti-Semitism in Europe Before the Holocaust* (Cambridge: Cambridge University Press, 2003), 158. However, in reality the congress was organized by the National Union of Christian Students of Romania and the Legion played only a marginal role in the event. See Roland Clark, "Printing a Pogrom: Violence

In the aftermath of the establishment of Antonescu's dictatorship, hundreds of Legionaries fled into German territory, with Horia Sima having managed to reach Berlin by April 9, 1941. On April 18, the Legionary refugees were informed that they would be held in certain camps due to the German government's alliance with Antonescu's new government. The Legionaries ended up being forced to stay largely in the concentration camps of Buchenwald, Dachau, and Oranienburg, although their conditions were not as poor as those of other prisoners.[116]

During the war Ion Antonescu fought the Soviet Union alongside Germany and its allies. According to Horia Sima, as well as Michel Sturdza, Antonescu had not set up a reliable government, giving power largely to sycophants who would later betray him, and he had essentially sabotaged Romania's ability to fully contribute to the war against the Soviets by his massacre of Legionaries and by holding thousands of other Legionaries in prison throughout the war.[117] Consequently, on August 23, 1944, King Michael I (who became King of Romania upon his return in 1940 after the expulsion of Carol) and a number of other political leaders arrested and imprisoned Ion Antonescu and switched sides, joining the Allies. As Horia Sima pointed out, Antonescu "was himself the victim of the political system he had created. He was devoured by the sharks he had gathered around himself."[118]

Upon King Michael's betrayal, the Third Reich government reacted by releasing the Legionaries from the camps in order to help them create an alternative Romanian government in the city of Vienna around which Romanian forces could rally. After certain groups of Legionaries disputed Horia Sima's leadership of the Legion, Sima managed to retain his position as Commander due to the fact that

and Print Communities in the Case of Captain Keller," in *Understanding Violence: Contexts and Portrayals*, ed. Marika Guggisberg and David Weir (Freeland, UK: Inter-Disciplinary Press, 2009), 133ff. In addition, it should be mentioned that Ion Mota had also reported that the cause of the pogrom was actually the initial violent attacks made by the Jews on the students at Oradea. See "Care Ardeal?," in Ion Mota, *Cranii de Lemn: Articole 1922-1936* (Bucharest: Editura Totul pentru *Ţară*, 1937).

116 Ronnett, *Romanian Nationalism*, 110, 220-21. On the experience in the camps, see also Horia Sima, *Prizonieri ai Puterilor Axei* (Madrid: Editura Miscării Legionare, 1990).

117 See Horia Sima, *Cazul Iorga-Madgearu* (Madrid: Editura Carpaţii, 1961); Horia Sima, *Pentru ce am pierdut războiul din rasarit şi am căzut în robia comunistă* (Madrid: Editura Biblioteca Documentară Generaţia Noua, 1973); Sturdza, *The Suicide of Europe*, 167ff.

118 Horia Sima as quoted in Sturdza, *The Suicide of Europe*, 165.

he had German support. On August 29, the Romanian National Government of Vienna was officially proclaimed under the presidency of Horia Sima.[119]

In Romania, by August 31, the Soviet army had entered the country looting and destroying homes, and raping and massacring parts of the local population. One possible reason for their barbaric behavior was that, as Dimitrie Gazdaru stated, Codreanu's teachings had such a great and lasting impact upon the Romanian populace, that when the Communists arrived in the country, "thrust by the Red hordes from the Russian steppes toward the civilized West" in 1944, they "found among the twenty million inhabitants fewer than a thousand Communists ...[who could] be entrusted with the Satanization of our country."[120]

Over the next months, King Michael, under Soviet pressure, increasingly placed Communists into positions of power. By May 7, 1945, the Romanian army serving Sima's government in Vienna had retreated and surrendered before Soviet and American forces. Also, by December 20, 1947, King Michael was forced to abdicate and the Romanian nation was taken over by a Communist regime.[121]

After being held as prisoners by the American forces, the captured Legionaries were investigated by the infamous Nuremberg Tribunal. After the facts and documents were reviewed by that court, the Legionary Movement was actually declared *not guilty* of "war crimes," "crimes against humanity," or "collaborationism" by April of 1947, and the Legionaries were therefore released.[122] This is a fact often ignored by mainstream historians who are apparently more often concerned with condemning the Legionary Movement and nationalism as a whole, instead of presenting an accurate account of history. Such historians most likely refuse to mention this information because they desire, as they often do, to incorrectly link the Legionaries with the Holocaust.

---

119 See Ilarion Ţiu, "National Government of Vienna: Political Component," *Transylvanian Review* 20, no. 2:2 (2011): 777-88. See also Horia Sima, *Guvernul National Român de la Viena* (Madrid: Editura Miscării Legionare, 1993).

120 Dimitrie Gazdaru, foreword to Codreanu, *For My Legionaries*, v.

121 Sturdza, *The Suicide of Europe*, lxiii–lxv, 252ff.

122 Mihail Fotin Enescu, ed., *Pozitia politică a Miscării Legionare în vederile Tribunalului International de la Nürnberg: Documente* (Bucharest: Editura Necoz Plus, 2005).

After attempting to organize committees to assist Romanian refugees, during the late 1940s, the Legionaries decided to collaborate with American military forces in Europe in order to combat the Communist regime in Romania. The Central Intelligence Agency and its Office of Political Coordination had begun the recruitment of Romanian refugees during that time to be trained and sent on missions into the East in order to combat Soviet influence. Romanians, many of them Legionaries, were trained at American bases and parachuted into Romanian territory to engage in sabotage, espionage, and guerilla warfare. These were essentially suicide missions and often ended in deadly last stands in the mountains between Legionary guerrilla groups and Communist forces; and while these activities were terminated by the early 1950s because they were largely unsuccessful, these missions were, for those Legionaries, heroic final battles against their Communist enemies.[123]

In Communist Romania, tens of thousands of Legionaries were arrested in 1948 so that "the prisons were filled to saturation with Legionaries."[124] From 1949 to 1952, the Communist regime initiated a barbaric program to "re-educate" Romanian nationalists, especially Legionaries, through the systematic application of torture in order to brainwash them and reduce them to psychological enslavement. This torture experiment, largely performed in Piteşti prison, forced former Legionaries to torture each other in turn and involved both physical torture and highly intense humiliation as psychological punishment. The program had been halted in 1952 after Ana Pauker, then the Communist dictator of Romania, had been removed from power. In order to publicly dissociate itself from the torture program, the Communist government placed some of the key torturers on trial in 1954 and condemned them to death.[125]

---

123 Kevin McDermott and Matthew Stibbe, *Revolution and Resistance in Eastern Europe: Challenges to Communist Rule* (Oxford: Berg, 2007), 83-85; Elizabeth W. Hazard, *Cold War Crucible: United States Foreign Policy and the Conflict in Romania, 1943-1953* (Boulder, CO: East European Monographs, 1996), 201; chapter 7, "Colaborarea cu Statele Unite si Franta," in Liviu Valenas and Mircea Dimitriu, *Miscarea Legionara intre adevar si mistificare* (Timişoara: Editura Marineasa, 2000).

124 Ronnett, *Romanian Nationalism*, 56.

125 Gheorghe Boldur-Lăţescu, *The Communist Genocide in Romania*, trans. Daniel Teodorescu (Hauppauge, NY: Nova Science Publishers, 2005), 21-22. On the Piteşti experiments, see also Dumitru Bacu, *The Anti-Humans: Student Re-education in Romanian Prisons* (Englewood, CO: Soldiers of the Cross, 1971), and Alin Mureşan, *Piteşti: Cronica unei sinucederi asistate* (Bucharest: Polirom, 2008).

However, the Communist regime still continued the torture of many Legionaries in prisons for decades afterwards.[126] Inside Romania, the only Legionaries who could survive as such were those who kept their beliefs hidden. Of special note are those who entered or were members the church or monasteries. In fact, monasteries were often accused of as being Legionary sanctuaries and monks as being the main supporters of the Legion.[127]

Codreanu's Legacy

Many Romanians, including clergymen, thus still retained their faith and belief in the Legion, albeit secretly, and this was essentially how the Legion survived in Romania. It survived because it had made such an impact and impression upon Romanians that it ingrained itself into the religion and tradition of the nation, and could thus survive even the heaviest persecution.

Outside of Romania, many Legionaries had gone into exile in various nations across Europe (most notably Germany, Italy, France, and Spain), Argentina, Chile, the United States, and Australia. Horia Sima himself and a number of other Legionaries ended up settling in Franco's Spain.[128] These Legionaries in exile collaborated with local Right-wing or nationalist organizations in the various countries they resided in and produced a vast amount of literature and translations of Legionary texts, as after Romania's fall to Communism the Legionaries believed that they should spread the story of their movement and its founder, hoping that it would inspire nationalists in other parts the world. This also resulted in a certain amount of influence on native nationalists or anti-Communist groups.[129]

Dr. Gazdaru has further pointed out that Right-wing youth groups all

126 See Ronnett, *Romanian Nationalism*, 233.

127 See George Enache, "Represiunea religioasă în România comunistă. Studiu de caz: 'Rugul aprins,'" *Analele Universității 'Dunărea de Jos' din Galați – Seria Istorie* 3 (2004): 135ff.

128 Ronnett, *Romanian Nationalism*, 226-29.

129 Scott Anderson and Jon Lee Anderson, *Inside the League: The Shocking Exposé of How Terrorists, Nazis, and Latin American Death Squads Have Infiltrated the World Anti- Communist League* (New York: Dodd, Mead, 1986), 30-37, 14-19, 270-93.

over the world have been increasingly influenced by the doctrine and story of Codreanu. According to Gazdaru, a significant demonstration of this fact was "the recent recognition of it by healthy-minded youth in Chile, whose spokesman, an eminent university professor, clearly declares that the anti-communist victory there has initiated posthumous victories for Corneliu Codreanu."[130] Also notable is Julius Evola's support of the Legionary idea in Italy, feeling that the teachings of Codreanu could provide a source of positive ideological and spiritual light for those in the Modern World.[131] Furthermore, by the year 1970, Franco's government in Spain supported the construction of a monument at Majadahonda dedicated to the martyrs Mota and Marin.[132]

After the fall of the Communist regime in Romania in 1989, Horia Sima and other Legionaries attempted to seize the opportunity for the revival of the Legionary Movement in Romania, and a number of Legionary parties and organizations were established during that same year. Sima attempted to provide support and communicated with them from a distance, although he could not enter Romania because he had been sentenced to death *in absentia* in 1946, and he most likely feared that his execution would mean the end of the Movement. The new Legionary groups, however, remained disunited and many engaged in petty quarrels with other groups, even after Sima's death in 1993.[133]

As a result of their disunity – and probably also their inability to adapt to the new social, political, and economic conditions of modern Romania – the Legionary Movement never successfully regained the status or strength it had, and Romania now possesses a number of organizations which claim to be the heirs of Codreanu's order, some of which are arguably only partly representative of the Legion and its principles.

---

130 Gazdaru, foreword to Codreanu, *For My Legionaries*, viii. Note that this foreword was written in 1976.

131 See "Appendix 1: Articles on Codreanu and the Iron Guard by Julius Evola," in Codreanu, *The Prison Notes*, 62ff.

132 Ronnett, *Romanian Nationalism*, 241. See also *Cultul delà Majadahonda si monumental Mota-Marin* (Madrid: Biblioteca Documentará Generacia Nouã, 1976).

133 See chapter 9, "Legiunea Revine în România," and chapter 10, "După Mortea Lui Horia Sima – 1993," in Valenas and Dimitriu, *Miscarea Legionara intre adevar si mistificare*.

While the Legion has dissolved and a direct revival of it is most likely impossible, its importance in our present situation is not whether it physically exists or may come to physically exist once more. The Legionary Movement, because of its determination to succeed despite all odds or obstacles, to remain true to its principles despite the dangers or hardships it faced, and to face what are clearly the most brutal forms of persecution, torture, and repression, and still, nevertheless, continue striving towards its goals, serves as a model, not just for Romanians, but for nationalists everywhere. The story of the Movement gives inspiration especially to those nationalists in the West, who now attempt to combat the most corrosive forms of cultural and ethnic decay.

This should perhaps not be seen as a source of political inspiration, but of moral and spiritual inspiration, as Codreanu himself believed that people's character was more important than the programs they may espouse. As Gazdaru stated, "the murder of Codreanu did not end his work, but, as did Golgotha for Christians, projected it for other peoples and into other times. He was not merely a genial exponent of the aspirations of his generation: he formulated ideals valid for all future generations."[134] For like the Legionaries of old, nationalists in the modern world must strive unshakably and steadfastly to realize their dreams and goals, no matter what dangers, difficulties, or tortures they may face on the path to a nationalist victory and the development of ethno-states for Europeans around the world.

---

134 Gazdaru, foreword to Codreanu, *For My Legionaries*, vii.

The Oath of Ranking Legionaries

Editor's Note: The following text is an English translation of the "Oath of Ranking Legionaries" delivered by Codreanu, which he and other top Legionaries took before the bodies of Mota and Marin in Bucharest on February 12, 1937.

Dear Comrades,

Whenever I was in front of a Legionary sacrifice, I have said: how terrible it would be if the supreme holy sacrifice of our comrades should institute a victorious caste which would open the doors to the business life of fantastic hits, to theft, to carousing, to the exploitation of others.

So that some have died, for the desires to gain enrichment, for the comfortable life and the debauchery of others!

Behold, now God has brought us here, before our faces, the greatest of sacrifices which the Legionary Movement could give.

Let us put the heart, mind, and body of Mota and his comrade Marin as the foundation of the Romanian Nation. As the basis for future Romanian advancements over the ages.

Let us put Mota and Marin as that on which future Romanian elite will be based, that which, will be required to make of this people what our minds hardly dare imagine.

You, who represent the very beginning of this elite, shall be bound by oath, that you will behave in such a way to truly be the healthy beginning, of the greatness of future Romanian elite, which will protect the entire Legion, so that it does not slip towards the ways of business, wealthy living, to immorality, to the satisfaction of personal ambitions or the lusts of mankind.

You swear that you understand, that there is no doubt in your conscience that Ion Mota and Vasile Marin did not make their enormous sacrifice for a few of us today or tomorrow, so that we may stuff ourselves with treats and feast on their graves. They have not died to overcome by their sacrifice a caste of exploiters in order to put ourselves in the palaces of this caste, continuing the exploitation of the country and the work of others, continuing the life of business, of luxury, and of debauchery.

In that case, the poor lot of Romanians through our victory, would only change the company of exploiters, while the country would be squeezed and would strain its exhausted energy to bear a new category of vampires that suck blood, which would be us.

Oh Mota, you have not died for that! You made your sacrifice for the people.

This is why you swear that you understand that being the Legionary elite means, in our language, not just to fight and win, but it means: Permanent sacrifice in the service of the people, because the idea of elite is linked to the idea of sacrifice, of poverty, of harsh and severe life, that where self-sacrifice ends, there also ends the Legionary elite.

We swear thus, so that we leave, by a covenant, successors to come to swear on the tomb of Mota and Marin on the following essential conditions of the elite, on which we ourselves swear:

1. To live in poverty, killing in ourselves the lusts of material enrichment.

2. To live a hard life and to severely banish luxury and indulgence.

3. To remove any attempt at the exploitation of man by man.

4. To permanently sacrifice for the country.

5. To defend the Legionary Movement with all our strength against anything that could lead it towards compromises or disrepute; or against anything that could lower even its highest moral standard.

MOTA and MARIN,

WE SWEAR!

A Word For My Legionaries

Editor's Note: The following is the text of a speech that was delivered by Codreanu in 1938 on the occasion of the anniversary of the founding of The Legion of the Archangel Michael. The audio of this speech was also recorded when it was delivered, and is the only surviving audio recording of Codreanu's voice.

Dear Comrades,

After fifteen years of struggle, persecution and sacrifices, the youth of Romania must know that the time of Legionary victory is not far.

All of the enemy's attempts against us will be crushed; all plans to tempt us, all attempts to buy our souls, all attempts to divide us, as well as any betrayals among ourselves, will fall to the ground.

Look them right in the eye – all your tyrants! Endure with resignation all blows, endure all pains, for our sacrifices will be the iron foundation, made of broken bodies and of tortured souls, for our victory.

Those from among us who will fall, will have the names and graves of heroes! While those who will kill us, will bear the name of traitor and will be cursed from generation to generation.

From the depths, the Legionary emerges victorious! With his soul of rock! Those believing they can defeat him, as well as those who think they can buy him, will soon realize - but too late - that they were mistaken!

Horia Sima's Description of Corneliu Zelea Codreanu

Editor's Note: The following is a description of Corneliu Zelea Codreanu excerpted from a section in Horia Sima's book, *The History of the Legionary Movement*, (Liss, England: Legionary Press, 1995), pp. 32-35. It is a somewhat idealized portrayal, but nevertheless allows one to comprehend Codreanu's character and how he was viewed by his followers.

From the first moment of meeting Corneliu Codreanu, the thing that was the most striking was his physical presence. No one would have been able to be near him without noticing it, without feeling himself attracted by it, and without asking who he was. His mere appearance in public excited curiosity. This young man seemed like a god come amongst mere mortals.

He was tall and possessed of a larger than average head, without being however, a giant of a man who could make others feel ill at ease. His development stopped exactly where it was necessary in order to endow him naturally with an air of distinction. Well proportioned, slim and supple, he was but muscle, resonance and style.

If one examined the perfectly rounded features of his face, the admiration increased. No false note disrupted the harmony of the whole. His face was oval, his complexion pale; his forehead upright with the eye arches slightly raised; his dense chestnut coloured hair was sharply delineated from his skin; his same coloured eyebrows neatly curved. Between his eyes two parallel folds highlighted his interior powers of concentration. His eyes were wide and green, a limpid green, warm and soothing, the nose straight and regular; the mouth beautifully drawn. A baritone voice, melodious and deep; long, fine hands that would have been the envy of any pianist; a regal bearing.

If we wanted to define him according to the artistic canons of our civilization, we would have to say that he was the synthesis of Nordic beauty with that ideal beauty of Ancient Greece. Even the Tharaud brothers in their book, *The Messenger of the Archangel*, and without a good word for the Captain, had commented upon "*his classical features.*"

Looking at him one felt overwhelmed, bewitched. His face exuded an irresistible fascination. He was "a living manifesto" as the legionaries used to say.

He was the leader without peer, the one who carries the day whatever the gathering, whatever the situation. In his presence, everyone else naturally took second place, and it was he alone who always remained the subject of general interest.

Without doubt there is in this world a host of individuals with some special feature, but who are empty within, who are not aware of any moral or spiritual impulse that corresponds to the physical gifts that nature has bestowed upon them. With Corneliu Codreanu, to this physical magnificence was attached an extraordinary interior richness. The acclamations of the crowd left him wholly untouched. The praise of him made him angry. He possessed only the pride of the fighter and the ambitions of the great reformers.

The common sense of the Captain was proverbial. In human relations he was possessed of a rare humility and a perfect tact. He was wholly incapable of being unjust to no matter whom, to do the least evil consciously. From this spiritual body comes, moreover, one of his great teachings: always act correctly and politely, even with your enemies; only use moral weapons in the struggle. A victory gained through treachery was vitiated at core and could not last.

Yet at the same time, when the situation required it, this same gentle soul would bubble with volcanic energy. His gestures, normally calm and precise, cut the air like a blade of steel. His tranquil features hardened and his eyes emitted flashes of lightning.

The main characteristic of his soul was kindness. If someone wanted to know the main reason why Corneliu Codreanu threw himself into such a difficult, almost impossible, struggle, the only true reply is that he had pity for the suffering of the people. His heart bled from a thousand wounds seeing the misery in which the Romanian peasants and workers were struggling. His love for his people had no limits! He was sensitive to every suffering afflicting the toiling masses. He had a reverence for the poor and gave over infinite attention to their dreams and hopes. The least complaint, the least request, was studied with the same seriousness as that accorded to grave political problems.

It is this immense love for the people which gives birth to and which propels the Legionary Movement. Into its foundations, he put the whole of his feelings and sacrifice. He joined his people with pride and devotion on its road of endless sufferings until the torturers took away his life. His death was a crime, not merely against the Romanian nation and the Legionary Movement, but against all the moral and spiritual principles of mankind that he defended and incarnated like all true martyrs. The future will surely be more gracious to him than was his own period.

Nevertheless, his sacrifice was not in vain! From beneath the rubble of a holocaust that should have marked the end of all hope, the tree of life of legionary doctrine pushes forth unendingly the immortal ideas of the Captain.

The central role of the Captain of the construction of the new Romanian conscience has been admirably described by Dr. Ion Banea. This comrade of the first hour, one of the most loved of his colleagues, and who, like him, died a martyr, characterized his leader thus:

"The Captain!

A steadfast marker, a frontier. A sword held between two worlds. An old world which he valiantly strives to overthrow; a new world that he creates, to which he gives life, which he calls into the light.

His figure in the ensemble of the nationalist movement since the war looms like a wall of fire about which all important events turn. He has been its inspiration, its motivator.

Forever at the front-line of the struggle, full of faith and resolve, never hesitating or seeking to avoid responsibility.

His life is interlaced with the struggle and with the nationalist movement to the point that there is no longer any room for a private life, everything within him constantly melting into one great gesture at the service of the national interest.

Predestined to sacrifice, he led a life vivid and tormented.

His life was full to the brim with action and threatened by all kinds of danger. He raised himself to breathtaking heights and sank into the abyss from which God alone, in whom he believed so strongly, could save him. Defying the view of a life of forced labour, he only wanted to see the greatness of Romanian national solidarity.

The terrible days of prison gnawed at his health, but he knew too the exhilaration of the most poignant moments, when tens of thousands of young people surrounded him and looked up to him.

He walked in step with his times, greeting with a smile on his lips, the sarcasm and the praise.

Truly comprehending courage, he dedicated his life to the struggle. He gave himself entirely to the Movement, asking nothing for himself.

His enemies wished for his death, but it only raise him ever higher.

The Captain! Thought, Decision, Action, Bravery, Life!"

Even today, we may join Ion Banea and say, although 30 years have passed since his infamous murder, that in spite of the wish of his enemies to see him crushed, Corneliu Codreanu has risen irresistibly in the conscience of the Romanian people becoming the spiritual home of the resistance of the invader from the East.

www.ingramcontent.com/pod-product-compliance
Lightning Source LLC
Chambersburg PA
CBHW050548270326
41926CB00012B/1963
* 9 7 8 1 9 1 3 1 7 6 5 9 4 *